Unexpected Parallels

Eastern Orthodoxy

and

The Church of Jesus Christ of
Latter-day Saints

M. Scott Bradshaw

2019

8/2019 First Paperback Edition

Unexpected Parallels: Eastern Orthodoxy and The Church of Jesus Christ of Latter-day Saints

© M. Scott Bradshaw
Pompano Beach, Florida
unexpectedparallels@gmail.com

Unless otherwise mentioned, all references to the Bible are to the LDS edition of the Holy Bible King James Version.

Besides the Holy Bible, the Church of Jesus Christ of Latter-day Saints considers the following books to be canonical: *The Book of Mormon, The Doctrine and Covenants,* and *The Pearl of Great Price.*

The Holy Scriptures cited in this book are available online in English and other languages at:
https://www.churchofjesuschrist.org/study/scriptures?lang=eng

To Brenda, my radiant eternal companion, in the year of our thirtieth anniversary.

To my parents, who taught me that reading is the key to learning and always encouraged my interest in foreign travel.

Contents

Author's Acknowledgments

This book is the result of more than two thousand hours of research and writing that I conducted over the course of nearly six years. It also draws on earlier reading and reflection dating as far back as the summer of 1985, when I attended a language study program in Moscow.

I've been called a *pioneer* for my research on the connections between Eastern Orthodoxy and The Church of Jesus Christ of Latter-day Saints. This is a title that I readily accept; however, I recognize that no pioneer reaches his destination without the support of others. There are always other travellers and at least a few trail markers, trail guides or rudimentary maps to help one along the way.

In this spirit, I wish to acknowledge the advice, suggestions and comments of the following individuals whose collective assistance has been invaluable on my journey:

I gratefully acknowledge the encouragement of **John W. Welch,** who met with me numerous times to discuss this project, offering historical and theological comments that were candid and helpful. Similarly, **Dennis B. Neuenschwander** provided consistent support and advice for my research, dating back almost to this project's inception. These men are distinguished leaders and pioneers in their own fields. Their support for this book has been particularly important.

Another important early supporter for my work was **Sergei Antonenko**, the editor of a well-known Moscow journal entitled *Science and Religion (Наука и Религия)*. Sergei published an article on parallels between Joseph Smith and Saint Seraphim of Sarov (1754-1833) under my name in March 2016, drawing from some of my early material. Sergei is a devout Russian Orthodox believer who has also written a book in Russian on Mormonism.[1]

Other helpful comments were provided by **James B. Lyon,** an expert on Southeast Europe who is my former classmate in Brigham Young University's Russian program and **Thomas F.**

Rogers, professor emeritus of Russian language and literature at Brigham Young University. Both have exposure to Orthodoxy, Church Slavonic and have broad knowledge of the languages, culture and history of the peoples in Eastern and Southeast Europe.

Editorial assistance was provided by **Brian Frastaci** (B.A., University of California at San Diego, suma cum laude, 2019). Brian is a skilled copy editor and was also able to assist with some of the Russian-language editing.

Vladimir Milocević kindly reviewed my manuscript from an Orthodox perspective. He also drafted biographical sketches for Orthodox saints from Serbia, Romania, Bulgaria and Georgia (given in Chapter 10). Vladimir studied Theology and Political Science at the University of Belgrade.

Preface

In this book, I describe a range of previously undiscovered parallels and correlations between the Eastern Orthodox Church and the Church of Jesus Christ of Latter-day Saints (the "restored Church of Jesus Christ" or simply, "the Church"). These are seen in the teachings and experiences of the Prophet Joseph Smith (1805–1844) and those of well-known Eastern Orthodox saints, including a number of Russian Orthodox saints. Important correlations are also seen between the Doctrine and Covenants[2] and the Eastern Orthodox liturgical (worship) calendar, which has its roots in the earliest centuries of the Christian era. As I show in Chapter 6, it is very unlikely that Joseph Smith had access to, or a knowledge of, Orthodox theology or an Orthodox calendar. With this in mind, I encourage readers to consider whether some of the connections that I describe are *providential,* meaning that they suggest a divine origin.

This book also includes several chapters with background information on Orthodoxy. These are intended to enhance appreciation for Orthodoxy among readers. Among these are an overview of Orthodoxy (Part I, Chapter 1); background on the Orthodox calendar (Part III, Chapter 7); an overview of the Orthodox Divine Liturgy, which is the primary worship service during which the Eucharist (the Lord's Supper or Holy Communion) is served; descriptions of Orthodox sacraments, or Gospel ordinances (Part IV, Chapter 8); and profiles of saints from a number of countries (Part IV, Chapters 9–13).

Other Christian writers have undertaken projects to build ties to Orthodoxy. Protestant author Daniel B. Clendenin included these thoughts in the preface to his second edition of precisely such a book:

> For far too long Christians generally have thought of our extended family as limited to either Catholic or Protestant communities. When we come to know this part of our Christian family . . . I am confident that we will be grateful for the many ways that Orthodoxy can enrich our own Christian experience.[3]

Although Clendenin and I write from different perspectives (he writes as a Protestant, and I as a Latter-day Saint), I echo his sentiments. My own experience in studying Orthodoxy has brought fresh insights and perspectives to my study of the Gospel and, in particular, has shed light on otherwise enigmatic references in Latter-day Saint scripture. As examples of this, several Orthodox saints and holy men may be referenced in specific prophetic verses of the Doctrine and Covenants (D&C 49:8; D&C 113:10 [interpreting Isaiah 52:6]; and D&C 133:26; see Chapter 5). Moreover, important sections of the Doctrine and Covenants suggest influences from Orthodox theologians from centuries past, yet there is no plausible way that Joseph Smith could have had access to the particular Orthodox writings in question. Of these, Sections 88 and 93 stand out; it is not surprising, thus, that the Lord chose *both* of these sections to instruct Church members of the need to study a broad range of literature from the "best books" and to learn about "countries and kingdoms" (D&C 88:79, 118; 93:53).

Perhaps the single most important commonality between the two churches is seen in the sacred visions, or *mystical experiences* (to use an academic term), of the holy men, monks, elders, and leaders, as the case may be, of the two churches. Both the restored Church of Jesus Christ and Eastern Orthodoxy have been blessed with the witnesses of men of great spiritual stature who testified of Jesus Christ and for the reality, love, and majesty of God. Several Orthodox saints have had visions of God in the form of brilliant light, have seen the personages of the Godhead, or have met the living Christ. Latter-day Saint leaders, including the Prophet Joseph Smith, have also experienced visions of God, have met the living Christ, and have experienced heavenly manifestations; some of these experiences have been documented in writing, while others remain unpublished.[4] The most glorious of these latter-day visions is the First Vision of Joseph Smith (1820), in which he saw the Father and Son as separate and distinct personages.

In describing commonalities between the two churches, I do not mean to gloss over doctrinal differences. These are real, of course, and are also numerous. Latter-day Saints believe that their prophets and apostles hold keys of priesthood authority that make them the Lord's authorized messengers on earth; thus, their teachings are received in the Church as the word of the Lord (see

D&C 1:38). The Eastern Orthodox Church sees itself as "the authentic continuation of the one, holy, catholic and apostolic Church" established by Jesus Christ and as the "Church of Councils, from the Apostolic Council in Jerusalem (Acts 15:5–29) to the present day."[5] It sees the continuation of apostolic authority in the work of bishops, all of whom are equal in authority (including with respect to the pope).

A major doctrinal difference is seen in the Latter-day Saint view that the personages of the Godhead (the Father, Son, and Holy Ghost) are separate and distinct beings, though their total unity and oneness is affirmed in Latter-day Saint teaching and scripture (2 Nephi 31:21; Mosiah 15:2–4; D&C 20:28; 130:22). In contrast, Orthodox teaching has at its core the Nicene-Constantinopolitan Creed (AD 325 and 381; usually simply referred to as the "Nicene Creed"[6]) and other doctrines that resulted from the first seven ecumenical councils (up to AD 781). The Nicene Creed is the authoritative statement that much of Christendom has turned to through the centuries in understanding the nature of the Father, Son, and Holy Spirit. The Nicene Creed defines Christ as being of "one Essence with the Father."

Despite the theological gap, the *experiences* of Orthodox holy men and Joseph Smith regarding the nature of God have commonalities. The most striking illustration of this is seen in Joseph Smith's First Vision (1820)[7] and the vision of the Holy Trinity seen by a Russian monk, Saint Alexander of Svir, in 1508. In his vision, Joseph saw a "pillar of light" descending upon him, "above the brightness of the sun." In the light, Joseph saw God the Father and Jesus Christ as separate personages "whose brightness and glory" defied description.[8] Similarly, Alexander saw the Father, Son, and Holy Spirit, or three angels representing them, as distinct persons, each wearing "most bright garments and clothed in white, beautiful in purity, shining more than the sun and illuminated with unutterable heavenly glory, and each holding a staff in his hand." According to Alexander's official biography, he understood these three beings in a way consistent with the Nicene Creed, that they were "one in Essence."[9]

The importance of actual *experience* with God in the Orthodox tradition is a theme that I come back to repeatedly in this book; however, undue focus on *experience* sets up a potential conflict

x

with established church dogma, teaching, and practice. What's more, it creates a potential for conflict with the whole idea of church authority. In Orthodoxy, the mystical experiences of saints are never cited to contradict the Nicene Creed or other points laid down in the seven Ecumenical Councils. Mystical or sacred experiences are studied only to better understand the *meaning* of dogma and the Holy Scriptures, or to attest to miracles. Moreover, the Orthodox monks who experienced sacred manifestations were invariably completely Orthodox. They were devoted to the Orthodox Church, its traditions, sacraments, and supported established authorities, though hermits sometimes went long periods of time without taking the Holy Communion (and they normally live as hermits only with the blessing of an elder or the abbot of a nearby monastery).

In the restored Church of Jesus Christ, this issue of experience or revelation versus authority was laid to rest less than six months after the Church was formally organized on April 6, 1830. No one in the Church was to receive revelations and commandments for the Church as a whole, except for Joseph Smith. His words were to be received as Moses'. Purported revelations for the Church received by anyone else were not to be accepted. This principle is still applied today—only Joseph's successors in the Presidency of the Church can declare revelation for the whole Church. In practice, this normally means that new revelation or major policy changes are accepted and declared by *fifteen* men: the President, his two counselors, and the full Quorum of the Twelve (see D&C 28).

Talking about sacred experiences carries another hazard. Some believers may assume that the receipt of unusual spiritual gifts or divine manifestations actually *defines* what it means to be Christian. It is not my intent to convey this meaning. While Latter-day Saint scripture teaches that glorious visions of Deity can occur in this life, these are very private matters about which members and leaders seldom speak (cf. Alma 12:9). Ultimately, accepting Christ and having faith in him is far more basic to our salvation, as is each believer's commitment to walk the path that Christ marked out for his followers (see 2 Nephi 31:19–20). The teaching and ministering of Church leaders and members normally focuses on topics such as the "first principles and ordinances of the

Gospel" (see the <u>fourth article of faith</u>), service to others, temple worship and other very basic subjects.

Author and editor Sergei Antonenko insightfully observed parallels in Latter-day Saint and Russian Orthodox *experience,* even if the outward forms of worship and governance of the two churches differ markedly. Of Orthodoxy and the Church of Jesus Christ of Latter-day Saints, he wrote:

> Both confessions seek the complete and original spiritual knowledge. Orthodox Christianity traces back to the ancient, undamaged Christian truth which is the axis of church history, keeping its own tradition, rejecting the liturgical and calendar changes of the West. Latter-day Saints accomplish their own sort of spiritual "jump over history," seeking to join with Christ through Prophetic revelation of recent times. Both are noted for uncompromising faith, a guarded attitude toward ecumenical contact and fidelity to conservative family values (in all likelihood, Mormons would agree with the Orthodox definition of the family as a "little church").
>
> **Another important point is that in both Orthodoxy and in Mormonism, the reverent, mystical experience of meeting the higher power is alive.** For both churches, Christ is not an abstract moral ideal, not a historical Jewish preacher and not a worldly, tolerant "teacher of life," but the living Son of God, the Redeemer and King of this world. Both Mormons and Orthodox believe in the possibility of real *theosis* (deification) of the individual, though they understand this joining of divine and human concepts in different ways. In the modern, Western Christian world, it is accepted to interpret verses of Holy Scriptures and Holy Tradition that testify of the light-bearing mystery of deification as being especially metaphysical [emphasis added).

Antonenko penned these comments as part of his introduction to an article that he published under my name in March 2016, in *Science and Religion* (*Nauka i religiya, Наука и Религия*), the respected Moscow journal of which he is now editor in chief. He is a devout Russian Orthodox believer and has also written a fine book in Russian on Mormonism.[10] In this same introduction, Antonenko also introduced me as a *pioneer* in researching Russian Orthodoxy from a Latter-day Saint perspective.

For Latter-day Saint readers, much of the research presented in this book should be seen as affirming that Joseph Smith was indeed a Prophet of God and that the revelations given to the world through Joseph Smith are of divine origin. My research suggests that Joseph's revelations have not just a nineteenth-century American historical context but also speak to the theological concerns of people (the Orthodox) far outside his historical and cultural frame of reference. In particular, my research underscores the importance of the temple in Latter-day Saint worship. Some of the most interesting correlations that I've uncovered in my research show that virtually all references to Latter-day Saint temples, temple sites, and temple ordinances in the Doctrine and Covenants find appropriate date and thematic links on the Eastern Orthodox calendar. The pattern is comprehensive, with numerous correlations to the feasts for the Prophet Elijah.

For Orthodox readers, many of the materials in this book underscore the tremendous spiritual stature of their saints. The richness, beauty, and ancient origin of Orthodox worship services and sacraments deserve serious study, as do the life stories of Orthodox saints. Orthodoxy has great appeal in its constancy, unchanging doctrines and modes of worship. This appeal is seen in the fact that several of the Orthodox writers whom I quote in this book are converts to Orthodoxy (Kallistos Ware, Frederica Mathewes-Green and Patrick B. O'Grady).

An important focus of this book is seen in the life and experiences of Saint Seraphim of Sarov (1754–1833), a Russian Orthodox monk whose fame among his countrymen today can hardly be overstated. Seraphim and several of the other monks profiled in this book were practitioners of a Christ-centered meditative practice called *Hesychasm*. Seraphim worked miracles and also prophesied of calamities that would befall his country and its believers. He also prophesied of a future period of spiritual renewal in the Russian Orthodox Church. The fulfillment of these prophecies is widely seen in the repression experienced in Russia during seventy years of Soviet rule, followed by the reemergence of the Russian Orthodox Church as a spiritual and social influence in Russian society.

Some of the parallels between Joseph Smith and Saint Seraphim are, simply put, completely stunning! On at least two occasions, Joseph Smith and Seraphim received revelations that were similar. One such revelation was received by Seraphim following three days of prayer. Seraphim heard the voice of God speaking to him, using words almost identical to some that the Lord spoke to Joseph Smith in 1820 during his First Vision. The other is seen in a vision of heaven that Seraphim experienced, which makes for interesting comparison to Joseph Smith's vision of the celestial kingdom, recorded in D&C 137. I describe these parallels and others in Chapter 9, "Saint Seraphim of Sarov."

I have organized this book in five parts with a glossary and recommended reading list at the end, as described here:

- **Part I (Chapters 1–2):** These chapters include background information on Eastern Orthodoxy and on *theosis*, or deification, which is the Orthodox teaching that believers can become gods, being deified by the very energy or light of God and transformed into the likeness of God. I show that the parallels between the teaching and experience of the two churches on this topic are deeper and more significant than previously understood.
- **Part II (Chapters 3–5):** This portion provides information on the Orthodox monastic tradition and how the lives of several Orthodox (and Catholic) monks over the centuries may fulfill Latter-day Saint prophecy.
- **Part III (Chapters 6–8):** The Orthodox calendar is described, as are several very interesting correlations to the dates and themes of key sections of the Doctrine and Covenants. The topic of whether Joseph Smith could have had access to an Orthodox calendar is explored.
- **Part IV (Chapters 9–14):** Profiles of several notable saints are given, including Saint Seraphim of Sarov (1754–1833) (Chapter 9); The Elders of Optina (Chapter 10); Saint Alexander of Svir (1448–1533) (Chapter 11); Saint Symeon the New Theologian (949–1022) (Chapter 12); and other saints and holy men (Chapter 13). Part IV ends with conclusions (Chapter 14).

- **Part V:** A detailed analysis of the Orthodox annual liturgical calendar is given, showing connections to themes and dates of the Doctrine and Covenants.
- **Glossary of Orthodox Terms**
- **Recommended Reading List**

Naturally, some readers may wish to visit the monasteries and churches that I describe. I do not discourage this, but would remind these readers that if they visit Orthodox holy sites, they should do so respectfully, quietly, and with the intent to learn from the tour guides. Questions should be addressed to guides, rather than to monks or clergy. The goal should be to *learn* about Orthodoxy *from* the Orthodox, not to persuade the guides or clergy of Latter-day Saint or other views. Visitors should dress modestly and neatly. Shorts for men are generally considered inappropriate. Women are normally encouraged to wear modest skirts or dresses and to wear a head scarf. Visitors should respect signs indicating where photography is prohibited, though on occasion, the tour guide or a monastery official may give their blessing (permission) for a few photos to be taken.

I have no political motive in publishing this book. Since the time when I first conceived this project, a number of events have intervened on the world stage that have added greater strain to US-Russian relations. Indirectly, these events have also taken a toll on the relations between the various Orthodox churches. This is seen in the decision by Ecumenical Patriarch Bartholomew in 2018 to recognize the Ukrainian Orthodox Church as "autocephalous," or independent. This is a decision that was firmly opposed by the Russian Orthodox Church. I do not take sides on this or other intra-Orthodox disagreements, nor do I intend that this book be construed as an endorsement of the policies of any government, on any topic.

If this book can help promote a positive image of Orthodoxy, or of Russian Orthodoxy, I will be pleased. If it can serve to build appreciation in the Orthodox community and in other Christian groups for the doctrines, teachings, and practices of the Church of Jesus Christ of Latter-day Saints, I will be equally pleased.

This book is not intended as a proselytizing tool or for use in Sunday meetings. Moreover, its writing was not requested by

Latter-day Saint leaders. I alone am responsible for the views expressed in this book.

M. Scott Bradshaw

August 13, 2019

---

[1] Sergey Antonenko, *Mormony v Rossii: Put' dlinoy v stoletiye* (Moscow: Rodina, 2007) = Сергей Антоненко, *Мормоны в России: Путь длиной в столетие* (Москва, Родина, 2007).
[2] Besides the Holy Bible, the Church of Jesus Christ of Latter-day Saints considers the following books to be canonical: *The Book of Mormon, The Doctrine and Covenants,* and *The Pearl of Great Price.* The Book of Mormon is a record of God's dealings with an ancient Israelite group that was led to the Americas by prophets about 600 BC. The most important part of The Book of Mormon is the book of   3 Nephi, which gives an account of Christ's appearance among this people following his resurrection in Palestine. The Doctrine and Covenants is a compilation of revelations given to Joseph Smith by the Lord (1820–1844), along with a few added by his successors. In these, the Lord speaks in the first person as with Moses and other Old Testament prophets. *The Pearl of Great Price* is a collection of writings of Moses and Abraham given to the world through Joseph Smith, along with twelve "Articles of Faith," Joseph's personal history, and an inspired revision of portions of Matthew, chapters 23–24. The Holy Scriptures can be found on the Church's   website   at: https://www.churchofjesuschrist.org/study/scriptures?lang=eng
[3] Daniel B. Clendenen, *Eastern Orthodox Christianity: A Western Perspective*, 2nd ed. (Grand Rapids: Baker Academic, 1994, 2003), preface.
[4] Boyd K. Packer, "The Temple, The Priesthood," April Conference 1993. Elder Packer stated in this talk, "There have been many visitations to the temple. President Lorenzo Snow saw the Savior there. Most of these sacred experiences remain unpublished."
[5] "Encyclical of the Holy and Great Council of the Orthodox Church," Holy and Great Council, https://www.holycouncil.org/-/encyclical-holy-council, para. 2 and 3.
[6] Translation of the Greek Orthodox Archdiocese of America.
[7] See in particular verses 8–20.
[8] Compare to the vision of Stephen as recorded in Acts 7:55–56.
[9] "The Life of Saint Alexander of Svir: Blessed Seer of the Holy Trinity," *The Northern Thebaid: Monastic Saints of the Russian North*, trans. Fathers Seraphim (Rose) and Herman (Podmoshnensky), with an

introduction by I.M. Kontzevitch (Platina, CA: St. Herman of Alaska Brotherhood, 1995), 110–139; and 123–124.

[10] Sergey Antonenko, *Mormony v Rossii: Put' dlinoy v stoletiye* (Moscow: Rodina, 2007) = Сергей Антоненко, *Мормоны в России: Путь длиной в столетие* (Москва, Родина, 2007).

Part I

An Overview of Eastern Orthodoxy

and

Theosis

1—Eastern Orthodoxy—A Short Overview

The term "Orthodox" is composed of two Greek words, orthos ("right") and doxa ("belief"), meaning right belief or right thinking. Orthodoxy is the form of Christianity that developed in the eastern portion of the Roman Empire. The Eastern Orthodox Church (of which Russian Orthodoxy is by far the largest branch) is the world's second largest Christian church, the largest being the Roman Catholic Church. These two are also the largest churches that trace their authority to the original twelve Apostles. There are over 250 million Orthodox believers in the world.

The Eastern Orthodox Church has no central governing authority but is rather a communion of fifteen independent churches that are referred to as "autocephalous," or self-governing. These autocephalous churches adhere to a common body of Orthodox beliefs, sacraments, liturgies, and practices that have been transmitted from generation to generation for many centuries. Each autocephalous church is headed by a *patriarch*.

Among the autocephalous churches are those of the Ecumenical Patriarchate of Constantinople, the Patriarchate of Alexandria, the Patriarchate of Antioch, the Patriarchate of Jerusalem, the Patriarchate of Russia, the Orthodox Church of Serbia, the Orthodox Church of Romania, the Orthodox Church of Bulgaria, the Orthodox Church of Georgia, the Orthodox Church of Cyprus, the Orthodox Church of Greece, the Orthodox Church of Poland, the Orthodox Church of Albania, and the Orthodox Church of the Czech lands and Slovakia.[1] The Ukrainian Orthodox Church was recognized as autocephalous in 2018, over the vehement objections of the Russian Orthodox Church. To this list, some would consider the Orthodox Church in America to be autocephalous as well. There are also several "autonomous" churches (in Finland, Japan, and China), and several national Orthodox churches or patriarchates that are not recognized as autocephalous (two in Ukraine; a few other examples include the Orthodox churches of Macedonia, Montenegro, and Belarus).[2] Most of the churches listed above are organized along national lines, with the exceptions of the ancient patriarchates of Alexandria, Antioch, and Jerusalem.[3]

2

The connection between church authority and governmental power is suggested by the largely national nature of most Orthodox churches. Some have called this "Caesaropapism," meaning that the church is subordinate to the state and is expected to serve state interests.[4] Given that this book is focused on building commonality between Christian churches, it does not explore this avenue of thought. It is enough to note here that the annals of Orthodox history are full of examples when church hierarchs and monks stood firm against immoral, wicked, or oppressive practices of their civil rulers, even if this carried dangers.

The ecumenical patriarch of Constantinople (modern Istanbul) is viewed as a "first among equals" and works to promote intra-Orthodox dialogue as well as dialogue with non-Orthodox faiths. The present patriarch, Bartholomew, is a recognized moral leader on the world stage. While relatively few Greeks still remain in Istanbul (former Constantinople), the Patriarchate of Constantinople also has spiritual stewardship over roughly seven million Orthodox believers globally, chiefly in the Greek diaspora abroad.[5]

The Eastern Orthodox Church has much in common with the Roman Catholic Church. Until the year 1054, the two were "undivided" and were considered one church. The two churches split that year, with the pope in Rome and the patriarch in Constantinople both excommunicating each other.

The two churches are otherwise quite close on points of theology. Both churches recognize the doctrines enunciated in seven ecumenical councils that took place between AD 325 and 787. These councils established doctrines that form a basic core of beliefs recognized by the Catholic and Orthodox faiths, as well as by many other Christians, including the dogma of the Holy Trinity. Both churches trace their authority and priesthood to the Apostles. The ordinances, or "sacraments," of the two churches are very similar, with both churches recognizing seven major sacraments.

An important exception to this general doctrinal alignment, however, is seen in Orthodox teachings on divine light and deification, or *theosis*, as taught by Saint Gregory Palamas (1296–1359). See Chapter 2 for more on these topics.

Of recent interest, a Holy and Great Council of the Orthodox Church was held in June 2016 on the island of Crete. This council was decades in the making. Some of the Orthodox faithful may have anticipated that this would ultimately be considered the "Eighth Ecumenical Council," or the first such council in over 1,200 years. The Council concluded on June 26, 2016. Representatives from ten of the (then) fourteen autocephalous Orthodox Churches[6] attended. The Churches of Antioch, Russia, Bulgaria, and Georgia declined to attend.[7] Given the absence of four delegations, it remains to be seen if the Council will achieve its intended recognition. Either way, the Council approved eight documents that, at least for the ten Churches that attended, are authoritative.

One of the eight documents approved at the 2016 Council specifically related to marriage and family.[8] The Orthodox Church, like the Catholic Church, recognizes marriage as one of the seven sacraments of the Church. In keeping with this view, this document stresses the importance of marriage between man and woman. Orthodox marriages must have the approval of the bishop (as do those for Roman Catholics and some other Christian groups), so that "the marriage may be according to God, not after their own desire."[9] The document cites an ancient letter on this point, from Ignatius the God-Bearer to Polycarp of Smyrna (both of these men, by the way, were disciples of John the Apostle). Civil marriage without the blessing of the Church "lacks sacramental character" and is "simply legalized cohabitation."[10] The Orthodox Church sees important symbolism in the fact that Christ's first miracle was performed at a wedding (John 2:2).[11] The Orthodox Church sees the family as a "small church" or as an "icon of the Church."[12] This document explains that faith in Christ is a "necessary condition of marriage" and "unity in Christ is the foundation of marital unity." It also states a strong position against "same-sex unions" and "any other form of cohabitation apart from marriage," and speaks of "grave consequences brought about by this crisis of the institutions of marriage and family."

On the topic of marriage, these lines from the entry on "Marriage" in *The Concise Encyclopedia of Orthodox Christianity* are of interest here. They show that the Orthodox Church teaches that marriage can have an eternal duration:

4

Through marriage, man and woman become "one flesh" (Eph. 5:31) and belong to each other eternally ("into the Kingdom"). Orthodox marriage is not seen as being only "Until death doth you part."

This same entry also states:

> This mystery of Christian marital love is everlasting because it flows out from Christ and makes the person eternal (deified by grace) through their partaking in the communion of the chosen one.[13]

The Roman Catholic Church also places great emphasis on marriage; however, the Catholic understanding of marriage does not seem to envision a union that endures beyond death.[14] This is evident from Pope Francis's 2016 document, *"Amoris Laetitia"* (meaning "the joy of love"), described below. During a 2014 summit on the "Complementarity of Man and Woman in Marriage," Pope Francis delivered a ten-minute address in which he explained that "the contribution of marriage to society is 'indispensable.'" The summit was attended by religious leaders from around the globe, including several senior Latter-day Saint leaders.[15] The pope noted that the institution of marriage and family is "in crisis," and observed that "we now live in a culture of the temporary, in which more and more people are simply giving up on marriage as a public commitment." He also mentioned the importance of marriage in the child's development, stating that children have a "right to grow up in a family, with a father and a mother capable of creating a suitable environment for a child's development and emotional maturity."[16]

In March 2016, Pope Francis issued a much-anticipated document, the "Post-Synodal Apostolic Exhortation *Amoris Laetitia*,"[17] which offers pastoral advice to the clergy on a variety of topics pertaining to marriage and family, including issues related to the divorce and remarriage of Catholics. This document is not intended to pronounce doctrine (this would be reserved for an "encyclical"), so there is no change in Catholic doctrine. The Exhortation followed two synods of bishops that took place in 2014 and 2015.

Notably, nothing in the document endorses same-sex marriage. In fact, it states that such unions "may not simply be equated with marriage." It does speak out against violence or aggression against homosexuals and calls for such persons and families to be treated with dignity and given appropriate pastoral care, to help them "fully carry out God's will in their lives."[18]

The Exhortation also reaffirms Catholic teaching on marriage in these terms:

> Christian marriage, as a reflection of the union between Christ and his Church, is fully realized in the union between a man and a woman who give themselves to each other in a free, faithful and exclusive love, who belong to each other *until death* and are open to the transmission of life, and are consecrated by the sacrament, which grants them the grace to become a domestic church and a leaven of new life for society [emphasis added].[19]

While there are many commonalities between the Catholic and Orthodox Churches, there are also points of differentiation. One of the more significant differences is that Orthodox parish priests may marry and have families, while Catholic clergy are expected to remain celibate; however, the Catholic position on this topic may change, since Pope Francis signaled a willingness in March 2017 to consider ordaining married men.[20]

There are also notable differences in the way that worship services are held. The liturgy in Orthodox services is chanted, or sung; in Catholic services, it is recited. In Orthodox services, the singing of hymns is a cappella, without instrumental accompaniment. Anecdotally, Orthodox sources sometimes explain this absence of musical instruments with a simple reply: the human voice is the only instrument created by God; therefore, it is the only instrument fit to praise him. In Catholic services, organs or even contemporary instruments are used. Organs in Catholic churches are among the grandest and oldest in the world.

Fasting has a great importance in Orthodox worship. In fact, the recent Holy and Great Council approved a document stressing the importance of fasting.[21] Orthodox believers are normally expected to fast from midnight the night before partaking of the Eucharist, or Holy Communion.

One of the most visible differences between Orthodox and Catholic worship is seen in the role of the artwork that adorns churches and the homes of believers. Catholic Churches often have works of art such as paintings or sculptures to promote a spirit of worship. The works of great Renaissance artists adorn churches in Italy and elsewhere. Orthodox churches usually have numerous icons, which are religious paintings of Christ, Mary, saints, martyrs, angels, and Biblical scenes. Miraculous powers are sometimes ascribed to particular icons; in fact, several dates on the Orthodox worship calendar commemorate miracles or great events attributed particularly to icons of Mary and the Christ child.[22] The icons are seen as means through which the Mother of God (*Theotokos*) makes manifest her mercy. The role of icons in worship was at times controversial in the early centuries of Christianity; however, the Seventh Ecumenical Council (AD 787) laid to rest the controversy, allowing for their use.[23]

As the use of icons has sometimes been misunderstood in the West, this quotation from the Seventh Ecumenical Council may provide helpful background:[24]

> "We define that the holy icons, whether in colour, mosaic, or some other material, should be exhibited in the holy churches of God. . . . We define also that they should be kissed and that they are an object of veneration and honour (timitiki proskynisis), but not of real worship (latreia), which is reserved for Him Who is the subject of our faith and is proper for the divine nature. The veneration accorded to an icon is in effect transmitted to the prototype; he who venerates the icon, venerated in it the reality for which it stands."[25] Orthodox writers clarify that not only is the honor or veneration of the believer passed through the icon to the sacred figure depicted thereon, but a blessing also returns from the icon to the believer.[26]

The theological understanding of icons is closely connected to Orthodox Christology. Christ is understood as having two natures, human and divine, and both aspects of this nature are believed to be present in an icon. The reasoning is essentially that if God can be present in a human form (Christ), then he can dwell in an icon.[27] From the Orthodox point of view, "the icon is a real incarnation of the image of Christ (or of the saints)." Rejecting this idea would be "tantamount to rejecting fundamental truths of the real incarnation of Christ."[28]

With this in mind, it is not surprising that miracles should be associated with icons. Moreover, the origin of icon painting is believed to trace back to Saint Luke the Evangelist. He is believed to have been the first icon painter, having painted Mary.

Figure 1.1: Christ Pantocrator Icon
Saint Catherine Monastery, Mount Sinai
Credit: Wikimedia Commons, public domain.[29]

The picture in Figure 1.1 is of *Christ Pantocrator,* which translates as "Christ Almighty," or "Christ Ruler of All." This icon is an outstanding example of Orthodox Christology. It dates to the mid-sixth century and is found in the St. Catherine Monastery on

Mount Sinai. It is the earliest surviving example of its type, showing Christ as a mature, powerful man, rather than as a younger, beardless boy. The two sides of his face are asymmetrical, representing the two halves of his nature, human and divine.

This icon has been copied and recopied thousands of times and is the most prevalent image of Christ in Orthodoxy. It is often found at the top of the center dome in an Orthodox Church, looking down on the worshipers as if from heaven.

Metropolitan Hilarion, a leading Orthodox writer, suggests that the Christ Pantocrator icon may have originally been painted based on an earlier image of Christ that, according to tradition, was made without human hands in a miraculous manner. Ancient sources report the existence of such an image, fixing its earliest location in Edessa (in modern Turkey).[30] Sources later state that it was located in Constantinople, where it seems to have disappeared from history in about 1204 when Western Crusaders pillaged the city.

Hilarion postulates that the famous Shroud of Turin—thought by Catholics to possibly be the actual burial shroud of Christ—may actually be the image of Christ that was made without human hands. In any case, the Christ Pantocrator image does bear general similarity to the face and proportions of the man in the famous Shroud of Turin.[31]

As in Roman Catholicism, Mary is venerated as the Mother of God. She is often referred to by Orthodox believers even in English by her Greek title, *Theotokos,* meaning "Mother of God."[32] Under Orthodox tradition, Mary is seen as having a special protective role over Christians and the Christian kingdoms of Byzantine and Slav rulers. There are even special "domains," or distinct regions, where Mary is believed to have a particular and special stewardship. One such domain is believed to be the Diveyevo Convent near Sarov, Russia. This convent has preserved Saint Seraphim of Sarov's (1754–1833) legacy; his relics (body) are housed there currently, as are a number of early notebooks of his sayings.

Another domain where Mary is said to have special stewardship is Mount Athos in Greece, a peninsula that has been known for centuries as the "holy mountain." Under Orthodox tradition, Mary visited Athos in company with John the Apostle while traveling from Joppa to Cyprus to see Lazarus. They were blown off course, landing near the present site of some of the monasteries on Athos. Mary was so captivated by the beauty of Athos that she asked her Son to give it to her as her garden. She is believed to have remained ever since the protector of Athos and of its monks.[33]

Today, Athos is the greatest spiritual center of the Eastern Orthodox Church. It is home to twenty monasteries, some dating back over a thousand years.[34] Its legal, religious, and cultural situation is unique. Athos retains a special status under the Greek Constitution and even under the treaties of the European Union, which Greece joined in 1981.[35] Athos is given special consideration with respect to the free movement of persons under the Schengen Agreement, which abolishes passport checks and establishes common visa requirements for travel *within* twenty-six signatory states in Europe. Women are not permitted to visit Athos (even female livestock animals are not kept there), and special visitor permits are required for men. The total exclusion of women underscores the strict code of sexual purity that the monks of Athos are expected to abide by.[36]

Although the deep reverence for Mary is shared with Roman Catholics, there are doctrinal differences in how her role is understood by the two faiths. The Orthodox Church does not accept the teaching of the Immaculate Conception, which is the idea that Mary was born without original sin, or related teachings, such as one that says Mary led a sinless life.[37]

One point of difference that figured large in the schism between the Catholic and Orthodox churches in 1054 is seen in variations of the Nicene Creed used by the Roman Catholic Church and the Eastern Orthodox Church. This creed was the outcome of the First and Second Ecumenical Councils, which were held respectively in AD 325 and 381. The Nicene Creed states basic beliefs on the nature of God and the relationship between the Father, Son, and Holy Spirit of the Holy Trinity. The Catholic version of the Nicene Creed adds words known as the *filioque*, which describe the Holy Spirit as proceeding from both the Father and the Son. The Eastern Orthodox form of the creed (which the Orthodox believe is the original form of the creed) omits these words, thus affirming that the Holy Spirit proceeds alone from the Father.

In the background over the controversy regarding the *filioque* is the topic of the pope's authority. With the emergence in the West of the *filioque* version of the Creed, the question arose: if the pope could change what was settled in the first two Ecumenical Councils (the dogma of the Trinity), what else could he change? Did the Roman pontiff have primacy over other ancient centers of Christianity, such as Constantinople (modern Istanbul), or of Antioch, Alexandria, and Jerusalem?

The issue of the pope's authority, or "primacy," has long been a concern of the Orthodox Church. As an illustration, a popular translation of Russian Orthodox services from the early twentieth centuries shows that Roman Catholics who wished to convert to Orthodoxy were required to renounce the "erroneous belief that the holy Apostles did not receive from our Lord equal spiritual power, but that the holy Apostle Peter was their Prince: and that the Bishop of Rome is his successor." They were also required to renounce the notion that the pope is infallible.[38]

There were other differences between the two churches that may also have contributed to the split in 1054. In the West, worship was only in Latin. In the East, worship was in Greek and numerous other languages. The Catholics used only unleavened bread; the Orthodox used leavened bread. The rupture seemed to have become irreparable after crusaders sacked Constantinople in 1204 as a culmination of the Fourth Crusade.

Periodic efforts have been undertaken over the centuries to reconcile the two churches. In recent decades, signs of possible rapprochement between the two churches can be seen. In 1965, the mutual excommunications of the pope and the patriarch of Constantinople were rescinded by both churches. This issue was the one that sparked the schism in 1054. In 2016, Pope Francis and Patriarch Kirill of the Russian Orthodox Church met in Havana, Cuba in a historic meeting that may eventually pave the way toward closer ties between these churches

In terms of the respective social missions of the two churches, Catholic educational and charitable activities are probably perceived as being more broad-based and active around the globe;

however, an internet search shows that there are large, well-funded Orthodox charities as well. For example, International Orthodox Christian Charities (IOCC) reports on their website that they have delivered over $580 million in relief and development aid since their inception in 1992. This is impressive by any measure.

The recent Holy and Great Council of the Orthodox Church in 2016 saw the approval of a document outlining the social mission of the Orthodox Church, including (among many other points) service to "the hungry, the poor, the sick, the disabled, the elderly, the persecuted, those in captivity and prison, the homeless, the orphans, the victims of destruction and military conflict, those affected by human trafficking and modern forms of slavery."[39]

Orthodoxy and the Language of Worship

Historically, Orthodox worship and that of Eastern Christianity in general has been in the vernacular of the people, or in a language intended to be widely understood, such as the Old Church Slavonic language that was created in the ninth century for worshippers in countries where Slavic languages are spoken. Early translations of religious materials were made in Syriac (second century), Coptic (second century), Armenian (fourth century), and Georgian (fifth century).[40] Catholic Mass, on the other hand, has been traditionally celebrated in Latin, though following Church reforms in the 1960s, services are widely available in local languages.

The most interesting illustration of the contrasting approaches of Eastern and Western Christianity on the topic of the language for worship services is seen in the mission of Constantine and Methodius to the Kingdom of Moravia in 862. In the ninth century, the patriarch of Constantinople sent two brothers, Constantine (later known as Cyril) and Methodius, on a mission to the Kingdom of Moravia,[41] which included parts of (modern) western Slovakia, Bohemia, southern Poland, and western Hungary. Their mission was to create a language for worship that would be understood by all speakers of Slavic languages. As part of this task, an alphabet also had to be created. This language and alphabet would serve as a vehicle for church services, worship, preaching, and the eventual translation of the scriptures. At the time, Slavic languages were closer to each other than they are now,

12

so seeking to create a mutually intelligible language for religious use by all Slavs was a realistic objective.

The brothers had unique preparation for such a task. Both had grown up in Thessalonica, in a region with many Slavs. According to Methodius's biographer, his intellect came to the attention of influential people at a young age. Even the Byzantine emperor explained that he expected to charge Methodius "with the government of a Slavic archontia [province]." The emperor also instructed him to "learn Slavic customs" and that "he would one day send him [Methodius] to be the teacher and first archbishop of the Slavs."[42] Later, Methodius was tonsured a monk and lived near Mount Olympus in Asia Minor (in Bithynia, not to be confused with Olympus in Greece). This also was a region heavily populated with Slavs.

Constantine, for his part, also exhibited a gift for learning. He attracted the attention of an imperial official who invited him to study in Constantinople. Constantine later filled a diplomatic mission to the Arab caliphate in Samarra. Subsequent to this, he went to Olympus to live with his brother. Both occupied themselves with academic pursuits during this time, in a place "surrounded by Slavs."

In 860, the two brothers filled a diplomatic and religious mission to Crimea and to Khazaria (a kingdom north of the Caspian Sea with borders extending to Crimea). The Khazar king had sent an emissary to the Emperor in Constantinople, asking for advice on matters of religion. It seemed that both Muslims and Jews were pressing the king to adopt their respective religions.[43] During this mission, the brothers gained even greater exposure to Slavic and other languages. Constantine reportedly studied Hebrew and "Samaritan books" (presumably the Bible), and is reported by his biographer to have found a copy of the Psalms and the Gospels in "Russian," though this statement has occasioned a good deal of debate (the Russians are not known to have had their own written language yet).[44]

In 862, the brothers began their mission to the Kingdom of Moravia, ultimately succeeding in their task to create a religious language for Slavs. The language they devised is known as "Old Church Slavonic," which over the centuries evolved into a similar liturgical language known as "Church Slavonic." This language is believed to be the oldest written Slavic language.[45] In centuries past, this language was used in Orthodox services in lands now within Bulgaria, Poland, the Czech Republic and Slovakia, Russia, Serbia, Montenegro, Bosnia and Herzegovina, the Republic of Macedonia, and Ukraine. Today it is mainly used in Russia, Serbia, and Bulgaria.

The brothers are sometimes also credited with having created the Cyrillic alphabet (named after Cyril), in which Russian and several other languages are written, though most scholars actually believe their creation was an alphabet known as "Glagolithic," which is quite different from the Cyrillic script. Glagolithic is not only different from Cyrillic but also from other known alphabets. The biographies of Cyril and Methodius and other ancient sources attribute this unique language to God, saying that it was revealed by God to these men.[46]

14

The Glagolithic script remained in use for a number of centuries and, in a few isolated cases, is still used today;[48] however, examples of documents in Cyrillic date back a thousand years or more.[49] The two alphabets were thus used simultaneously for a number of centuries for the same Old Church Slavonic language.

Upon arriving in Moravia, Cyril and Methodius soon encountered opposition from German clergy, who were Roman Catholic and objected to the plan to translate religious materials into a Slavic language. These clergy were advocating a view that has been called "trilingualism," or the notion that only Hebrew, Greek, and Latin were "sanctified languages" that could properly be used for Christian worship and for written religious works, such as translations of the Bible.[50]

This controversy prompted Constantine (Cyril) and Methodius to travel to Rome in AD 867 in order to discuss the language question with the pope. They also brought with them the relics of Saint Clement, which Constantine had providentially discovered during an earlier diplomatic mission to Crimea.[51]

Clement is considered by Roman Catholics to have been one of the early popes.

Figure 1.3: Basilica San Clemente, Rome.

15

While traveling to Rome, the brothers passed through Venice, where they defended their decision to translate the liturgy into Slavonic. Cyril delivered an apologia defending their actions, asking, "does not the rain fall equally upon all people, does the sun not shine for all, and do we not all breathe the air in equal measure?" During his speech, Cyril pointed out that many peoples have their own language for worship: the "Armenians, Persians, Abasgians, Iberians, Sogki, Goths, Avars, Turks, Khazars, Arabs, Egyptians, Syrians, and many others besides."[52] In citing these examples, Cyril demonstrated the "ecumenicity of Byzantium, which, precisely through recognizing and respecting the spiritual freedom of the peoples around it, ensured recognition of its own supremacy."[53]

The fact that the brothers arrived in Rome in possession of Clement's relics helped assure their success in seeking the pope's blessing for their mission. In fact, the presence of these relics caused a sensation in Rome. Pope Hadrian II and his retinue greeted the brothers and the relics at the gate of the city. Miracles were also reportedly occasioned by the arrival of the relics. The brothers presented the pope with Slavic religious books, and he later put them on the altar of a church to consecrate them.

The pope took other steps to ensure acceptance among the clergy and people of the Slavic language and script that Cyril and Methodius had devised. He personally ordained Methodius a priest and arranged for hand-picked bishops to similarly ordain some of the Slavs who accompanied Cyril and Methodius. These newly ordained men were then invited to assist in celebrating a mass in Slavonic at Saint Peter's Basilica.[54]

Unfortunately, Cyril died in Rome a year later in February 869. He was tonsured a monk a few weeks before his death, taking the name Cyril (having been known previously as Constantine). The pope offered his own tomb in Saint Peter's Basilica for Cyril, but Methodius asked that he be buried underneath Saint Clement's Church, where Clement's relics had been placed. The funeral was conducted with the dignity that would otherwise be seen only for a pope's funeral. Now known as the Basilica of Saint Clement, the church and its foundations make for an interesting visit. [55]

Excavations that were commenced in the nineteenth century have uncovered the location where Cyril's body was buried in the ninth century (though it was reportedly removed in 1788).[56] The spot is appropriately marked by plaques in various languages, including Russian, acknowledging Cyril's role in helping lay the groundwork for the Christianization of Slavic lands. Beautiful frescos from the twelfth century line the walls. One tells the story of the miraculous discovery of Clement's remains in Crimea by Cyril during his earlier diplomatic mission.[57]

The story of the mission of Cyril and Methodius to Moravia and subsequent journey to Rome underscores just how paradoxical relations between the Orthodox and Catholic Churches can be. In the ninth century, the two were still an "undivided" church, the "universal" Christian church, yet their respective approaches to the topic of liturgical language were vastly different. Eastern (later Orthodox) worship was usually in the vernacular, or local language of the people, while Western (later, Catholic) worship was in Latin. In the end, Cyril's death in Rome helped create a modest but lasting link between Rome and Orthodoxy; the site of Cyril's tomb is now a location for quiet veneration by both Catholic and Orthodox believers.

Consistent with the Orthodox focus on making worship services available in local languages, translations of the Bible into Old Church Slavonic emerged earlier than some the more famous translations in the West. For example, the Ostromir Gospels date to 1056–57. This beautiful volume of 294 pages is considered the oldest book in the East Slavic language (i.e., a precursor to modern Russian). It is a lectionary, with Gospel readings organized by week and feast.

Beyond the mere beauty of the Ostromir Gospels and their linguistic significance, this volume is important because it is tangible proof that the scriptures were read to worshippers during Orthodox services. Moreover, they were read in a language that was understood by the people. The Russian National Library has a full set of high-resolution scans online of the Ostromir Gospels, organized by weekly readings. The first page is shown here, that of the Gospel of John, Chapter 1.

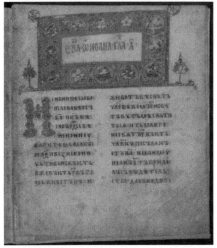

Figure 1.4 The Ostromir Gospels, John Chapter 1
Lectionary for Sunday and feast day readings, 1056-1057.
Credit: Russian National Library.[58]
Contrast the date of the Ostromir Gospels, 1056–57, with that of early translations of the Bible in English. John Wycliffe's translations of the Bible came late in the fourteenth century. William Tyndale's translation in English came over a century later, starting with the New Testament (1525). Tyndale was put to death in 1536 for heresy. Reportedly, thousands of copies of his translation of the New Testament had been printed before he died. Other early printings of Bibles in Slavic languages include the Prague Bible (Czech), which was printed in 1488, building on the work of men such as Jan Hus, who preached in Czech (ca. 1400) at the Bethlehem Chapel in Prague. Hus sought to reform church practices from within, and by preaching in Czech (instead of Latin) he has been seen a nationalist figure among Czechs. Hus suffered a martyr's death in 1415. The esteem with which he is held today in the eyes of his countrymen is suggested in the size and location of his statue, which is prominently placed, literally larger than life, in the Old Town Square in Prague. The Vaclav Havel International Airport in Prague also has a series of informative wall panels that tell his story in considerable detail.

Another notable early figure who was involved in translating and publishing the Bible in Eastern Europe was Francysk Skaryna (1494–1536),[59] who remains relatively unknown in the West. Skaryna is a national hero in Belarus.[60] A university in Belarus is named for him, the Francisk Skorina Gomel State University. In

1517, Skaryna was engaged in translating the Bible into Belarusian (which he referred to as "Russian") and printing portions of it in individual books from Prague.

The title page to Skaryna's Bible publications contained this introductory wording:

> Translated by Doctor Francis Skorina of the Renowned City of Polotsk to the Honour of God and the Good Edification of Common People.[61]

Skaryna's reference to "Common People" brings to mind a familiar quotation from William Tyndale, who almost simultaneously was engaged in translating and publishing the Bible into English. Tyndale stated to a clergyman of his day:

> If God spare my life, before very long I shall cause a plough boy to know the scriptures better than you do!

Later, in 1525, Skaryna also published a Slavonic version of the Acts and Epistles, from Vilnius, Lithuania. In the preface to this publication, Skaryna used this reasoning to support his intention to render the New Testament in the local languages of the day:

> The prophets were given the spirit to speak only in Hebrew or Chaldaic. To the Apostles on the other hand, and to all those who believe in Christ, the Holy Spirit was given, so that they could proclaim the divine truth, the word of salvation and the kingdom of God in all languages under the sun.[62]

Skaryna's translation raised eyebrows in some respects; his published volumes showed his name as translator and publisher and also included his printer's mark. Published Bibles in those days never included such indicia.

The first full, printed Bible in Slavonic appeared in 1580–81. It has been estimated that between one thousand and four thousand copies of this book, known as the Ostrog Bible, were eventually published.[63] One such copy is on display in a glass case in the library of the St. Vladimir's Orthodox Seminary in Crestwood, New York. Contrast this number of copies with the number of

German Bibles that Johannes Gutenberg printed over a century before in the 1450s, which scholars estimate was between 160 and 200.

The Ostrog Bible was later republished in Russia in 1663. In 1751, a third printing of the Bible in Church Slavonic was published with the support of the Russian empress Elizabeth. A revised version of this Bible, called the Bible of Elizabeth (1756), is considered the authorized version of the Bible by the Russian Orthodox Church.

The defeat and expulsion of French troops from Russia in 1812 brought a renewed effort to make the Bible available in Russia. A British newspaper printed this letter from one Mr. Paterson in 1813, attesting to extraordinary developments in this regard, including the creation of a Russian Bible society with the support of the emperor himself and many church officials, both Orthodox and non-Orthodox:

Extract of a Letter from Mr. Paterson, dated St Petersburg,

30th January 1813.

The hope you expressed in your last letter, that the day [illegible] "from on high" was about to visit the Russians, has, I trust, in part been already fulfilled. His Imperial Majesty and his Ministers have taken up the plan of establishing a Bible Society here, on an extensive scale, very warmly, and have done even more than I could ask for. . . . The Ukaze permitting this was signed by his Majesty, on the 6th December, and published by the Senate on the 2d January: About 40 persons of all ranks and of all religions, met on the 11th, to form themselves into a Society. We had the Metropolitan of the Russian Church, and the Metropolitan of the Catholics present; one spirit animated the whole, and all rejoiced at having an opportunity of uniting together in good cause. Perhaps such an assembly never met on earth; they manifested their zeal by their deed; 15,000 roubles were almost immediately subscribed, although our number was so small. I have no doubt of this becoming, at least, the third Bible Society in the world. The field is ample, extending from the Frozen Ocean to the Black Sea and the borders of China, and from the Baltic to the Eastern Ocean.

During the 1820s, portions of the Bible, including the New Testament, became available in the Russian language, with a complete translation published by 1876. During this time, Slavonic language Bibles were also increasingly available in Russia.

Representatives of the Russian Bible Society undertook far-flung missions on behalf of their society, extending their translation and publishing efforts to regions and tribes across the Russian Empire. In doing so, they did not proselytize or attempt to convert the locals to Protestant churches or to the Roman Catholic faith. It was expected that non-Christians who were baptized would join the "established church," meaning the Russian Orthodox Church.

With this in mind, the Russian emperor Alexander declared in 1817:

> I consider the progress of Bible Societies in Russia and the whole world, and their success among Christians, Heathens and Mahometans, as a signal instance of the grace of God . . . that the saving light of Revelation might be extended to all the nations of the empire.[64]

The emperor himself joined the Russian Bible Society and issued a decree instructing the clergy to consider the dissemination of the scriptures among the people as an "imperative duty."[65]

The Russian Bible Society still exists today. Throughout its history, it has been responsible for publishing the Bible not only in Russian but also many other languages of peoples native to Eurasia.[66]

A widely read nineteenth-century literary work in Russian attests to the growing influence of the Bible and Eastern Orthodox spirituality within Russian society during that time. Entitled in English *The Way of a Pilgrim*, or *Pilgrim's Tale*, this work was first published anonymously in Kazan, Russia in 1884. It tells the story of a Christian wanderer who reflects on the meaning of Paul's admonition to "pray without ceasing" (1 Thessalonians

21

5:17), learns the "Jesus Prayer," and meets other believers while traveling.

The Way of the Pilgrim also illustrates the spiritual power of the Jesus prayer, the practice of which was a central feature of *Hesychasm*. This method of prayer involved the continual, silent repetition of the words: "Lord Jesus Christ, Son of God, have mercy on me, a sinner."

The work starts with this statement:

> By the grace of God I am a Christian man, by my actions a great sinner, and by calling a homeless wanderer of the humblest birth who roams from place to place. My worldly goods are a knapsack with some dried bread in it on my back, and in my breast pocket a Bible. And that is all.[67]

The unnamed wanderer is later robbed of his earthly possessions, including his Bible and other religious books. Greatly distraught, he subsequently explains his predicament to a passing military officer who is fortuitously able to restore the stolen Bible and other religious books to their owner. The Way of the Pilgrim describes the wanderer's reaction as he once again holds his Bible and books:

> Now that I had my books again, I was so glad that I did not know how to thank God. I clasped the books to my breast and held them there so long that my hands got quite numbed. I shed tears of joy, and my heart beat with delight. The officer watched me and said, "You must love reading your Bible very much!" But such was my joy that I could not answer him, I could only weep. Then he went on to say, "I also read the Gospel regularly every day, brother." He produced a small copy of the Gospels, printed in Kiev and bound in silver, saying, "Sit down, and I will tell you how it came about."[68]

The military officer then proceeds to tell of his miraculous conversion to Christ and recovery from alcoholism, aided in great measure by his regular reading of a Slavonic Bible that, at least at first, he could barely understand.

Ironically, by the nineteenth century, the Church Slavonic language had become increasingly difficult for Russians to understand. Thus, the story describes the military officer's early experiences in trying to read the Slavonic Bible:

> I opened it, took a glance, and said, "I cannot accept it. I am not used to Church Slavonic and don't understand it." But the monk went on to assure me that in the very words of the gospel there lay a gracious power, for in them was written what God Himself had spoken. "It does not matter very much if at first you do not understand; go on reading diligently."[69]

The difficulty for Russians in understanding Church Slavonic was commented upon by newspapers in the West during the nineteenth century. Several English newspapers ran an article in 1855, explaining:

> And it [Church Slavonic] is no more understood by the Russian people than Latin is now by the Italian peasant. Only the learned are acquainted with it, and they study it as they would study dead language. Now, this ancient version of the Bible (after the precedent of the Vulgate of the Latin Church), has become the authorised Bible of the Russian Church; it alone is in the hands of the clergy, it alone is used for public worship, and it is from this text, now become unintelligible to the people, that the priests, every Sunday, read long portions, taken from the Gospels, the Epistles, the Psalms, and other books. The priests themselves hardly understand what they read.

The case is undoubtedly overstated. Many Russians still prefer the Church Slavonic, since it is part of their spiritual tradition, and with a little effort, Russians can learn to understand it reasonably well. The fact that much of the Divine Liturgy is repeated from week to week in the same words—and printed service books are also available—helps ensure that the words are understood.

To a certain extent, one could draw an analogy between Church Slavonic and the continued use of the King James Bible by many English-speaking Christians, including Latter-day Saints. This translation of the Bible is four hundred years old and draws heavily from language penned by William Tyndale five hundred years ago.

Some of the syntax, vocabulary, and grammar of this translation of the Bible are difficult to understand today, even for native English speakers. Yet the King James translation of the Bible is viewed by many (including many Latter-day Saints)[70] as a priceless part of their spiritual heritage. For these Christians, the use of contemporary language in addressing God or reading the Bible just doesn't sound dignified or reverent.

On the other hand, to make the analogy between the King James Version and Church Slavonic, one would have to imagine a King James Bible written in an alphabet containing additional letters compared to standard English (there are forty letters in Church Slavonic to Russian's thirty-three), with vocabulary even more distant from daily use than that of the King James to today's.

The Way of the Pilgrim also illustrates the spiritual power of the Jesus prayer, the practice of which was a central feature of *Hesychasm.*

---

[1] This list is taken from the website for the recent Holy and Great Council that was held in Crete in June 2016, accessed July 22, 2019, https://www.holycouncil.org/churches.

[2] A website advertising itself as the largest Pan-Orthodox information source on the web gives a helpful list of the various branches of Orthodoxy, accessed July 22, 2019, http://theorthodoxchurch.info/main/church/non-canonical-orthodox-churches/.

[3] In view of the largely national-nature of most Orthodox churches, there is an apparent connection between church authority and governmental power in Orthodoxy. Some have called this "Caesaro-papism." This term is sometimes understood to mean that the church is subordinate to the state and is expected to serve state interests (see Ware, The Orthodox Church, 40-41). It is not this book's purpose to explore or establish this point. In any case, any such research would also need to take into account the many instances in Orthodox history when the church has served as an important moral compass, when church heirarchs, clergy and monks stood firm against immoral, wicked or oppressive practices of their civil rulers.

[4] See Timothy Ware (Bishop Kallistos of Kokleia), *The Orthodox Church* (London and New York: Penguin Books, 1997), 40–41.

[5] See generally, John Anthony McGuckin, "Constantinople, Patriarchate of" in John Anthony McGuckin, ed., *The Concise Encyclopedia of Orthodox Christianity* (Malden, MA: Wiley Blackwell, 2014), 114.

[6] The Ukrainian Orthodox Church had not yet been recognized as autocephalous.

[7] See generally, "The Holy and Great Council: Pentecost 2016," Holy and Great Council, accessed July 22, 2019 https://www.holycouncil.org/home. The Church of Antioch reportedly pulled out due to a disagreement with the Church of Jerusalem over jurisdiction in Qatar. The Churches of Bulgaria and Greece reportedly had concerns about some of the documents slated for approval at the Council. The Russian Church declined to attend, based on the anticipated absence of Antioch, Bulgaria, and Georgia.

[8] See "The Sacrament of Marriage and its Impediments," Holy and Great Council, accessed July 15, 2019, https://www.holycouncil.org/-/marriage.

[9] Holy and Great Council, "Sacrament," para. 3.

[10] Holy and Great Council, "Sacrament," para. 9.

[11] Holy and Great Council, "Sacrament," para. 2.

[12] Holy and Great Council, "Sacrament," para. 4.

[13] Dan Sandu, "Marriage," in McGuckin, *Encyclopedia of Orthodox Christianity,* 307–9.

[14] See "Post-Synodal Apostolic Exhortation *Amoris Lætitia* of the Holy Father Francis" (Vatican Press: March 19, 2016), PDF, https://w2.vatican.va/content/dam/francesco/pdf/apost_exhortations/documents/papa-francesco_esortazione-ap_20160319_amoris-laetitia_en.pdf. See paragraph 163: "Yet if a couple can come up with a shared and lasting life project, they can love one another and live as one until *death do them part,* enjoying an enriching intimacy"; paragraph 214: "It needs to be stressed that these words cannot be reduced to the present; they involve a totality that includes the future: '*until death do us part*'"; paragraph 292: "Christian marriage, as a reflection of the union between Christ and his Church, is fully realized in the union between a man and a woman who give themselves to each other in a free, faithful and exclusive love, *who belong to each other until death* and are open to the transmission of life, and are consecrated by the sacrament, which grants them the grace to become a domestic church and a leaven of new life for society" [emphasis added].

[15] Jason Swensen, "President Eyring Champions Marriage at Interfaith Gathering," *Church News*, November 18, 2014, https://www.churchofjesuschrist.org/church/news/president-eyring-champions-marriage-at-interfaith-gathering?lang=eng, and Paul S. Edwards and Tad Walch, "Vatican brings faiths, including LDS, together in historic conference on marriage, family," November 16, 2014, *Deseret News*, http://www.deseretnews.com/article/865615664/Vatican-brings-faiths-including-Latter-day Saint-together-in-historic-conference-on-marriage-family.html, both accessed July 22, 2019.

[16] "Pope Francis's opening address to Humanum conference," Catholic

Herald, November 17, 2014, accessed July 22, 2019, https://catholicherald.co.uk/news/2014/11/17/full-text-pope-franciss-opening-address-to-humanum-conference/

[17] "Apostolic Exhortation," cited above at note 12.

[18] Jimmy Akin, "Pope Francis's New Document on Marriage: 12 Things to Know and Share," Catholic Answers, April 7, 2016, accessed July 22, 2019, https://www.catholic.com/magazine/online-edition/pope-franciss-new-document-on-marriage-12-things-to-know-and-share.

[19] "Apostolic Exhortation," para. 292.

[20] Crux staff, "Pope Francis signals openness to ordaining married men," March 8, 2017, Crux, Crux Catholic Media, accessed July 22, 2019, https://cruxnow.com/global-church/2017/03/08/pope-francis-signals-openness-ordaining-married-men/.

[21] Holy and Great Council, "The Importance of Fasting and Its Observance Today," accessed July 22, 2019, https://www.holycouncil.org/-/fasting.

[22] See for example the Donskoi Icon of the Mother of God, commemorated on August 19 in the Julian calendar. This icon was carried by Russian troops into battle against their Tatar overlords in 1380, when the Russians defeated these enemies for the first time in over a century and a half of domination. Later, in 1591, it was once again carried into battle as Tatar forces besieged Moscow. See "The Donskoi Icon of the Mother of God," Holy Trinity Russian Orthodox Church, accessed July 22, 2019, http://www.holytrinityorthodox.com/calendar/los/August/19-05.htm.

[23] For a general discussion of images and artwork from a Catholic perspective, see Kevin Knight, "Veneration of Images," New Advent, http://www.newadvent.org/cathen/07664a.htm.

[24] Metropolitan Hilarion Alfeyev, The Architecture, Icons, and Music of the Orthodox Church, vol. 3 of Orthodox Christianity, trans. Andrei Tepper (Yonkers, NY: St. Vladimir's Seminary Press, 2014), 127–134. This legend is also mentioned in a nineteenth-century English language source referenced in Chapter 6: Richard Lister Venables, Domestic Scenes in Russia: In a Series of Letters (London: J. Murray, 1856), 67; note that an 1839 edition also exists.

[25] "Sunday of Orthodoxy," Greek Orthodox Archdiocese of America, accessed July 22, 2019, https://www.goarch.org/sunday-of-orthodoxy.

[26] Theodor Damian, "Icons," in McGuckin, Encyclopedia of Orthodox Christianity, 270.

[27] Compare to Doctrine and Covenants 93:35, "The elements are the tabernacle of God . . ."

[28] Damian, "Icons," 270.

[29] https://commons.wikimedia.org/wiki/File:Spas_vsederzhitel_sinay.jpg; uploaded December 25, 2011, by Brandmeister~commonswiki.

[30] This legend is also mentioned in a nineteenth-century English language source referenced in Chapter 6: Richard Lister Venables, *Domestic Scenes in Russia: In a Series of Letters* (London: J. Murray, 1856), p. 67; note that an 1839 edition also exists.

[31] Metropolitan Hilarion Alfeyev, *The Architecture, Icons, and Music of the Orthodox Church*, vol. 3 of *Orthodox Christianity*, trans. Andrei Tepper (Yonkers, NY: St. Vladimir's Seminary Press, 2014), 127–134.

[32] Antonia Atanassova, "Theotokos, the Blessed Virgin," in McGuckin, *Encyclopedia of Orthodox Christianity*, 483–87.

[33] Graham Speake, *Mount Athos: Renewal in Paradise* (New Haven, CT: Yale University Press, 2002), [17]–18.

[34] For example, the existence of one of the leading monasteries on Athos, Vatopedi, can be documented back to at least 985 and may have been founded on the site of a monastery as old as the fourth century. This particular monastery has a notable library, housing valuable, rare documents and books. See "A Pilgrim's Guide to the Great and Holy Monastery of Vatopaidi," Pravoslaviye, accessed July 20, 2019, http://www.pravoslavieto.com/manastiri/aton/vatoped/guide_vatopedi.htm.

[35] See Agreement on the Accession of the Hellenic Republic, Final Act, "Joint Declaration concerning Mt. Athos," EUR-Lex, Publications Office of the EU, accessed July 21, 2019, http://eur-lex.europa.eu/legal-content/EN/TXT/?uri=CELEX:42000A0922(06).

[36] See generally "Mount Athos," Mount Athos Area Organization, accessed July 20, 2019, http://en.mountathosarea.org/our-area/mount-athos/.

[37] St. John Maximovith, *The Orthodox Veneration of the Mother of God*, trans. Fr. Seraphim Rose (Platina, CA: St. Herman of Alaska Brotherhood, 2012), 47–61.

[38] Isabel Florence Hapgood, *Service Book of the Holy Orthodox-Catholic Apostolic Church* (1906; repr., Englewood, NJ: Antiochian Orthodox Christian Archdiocese of North America, 1996), 455–56.

[39] "The Mission of the Orthodox Church in Today's World," Holy and Great Council, accessed July 20, 2019, https://www.holycouncil.org/-/mission-orthodox-church-todays-world.

[40] Dimitry Pospielovsky, *The Orthodox Church in the History of Russia* (Crestwood, NY: St. Vladimir's Seminary Press, 1997), 5. A mid-second-century translation of the Gospel of John on papyrus is found in the Bodmer collections in Switzerland. See Daniel Brierton Sharp, *Papyrus Bodmer III: An Early Coptic Version of the Gospel of John and Genesis 1–4:2* (Berlin: Walter de Gruyter, 2016).

[41] *Encyclopedia Britannica*, s.v. "Moravia: Historical Region, Europe," accessed July 20, 2019, https://www.britannica.com/place/Moravia. See also the description of Great Moravia in Anthony-Emil N. Tachiaos, *Cyril*

and Methodius of Thessalonica: The Acculturation of the Slavs (Crestwood, New York: St. Vladimir's Seminary Press, 2001), 57–64. My sketch of Cyril and Methodius is based mainly on this work.

[42] Tachiaos, *Cyril and Methodius,* 21.

[43] Tachiaos, *Cyril and Methodius,* 39–40.

[44] Tachiaos, *Cyril and Methodius,* 42

[45] Historical sources provide some clues that an earlier Slavic or Russian script may have existed, but the case is inconclusive at best. When traveling in Crimea on an earlier diplomatic mission in about 860, Cyril reportedly saw a Gospel and Psalter written in "Russian letters." There is also that case of unusual letters etched on stones on the Black Sea shore, which some scholars think may be an earlier Slavic script. See Tachiaos, *Cyril and Methodius,* 42–45. To these facts, one can add stories of the "Black Sea Rus," who, based on some early accounts, were believed to have been Goths who had their own church and missionary program as of the fourth century. The first Christian diocese of Rus was created by Cyril in 860 in Tmutarakan', which is located today in Russia across from the Crimean Peninsula. Early sources also mention liturgical materials in "Rus letters," but interpretations of these accounts vary widely. See Pospielovsky, *Orthodox Church,* 17–18.

[46] Tachiaos, *Cyril and Methodius,* 72. For notes on the alphabet created by Cyril and Methodius, see James H. Billington, *The Icon and the Axe: An Interpretive History of Russian Culture* (New York: Vintage Books, 1970), 629.

[47] https://commons.wikimedia.org/wiki/File:Saint_Cyril_tomb_in_San_Clemente_(2).jpg; uploaded November 6, 2017, by Harke.

[48] Glagolithic is used by a few islands in the Adriatic. See Pospielovsky, *Orthodox Church,* 18.

[49] Ivan G. Iliev, "Short History of the Cyrillic Alphabet," *International Journal of Russian Studies,* no. 2 (2013), http://www.ijors.net/issue2_2_2013/articles/iliev.html.

[50] Tachiaos, *Cyril and Methodius,* 78.

[51] Tachiaos, *Cyril and Methodius,* 45–46.

[52] Tachiaos, *Cyril and Methodius,* 83.

[53] Tachiaos, *Cyril and Methodius,* 84.

[54] Tachiaos, *Cyril and Methodius,* 85.

[55] Tachiaos, *Cyril and Methodius,* 87–90.

[56] Tachiaos, *Cyril and Methodius,* 91.

[57] Tradition holds that Clement was sent to Crimea as a prisoner, where he preached the gospel to slaves and prisoners. He died while in Crimea.

[58] Available at http://expositions.nlr.ru/ex_manus/Ostromir_Gospel/_Project/page_Manuscripts.php?dir. The main page for the Russian National Library

(English) is http://www.nlr.ru/eng/.

[59] There are several variations on the spelling of his name in English. I use *Francysk Skaryna*, which is commonly used on the internet. The spelling of his name as attached to the Francisk Skorina Gomel State University, a major Belarusian university, is taken directly from that university's webpage (see http://www.gsu.by/en).

[60] A.V., "Francysk Skaryna, the Martin Luther of Belarus," *The Economist*, January 2017, https://www.economist.com/blogs/prospero/2017/01/slavic-scholar, and "Francysk Skaryna," Belarus: The Official Website of the Republic of Belarus, Belarus.by, http://www.belarus.by/en/about-belarus/famous-belarusians/francysk-skaryna, both accessed July 22, 2019. The website of the National Library of Russia hosted an exhibit in 2017 entitled "500 Years of the Skaryna Bible," which includes background information on Skaryna and his Bibles, as well as digital images, available at http://expositions.nlr.ru/eng/faust/skorina.php. A digital image of the title page to Skaryna's Bible publications is available online at Wikipedia, s.v. "Francysk Skaryna," https://en.wikipedia.org/wiki/Francysk_Skaryna#/media/File:Biblia_Ruska.jpg. A nineteenth century British bibliographic note provides interesting background on Skaryna: see Thomas Joseph Pettigrew, *Bibliotheca Sussexiana a Descriptive Catalogue, Accompanied by Historical and Biographical Notices, of the Manuscripts and Printed Books Contained in the Library of His Royal Highness the Duke of Sussex* (London: Longman and Co., 1839), 244–245, https://play.google.com/books/reader?id=qriEbnTE7pgC&printsec=frontcover&output=reader&hl=en&pg=GBS.PR10. Biographical information on Skaryna is found in G. Pichura, "The Engravings of Francis Skaryna in the Biblija Ruska (1517-1519)," *Journal of Byelorussian Studies* 1, no. 3 (1967), [146]–167, available at http://belarusjournal.com/sites/default/files/JBS_1967_1_The%20Engravings%20of%20Francis%20Skaryna%20in%20twentiethe%20Biblija%20Ruska.pdf.

[61] Image available on the website of the National Library of Belarus, under the heading "Francisk Skorina: A Journey to the Fatherland," accessed August 2, 2019, http://content.nlb.by/content/dav/nlb/portal/content//File/Portal/Novosti/2012/October/2012.10.05/Skorina_portal/19.jpg. Translation from Francis J. Thompson, "Slavonic and Other Translations of the Bible," in Joze Krasove, ed., *The Interpretation of the Bible: The International Symposium in Slovenia*, Journal for the Study of the Old Testament, Supplement 289 (Sheffield, England: Sheffield Academic Press, 1998), 667.

[62] Cited in Alexander Nadson, "Francis Skaryna, the first Belarusian

printer and Bible scholar," Pravapis.org, Pravapis.org and Uladzimir Katkouski, June 14, 2001, accessed July 15, 2019, http://www.pravapis.org/art_skaryna1.asp.

[63] Thompson, "Slavonic and Other Translations," 677.

[64] Henry Augustus Zwick and John Golfried Schill, *Calmuc Tartary; or a Journey from Sarepta to Several Calmuc Hords of the Astracan Government; from May 26 to August 21, 1823 Undertaken on Behalf of the Russian Bible Society* (London: Holdsworth and Ball, 1831), 18.

[65] Zwick and Schill, *Calmuc Tartary,* 18.

[66] The Russian Bible Society's website is found at http://www.biblia.ru/en/?lang=e.

[67] *The Way of a Pilgrim and the Pilgrim Continues his Way,* trans. R.M. French, (1965; repr., New York: Harper, 1991), 4.

[68] *Way of a Pilgrim*, 11.

[69] *Way of a Pilgrim*, 11.

[70] The Church of Jesus Christ of Latter-day Saints uses the King James Version of the Bible in English-language settings.

2—Theosis, or Deification

Theosis is the idea that Christian believers can become gods, being deified by the grace or energies of God and transformed into the likeness of God. This is a distinctive Orthodox doctrine that has roots in the earliest centuries of Christianity and verses of scripture (notably, Psalms 82:6 and 2 Peter 1:4). Theosis has sometimes been compared and contrasted with Latter-day Saint teachings of "exaltation" and "eternal life"—the idea that believers as married couples can become gods. In the restored Church of Jesus Christ, this notion traces back to Doctrine and Covenants 132 (revealed on July 12, 1843) and a famous talk delivered by Joseph Smith, the King Follet sermon.

The doctrine that believers can become gods was taught by the Prophet Joseph Smith in his famous King Follett sermon, given on April 7, 1844, only months before his death:

> Here, then, is eternal life—to know the only wise and true God; and you have got to learn how to be gods yourselves, and to be kings and priests to God, the same as all gods have done before you, namely, by going from one small degree to another, and from a small capacity to a great one; from grace to grace, from exaltation to exaltation, until you attain to the resurrection of the dead, and are able to dwell in everlasting burnings, and to sit in glory, as do those who sit enthroned in everlasting power.[1]

Many of the men who have served as President of the Church since Joseph Smith have affirmed this same doctrine. Brigham Young stated in 1852:

> The Lord created you and me for the purpose of becoming Gods like Himself; when we have been proved in our present capacity, and been faithful with all things He puts in our possession. We are created, we are born, for the express purpose of growing up from the low estate of manhood, to become Gods like unto our Father in heaven. That is the truth about it, just as it is.[2]

Lorenzo Snow, the fifth President of the Church, gained an understanding of this doctrine through personal revelation four years before Joseph Smith taught this truth in the King Follett sermon, and three years before Doctrine and Covenants 132 was recorded. President Snow described this revelatory experience in these words:

> [The] Spirit of the Lord rested mightily upon me—the eyes of my understanding were opened, and I saw as clear as the sun at noonday, with wonder and astonishment, the pathway of God and man. I formed the following couplet which expresses the revelation, as it was shown me . . .
>
> As man now is, God once was: As God now is, man may be.[3]

More recently, President Gordon B. Hinckley reaffirmed this doctrine. According to an article on the Church's website, when President Hinckley was asked about this doctrine in 1997, he stated:

> That gets into some pretty deep theology that we don't know very much about. . . . Well, as God is, many may become. We believe in eternal progression, very strongly.[4]

Earlier, in the General Conference of October 1994, President Hinckley stated, "The whole design of the gospel is to lead us onward and upward to greater achievement, even, eventually, to godhood."[5]

On the surface, the parallels between theosis and exaltation seem inviting and even compelling; however, as one looks more deeply, there are significant differences in how the two churches understand these teachings.

One Latter-day Saint scholar, Terryl Givens, underscores the flaw in seeking simplistic comparisons between Orthodox and Latter-day Saint teachings on this topic. He gave an interview for an LDS Perspectives Podcast, where he states, in part:

> It's easy to find abundant quotations taken out of context that seem to perfectly parallel Joseph Smith's King Follett teaching that we can become God or like God. The problem is that for virtually all of western theological history, there has been in place a radical, ontological divide between the divine and the human.[6]

32

The "ontological gap" is essentially that God is eternal and humankind is his creation. Under Orthodox thinking, God is the only self-existing reality in the universe. Humans did not exist prior to their creation.

Orthodox sources articulate this same concern. Consider this comment from OrthodoxWiki:

> The Mormons' belief differs with the Orthodox belief in deification because the Latter-Day Saints believe that the core being of each individual, the "intelligence" which existed before becoming a spirit son or daughter, is uncreated or eternal. Orthodox deification always acknowledges a timeless Creator versus a finite creature who has been glorified by the grace of God.[7]

This same source also mentions the rejection of Trinitarian theology by the restored Church of Jesus Christ, which plays an important role in Orthodox teachings on theosis. One of the chief hurdles for dialogue here is that Orthodox Trinitarian theology holds that God is unknowable in his Essence, though he can be encountered, seen and partly understood in his Energy—meaning bright, uncreated light that is considered to be part of God, but not his "Essence." It is through this Energy of God that the faithful can be deified, or experience theosis. This Energy can transfigure the body, bathing it in light. This is the light that will shine from the faithful in the resurrection, and which on occasion has shined from numerous saints and monks during this life. This essence-energy distinction is essential in understanding Orthodox theology on deification.

The most well-known proponent of the essence-energy distinction was Saint Gregory Palamas (1296–1359). His writings constitute the most authoritative source to which Orthodoxy looks to understand deification and the essence-energy distinction. Palamas's views were not just based on the prior teachings of patristic writers. He drew heavily from the experiences of monks on Mount Athos in Greece. In fact, a significant number of the leading monks of Athos signed a declaration affirming Palamas's views, attaching their own names and asserting (modestly) that they know these things from their own "small experience."[8]

Over the centuries, some of the monks on Athos had encountered God in the form of bright light and had even experienced the transfiguration of their bodies. This light is believed to be the same light that shined from Christ's face on the Mount of Transfiguration as described in Matthew 17. It is referred to in Orthodox writings as the "Uncreated light" or "Tabor light" (the Transfiguration is believed to have occurred on Mount Tabor in Orthodox teaching).

In one of the greatest theological debates in history, Palamas prevailed in convincing Orthodox church authorities that monks really could see (and did see) this divine light, and that it was possible for humans to see God, or the energies of God in the form of this great light.[9]

The principal adversary of Palamas in this debate was one Barlaam. Influenced by Neoplatonic Greek philosophy, Barlaam, rejected the notion that man can see or have direct experiences with God. Barlaam maintained that God is unknowable and cannot be perceived by human senses, stating bluntly that the light spoken of by Palamas and the monks "does not exist." As Orthodox scholar John Meyendorff put it, Barlaam was essentially saying, "The monks claim to see God Himself; but direct vision of God is impossible!"

Barlaam was shocked in particular by the claim of these monks "that the human body, and not only the mind, could be transfigured by divine light and contributed to the knowledge of God."

In response to Barlaam's arguments, Palamas affirmed that Church Fathers and monks had indeed seen the Uncreated light, however, he was vague on the details in this regard, writing cautiously so as to not subject sacred things to ridicule. Palamas clarified that, even if mortals can experience the Uncreated light, "[n]o one has ever seen the fullness of this Divine Beauty."

The icon in Figure 2.1 is one of the most famous in the Orthodox Church. The story of the transfiguration as told in the New Testament (Matthew Chapter 17) holds immense doctrinal importance in Orthodoxy and in the writings of Palamas. The light that shined from Jesus' countenance during the transfiguration is believed to be the deifying Energy of God, part of God, but not his

"Essence" which is deemed unknowable. This light is believed by the Orthodox to have shined from saints on many occasions and will cause the faithful to shine in the resurrection.

At least with respect to mortal beings, Latter-day Saint scripture may agree in part with Palamas on this point. The Pearl of Great Price confirms: "no man can behold all my glory, and afterwards remain in the flesh on the earth" (Pearl of Great Price, Moses 1:5).

The conflict between the opposing views articulated by Barlaam and Palamas was decided in favor of Palamas by two councils of the Eastern Orthodox Church, held in June and July 1341. Ultimately, a decisive voice in settling this controversy was heard in the declaration of the monks of Mt. Athos, who in 1341, affirmed the views of Palamas, stating that his doctrines were taught in scripture and received from the fathers. With self-effacing modesty, the monks of Athos declared that they knew of these things from their "own small experience," signing their names and often adding words such as "the least of the monks," or "least of the hieromonks" next to their names.

Figure 2.1: The Transfiguration of Jesus
Theophenes the Greek, ca. 1408
Tretyakov Museum, Moscow
Credit: Photo by the author

The victory of Palamas in this debate and ensuring events were nothing short of high drama. Palmas himself was later imprisoned for three years for advocating this view after the prevailing doctrinal and political "winds" shifted against him in Constantinople. The debate eventually stirred public passions and has been cited as a contributory cause for a civil war that raged in Byzantium.

Outside of scholarly circles and the Orthodox Church, the story of Palamas is poorly known, but deserves to be better known. His contribution to Eastern Orthodoxy is immense, standing for the proposition that people actually could have personal encounters with God, in a very real sense.

The focus on the "Energy" of God is unique to Orthodoxy and is not accepted as doctrine in the Roman Catholic faith; however, recent decades have seen small efforts by the Catholic Church towards attempting reconciliation over the theology of Palamas and the Hesychasts. In 1996, Pope John Paul II delivered a series of addresses in which he called out aspects of Eastern Orthodox worship for praise. Of the Hesychast controversy from the fourteenth century, he had this to say:

> The Hesychast controversy marked another distinctive moment in Eastern theology. In the East, Hesychasm means a method of prayer characterized by a deep tranquility of the spirit, which is engaged in constant contemplation of God by invoking the name of Jesus. There was no lack of tension with the Catholic viewpoint on certain aspects of this practice. However, we should acknowledge the good intentions which guided the defense of this spiritual method, that is, to emphasize the concrete possibility that man is given to unite himself with the Triune God in the intimacy of his heart, in that deep union of grace which Eastern theology likes to describe with the particularly powerful term of "theosis," "divinization."[10]

The Roman pontiff uses conciliatory terms. He acknowledges the "tension" that once existed over Hesychasm and refers to "good intentions." Still, a gap exists between Catholic and Orthodox theology on this point. In referring to unification "in the intimacy of his heart," the pope seems to be downplaying the more visible aspects of theosis that the monks claimed to experience: the purification and transfiguration of their very bodies.

As this book shows, the writings of Palamas should be of great interest to Latter-day Saint scholars. His writings and those of other Orthodox saints and theologians have analyzed the descriptions of heavenly light given in the New Testament. The verses they have studied include the account of the Transfiguration of Christ (Matthew 17) and John Chapter 1, verses 4-9, which speak of Christ as "the true Light, which lighteth every man that cometh into the world" (v. 9). Their conclusions show similarity to the teachings on divine light and seeing God of Sections 88 and 93 of the Doctrine and Covenants.

Orthodox scholars have analyzed not just New Testament accounts for insights into the nature and workings of this heavenly light. They also turn to the actual experiences of Orthodox saints from eras past. An interesting illustration of this is seen in the writings of Metropolitan Kallistos (Timothy) Ware, a leading Orthodox scholar who taught at Oxford for over thirty years. In his book entitled *The Orthodox Church*, Ware cites the example of Saint Seraphim of Sarov (1754–1833) to illustrate deification. As pointed out in the preface, Seraphim was a contemporary of Joseph Smith. The two received similar revelations on at least two occasions. Several aspects of their teachings and experience align in interesting parallels (see Saint Seraphim of Sarov, Chapter 9).

Ware cites a famous incident from November 1831, when Seraphim and a lay disciple were transfigured in a blaze of heavenly light. This account has been widely reproduced on the internet and is referenced in Seraphim's biographies.

Of this transfiguring event that was experienced by Seraphim and his disciple, Nikolay Motovilov, Ware writes:

> The whole passage is of extraordinary importance for understanding the Orthodox doctrine of deification [theosis] and union with God. It shows how the Orthodox idea of sanctification includes the body: it is not Seraphim's (or Motovilov's) soul only, but the whole body which is transfigured by the grace of God.[11]

The references to light, being "filled with light" and seeing God are an important part of how deification is understood in Orthodoxy. Saint Symeon the New Theologian (see Chapter 12) described glorious encounters with God in the form of brilliant light, not even knowing whether he (Symeon) was "clothed with a body" or not, due to the pervasive, glorious light (regarding the bodily aspect, compare to 2 Corinthians 12:2; D&C 137:1; and 3 Nephi 28:15). Several other Orthodox saints use this same terminology in describing their mystical or sacred visions, including Saint Seraphim in his vision of heaven, and Saint John the Ladder, who met an angel and asked about the nature of the Trinity or Godhead (see Chapter 6, under "The Nature of the Godhead [2 April 1843])."

Once Latter-day Saint readers begin to understand theosis, or "deification," as a doctrine that involves an eventual change in our bodies, a whole range of possible parallels to Latter-day Saint scripture are opened up. In this connection, readers can study the Latter-day Saint Topical Guide for keywords "purification" and "sanctification." A few of the verses worth studying would include Doctrine and Covenants 50:24; 84:33; 88:49, 67; 131:8; Alma 5:14 ("image in your countenance"; cf. Psalms 17:15); Alma 5:21; 3 Nephi 19:25–28; and Moroni 7:48 (similar to 1 John 3:3, "purified even as he is pure").

In a broader sense, Ware's discussion of the event involving Seraphim and Motovilov raises some interesting possibilities for this book. If a noted scholar such as Ware can cite this mystical or sacred experience from 1831, to illustrate Orthodox teachings, might Latter-day Saint readers point to similar experiences of Joseph Smith or other early Latter-day Saint elders in order to illustrate and discuss possible parallels to Orthodoxy? Or to underscore the sacred and actual nature of *their* experiences?

Joseph Smith and early Latter-day Saint elders also shined this very light on occasion. Outpourings of heavenly light among Latter-day Saint elders in Kirtland (1830–37) are particularly well documented. In the 2012 book by Karl Ricks Anderson entitled *The Savior in Kirtland*, Anderson provides details concerning many such outpourings of divine light among Latter-day Saint elders in Kirtland, including transfiguring events, appearances of both the Father and the Son, and visions of Christ.[12]

Joseph Smith in particular experienced these outpourings of light. His countenance was said to have glowed on occasion in an unusual way when he received revelations.[13] Anderson documents events that are not well known, involving numerous Latter-day Saint elders and witnesses.

The following are a few highlights of the sacred experiences of Latter-day Saint elders in Kirtland (1830–1837) that Anderson presents, drawing upon years of research into first-hand accounts:

- Thirty people saw a pillar of light above the spot were baptisms were performed (November 1830);

- Fifteen witnesses saw Joseph Smith illuminated with a divine light: "All at once his countenance changed and he stood mute. . . . He got so white that anyone who saw him would have thought he was transparent";

- Twenty-two witnesses saw the glory of the Lord shining, as Lyman Wight's "countenance was a brilliant, transparent white";

- Twelve witnesses on February 16, 1832 saw Joseph Smith and Sidney Rigdon as they experienced their remarkable vision of heaven, the three heavenly degrees of glory; during this time, Joseph's countenance was said to shine "as if it were transparent";

- One hundred witnesses on January 28, 1836 saw a pillar of fire rest down upon the heads of some of the brethren; Roger Orton was enveloped in the light.[14]

As discussed in the Preface, this is an area where the experiences of Latter-day Saints and Orthodox saints align, even though the doctrinal understanding of this light is different.

In terms of vocabulary, the terms "deification" or "divinization" are at times used interchangeably with the word *theosis*. Language referring to theosis or deification is used in the writings of early church fathers in a variety of ways. The most relevant for this discussion are metaphorical and realistic uses. In this range of meaning, these terms assert that the believers incorporate "some of the divine attributes in their own lives by imitation," or even that the believers are transformed into the likeness of God. This latter possibility is based on a notion that believers actually participate in God by partaking of the divine nature, a possibility referred to in 2 Peter 1:4, which states:

> Whereby are given unto us exceeding great and precious promises: that by these ye might be partakers of the divine nature, having escaped the corruption that is in the world through lust.

For Latter-day Saints, this transformation occurs as Church members receive and enjoy the gift of the Holy Ghost following baptism, remember their divine identity as children of God, and make, keep, and remember sacred temple covenants. A vital aspect of these covenants is seen in temple marriage between a man and a woman, or eternal marriage.[15] For Latter-day Saints, these marriages are solemnized in temples around the world. As of the date of this writing, there are over 150 functioning temples where such marriages can be performed; these are accessible to a broad part of humanity and the number keeps growing.

The Orthodox Study Bible provides this commentary on the verse quoted above (2 Peter 1:4), giving a concise overview of key concepts related to deification, or theosis:

> Being renewed by God's power, we become partakers of the divine nature. This does not mean we become divine by nature. If we participated in God's essence the distinction between God and man would be abolished. What this does mean is that we participate in God's energy, described by a number of terms in scripture, such as glory, life, love, virtue, and power. We are to become like God by His grace, and truly His adopted children, but never become God by nature. According to some Church Fathers, this especially occurs through the Eucharist, for when Christ's Body and Blood become one with ours, we become Christ-bearers and partakers of the divine nature.[16]

Scholars of theosis trace Orthodox teachings on theosis back to the earliest centuries after Christ. Saint Justin Martyr (AD 100–165) and Saint Irenaeus, bishop of Lyon (AD 130–202) are the earliest Christian writers to teach that believers can become gods. Both men cited Psalms 82:6 and other verses of scripture for support of this idea. Psalms 82:6 states:

I have said, Ye are gods; and all of you are children of the most High.

Irenaeus wrote that Christ "became what we are in order to make us what he is himself."[17] In these words, Irenaeus articulated what scholars have referred to as the "exchange formula," meaning that God lowered himself to take on human form, so that humans could be raised to become as he is. Other early church fathers expressed the same idea, sometimes in slightly different terms.

Below are a few examples of the "exchange formula," quoted in a 2009 book by Norman Russell. In this particular work, he simplifies the scholarship, vocabulary, and concepts related to theosis, making them accessible to ordinary readers:

> The Word of God became man so that you too may learn from a man how it is even possible for a man to become a god (Clement of Alexandria, ca. 150–ca. 215).

> He became human that we might become divine (Athanasius, 296–373).

> Let us become as Christ is, since Christ became as we are; let us become gods for his sake, since he became man for our sake (Gregory of Nyssa, 335–394).

> He became like us, that is, a human being, that we might become like him, I mean gods and sons. On the one hand he accepts what belongs to us, taking it to himself as his own, and on the other he gives us in exchange what belongs to him (Cyril of Alexandria, 378–444).[18]

The writings of Irenaeus in particular carry great authority. He was a disciple of Polycarp, who in turn was a disciple of John the Apostle. Irenaeus thus had a very close link to one of the original Apostles. He is noted for articulating doctrines that he believed Christians should accept as correct. He also wrote against views that were "heretical," which he believed should not be accepted by Christians. Irenaeus is credited with establishing which of the many Gospel accounts of Christ's ministry should be accepted as authentic, or "canonical." The fact that Christians today recognize the Gospels of Matthew, Mark, Luke, and John as canonical can be traced, in significant measure, to Irenaeus's influence.

The modern relevance of theosis is suggested by the number of hits that turn up on a Google search of the internet in English: about 400,000. Most of these are seen in contexts involving discussions of Eastern Orthodox theology. A search of the term *deification* turns up nearly four million hits, though some of these have no relation to Orthodox theology. Over 200,000 hits turn up on Google for the Russian term "обожение" (deification), many of which are substantial web pages maintained by church organizations.[19]

While deification or theosis is an ancient Christian doctrine, it was "rediscovered" by scholars in the twentieth century. This process began first in Paris among scholars who wrote in French. Myrrha Lot-Borodine published a series of articles in 1932–33, in *Reveue d'histoire des religions*, dealing with the importance of deification in the Orthodox tradition.[20] Vladimir Lossky published a work in French on Orthodox theology and deification in 1944, which was later translated into English and published in 1957 as *The Mystical Theology of the Eastern Church*. This book is credited with having been very influential in explaining deification to a Western audience. Influential Russian Orthodox émigré scholar John Meyendorff began writing in Paris on theosis and other Orthodox topics in the 1950s.[21] Meyendorff later lectured and served at various times on the faculties of Harvard, Columbia, and Fordham Universities. He also served as Dean of St. Vladimir's Seminary in New York from 1984 until the time of his death in 1992.[22]

A growing body of scholarly literature in English also attests to the interest in theosis among not just the Eastern Orthodox faithful but among scholars and believers from other Christian traditions. In fact, there has been a proliferation of books on theosis in recent years. An example is seen in a 2012 book containing articles on theosis by several different authors, including one by a writer who discusses scholarship of Baptist theologians who borrow the idea of theosis "to develop an understanding of the terms 'union with God' or 'participation in God.'"[23] Another illustration of this is seen in the work of a Finnish Lutheran theologian, who asserts that Martin Luther accepted the idea of "the deification of the Christian."[24]

Early Christian church fathers recognized that the idea of theosis embraces several biblical concepts. For example, according to scholar Norman Russell, Saint Cyril of Jerusalem (AD 313–386) listed justification, sanctification, adoptive sonship, sharing in the Spirit, and partaking of the divine nature as being included within the idea of theosis.[25]

The terms listed by Cyril relate to the salvation of the individual. Other writers, such as Saint Maximus the Confessor (AD 580–662), saw theosis in terms of broader "cosmic theology," emphasizing themes like making mankind equal with angels, abolishing the law of sin, or destroying the tyranny of Satan.

Russell quotes Maximus, listing seven themes, or "mysteries," which Christ brought into being:

- theology, by which we attain knowledge of God through the incarnate Word;
- adoption as sons and daughters, which is brought about by baptism and maintained by keeping the commandments;
- equality with the angels, which was achieved for us by Christ's sacrifice on the Cross, which united heaven and earth in his person
- participation in eternal life, by feeding on the Word as the bread of life, both through meditating on the Scriptures and through sharing in the Eucharist;
- restoration of human nature, by Christ's healing of the interior conflicts of the human will in his representative humanity;
- abolition of the law of sin, by which Christ has freed us from the terrible compulsiveness of sin if we freely choose to accept the mystery of salvation; and
- *destruction of the tyranny of the evil one*, which was brought about because the flesh defeated in Adam proved victorious in Christ [emphasis added; compare bold wording to wording below from D&C 19].[26]

While Maximus and Russell refer to these themes in the context of theosis, Latter-day Saints would see these as illustrations of the scope and reach of the atonement of Jesus Christ. Latter-day Saint scripture also supports a broad, cosmological dimension of Christ's atoning sacrifice, as do some Eastern church fathers who wrote regarding theosis. Either way, the doctrines of the two churches intersect in many ways on these points, even if the terminology differs.

Consider these words spoken by the Lord to Joseph Smith in Doctrine and Covenants 19. In this section, the Lord himself uses cosmological themes similar to those articulated by Maximus in describing Christ's suffering and his eventual destruction of the devil. Compare these words to the last point above from Maximus:

> **2** I, having accomplished and finished the will of him whose I am, even the Father, concerning me—having done this that I *might subdue all things unto myself*—

> **3** Retaining all power, even to the *destroying of Satan* and his works at the end of the world, and the last great day of judgment . . . [emphasis added].

Doctrine and Covenants 88:6 contains this interesting description of Christ's descent "below all things," a phrase that also suggests a cosmic struggle:

> He that ascended up on high, as also he descended below all things, in that he comprehended all things, that he might be in all and through all things, the light of truth;

Reminiscent of the "exchange formula," here we read that Christ lowered himself—or "descended"—so that his holy influence in the form of divine light (the light of Christ or light of truth) would permeate all things. Latter-day Saints see this "descent" not just in Christ's crucifixion on the cross; more important was his suffering in Gethsemane, where he bore a burden exceeding the excruciating physical pain of the Cross. While in the garden, Jesus took on him full weight of the sins of the world, as well as the "pains and sicknesses of his people" (see Alma 7:11). Luke describes the Savior's suffering in Gethsemane as being so intense that "his sweat was at it were great drops of blood falling" (Luke 22:44). In Doctrine and Covenants 19:18, the Lord describes his sufferings as having been so severe that they caused him "to tremble because of pain, and bleed at every pore, and to suffer both body and spirit—and would that I might not drink the bitter cup and shrink."

The "descent" or "lowering" of Christ makes for interesting comparison to verses penned by Nephi in the Book of Mormon. As given in 1 Nephi 11, the prophet Nephi recorded the following vision of Mary and the Christ-child, ca. 600 BC:

> **14** And it came to pass that I saw the heavens open; and an angel came down and stood before me; and he said unto me: Nephi, what beholdest thou?
>
> **15** And I said unto him: A virgin, most beautiful and fair above all other virgins.
>
> **16** And he said unto me: *Knowest thou the condescension of God?* . . .
>
> **20** And I looked and beheld the virgin again, bearing a child in her arms [emphasis added].

The angel's question to Nephi regarding the "condescension of God" invokes familiar imagery from patristic writings on theosis, or deification. As mentioned above, Irenaeus wrote that Christ "became what we are in order to make us what he is himself," meaning that God lowered himself to take on human form, so that humans could be raised to become as he is. In this light, Orthodox theology may offer an interesting framework for understanding the words the angel spoke to Nephi, and this framework aligns nicely with Latter-day Saint scripture and commentary.

Consider the following excerpt from the article on this topic in *The Encyclopedia of Mormonism*:

> The word "condescension" implies *"voluntary descent,"* "submission," and "performing acts which strict justice does not require." This definition is particularly applicable to Jesus in the portrayal of him by prophets who lived before his birth and who affirmed: "God himself shall come down" to make an Atonement (Mosiah 15:1); "the God of Abraham, and of Isaac, and the God of Jacob, yieldeth himself . . . into the hands of wicked men" (1 Nephi 19:10); "the great Creator . . . suffereth himself to become subject unto man in the flesh" (2 Nephi 9:5); and "he offereth himself a sacrifice for sin" (2 Nephi 2:7). "The Lord Omnipotent," said King Benjamin, "shall come

down from heaven among the children of men, and shall dwell in a tabernacle of clay" (Mosiah 3:5) [emphasis added].[27]

In short, the angel's words spoken to Nephi fit nicely in the context of concepts associated with theosis.

A simplified description of theosis theology can be found in a book entitled, *Theosis: The True Purpose of Human Life*.[28] This book was published in 2006 by Abbot George of the Holy Monastery of Saint Gregorios on Mount Athos in Greece. It is available for download free of charge on the internet in numerous languages. Abbot George's book is short, only having eighty-six pages in the English version. It is easy to read and the doctrines it teaches can be readily understood by readers outside of the Eastern Orthodox tradition.

Besides its short length and simplicity, the abbot and other monks on Mount Athos have inherited a spiritual tradition that is at the very core of Eastern Orthodoxy. For the last thousand years, Athos has been the heart of the Eastern Orthodox faith. It is so sacred to the Orthodox tradition that it is referred to as the "Holy Mountain." Some of the predecessors to today's monks on Athos have experienced visions of God and have enjoyed glorious spiritual manifestations. Accordingly, Abbot George and those of his tradition are well situated to instruct readers on the true meaning of theosis as understood in the Eastern Orthodox tradition.

Here are several explanations and definitions of theosis contained in Abbot George's book:

- Theosis is personal communion with God "face to face."
- The Church Fathers say that God became man in order to make man a god. If God had not taken flesh, man would not be able to achieve Theosis.
- [Theosis] can become a present reality for those who are willing to tread the path, and so it is not exclusively an after-death experience. With Theosis death is transcended. St. Paul alludes to this when he says, "it is no longer I who live, but Christ who lives in me."

- The only truly Orthodox form of pastoral guidance is that which is intended to lead to Theosis, and is not, as in Western Christianity, aimed at a moral perfection for man which does not depend on God's Grace.
- He [God] does not wish him [humankind] simply to be a being with certain gifts, certain qualities, a certain superiority over the rest of creation, He wishes him to be a god by Grace.
- Since man is "called to be a god" (i.e. was created to become a god), as long as he does not find himself on the path of Theosis he feels an emptiness within himself.
- Those who wish to unite with Jesus Christ, and, through Christ, with God the Father, recognise that this union is realised in the body of Christ, which is our Holy Orthodox Church.[29]

Abbot George would be heavily drawing his writings here from his fellow Athonite monk from the fourteenth century, Saint Gregory Palamas.

Of theosis, Gregory wrote:

- The glory, kingdom, and radiance shared by God and His saints are one and the same.
- The divine light is given by measure and is received to a greater or lesser extent, being distributed, undividedly divided, according to the worthiness of the recipients.[30]

Niketas Stethatos, a disciple of Saint Symeon the New Theologian (see Chapter 12), wrote this of the divine union with God and deification:

He who wholeheartedly and assiduously directs himself towards God attains such virtue of soul and body that he becomes a mirror of the divine image. He is so comixed with God, and God with him, that each reposes in the other. Because of the richness of the gifts of the Spirit that he has received, henceforth he is and appears to be an image of divine blessedness and god by adoption, God being the perfector of his perfection.[31]

Stethatos was the disciple whom Saint Symeon charged with editing his writings and transmitting his teachings. With this in mind, the writings of Stethatos likely reflect the instruction of Saint Symeon himself.

Latter-day Saint readers may have a guarded reaction to concepts involving God dwelling in humankind or reposing in the believer, a concept sometimes referred to as divine *indwelling* by scholars of theosis. Joseph Smith stated in Doctrine and Covenants 130:3 that "the idea that the Father and the Son dwell in a man's heart is an old sectarian notion, and is false."

For context, Latter-day Saint scripture testifies to the real possibility of the believer meeting Christ (receiving the "other" or "Second" Comforter) and receiving Christ *"in himself"* in the form of divine light (see for example 3 Nephi 19:29–30; D&C 88:50; and 93:35). Moreover, it was in the context of John 14:23 and a discussion of the *other Comforter* that Joseph spoke the comments about the "sectarian notion," so in Doctrine and Covenants 130:3 Joseph certainly was not dismissing the idea that believers could shine with heavenly light. In fact, Joseph himself and numerous Latter-day Saint elders in Kirtland, Ohio (1831–37) had experiences when they were filled with light. These have been meticulously documented by Karl Ricks Anderson, as described above.

Orthodox writers also attest to the real possibility of meeting God and of receiving his indwelling. As seen in the lives of Orthodox saints, this experience is sometimes observable outwardly, in the form of radiant light shining from the faces and bodies of saints. Many such accounts exist in Orthodox hagiography, or the life stories of saints, and while Orthodox hagiographic writings often follow formulas or recognized patterns in how the life of the saint in question is described, by no means do they *all* describe occurrences when heavenly light shined from the saint.

This book proposes that hagiographic accounts of heavenly light be taken seriously; they align nicely with Biblical accounts regarding Moses (Exodus 34:35); the story of Christ's transfiguration in Matthew 17:2; The Book of Mormon account of Abinadai (Mosiah 13:5); the account of the transfiguration of the twelve disciples recorded in 3 Nephi 19:25; Sections in the Doctrine and Covenants that describe divine light; and the research described by Karl Ricks Anderson in his 2012 book, *The Savior in Kirtland,* described above.

In the teachings of the Orthodox Church (best articulated by Saint Gregory Palamas), this light is "Uncreated" and is deemed to be the very energies of God (but not his Essence).

The descriptions of this light given by Orthodox writers are similar to the "light of Christ" referred to in the Doctrine and Covenants (see D&C 88:6–13), except that for the Orthodox, this light is part of God himself, his Energy.

Quoted here are verses 11–12 of Doctrine and Covenants 88:

> **12** Which alight proceedeth forth from the presence of God to fill the immensity of space—

> **13** The light which is in all things, which giveth life to all things, which is the law by which all things are governed, even the power of God who sitteth upon his throne, who is in the bosom of eternity, who is in the midst of all things.

When the Savior visited the ancient habitants of the Americas following his resurrection (ca. AD 34), the light shining from his countenance purified and sanctified his disciples to the point that they glowed just as he did. The account below shows the *effect* of the light of Christ. It also presents a case from Latter-day Saint scripture of what Orthodox readers might call deification or theosis:

> **28** Father, I thank thee that thou hast purified those whom I have chosen, because of their faith, and I pray for them, and also for them who shall believe on their words, that they may be purified in me, through faith on their words, even as they are purified in me.

> **29** Father, I pray not for the world, but for those whom thou hast given me out of the world, because of their faith, that they may be purified in me, that I may be in them as thou, Father, art in me, that we may be one, that I may be glorified in them.

> **30** And when Jesus had spoken these words he came again unto his disciples; and behold they did pray steadfastly,

without ceasing, unto him; *and he did smile upon them again; and behold they were white, even as Jesus* [emphasis added].

Orthodox writers have described this light. The quotes below are just a small sampling of how it is described.

Here are some quotations from Palamas regarding this light:

- This light is not the essence of God, for that is inaccessible and incommunicable; it is not an angel, for it bears the marks of the Master. Sometimes it makes a man go out from the body or else, without separating him from the body, it elevates him to an ineffable height. At other times, it transforms the body, and communicates its own splendour to it when, miraculously, the light which deifies the body becomes accessible to the bodily eyes.[32]

- Nevertheless, He who shone with this light proved in advance that it was uncreated by referring to it as the kingdom of God.[33]

- May we all be delivered from such a fate by the illumination and knowledge of the pre-eternal, immaterial light of the Lord's transfiguration, to His glory and the glory of His Father without beginning and the life-giving Spirit, whose radiance, divinity, glory, kingdom and power are one and the same, now and forever and unto the ages of ages. Amen.[34]

The "Declaration of the Holy Mountain" by the monks of Athos, which Palamas himself wrote, gives this description of the light, quoting earlier church fathers:

> And St. Maximos [Maximus the Confessor], when speaking about Melchisedec, writes that this deifying grace of God is "uncreated", declaring it to be "eternally existent, proceeding from the eternally existing God"; and elsewhere in many places he says it is a light, ungenerated and completely real, that it is manifested to the saints when they become worthy of receiving it, though does not come into being merely at that moment. He also calls this light "the light of utterly inexpressible glory and the purity of

50

angels"; while St. Makarios calls it the nourishment of the bodiless, the glory of the divine nature, the beauty of the age to come, divine and celestial fire, inexpressible noetic light, foretaste and pledge of the Holy Spirit, the sanctifying oil of gladness.[35]

Elder Sophrony, the biographer of Saint Silouan the Athonite (1866–1938; see Chapter 13), describes this light as follows:

> Uncreated light, like the sun, lights up the spiritual world and makes visible the way of the spirit which otherwise cannot be seen. Without this Light man can neither apprehend nor contemplate, still less perform the commandments of Christ, for he dwells in darkness. Uncreated light bears within it eternal life and the force of divine love. Indeed, it is itself both divine love and divine wisdom, indivisibly one in eternity.[36]

It is evident that the two churches are talking about the same light or phenomenon but understanding it in differing ways.

In the teachings of both churches, this light is "Uncreated," or was "not created" (see D&C 93:29; it seems the Lord is giving a divine nod here to Palamas); however, the same verse that uses the term "not created" (93:29) also states that "man was in the beginning with God" and seems to equate man with (or trace mankind's origin to) "intelligence, or the light of truth."

For the full context, Doctrine and Covenants 93:29 states as follows:

> **29** Man was also in the beginning with God. Intelligence, or the light of truth, was not created or made, neither indeed can be.

This is where the two churches part company doctrinally. In Orthodoxy, the only eternal reality is God. His Energy (the light) is also eternal, because it is part of God, but it is not part of his unknowable, actual Essence. Man is considered to be a created being, thus cannot have an eternal existence. Yet, Doctrine and Covenants 93 refers to a preexistent and even eternal origin of the spirits or souls of mankind.

Other teachings in Section 93 may help bridge this theological gap. The revelation was given, in part, to help the Church and the world "know what [we] worship" (93:19). We don't worship the light. It isn't God, but rather, it emanates from God. Thus, the light is indeed eternal, but it isn't God and isn't part of God, but it is closely associated with God. Moreover, it seems from Doctrine and Covenants 93 that man's spirit was created out of this light.

This section also provides a revealed rationale for why God and material elements go hand-in-hand:

> "The elements are the tabernacle of God; yea, man is the tabernacle of God, even temples." "[S]pirit and element inseparably connected, receive a fullness of joy" [v. 35 and 33, open citation].

Thus, in order for God to experience the "fullness of joy," (and to embody perfection) he too needs the elements; therefore, God has a body, just as does Christ (see D&C 130:22).

Interestingly, the use of the term "indeed" as used in verse 29 (quoted above) suggests that the Almighty is responding to an assertion already made (and that is well known in at least part of the world); to this author's knowledge, only the writings of Gregory fit the context.

Once Latter-day Saint readers begin to understand theosis as a doctrine that involves an eventual change in our bodies, a whole range of possible parallels to Latter-day Saint scripture are opened up. In this connection, readers can study the Latter-day Saint Topical Guide for keywords "purification" and "sanctification." A few of the verses worth studying would include Doctrine and Covenants Sections 50:24; 84:33; 88:49; 131:8; Alma 5:14 ("image in your countenance"; compare to Psalms 17:15); 3 Nephi 19:25–28; and Moroni 7:48 (similar to 1 John 3:3, "purified even as he is pure").

This discussion of visions of the Uncreated light or transfiguring experiences among Orthodox or Latter-day Saint believers should not cause readers to misunderstand Latter-day Saint (or Orthodox) doctrine. Visions of Deity or transfigurations are not commonly spoken of among Latter-day Saints, nor are they treated as prerequisites in this life for our future salvation; however, there is ample basis in Latter-day Saint doctrine to assume that some believers *may* meet the Savior in this life or have other sacred experiences with God. These form interesting points of comparison with Orthodoxy.

The public discourses of Church leaders generally emphasize basic principles of the Gospel, such as faith, repentance, baptism, and the gift of the Holy Ghost, or the importance of other basic topics, such as service to others or temple ordinances, rather than discussing sacred or mystical experiences.

The Book of Mormon teaches that all who are baptized, receive the Holy Ghost, and exercise faith in Christ are on the path that leads to eternal life.

This principle is taught in 2 Nephi 31:

> **19** And now, my beloved brethren, after ye have gotten into this strait and narrow path, I would ask if all is done? Behold, I say unto you, Nay; for ye have not come thus far save it were by the word of Christ with unshaken faith in him, relying wholly upon the merits of him who is mighty to save.
>
> **20** Wherefore, ye must press forward with a steadfastness in Christ, having a perfect brightness of hope, and a love of God and of all men. Wherefore, if ye shall press forward, feasting upon the word of Christ, and endure to the end, behold, thus saith the Father: Ye shall have eternal life [see also 3 Nephi 27:16, 20].

In a similar vein, Metropolitan Ware presents an important perspective in discussing theosis. While glorious transfiguring events can occur in this life, these are the exception rather than the rule. Yet, these are experiences that all the righteous can anticipate in the day of Resurrection:

> The full deification of the body must wait, however, until the Last Day, for in this present life the glory of the saints is as a rule an inward splendor, a splendor of the soul alone; but when the righteous rise from the dead and are clothed with a spiritual body, then their sanctity will be outwardly manifest. "At the day of Resurrection the glory

of the Holy Spirit comes out from within, decking and covering the bodies of the saints—the glory which they had before, but hidden within their souls. What a person has now, the same then comes forth externally in the body." The bodies of the saints will be outwardly transfigured by divine light, as Christ's body was transfigured on Mount Tabor. "We must look forward also to the springtime of the body."

But even in this present life some saints have experienced the firstfruits of this visible bodily glorification. Saint Seraphim of Sarov is the best known, but by no means the only, instance of this.[37]

---

[1] See Joseph Smith Jr., The King Follet Sermon, *Ensign* April 1971; *Teachings of the Prophet Joseph Smith,* ed. Joseph Fielding Smith, public domain reprint of the original 1924 edition, 346–47; see also "Discourse, 7 April 1843, as reported in the *Times and Seasons*," available at https://www.josephsmithpapers.org/paper-summary/discourse-7-april-1844-as-reported-by-times-and-seasons/3; the discourse is recorded in Wilford Woodruff's diary, April 7, 1844, pp. [133]–[140], available online at http://josephsmithpapers.org/paperSummary/discourse-7-april-1844-as-reported-by-wilford-woodruff.

[2] Brigham Young in *Journal of Discourses* 3, August 8, 1852, p. 93; available online in beta version, accessed March 30, 2019, http://jod.mrm.org/1; and https://contentdm.lib.byu.edu/digital/collection/JournalOfDiscourses3/id/290/rec/1.

[3] *Teachings of the Presidents of the Church: Lorenzo* Snow, chap. 5, s.v. "From the Life of Lorenzo Snow" (2011).

[4] "Becoming Like God," The Church of Jesus Christ of Latter-day Saints, Intellectual Reserve, https://www.lds.org/topics/becoming-like-god?lang=eng.

[5] "Becoming Like God."

[6] "Becoming Like God with Terryl Givens," November 8, 2017, in *LDS Perspectives Podcasts* (episode 63), https://ldsperspectives.com/2017/11/08/becoming-like-god-terryl-givens/. See also Terryl L. Givens, *When Souls Had Wings: Pre-Mortal Existence in Western Thought,* (Oxford and New York: Oxford University Press, 2010), and Andrew C. Skinner, *To Become Like God: Witness of our divine Potential,* Kindle (Salt Lake City: Deseret Book, 2016), chap. 6, location 1457; and David L. Paulsen and Donald W. Musser, eds., *Mormonism in Dialogue with Contemporary Christian Theologies*

(Macon, GA: Mercer University Press, 2007), for example pp. 301, 526.
[7] OrthodoxWiki, s.v. "Theosis," under "Deification in Mormonism," accessed June 1, 2019, at https://orthodoxwiki.org/Theosis. See also Bill McKeever, "Godhood and Theosis," Mormonism Research Ministry, http://www.mrm.org/exaltation.
[8] Vol. 4 of *The Philokalia: The Complete Text Complied by St. Nikodimos of the Holy Mountian and St. Makarios of Corinth,* ed. and trans. G.E.H. Palmer, Philip Sharrard, and Kallistos Ware (London: Faber & Faber, 1995), 424–25.
[9] My discussion of Palamas and Barlaam is taken from John Meyendorff, *St. Gregory Palamas and Orthodox Spirituality* (St. Vladimir's Seminary Press: Crestwood, NY, 1974), 90. The revival of interest in Palamas' views and teachings on divine light and theosis is credited in significant measure to this book. It was first published in French as See "St Grégoire Palamas et la mystique orthodoxe," *Maitres spirituels,* n. 20 (Paris: Éditions du Seuil, 1959).
[10] Pope John Paul II, "Eastern theology has enriched the whole Church," *L'Osservatore Romano,* August 21, 1996, accessed August 5, 2019, https://www.catholicculture.org/culture/library/view.cfm?recnum=5660.
[11] Timothy Ware (Bishop Kallistos of Kokleia), *The Orthodox Church* (London: Penguin Books, 1997), 120. Ware is the best-known English-language scholar of Orthodoxy. For a short overview of his thoughts on Orthodoxy, see "Becoming Orthodox," interview with Timothy Ware, *A Journal of Orthodox Faith and Culture: The Road to Emaus* 3, no. 3 (#10), PDF, pp. 46–54, http://www.roadtoemmaus.net/back_issue_articles/RTE_10/Bishop_Kallistos_Ware_on_Personhood.pdf.
[12] Karl Ricks Anderson, *The Savior in Kirtland: Personal Accounts of Divine Manifestations* (Salt Lake City: Deseret Book, 2012). Anderson's book is well researched and contains footnotes to original sources. It was the product of many years of research that he originally undertook at the suggestion of Latter-day Saint Apostle Neal A. Maxwell (1926–2004), who commented that there was a lot of "Christology" in the accounts of Church history in Kirtland. Anderson is the author of another popular book; see Karl Ricks Anderson, *Joseph Smith's Kirtland: Eyewitness Accounts* (1996). This work contains numerous accounts of the pentecostal outpourings of the Spirit and other events associated with the dedication of the Kirtland Temple.
[13] Anderson, *Savior in Kirtland,* 149, 153–55, 180–81.
[14] Anderson, *Savior in Kirtland,* 148–52.
[15] See generally Elder David A. Bednar, "Exceeding Great and Precious Promises" (October 2017 general conference), The Church of Jesus Christ of Latter-day Saints, Intellectual Reserve, https://www.lds.org/general-conference/2017/10/exceeding-great-and-

precious-promises?lang=eng.

[16] *The Orthodox Study Bible*, note under 2 Peter 1:4 (Thomas Nelson, 1993).

[17] Quoted in Norman Russell, *Fellow Workers With God: Orthodox Thinking on Theosis* (Crestwood, NY: St. Vladimir's Seminary Press, 2009), p. 23; Norman Russell, *The Doctrine of Deification in the Greek Patristic Tradition (*Oxford: Oxford University Press, 2004), p. 106. See the review of Russell's 2004 work by Jordan Vajda in *BYU Studies* 46, no. 1 (2007), pp. 161–164.

[18] Russell, *Fellow Workers*, 39.

[19] All searches conducted from my home in Switzerland on Google.com, March 14, 2019.

[20] Myrrha Lot-Borodine, "La Doctrine de la déification dans l'Eglise greque jusqu'au XI siècle," in *Revue d'histoire des religions* nos. 105–107, 1932–33.

[21] "St Grégoire Palamas et la mystique orthodoxe," *Maitres spirituels*, no. 20 (Paris: Éditions du Seuil, 1959); later published in English as John Meyendorff, *St. Gregory Palamas and Orthodox Spirituality* (Crestwood, NY: St. Vladimir's Seminary Press, 1974).

[22] St. Vladimir's has a fine library; much of my research has been conducted using the resources of this institution, including books published by the St. Vladimir's Seminary Press.

[23] Mark S. Medley, "Participation in God: The Appropriation of *Theosis* by Contemporary Baptist Theologians, in Vladimir Kharlamov, ed., vol. 2 of *Theosis: Deification in Christian Theology,* Princeton Theological Monograph Series, no. 156 (Eugene, OR: Pickwick, 2011), 205.

[24] Russell, *Fellow Workers*, 18

[25] Russell, *Fellow Workers*, 44, 45.

[26] Russell, *Fellow Workers*, 46.

[27] Brian Merril, "The Condescension of God," *The Encyclopedia of Mormonism*, 200, accessed July 22, 2019, https://eom.byu.edu/index.php/Condescension_of_God.

[28] Archimandrite George, *Theosis: The True Purpose of Human Life* (Mount Athos, Greece: Holy Monastery of Saint Gregorios, 2006), PDF, http://orthodoxinfo.com/general/*theosis*-english.pdf.

[29] George, *Theosis*, [9], 24, 13, [19], 42, 22, and [34].

[30] Saint Gregory Palamas, *The Homilies,* ed. and trans. Christopher Veniamin, with assistance from the Monastery of St. John the Baptist, Essex, England (Dalton, PA: Mount Thabor Publishing, 2016), homily 35, para. 16, p. 280.

[31] Vol. 4 of *The Philokalia: The Complete Text Complied by St. Nikodimos of the Holy Mountian and St. Makarious of Corinth,* ed. and trans. G.E.H. Palmer, Philip Sharrard, and Kallistos Ware (London: Faber & Faber, 1995), [139].

[32] Saint Gregory Palamas, *The Triads*, ed. John Meyendorff, trans. Nicholas Gendle, with a preface by Jaroslav Pelikan (Mahwah, NJ: Paulist Press, 1983), p. 57, para. 9.

[33] Saint Gregory, *Homilies*, homily 34, para. 12.

[34] Saint Gregory, homily 34, para. 18.

[35] Vol.4 of *The Philokalia*, 419.

[36] Archimandrite Sophrony, *The Monk of Mount Athos: Staretz Selouan 1866–1938* (Crestwood, NY: St. Vladimir's Seminary Press, 1997), 108–9.

[37] Ware, *Orthodox Church*, 233.

Part II

Monks Who Fulfill Prophecy

3—Monks as Prophets

Timothy (Kallistos) Ware is the author of a widely read introduction to Eastern Orthodoxy, aptly entitled *The Orthodox Church*. In his book, Ware makes a bold assertion that can be used to frame an important discussion in this book. He articulates a fundamental difference between Christian theology in the West and that of Eastern Orthodoxy:

> Latin Scholastic theology, emphasizing as it does the essence [of God] at the expense of persons, comes near to turning God into an abstract idea. He becomes a remote and impersonal being, whose existence has to be proved by metaphysical arguments—a God of philosophers, not the God of Abraham, Isaac and Jacob. Orthodoxy, on the other hand, has been far less concerned than the Latin west to find philosophical proofs of God's existence; what is important is not that we should argue about the deity, but that we should have a direct and living encounter with a concrete and personal God.[1]

Ware's statement illustrates a point sometimes made in describing Orthodox theology: that it is *experiential* in nature, based on "direct and living encounter[s] with a concrete and personal God."

This *experiential* side of Orthodoxy is reflected in the lives of the monks and saints profiled in this book. Over the many centuries since the era of the original Apostles, these men have had *personal experiences* with the divine—some have worked miracles through faith in Christ, while others have seen visions and have met God in the form of bright light; in a few cases, some have actually met the Savior. Moreover, Christianity has benefited from their personal witnesses at critical junctures, when topics of theological importance were at stake or in eras when the survival of Christianity in entire countries or regions was potentially in peril.

Many of the men profiled in this book would be termed "mystics" by scholars. This term could cause some readers to immediately react with skepticism. For some, this word could seem to imply paranormal experiences, such as extrasensory perception or seeing

UFOs. For others, the meaning might suggest dark, occult-like occurrences or drug-induced states of mind.

Actually, the term "mystic" is also often used in a Christian context by scholars. A popular book on Christian mysticism written by Stephen Fanning demonstrates this kind of usage. He uses a definition for "mystic" that emphasizes "direct intuition or experience of God."[2] Fanning devotes several pages each to Saint Symeon the New Theologian (949–1022) and Saint Seraphim of Sarov (1754–1833), both of whom are discussed extensively in this book. Interestingly, Fanning also lists Joseph Smith among the Christian mystics, quoting Joseph's own account of the First Vision and the later appearance of the angel Moroni.[3]

A leading Orthodox authority, Metropolitan Hilarion (Alfeyev), comments that the term "mysticism" was not used by Church Fathers; however, in examining the underlying Greek word in question, he concludes that it can be equated with the "vision of God" or "vision of the divine light."[4] With the above points in mind, this book uses the term "mystic" and "mysticism" in a Christian context, sometimes substituting a phrase Latter-day Saint readers will more readily accept: "sacred experiences."

In a broad sense, the monks and clerics described in this book can be called *prophets* (though the Orthodox faithful would not ordinarily use this term in referring to these men). This term is used in Doctrine and Covenants 133:26, a prophecy which is discussed in this book at length and fits quite well as a title for some of the great monks described in this book. For how the term *prophets* might apply to a broad range of inspired religious leaders of various religious traditions, consider this quotation from an early Latter-day Saint leader and historian, B. H. Roberts (1857–1933):

> This is the Mormon theory of God's revelation to the children of men. While The Church of Jesus Christ of Latter-day Saints is established for the instruction of men; and is one of God's instrumentalities for making known the truth yet he is not limited to that institution for such purposes, neither in time nor place. God raises up wise men and prophets here and there among all the children of men, of their own tongue and nationality, speaking to them

through means that they can comprehend; not always giving a fullness of truth such as may be found in the fullness of the gospel of Jesus Christ; but always giving that measure of truth that the people are prepared to receive.[5]

While some religious figures throughout history may merit the title of *prophet,* this term also has a more specific meaning within Latter-day Saint teaching. The term does not refer just to a person who predicts the future; rather, it is understood as applying to a person who speaks the word of the Lord. In the restored Church of Jesus Christ, the term *prophet* is normally reserved for the President of the Church (who is deemed *the Prophet* for the whole world, not just for Latter-day Saints) and, in a secondary sense, it is applied to his two counselors in the First Presidency and to the members of the full Quorum of the Twelve Apostles. These fifteen men are considered *prophets, seers, and revelators.* They are deemed to hold all the keys of God's authority that are conferred upon men on earth; however, the President, or Prophet, is the only one of the fifteen who is authorized to exercise these keys in full. Pronouncements of the Prophet alone, the First Presidency collectively, or of the fifteen men comprising the First Presidency and Quorum of the Twelve speaking jointly, can be considered authoritative. The most important pronouncements normally will be signed by all fifteen men.

The most notable early example of a monk with prophetic gifts was Saint Anthony the Great (ca. 251–357). Anthony is regarded as the founder of Christian monasticism. He spent much of his life living in remote locations in Egypt where he cultivated spiritual gifts and lived an austere life. Even though he sought seclusion in the wilderness, Anthony also employed these gifts in counseling others, exemplifying a quality of prayerful watchfulness. The theme of watchfulness is one seen repeatedly in Orthodox monastic literature. Interestingly, this is also a recurring theme in the Book of Mormon and Doctrine and Covenants.[6]

As an illustration of this sort of watchful, prophetic service, consider this story regarding Father Anthony (also spelled *Antony*):

It happened that when two of the brethren were journeying to him [Saint Antony], the water gave out on the journey:

61

the one died and the other was on the point of dying. He no longer had strength to go, but lay on the ground expecting to die also. Antony, sitting on the mountain, called two monks who happened to be there, and urged them to hasten, saying: "Take a jar of water and run down the road towards Egypt; for two were coming, one has just died, and the other will unless you hurry. This has just now been revealed to me as I was praying." The monks, therefore, went and found the one lying dead and buried him. The other they revived with water and brought him to the old man. The distance was a day's journey. Now, if anyone asks why he did not speak before the other man died, his question is not justified. For the decree of death was not passed by Antony, but by God who determined it for the one and revealed the condition of the other. As for Antony, this alone was wonderful, that as he sat with sober heart on the mountain, the Lord showed him things afar off.[7]

Stories such as this were passed down through the ages, causing some young monastic novices to strive to develop spiritual gifts that they could use to counsel and instruct others (on the other hand, many other monks sought primarily to save their souls through religious devotion and acts of asceticism). Understanding this context is important, as the men described in this book all exemplified these gifts and this commitment to serving others.

In a broader sense, the service of Anthony may have impacted the Christian world in another fundamental way. The story is told that during the discussions at the Council at Nicaea (AD 325), Anthony bore a stirring witness for Christ.[8] The sight of this humble old man (then about seventy-four years old), with no ecclesiastical position (other than as a deacon), speaking for the divinity of Christ, made a lasting impression.[9] Anthony's words may have helped counter the influence of Arianism, a branch of early Christianity that denied the divinity of Christ. Supporters of Arianism held that Christ must "be deemed a creature who has been called into existence out of nothing and has had a beginning." This teaching was deemed to undermine the Christian doctrine of redemption from sin, "since only he who was truly God could be deemed to have reconciled humanity to the Godhead." Under Arianism, the Son could have no "direct knowledge of the Father, since the Son is finite and of a different order of existence."[10] The Council ultimately rejected the views of Arianism, opting for a definition of God where Christ was seen as consubstantial or "of one Essence" with the Father, and was both God and the Son of God.

As an outcome of the Council at Nicaea (AD 325) and a later Council at Constantinople (AD 381), the Nicene Creed was written. While Latter-day Saints do not accept this or other creeds of Christian churches (see Joseph Smith History—1:19), the alternatives need to be considered. How might Christianity have changed if the Arian view of Christ had prevailed; that is, if it were accepted that Christ was really only a finite being and not God? Could Christian believers truly exercise faith in a being who was a *created being* (rather than an infinite being), who had no real ability to reconcile man to God and, for that matter, who could not personally have any direct knowledge of God?

Anthony and many of the men profiled in this book were "ascetic" monks. This means that they led simple lives involving not only religious pursuits, but also physical labor, frequent fasting, the avoidance of pleasure, and sometimes exposing themselves to discomfort. The purpose of these rigorous labors was to create a condition of humility and dependence on the Lord, with the ultimate aim of securing salvation, drawing nearer to God, and developing spiritual gifts. As odd or as misguided as ascetic practices may seem to modern readers, many of these men actually achieved great heights of spirituality.[11]

Eastern Orthodox monks invariably are students of the Holy Bible and other Christian writings; however, their method of learning from the Bible does not necessarily involve scholarly exegesis. They learn passages by heart and apply the principles to their own lives (compare to 1 Nephi 19:23). Saint Anthony said, "Wherever you go, always have God before your eyes; whatever you do, have the testimony of the Holy Scriptures." As one writer put it, "they learned the Bible through experience and understood it by carrying it into effect."[12]

Lest readers should condemn these men as engaging in practices the Lord would disapprove of, we only need to read some of the stories of Old Testament prophets to see examples of men who pleased and obeyed God through what, to modern understanding, would be extreme or unusual endeavors. The Lord commanded Isaiah to walk about nude and shoeless for three years, "for a sign and wonder upon Egypt and upon Ethiopia" (Isaiah 20:2–4). Yet Isaiah is one of the greatest Old Testament prophets. Jesus himself endorsed the words of Isaiah while teaching the inhabitants of ancient America (3 Nephi 23:1).

Consider also the case of Ezekiel, who was commanded by God to lie on his left side for 390 days for the "iniquity of the house of Israel" (Ezekiel 4:4–5), and then to lie on his right side for forty more days "for the iniquity of the house of Judah" (Ezekiel 4:6). Ezekiel was also to cook his food over a fire made with human dung, while lying on his side, doing all of this in the sight of the people (Ezekiel 4:12). Yet this same Ezekiel is esteemed a great prophet by Jews and Christians of all denominations. He left us with precious prophecies and revelations, such as his reference to the sticks of Joseph and Judah (Ezekiel 37:15–20), prefiguring (from a Latter-day Saint point of view) the future coming forth of the Book of Mormon (the "stick of Joseph"). Ezekiel also foretold in detail the scattering of Israel (Ezekiel 6:8; 11:16; and 12:13–15), calamitous warfare that will precede Christ's Second Coming (Ezekiel 38–39) and other events of the last days, including the building of a Temple in Jerusalem (Ezekiel 40–47) and the gathering of Israel (Ezekiel 11:17; 20:41–42; and 28:25–26).

Throughout Orthodox history, monks have played an important role in defending or helping define what was viewed as correct Orthodox doctrine. Their saintly lives, spiritual gifts won them the admiration and support of the people. There is a striking correlation between difficult times when national survival or the survival of Christianity in entire nations or regions was potentially in question, on the one hand, and the service of famed monks who enjoyed spiritual gifts, including prophetic gifts. In short, the monks played a role in preserving divine truth. Here are a few illustrations of monks who are profiled in this book:

Figure 3.1: Saint Symeon the New Theologian (949–1022).

Credit: Wikimedia Commons, public domain.[13]

The icon at right depicts Symeon conversing with the Lord as both radiate heavenly light.

Saint Symeon was a monk who met God in the form of brilliant light on several occasions. His first-hand descriptions of these encounters are touching and utterly convincing. According to at least one published account, he reports that he personally met the Savior, calling him his "gentle Master." Symeon is considered a saint in both the Eastern Orthodox and Roman Catholic traditions. He died only three decades before the permanent schism, or split, between Catholicism and Orthodoxy in 1054. He is a saint in both the Catholic and Orthodox traditions.

Saint Gregory Palamas (1296–1359). Palamas defended the notion that monks on Mount Athos in Greece had seen or experienced the light of God, the "Uncreated" or "Tabor" light. To this day, the writings of Palamas constitute the most important source for the Eastern Orthodox Church in articulating the idea of *theosis,* or deification. His writings helped Orthodoxy preserve the vitality of theosis theology, an ancient Christian teaching that presents interesting parallels to Latter-day Saint doctrines recorded in

Doctrine and Covenants 88 and 93. The writings of Palamas also may have helped preserve the spiritual strength of Orthodoxy for the coming centuries, during which the Greek Church (i.e., Eastern Orthodoxy) would come under the domination of the Turkish Empire, beginning with the fall of Constantinople in 1453. Palamas himself was taken prisoner by Turkish forces and treated well, showing that Christians and Muslims could coexist.

Figure 3.2: Saint Gregory Palamas, Vatopaidi Monastery, Mount Athos
Credit: Wikimedia Commons, public domain.[14]

Sergius of Radonezh (1314/22–1392). Sergius is the single greatest figure in the history of the Russian Orthodox Church. The monastery he founded outside of Moscow in Sergiyev Posad, the "Trinity Lavra," remains to this day one of the most important of the Russian Orthodox Church. He experienced and worked his share of miracles, opening a miraculous well of water by his prayers, seeing the Holy Spirit descend as fire upon the sacrament table, radiating holy light from his face, as did Christ on the Mount of Transfiguration, and meeting John the Apostle, who according to tradition appeared to him along with Mary and Peter. He also sent followers out to distant regions to Christianize the people.

His leadership and political acumen helped bring peace among warring Russian princes. He blessed Russian troops who went out to face their enemies on the battlefield at Kulikovo (1380), where Russian forces defeated a Mongol-Tatar army for the first time in well over a century after all the fall of Kiev (1240).

Above right: "Saint Sergius' Labors" (1896)
Credit: Mikhail Nesterov (d. 1942). Wikiart, public domain.[15]

Figure 3.4: Appearance of the Holy Trinity to Alexander of Svir
Holy Trinity St. Alexander of Svir Monastery, Trinity Church.
Credit: Photo by author.

Saint Alexander of Svir (1448–1533). Alexander was born on the feast day of the Old Testament prophet Amos. Interestingly, Joseph Smith was killed on the feast day of Amos. Joseph cited Amos 3:7 to support the idea that God spoke to the world through prophets.

Alexander is the only saint in the Russian Orthodox tradition to have experienced a vision of the entire Holy Trinity. In 1508, he saw a vision of the Father, Son, and Holy Spirit, or of three angelic beings representing the Trinity, "one in Essence." The Russian Orthodox Church compares his experience with Abraham's vision of the Lord as recorded in Genesis 18, in which Abraham saw the Lord (18:1) and "lo, three men stood by him" (18:2). Alexander's vision came during an era when the dogma of the Trinity and the divinity of Christ (and the role of monasticism) had come under attack by the so-called "Judaizers." These individuals questioned some fundamental aspects of the Eastern Orthodox tradition, including the divinity of the Son of God. Alexander's lifetime also preceded the rise of Ivan the Terrible, whose armed followers oppressed and brutalized many people, particularly in Alexander's home region of Novgorod.

The icon in Figure 3.4 is without a doubt the most studied of all Russian religious artworks.[16] It depicts an event referred to in the Orthodox Church as the "Hospitality of Abraham" (Genesis 18:1-2). Saint Alexander's experience is similar to how the Orthodox Church understands the meaning of these verses in Genesis—that they describe an appearance of the Father, Son, and Holy Ghost to Abraham.

Figure 3.4: The Trinity
Andrei Rublev
Early fifteenth century
The Tretyakov Museum, Moscow
Credit: Photo by the author

Saint Seraphim of Sarov (1754–1833). Numerous interesting parallels to Joseph Smith and Latter-day Saint doctrine are seen in the life of Seraphim. He worked many miracles and taught doctrines about seeing God and divine light that find close

parallels in some of Joseph's teachings. Seraphim also prophesied of future calamities for Russia, the fulfillment of which has widely been seen in the brutal rise of Soviet Communism, whose leaders repressed Orthodoxy and imprisoned and killed monks and clerics. Seraphim also prophesied of the rebirth of Orthodox Christianity in

68

Russia. The collective memory in Russia of his miracles and ministry, as well as that of the equally famed monks of the Optina Monastery, helped keep Christianity alive during the years of Soviet repression. An article that I wrote on parallels between Joseph Smith and Saint Seraphim was published in March 2016 by *Science and Religion* (*Nauka i religiya*, *Наука и Религия*), a respected Moscow journal.

Figure 3.5: Saint Seraphim Praying with Upraised Arms
Credit: Adobe Stock photo.[17]

Seeking personal experience with Christ is not just the aim of monks; it is the focus of Eastern Orthodoxy. Ordinary believers seek Christ through participation in church worship—particularly through the Divine Liturgy service (the Eucharist service, or Lord's Supper). Orthodox scholar Andrew Louth underscores the importance of not just getting dogma right, but also of [seeking] "a genuine encounter with the Person of Christ, witnessed in the Scriptures, safeguarded in the definitions of Church Councils, and experienced in the sacraments of the Church."[18] The study of the Scriptures, the writings of Church Fathers, and the lives of saints are "ways of encountering Christ." Prayer and openness to Christ's voice are vital to such encounters and help open us to "inner transformation, to a fundamental repentance."[19]

This experiential side of Orthodoxy is emphasized by many writers. Frederica Mathewes-Green authored a reader-friendly guide to Orthodoxy in 2015. In her introduction, she apologizes for writing a book in the first place: "Having pled for the superiority of direct experience over writing a book, here we are— at the beginning of a book."[20]

Similar to Orthodoxy, many of Joseph Smith's teachings are also *experiential* as they are based on actual encounters with God the Father, Jesus Christ, and holy angels; however, Joseph's authority in the eyes of Latter-day Saints is broader. Doctrine and Covenants 21:4–5 records the Lord's command to the Church: to "give heed to all his [Joseph's] words." Joseph was a revelator, as was Moses. He spoke for God as a living oracle (see D&C 90:4–5; 124:39, 126). In many of Joseph's revelations, God speaks in the first person.

As in Orthodoxy, Latter-day Saint members seek to draw closer to Christ (or have personal experiences with Christ, to use the Orthodox terminology) through the Sunday worship experience and temple attendance. Parents are encouraged to help children study and learn about the Holy Scriptures at home, all with the aim of helping them come to Christ. The Church's Sunday curriculum was overhauled in 2019 and aligned across age groups and integrated into a study plan that parents can discuss at home with their children. The new program is called, "Come Follow Me," invoking the Savior's invitation to follow in his footsteps, by living Gospel truths and principles in their daily lives.[21]

The Protestant world in which Joseph Smith grew up was one that denied the possibility of revelations and visions, and rejected the idea that man could have direct experience with God. Consider this familiar quote in which Joseph described the reaction of the unnamed Methodist minister upon hearing Joseph's account of seeing God the Father and his Son Jesus Christ in a vision:

> I was greatly surprised at his [i.e., the minister's] behavior; he treated my communication not only lightly, but with great contempt, saying it was all of the devil, that there were no such things as visions or revelations in these days; that all such things had ceased with the apostles, and that there would never be any more of them.[22]

The minister's words represent the views that prevailed among Protestant ministers in Joseph's day: there would never again be any visions or revelations.

Readers may consider (and speculate) for a moment what might have occurred if Joseph Smith were to have been born in Russia or Greece and had told such a tale to an Orthodox priest or monk. Very possibly, the clergy, or his parents, or at least some of his friends and neighbors, would have accepted Joseph's words and might have encouraged him to go serve in a monastery. In Russia, they might have drawn parallels to Saint Alexander of Svir's vision of the Trinity. Joseph might have grown to be a towering figure in Orthodox spirituality (again, this is obviously speculation).

Consider this story from the early twentieth century regarding Elder Paisios of Mount Athos in Greece (now *Saint Paisios;* he was canonized in 2015). Paisios is a modern example of an Eastern Orthodox monk who is reported to have achieved great spirituality.[23] His biography recounts an interesting story from his youth of a vision he had of the Savior before entering the monastery.

At age fifteen, a friend of his brother, named Costen, spoke with young Paisios (then named Arsenios) to convince him to abandon his Christian faith. Costen was determined to "make him give up all this stuff" about Christianity and spoke of Charles Darwin and the theory of evolution. Young Paisios was a bit shaken by this talk, but still maintained his faith in the Lord. This is his account of what he told Costen and of what he did next:

> "I'll go and pray, and, if Christ is God, He'll appear to me so that I'll believe. A shadow, a voice— He'll show me something." That's all I could come up with.
>
> So, I went and began to pray and make prostrations, which I did for hours, but—nothing happened. Finally, I stopped in a state of exhaustion. Then something Costen had said came to mind: "I can accept that Christ is an important man," he had told me, "righteous and virtuous, Who was hated out of envy for His virtue and condemned by His countrymen." I said to myself, "Since that's how Christ was, even if He was only a man, He deserves my love, obedience, and self-sacrifice. I don't want paradise—I don't want anything. It is worth making every sacrifice for the sake of His holiness and kindness."
>
> God was waiting to see how I would deal with this temptation. And after this Christ Himself appeared to me in a great light. He was visible from the waist up. He looked on me with tremendous love and said to me, "I am the resurrection, and the life: he that believeth in Me, though he were dead, yet shall he live. He was holding open the Gospel in His left hand, where the same words were written."[24]

Paisios prayed for confirmation of his Christian faith at a time when the young people of his era were questioning the relevance of Christianity in an age of science. Paisios's faith and love for Christ led to a wondrous vision that confirmed the most basic of

Christian tenets: that Christ did rise from the dead and is "the Resurrection and the Life."

The parallels to Joseph Smith are also interesting. Both were almost the same age at the time of their respective visions. Both prayed because they were experiencing confusion over religious topics. In the case of Paisios, his faith in Christ was challenged, but later greatly fortified though his beautiful vision of Christ. For Joseph, the region where he lived was full of preachers of various Protestant groups, many of whom claimed to be correct in their religious views, while claiming that the others were in error. Joseph wanted to know which, if any, of these groups was right and which church he should join in order to seek salvation. His humble prayer was also answered, as in the case of Paisios, with a beautiful vision which Latter-day Saints call the First Vision (1820). Through his vision, Joseph saw God the Father and his Son Jesus Christ standing side by side.

Latter-day revelation contains verses of scripture that make abundant allowance for Christians of any tradition to experience miracles. Having faith in Christ is the key. Consider these verses from Moroni 7:

> 27 Wherefore, my beloved brethren, have miracles ceased because Christ hath ascended into heaven, and hath sat down on the right hand of God, to claim of the Father his rights of mercy which he hath upon the children of men?
>
> 28 For he hath answered the ends of the law, and he claimeth all those who have faith in him; and they who have faith in him will cleave unto every good thing; wherefore he advocateth the cause of the children of men; and he dwelleth eternally in the heavens.
>
> 29 And because he hath done this, my beloved brethren, have miracles ceased? Behold I say unto you, Nay; neither have angels ceased to minister unto the children of men.

Moreover, the Restoration through Joseph Smith was occasioned not because *no* faith in Christ remained on the Earth, but rather so that faith might *increase* (see D&C 1:21).

[1] Timothy Ware (Bishop Kallistos of Kokleia), *The Orthodox Church* (London: Penguin Books, 1997), 120.

[2] Stephen Fanning, *Mystics of the Christian Tradition* (London: Routledge, 2001), 2, citing Evelyn Underhill.

[3] Fanning's listing of Joseph Smith's visions in a matter-of-fact way alongside great and noted Christian monks and saints is an encouraging development and should be welcomed by Latter-day Saints.

[4] Hilarion Alfeyev, *St. Symeon the New Theologian and Orthodox Tradition*, Oxford Early Christian Studies (Oxford University Press, 2005), 5–6.

[5] B. H. Roberts, *Defense of the Faith and the Saints* (Salt Lake City, 1907; Project Gutenberg, 2014), [512–13], http://onlinebooks.library.upenn.edu/webbin/gutbook/lookup?num=47730.

[6] See Doctrine and Covenants 20:42; 42:76; 45:44; 46:27; 50:46; 61:38; 82:5; 84:111; 101:12; 133:11. In the Book of Mormon, see Jacob 5:12; Mosiah 4:30, 23:18; Alma 6:1; 15:17; 34:39; 3 Nephi 1:8, 18:15; Moroni 6:4.

[7] Athanasius, *The Life of Antony,* ed. Robert T. Meyer, no. 10 of *Ancient Christian Writers: The Works of the Fathers in Translation,* eds. Johannes Quasten and Joseph C. Plumpe (Washington, DC: The Newman Press: 1950), p. 70, para. 59.

[8] No manuscript with the original records of the Council of Nicaea is known to exist. The text of the Creed is known only through the other records, chiefly those of the Fourth Ecumenical Council in 451. See generally Tarmo Toom, "Council of Nicea I (325)," in *The Concise Encyclopedia of Orthodox Christianity*, ed. John Anthony McGuckin (Malden, MA: Wiley Blackwell, 2014), 133.

[9] George Poulos, *Orthodox Saints 1: Spiritual Profiles for Modern Man, January-March* (Brookline, MA: Holy Cross Orthodox Press), pp. 57–58, under "January 17."

[10] Encyclopedia Britannica Online, s.v. "Arianism," accessed July 22, 2019, https://www.britannica.com/topic/Arianism.

[11] I am conscious of the fact that monasticism may be difficult for some Latter-day Saint readers to appreciate, given that eternal life and godhood (D&C 132:19), in the Latter-day Saint understanding, are linked to marriage and family. In this context, readers might find insight in studying Isaiah 56:4-5 and applying it figuratively to monks, nuns and clergy for whom sexual abstinence is required. See also comments of Elder Dallin H. Oaks, "Sacrifice," April Conference 2012, "Latter-day Saints have no tradition of service in a monastery, but we can still understand and honor the sacrifice of those whose Christian faith motivates them to devote their lives to that religious activity."

[12] Alfeyev, *St. Symeon*, 46 (both quotations).

13
https://commons.wikimedia.org/wiki/File:Symeon_the_New_Theologian.
jpg; March 22, 2008, uploaded by Mladifilozof.
[14] https://commons.wikimedia.org/wiki/File:Palamas_Vatopaidi.jpg
October 27, 2011, uploaded by lamprotes.
[15] https://www.wikiart.org/en/mikhail-nesterov/saint-sergius-labours-
1896; last edit: March 14, 2012 by xennex.
[16] For a study of this icon, see Gabriel Bunge, The Rublev Trinity: The
Icon of the Trinity by the Monk-Painter Andrei Rublev, forward by
Sergei S. Averintsev, trans. Andrew Louth (Yonkers, NY: St. Vladimir's
Seminary Press, 2007).
[17] DATEI-NR.: 259960997
[18] Andrew Louth, Introducing Eastern Orthodox Theology (Downers
Grove, IL: InterVarsity Press, 2013), xviii–xix (open citation).
[19] Louth, Introducing Eastern Orthodox Theology, 7 (open citation).
[20] Frederica Mathewes-Green, Welcome to the Orthodox Church: An
Introduction to Eastern Orthodox Christianity (Brewster, MA: Paraclete
Press, 2015), xvii. Mathewes-Green's husband is an Orthodox priest.
She herself was raised Roman Catholic, but later abandoned her
Christianity and considered herself Hindu. She experienced a spiritual
conversion after graduating for college, later converting to Orthodoxy.
She is a prolific writer and has been involved in causes ranging from
feminism to right-to-life advocacy. See "Why Frederica Mathewes-
Green Loves Icons," interview by Dick Staub, Christianity Today,
September 2003, accessed July 24, 2019,
https://www.christianitytoday.com/ct/2003/septemberweb-only/9-8-
22.0.html.
[21] The family and individual curriculum for 2019 (the first year it was
introduced) is found at this link:
https://www.churchofjesuschrist.org/study/manual/come-follow-me-for-
individuals-and-families-new-testament-2019/title?lang=eng
[22] Joseph Smith History—1:21
[23] See Hieromonk Isaac, Elder Paisios of Mount Athos, trans. Hieromonk
Alexis and Fr. Peter Heers, eds. Hieromonk Alexis (Trader), Fr.
Evdokimos (Gorantis), and Philip Navarro (Chalkidiki, Greece: Holy
Monastery Saint Arsenios the Cappadocian, 2012).
[24] Isaac, Elder Paisios, 23–24.

4–The *Philokalia* and the Monastic Tradition

The men who are described in this book were all monks, and many were *hesychasts,* meaning that they practiced silent meditation focused on Christ. A good case can be made that some of these men fulfill Latter-day Saint prophecy. With this in mind, some background first on monasticism in Eastern Orthodoxy may be helpful.

Unlike in the Roman Catholic faith, there are no religious orders of monks in Eastern Orthodoxy, but each monastery does have its own "rule" or governing principles. A monk is normally subject to an "elder" or spiritual guide (who may or may not hold the Orthodox priesthood).

Many monks described in this book read and studied an important collection of writings known as the *Philokalia* in Greek, or *Dobrotolyubie* in Church Slavonic. The *Philokalia* was first compiled and translated by Macarius of Corinth and Nicodemus the Hagiorite in Greek. When their work appeared in print in 1782, Paisius Velichkovsky (1722–1794) translated and incorporated it into his Slavonic *Dobrotolyubie*. His work was published in 1793, in Moscow. Reportedly, twenty-four or thirty-six texts in this 1793 work came from the *Philokalia* of Macarius and Nicodemus.[1]

The publication of the *Dobrotolyubie* made an immense contribution in strengthening Hesychasm among the monks. The *Philokalia* and *Dobrotolyubie* are the most influential books in the history of Eastern Orthodoxy, outside of the Bible.

As is described in this book, some of the monks who studied the *Dobrotolyubie* (hereafter, this book uses the term *Philokalia*) became known for spiritual gifts. Their service to their countrymen so marked Russian society that people small and great came for spiritual advice. The memory of these monks, such as those of the Optina Monastery (shown on the cover of this book; see Chapter 10) and Saint Seraphim of Sarov, helped keep alive faith in Christ during the repressive decades of Soviet rule (1917–1991). When restrictions on religious activity began to be relaxed in the late 1980s, many Russians flocked back to Orthodox churches, inspired in great measure by the memory of these earlier monks of great fame. The fact that Russians were interested in returning to Orthodoxy or in joining other Christian groups after the fall of Soviet communism can be traced, in significant measure, to the service of men like Seraphim and the monks of Optina in the nineteenth century. This fact should make the story of the *Philokalia* of interest to Christians of all denominations and churches.

The creator of the version of the *Dobrotolyubie* was Paisius Velichovsky, a monk of very great renown.[2] Paisius was Ukrainian-born, but served, successively, in Kiev (Ukraine), Mount Athos (Greece), Moldavia, and Romania. As a young man Paisius heard a metropolitan from Romania celebrate the liturgy in Romanian and was deeply touched. He reportedly wrote that in his soul was "born a great love for the Moldavian [i.e., Romanian] language and its God-protected people; still more, from this moment, my soul was set on fire with the desire to become a monk in a foreign land."[3]

Paisius himself sensed a great mission as he embarked on his publication and translation projects that are included the *Philokalia*. Consider these remarkable words, in which he sees a special purpose for the writings of the early Church Fathers, which had been preserved "so that in the last times this divine work would not fall into oblivion":

> Let it be known that this divine work of sacred mental prayer [i.e., the Jesus Prayer practiced by Hesychasts] was the unceasing occupation of our God-bearing Fathers of antiquity, and in many desert places as well as in coenobitic monasteries it shone forth like the sun among monks: on Mount Sinai, in Scetis of Egypt, on the Mount of Nitria, in Jerusalem and in the monasteries which are about Jerusalem, and in a word—in the entire East, in Constantinople, on Mount Athos and in the islands of the sea; and in the latest times, by the grace of Christ, in Great Russia also. By this mental heedfulness of sacred prayer, many of our God-bearing Fathers, being kindled by a seraphimic flame of love for God, and after God for their neighbor, became the strictest keepers of God's commandments, and having purified their souls and hearts of all the faults of the old man, they were enabled to be

chosen vessels of the Holy Spirit. Being filled with various divine Gifts, they were manifested by their lives as lamps and fiery pillars in the world, having performed numberless miracles, by deed and word they brought an incalculable multitude of human souls to salvation. Many of them, being moved by a secret divine inspiration, wrote books of their teachings concerning this divine mental Prayer, in accordance with the divine Scriptures of the Old and New Testaments, which books are filled with the wisdom of the Holy Spirit. And this was by the special Providence of God, so that in the last times this divine work would not fall into oblivion. Many of these books, by God's allowance because of our sins, were destroyed by the Saracens [Turks] who subjugated the Greek kingdom; but some of them by God's Providence have been preserved in our times.[4]

The mention of "secret divine inspiration" could either cause readers to dismiss Paisius as a crank, or on the other hand, to believe that there may yet be a bonanza or hidden trove of important manuscripts to be discovered. His meaning isn't clear. Possibly, Paisius was simply making assumptions about events from centuries past (the Turkish capture of territories that used to be Byzantine; i.e., the capture of Constantinople in 1453). Either way, the credibility of Paisius and the importance of his influence on monasticism in Russia, Romania, and other countries of the region is beyond question.

One Orthodox writer referred to Paisius as a "new Moses . . . who collected a number of books by the ancient holy ascetics, and gave it the name Philokalia (Dobrotolyubie) . . . [that] includes true instruction for all who seek salvation—not only for monastics, but also for laymen.[5]

While living on Mount Athos in Greece, Paisius had a growing number of disciples, which necessitated construction of accommodations for them. As their number grew and he introduced innovations into the daily routine of his monks, Paisius began to face opposition. The challenges arose in particular as a result of his particular emphasis on older Greek patristic texts in his translations, rather than more recent Greek religious scholarship, and for his focus on the Hesychast tradition and the repetition of the Jesus Prayer.

Figure 4.1: Saint Paisius Velichkovsky
Credit: Wikimedia Commons, public domain.[6]

Paisius and his followers eventually moved to Romania, where they occupied two different monasteries through the years, benefiting from the patronage of Prince Gregory III of Moldavia, who wished to have Paisius "preside over the

revival of monastic life of his country."[7] As with the other monks described in this book, Paisius is said to have had great spirituality. As an older man, he "had the gift of tears in abundance, and once had a vision of Christ during the Divine Liturgy (the Eucharist worship service) that left him in a state of ecstasy for five hours."[8]

One of the spiritual practices promoted by the *Philokalia* is the silent, constant repetition of the Jesus Prayer, usually in these terms: "Lord Jesus Christ, Son of God, have mercy on me, a sinner." The monks who practice this prayer are known as

Hesychasts. The New Testament basis for this practice is seen in 1 Thessalonians 5:17, which states, "Pray without ceasing."

The aim of this spiritual practice is to center one's entire being on Christ. The literature on this practice is abundant, as is the number of monks and others who have found this practice invaluable in drawing closer to the Lord. On the other hand, numerous writers caution that an Orthodox believer seeking to practice the Jesus Prayer needs a spiritual guide or elder to assist. Breathing practices have often been linked to meditation using the Jesus Prayer, though whether true Hesychast prayer needs to involve breathing exercises or not is contested by different writers.

While Latter-day Saints are not taught meditation of this sort, the Book of Mormon and the Doctrine and Covenants do teach the need for constant prayer. Amulek (Alma 34:26–27) urges us to offer prayer in all circumstances: over our flocks and herds, for our crops, and against our enemies, including the devil. We are to pray vocally in private and in our hearts:

> **26** But this is not all; ye must pour out your souls in your closets, and your secret places, and in your wilderness.
>
> **27** Yea, and when you do not cry unto the Lord, let your hearts be full, drawn out in prayer unto him continually for your welfare, and also for the welfare of those who are around you.

Jacob also teaches of continual prayer (2 Nephi 9):

> **52** Behold, my beloved brethren, remember the words of your God; pray unto him continually by day, and give thanks unto his holy name by night. Let your hearts rejoice.

Alma too urges us to "pray continually," so that we are "not tempted above that which [we] can bear" (Alma 13:28).

In a similar vein, the Lord instructed Oliver Cowdery to direct all his thoughts to God (D&C 6):

> **36** "Look unto me in every thought; doubt not, fear not."

The Lord told Joseph Smith likewise (D&C 10).

5 Pray always, that you may come off conqueror; yea, that you may conquer Satan, and that you may escape the hands of the servants of Satan that do uphold his work.

Other verses of the Doctrine and Covenants teach that Latter-day Saints should "treasure" words of scripture in their hearts; we are to let the "solemnities of eternity rest upon [our] minds" (D&C 43:34) and let "virtue garnish [our] thoughts unceasingly" (D&C 121:45).

According to tradition, the *Dobrotolyubie* was brought to the famed Optina monastery in Russia by Elder Leonid, who had been a disciple of Elders Theodore of Svir and Cleopas of Valaam. Both of these men were disciples of Saint Paisius.[9] The early Elders of Optina were also contemporaries of Saint Seraphim. The service and miracles that these men performed during the course of a century (1829–1923) left an indelible example of Christian faith that is still cherished by Russian Orthodox believers. More about the Optina elders will be discussed in Chapter 10.

The influence of Paisius was felt not only in Russia. As with the Elders of Optina, miraculous occurrences are associated with Hesychast monks living outside of Russia as well. The stories of Hesychast monks and the monks described by Saint Gregory Palamas (1296–1359) tell of outpourings of heavenly light, of glorious visions, and even of monks being transfigured.

A history of the Romanian Orthodox Church tells the story of one of the disciples of Paisius, John of Moldavia. John related the following to an abbot known as Parthenius in the mid-nineteenth century, describing his training by Paisius and efforts to learn the art of Hesychast prayer, along with the resulting joy and spiritual gifts he experienced. John's spiritual experiences serve as classic illustrations of visions of the Uncreated light, which are associated with the experiential side of theosis. Abbot Parthenius published this account in the 1850s in Russia:

> Hear me, sinner that I am. I am going to reveal to you a secret, but keep it while I'm alive. I am going to give you part of my treasure. Don't hide it; when the time comes, share it with others. . . . I began to practice it [Hesychast prayer]. This prayer seemed so sweet to me that I loved it above everything. . . . Living in this way, many years

passed, and, little by little, the prayer began to take root. . . . An indescribable joy descended into my heart and the prayer began to act in me. . . . In truth, my child, the Kingdom of God is within us. An indescribable love for all men was born in me, and also tears. If I desired it, I could cry without ceasing. The Holy Scriptures, particularly the Gospels and the Psalter, became for me so sweet that I was not able to stop tasting them. . . . Often, I would stand up in the evening and read the psalms or to say the Jesus Prayer, and I was seized, drawn outside of myself, I don't know where, in the body or out of the body, I don't know, God knows. And when I returned to myself, it would be day.[10]

About 1925, an elderly Orthodox priest related a story involving this same John of Moldavia. When he was a young priest, many years before, he saw a light at his window one night and heard a voice commanding him to take the Holy Communion to this same John of Moldavia, then on his deathbed. Although frightened, the young priest obeyed and set off for the three-kilometer walk to the cave where John lived. As he walked through the night, the priest was led by a miraculous light, which went before him as he walked. There in the cave, he indeed found John, who said, "Father, fear nothing! Come and give me Communion, so that I may depart from this world!" The priest did as instructed, after which the two conversed for a time and the priest left. Three days later, the priest returned to the cave, and found all as it was when he last saw John; however, the body was not there, and was never found, leading some to believe his body had been "miraculously hidden."[11]

Eldership in Orthodox Monasticism

Paisius, Seraphim, the Elders of Optina, and others described in this book are outstanding examples of men who are referred to as "elders" in the Orthodox monastic tradition. In an Orthodox monastic community, the idea of obedience is tied to accepting the spiritual guidance and instructions of one's elder (in Russian *starets,* or старец[12]). The concept of obedience also extends to elders' lay disciples and to those who come for advice: the elders

81

give advice and the disciple or visitor is left with the choice of whether to heed or disregard the counsel.

Interesting background on the Orthodox concept of "eldership" is found in a book published by the Optina Monastery Press. Entitled *The Reverend Optina Elders*,[13] this book devotes much of the first chapter to the history of "eldership" (*starchestvo*, or старчество), both in Russia and going back to ancient times elsewhere.

In this particular book, the unnamed author[14] affirms that eldership existed before Christ, starting from the first chapter of Genesis and continuing throughout the whole Old Testament until the birth of the Savior. He lists prophets such as Elijah, Elisha, Samuel, and Daniel among the great elders. No documents are cited, so presumably this assertion is based on a reading of the Old Testament.

Unlike parish priests or the clergy, an Orthodox monastic elder does not necessarily hold the Orthodox priesthood—some do; some don't. Orthodox eldership generally sits outside the formal structure of the Orthodox Church, though a monastery is normally under the jurisdiction of an Orthodox bishop.

Figure 4.2: Angel with a Trumpet, Optina Monastery
Credit: Photo by the author

Each monastery is free to set its own "rule" or set of regulations, a fact which gives the individual monastery considerable latitude in setting its daily routine or in prescribing the duties and roles of its monks. Some monks who start their service in a monastery later receive the blessing of their elder or abbot to seek isolation in the wilderness or "desert" (even wooded wilderness areas are referred to as a "desert") and live as a hermit. Others live in "sketes" (scetis) which are smaller monastic residences consisting of only a few monks, with a dozen being the ideal size. Some of the famed Orthodox monks described in this book started their service as hermits, eventually gaining fame that, ironically, they may never have expected to find by seeking isolation in the wilderness.

Monastic elders are invariably completely devoted to the Orthodox Church, its sacraments and traditions; however, any influence or recognition they gain is not by virtue of position in the Church hierarchy, but as a result of their love, wisdom, sound spiritual counsel, and gifts of the Spirit. The elder may possess the gift of clairvoyance (*prozorlivost'*, or прозорливость), which is sometimes translated as "discernment." The elder remains in a state of penitent prayerfulness and has the gifts of working miracles and prophesying. The elder can look into the deepest recess of a human soul and perceive the very inception and causes of sin; and, thus knowing the soul of his disciple, he can point him or her on a straight path to salvation.

According to one leading Orthodox source on the internet, "an elder is one who, through inward purification, has become a vessel and conduit of the action of the Holy Spirit." This same source explains that the ministry of the Optina Elders was transmitted "from one Elder to the next, in a remarkable chain of sanctity that lasted a full century."[15]

The author comments that while the ancient eldership of Palestine and the Byzantine tradition in Constantinople did indeed provide spiritual food to even laypeople, this service to the community and society as a whole was not as systematic or continual as was seen in Russian eldership. The author traces some examples going back centuries in Russia. He sees the modern revival of eldership in Optina and elsewhere in Russia as arising through the service of Paisius.

[1] John A. McGuckin, "The Life and Mission of St. Paisius Velichkovsky, 1722–1794: An Early Modern Master of the Orthodox Spiritual Life," in *Spiritus: A Journal of Christian Spirituality* 9, no. 2 (Fall 2009), 157–73.

[2] Regarding Paisius Velichkovsky, see generally Metrophanes, *Blessed Paisius Velichkovsky: The Man Behind the Philokalia*, trans. Seraphim Rose (Platina, CA: Saint Paisius Abbey, St. Herman of Alaska Brotherhood, 1994); and McGuckin, "Life and Mission," 157–73.

[3] McGuckin, "Life and Mission," 157–73. Available at this link, accessed July 24, 2019, https://stpaisiusmonastery.org/about-the-monastery/life-of-st-paisius/the-life-and-mission-of-st-paisius-velichkovsky-1722-1794/.

[4] Paisius Velichkovsky, "The Scroll," in *Little Russian Philokalia* (Alaska: New Valaam Monastery, 1994), 21.

[5] Helen Kontzevitch, *Saint Seraphim: Wonderworker of Sarov and his Spiritual Inheritance* (Wildwood, CA: St. Xenia Skete, 2004), 16.

[6] https://commons.wikimedia.org/wiki/File:Paisius.jpg; uploaded November 29, 2006, by Roman Z.

[7] McGuckin, "Life and Mission," under "A Coming Home."

[8] McGuckin, "Life and Mission," under "Paisius' Enduring Influence."

[9] See the "Holy Elders of Optina: Commemoration of October 11/24," accessed July 1, 2019, http://www.pravoslavie.ru/english/65171.html. It appears that some of this material is quoted from the biography of Elder Leonid, published by St. Herman of Alaska press. The references to Alexander and Valaam show that these two men came from monasteries of great renown.

[10] Seraphim Jonata, *Romania: Its Hesychast Tradition and Culture* (Wildwood, CA: St. Xenia Skete, 1992), 175. Jonata's book gives a detailed and well-documented account of *Hesychasm* in Romania.

[11] Jonata, *Romania*, 176.

[12] This is not the same term used for a Latter-day Saint "elder"; this term is instead *stareyshina*, or старейшина.

[13] *Prepodobnyye stareyshiny Optiny: zhitiya i nastavleniya*, 2nd ed. (Kozelsk', Russia: Vvedenskiy muzhskoy monastyr' Optina Pustyn', 2014) = *Преподобные старейшины Оптины: жития и наставления,* Издание 2-е (Козельск: Введенский мужской монастырь Оптина Пустынь, 2014)

[14] Books written by monks are often anonymous.

[15] "Holy Elders of Optina: Commemoration of October 11/24," Orthodox Christianity, accessed July 24, 2019, http://www.pravoslavie.ru/english/65171.htm. When I toured Optina in 2015, our guide was asked by one of the tourists in our group (such visitors are normally referred to as "pilgrims") whether there are any such notable elders today in the Russian Orthodox Church as there were in the Optina of the nineteenth century. The guide replied that, to her knowledge, there were not. She explained that she had asked the same

question of others. The conclusion she drew after conversations was that, simply put, something had been lost; a chain had been broken. The great tradition of eldership had taken centuries to develop, whereby younger monks were nurtured spiritually by older, experienced elders. She explained that under the Soviet system, this spiritual knowledge was so severely damaged that there simply hasn't been time yet to rebuild it. These are, of course, only the remarks of one person, filtered through my recollections.

5—Orthodox Monks Who Fulfill Prophecy

A plausible case can be made that some Orthodox (and Catholic) saints described in this book are actually referenced in the Doctrine and Covenants. Three verses deserve careful consideration in this regard. These are Doctrine and Covenants Sections 49:8; 133:26; 7; and 113:10.

A detailed discussion of how these verses fit the stories of specific saints of the Eastern Orthodox (and Roman Catholic) tradition is given below.

Doctrine and Covenants 49:8

Perhaps the plainest example, Doctrine and Covenants 49:8 mentions "holy men" in an enigmatic context and cannot be deciphered solely with reference to known Latter-day Saint historical sources. These "holy men" may include some of the very saints profiled in this book (or others of their tradition). The verse states:

> Wherefore, I will that all men shall repent, for all are under sin, except those which I have reserved unto myself, holy men that ye know not of.

Latter-day Saint readers might assume at first glance that the "holy men" in question are "translated beings." Under Latter-day Saint doctrine, these are mortals who have been transfigured by the Holy Spirit to the point that they receive a lasting change in their bodies. In the case of the "three Nephites," this change made it possible for them to remain in a mortal condition for ages, until the Lord returns in glory. These individuals do not experience pain or sorrow, except for the sins of the world. Their purpose is to bring souls to Christ. These three were caught up to heaven, where they heard and saw things so glorious that they could not speak of them. They cannot be harmed by wild beasts or flames, nor can they be contained in pits or prisons (3 Nephi 28). Latter-day Saints believe that John the Beloved (i.e., John the Apostle) is one such being (see John 21:22 and D&C 7).

86

In fact, the date of this revelation (7 May 1831) suggests that the identity of these "holy men" is unknown to the restored Church of Jesus Christ and does not refer to any known "translated beings." For example, the "three Nephites" are known throughout the Book of Mormon, which was printed in March 1829; information regarding John the Beloved is found in Doctrine and Covenants 7 (April 1829), and the account of Enoch and his people who were "received into [God's] own bosom" was known by February 1831, when the "Book of Moses" was revealed to Joseph Smith (see Moses 7:69 and Genesis 5:24).[1] Thus, all these were *known* to the Church at the time of this revelation. So, this verse does not refer to any "translated" beings who are known at this time to Latter-day Saints.

Whom, then, does this verse refer to? This book proposes that it may refer to noted monks and saints within the Eastern Orthodox or Roman Catholic traditions, such as Saint Seraphim of Sarov (who died in 1833) or the monks of Optina (see Chapter 10) or monks from earlier eras.

Doctrine and Covenants 133:26

One of the most enigmatic prophecies in the Doctrine and Covenants concerns the "prophets" of the "north countries" mentioned in Doctrine and Covenants 133:26. This verse states:

> And they who are in the north countries shall come in remembrance before the Lord; and their prophets shall hear his voice, and shall no longer stay themselves; and they shall smite the rocks, and the ice shall flow down at their presence.

This verse contains several curious references to stories and prophecies of the Bible. One reads of "prophets" and the people of the "north countries." There is an allusion to a story recorded in the Book of Numbers, when Moses "smote" the rocks, causing water to flow forth (Numbers 20:11). One also reads a prophecy of the ice melting at the very "presence" of these prophets.

Just who are these prophets of the "north countries"?

Several early Latter-day Saint apostles commented on this verse and on this particular point. From their words, it is evident that readers will need to look *outside* the Latter-day Saint tradition to find these prophets. Early Latter-day Saint Apostles Orson Pratt, Franklin D. Richards, Wilford Woodruff, and Heber C. Kimball made statements that seem to point in this direction.

The specific statements made by these leaders are worth quoting, so they are given here. Readers should keep in mind that the time frame and specific geography (other than "north") for these predictions are not specified, neither in the Doctrine and Covenants nor in the statements referred to in this book. For that matter, they may even pertain in part to events in the spirit world. Latter-day Saint Apostles have emphasized that the work of the Church and the gathering of Israel are taking place on both sides of the veil—here on earth and in the spirit world.[2]

Regarding these prophets, Elder Woodruff (who later became President of the Church) stated in 1857:

> Again, here are the ten tribes of Israel, we know nothing about them only what the Lord has said by His Prophets. *There are Prophets among them*, and by and by they will come along, and they will smite the rocks, and the mountains of ice will flow down at their presence . . . and the men will have to be ordained and receive their Priesthood and endowments in the land of Zion, according to the revelations of God [emphasis added].[3]

Apostle Orson Pratt gave a lengthy discourse in 1875, quoting scriptures regarding the gathering of Israel in the last days, including from the lands of the north. Some of his discourse is speculation, no doubt; however, he comments regarding these prophets of the north are of interest here:

> *Do not think that we are the only people who will have Prophets. God is determined to raise up Prophets among that people*, but he will not bestow upon them all the fullness of the blessings of the Priesthood. The fullness will be reserved to be given them after they come to Zion. But Prophets will be among them while in the north, and a

portion of the Priesthood will be there; and John the Revelator will be there, teaching, instructing and preparing them for this great work; for to him were given the keys for the gathering of Israel" [emphasis added].[4]

Elder Richards stated in 1884, "The north country will yield up its multitude, with John the Apostle, who is looking after them. They also will come to Zion and receive their crowns at the hands of their brethren of Ephraim."[5]

The comments of these men track Doctrine and Covenants 133:26 in some respects and may also incorporate elements from other verses of this same section (such as verse 32). Some of their remarks refer to John the Revelator. The inspiration for their references to John may have originated in a reading of Doctrine and Covenants 7, which pertains to John, or in the following statement that Joseph Smith made in June 1831:

> John the Revelator was then among the Ten Tribes of Israel who had been led away by Shalmaneser, king of Assyria, to prepare them for their return from their long dispersion.[6]

The references to John the Apostle in these statements are interesting, because there are numerous documented appearances of John to the Orthodox saints profiled in this book. Some of these are discussed below.

As a first point of analysis in discussing the prophecy in Doctrine and Covenants 133:26, consider the wording relating to "smiting the rocks." The theme of causing water to flow is seen in miracles worked by Moses (see Exodus 17:6; Numbers 20:11; Deuteronomy 8:15). The Book of Isaiah and the Psalms contain references to this event and others when the children of Israel were blessed with water (2 Kings 2:21–22; Isaiah 48:21; Psalms 78:15, 16, 20). This theme is also seen in prophecies for the future (see for example Isaiah 12:3; 35:7; Ezekiel 47).

The hagiography or life stories (*vita, zhitiya*) of Catholic and Orthodox saints also contain such stories. These traditions seem to build on the stories recorded in the Old Testament, which are referred to above, when Moses caused water to flow from rocks.

In dictating a revelation referring to prophets causing water to flow from rocks (D&C 133:26), Joseph gave the world a prophecy that was consistent with a long line of stories from Christian tradition, dating back to at least the Apostle Peter. Historians should take note of this point. How much exposure might Joseph have had to these stories? As to the Orthodox saints, the likely answer is "zero"; however, as to Catholic saints and tradition, it is possible Joseph may have been exposed to stories of miraculous wells of water. Either way, this is an area where Joseph's prophecies seem to put him in dialogue with cultures and traditions of which he could have had little or no knowledge.

Here are a few highlights from these stories:

- **Saint Peter.** Catholic tradition holds that Saint Peter preached to his guards while in Rome's Mamertine Prison, converting and baptizing both the guards and forty-seven others. He miraculously caused water to flow from the rocks so their baptisms could be performed. An article in *The Telegraph* reported that archaeological work at the site of this prison has lent credibility to the story of Peter's miracle.[7] Tradition holds that Peter and Paul were killed in Rome; the tradition related to their death seems to have been accepted by Latter-day Saint authorities.[8]

Figure 5.1: The Mamertine prison in Rome (Carcere Mamertino) near the Forum in Rome
Credit: Wikimedia Commons.[9]

- **Saint Andrew.** Orthodox sources report that the Apostle, Saint Andrew (Peter's brother) is also said to have struck

90

the rocks to miraculously fetch water.[10]   Andrew is also
said to have preached the gospel in what today is Ukraine
and Russia.

A Romanian Orthodox tradition also holds that Andrew
lived in a cave in Dervent, Dobrogea, in southern Romania
for twenty years.[11]

Figure 5.2: Cave of Saint Andrew, Romania
Credit: Wikimedia Commons.[12]

- **John the Apostle (John the Theologian, in Orthodoxy).**
  Orthodox tradition tells of a prophecy by Saint John made
  while he labored in the vicinity of Hierapolis and
  Colossae, that "the community would soon be blessed with
  a miraculous well to which the ailing could go for cure."
  The prophecy came true and the people attributed the
  miraculous appearance of water to Saint Michael, the
  archangel. Later, a church was dedicated to John's name.
  Subsequent to this time, local pagans sought to destroy the
  well by diverting the nearby Chryssos River, but the well

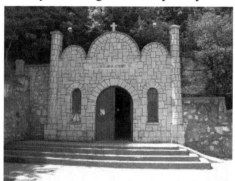 was rescued by
  the appearance
  of Michael the
  archangel, who
  descended from
  heaven with a
  flaming sword,
  which he used
  to separate the
  river into two
  currents,
  causing the water to flow permanently around the well
  rather than destroy it. This miracle is commemorated on
  the old Orthodox calendar on September 19 and on the
  new (Revised Julian) Orthodox calendar on September 6.[13]
  There are interesting correlations between this event on the
  Orthodox calendar and Doctrine and Covenants 128,
  which are described in Part V under "September 6/19—
  Angel Michael At Colossae, Doctrine and Covenants 128."

- **Saint Sabbas the Sanctified (also Sabas) (439–532)**. Sabbas was a Palestinian monk who founded a number of monasteries, including one in the vicinity of Jerusalem known in Arabic as Mar Saba or the Monastery of Saint Sabbas the Sanctified (the Great Lavra). He entered a monastery at age eight and became a great student of the scriptures. Later, after being tonsured as a monk, he "attained such perfection in fasting and prayer that he was given the gift of wonderworking." During a drought, the prayers of Sabbas caused a spring of water to well up at the Great Lavra. He also created the "Jerusalem *Typikon*," or first instruction guide on the order of church services used in monasteries around Jerusalem.[14] The efforts of Sabbas to standardize worship are cited by authorities as an important contribution to what later emerged in Constantinople in the eighth century and later as the Byzantine Rite, forms of worship still used today in the Eastern Orthodox Church.

Figure 5.3 The Monastery of Saint Sabbas the Sanctified (the Great Lavra), or Mar Saba in Arabic
Credit: Adobe Stock photo[15]

- **Saint Amatus (Amé or Aimé in French) (ca. 570–630)**. Amatus was a Catholic monk who lived as a hermit in the cliffs above the Saint Maurice Abbey in Switzerland. His parents are said to have been of noble lineage from the city of Grenoble in France. He was in fact raised at the abbey, having been brought there by his father as a "gift to God." Thus, like the Prophet Samuel of old, he was raised in a sacred setting by men of God. He is said to have smitten the rocks to miraculously bring forth water during the three years (611–614) he lived in the location.[16] His short biography, written by another monk of the same monastery, contains this account. The writer claims to have himself seen the spring and a leaden basin that Amatus caused to be put in place:

> The Lord worked yet another miracle through this man. Since his servant had been bringing him water for the last year from the stream in the valley, Amé, who was compassionate for his troubles, said to the brethren: "Let's go and approach that rock down there, and let's pray to God for he can make water come from the stone." When the prayer was finished, each [man] got up and with the staff he held in his hand, the man of God struck the rock; from which a spring gushed out, which remains inexhaustible; he commanded that we place there a leaden basin. I have seen it myself full, continuously spilling out water.[17]

Other miracles are attributed to Amatus. Once as an enormous boulder started rolling from the top of the mountain, headed straight for his cell (room), Saint Amatus is said to have made the sign of the cross and then spoken these words: "In the name of Jesus Christ, I command you not to descend lower!" The rock was just above the roof of his cell when it stopped short at his command, as if suspended on the mountain.

A discussion of the monastery where Amatus served, the Abbey of Saint Maurice, is included in Part V of this book, in connection with Doctrine and Covenants 84.

Figure 5.4: Chapel in the Cliff – Chapelle de Notre Dame du Scex, Saint Maurice Abbey, Switzerland Credit: Wikimedia Commons.[18]

- **Saint Sergius of Radonezh (1314/22–1392).** Sergius is the most famous of all Russian monks.[19] When some of his monastic brethren murmured that water was in short supply in the vicinity of the monastery, Sergius knelt in prayer and specifically asked the Lord to bring water from rocks, as the Lord had done for Moses. His prayer was answered. This account is told in his biography.[20]

Returning to Doctrine and Covenants 133:26—stories widely told of Seraphim suggest that he may represent a plausible fulfillment of the prophecy in Doctrine and Covenants 133:26. He too is reported to have stuck the rocks in order to fetch water. An account published in an Orthodox journal, *The Road to Emmaus,* tells of his appearance in the 1960s (about 130 years after his death), near the site of his former monastery, which then was a secret Soviet nuclear facility. Seraphim was reportedly dressed in white, carrying a staff with which he struck the ground. A spring of water burst forth, causing such a stir among local believers that the site became a place of religious pilgrimage.[21]

This wasn't the first well of water miraculously associated with Seraphim in that vicinity. Orthodox tradition tells of an earlier well that was opened by Mary in 1825, who appeared to Seraphim in company with Saint Peter and Saint John the Evangelist;[22] however, in the incident described above from the 1960s, it was Seraphim himself who reportedly struck the rocks. Seraphim's leading biography in English describes four appearances of John the Apostle (the Evangelist) along with Mary.[23]

Earlier apparitions of Seraphim in this same vicinity reportedly had already caused commotion among Soviet troops. According to this same Orthodox journal:

> He [Seraphim] was seen by many of the soldiers who reported being approached by an old man in a white robe with a staff. Shouting at him to halt, they shot at close range but the bullets never touched him. This became such a common occurrence that when a shaken new recruit came to report his first sighting to his superiors, he was simply told to forget it.[24]

It is not known if any writer or journalist has attempted to independently verify these stories. In fact, given the reported tie to a secret Soviet nuclear installation, it may not even be possible to assess their truth: the records of these incidents could be considered "state secrets." Yet, clearly the editors of *The Road to Emmaus* took them seriously.

In case some readers are tempted to see these stories as mere fables, two observations would seem to lend a measure of credibility to the journal in question. Metropolitan Timothy Kallistos Ware himself gave an interview for this journal.[25] Ware is undoubtedly the greatest living scholar of Orthodoxy in the English-speaking world. In addition, a respected Orthodox magazine editor, Sergei Antonenko, thought enough of these stories to publish this author's article in which they are cited.

Regardless of whether these accounts are totally accurate, other materials in this book also connect Seraphim to the prophecy recorded in Doctrine and Covenants 133:26.

The reference to the "north countries" in Doctrine and Covenants 133:26 is a clear allusion to the ten "lost tribes" of Israel, which were led away captive by the Assyrians about 721 BC. According to biblical prophecy, the lost tribes will eventually be gathered from around the world, and some will be led from the lands of the north. Speaking through the Prophet Jeremiah, the Lord spoke of a future time when people would say, "The Lord liveth, which brought up and which led the seed of the house of Israel out of the north country" (Jeremiah 23:8; see also 3:12, 18; 31:8; and Zechariah 2:6).

The Book of Isaiah makes reference to this gathering as well:

> "I will say to the north, Give up; and to the South, Keep not back: bring my sons from far, and my daughters from the ends of the earth" (Isaiah 43:6; see also Isaiah 49:12).

Russia is so vast that it covers nearly 180 degrees of the northern expanse of the Earth. Accordingly, a part of the fulfillment of these ancient prophecies (at least those pertaining to the "north") will inevitably be associated in some measure, great or small, with the lands of Russia or the former USSR.

With these geographical considerations in mind, it is fair to see the Christianization of many of these lands and regions of the "north" as part of, or a precursor to, the gathering of the lost tribes of Israel referred to by ancient and modern prophets. Christ is the very God of Israel (1 Corinthians 10:4). As these peoples take steps towards Christ, they also begin the process of being "gathered." Conditions of religious tolerance and pluralism that exist in many countries make this modern gathering possible. From the Latter-day Saint perspective, this gathering is occurring as local converts (in any country) join the Church and are thus "gathered" to local Church units[26] (Orthodox materials sometimes speak of gathering the people of the world to the Eucharist, a similar idea).

As additional evidence that the peoples of the lands of Russia and the former USSR are within the scope of these prophecies, one could also cite anecdotal stories concerning the patriarchal blessings of Latter-day Saint converts. Stories are occasionally told that the patriarchal blessings of Latter-day Saints in former Soviet-bloc nations are indicating tribal affiliations other than Ephraim and Manasseh.[27] These blessings are a very personal and private matter, so such stories are normally only told and heard through word-of-mouth among friends and acquaintances.

As an extremely interesting exception to this general rule, Sister Wendy W. Nelson, the wife of President Russell M. Nelson, recounted an experience she had in Moscow in 2013 while meeting with Latter-day Saint women.

> When I stepped to the pulpit to speak, I found myself saying something I'd never anticipated. I said to the women: "I'd like to get to know you by lineage. Please stand as the tribe of Israel that represents the lineage declared in your patriarchal blessing is spoken."
>
> "Benjamin?" A couple of women stood.
>
> "Dan?" A couple more.
>
> "Reuben?" A few more stood.
>
> "Naphtali?" More stood.
>
> As the names of the twelve tribes of Israel were announced—from Asher to Zebulun—and as the women stood, we were all amazed with what we were witnessing, feeling, and learning. How many of the twelve tribes of Israel do you think were represented in that small gathering of fewer than 100 women on that Saturday in Moscow?
>
> Eleven! Eleven of the twelve tribes of Israel were represented in that one room! The only tribe missing was that of Levi. I was astonished. It was a spiritually moving moment for me.[28]

That important events for Latter-day Saints would eventually be associated with Russia is seen from an 1843 statement made by Joseph Smith. In 1843, Joseph called Brother George J. Adams to fill a mission to Russia to

> introduce the fullness of the Gospel to the people of that vast empire, and [to this] is attached some of the most important things concerning the advancement and building up of the kingdom of God in the last days, which cannot be explained at this time.[29]

Returning to Seraphim and the prophecy in Doctrine and Covenants 133:26: another aspect of that prophecy is the reference to ice melting ("flowing down").[30] Indeed, the ice has melted in the far reaches of Russia, in more ways than one. During the Cold

War, Russian writers sometimes used the analogy of "ice" to describe the atmosphere of oppression under Soviet power. For example, during the initial years of Nikita Khrushchev's rule in the Soviet Union (mid-1950s–early 1960s), he relaxed the rules of censorship and released many political prisoners from prison. This period is referred to in history books as the "Thaw" (in Russian, "Ottepel'," or "Оттепель"). Eventually, the "climate" in the Soviet Union thawed to such an extent that Soviet power collapsed in late 1991.

When one considers actual developments in the weather, not just the political conditions, this prophecy of the Doctrine and Covenants also fits the situation. The scientific basis for global warming, or climate change, started gaining broad acceptance in 1988, when Dr. James Hansen appeared before the US Senate Committee on Energy and Natural Resources. *The New York Times* reported in June 1988 that the earth was warmer in the first five months of that year than at any time in the prior 130 years.[31]

The year of 1988 also happened to coincide roughly with the period in which dramatic events began to reshape the Soviet Union. The Orthodox Church was also commemorating the thousand-year anniversary of the introduction of Christianity into ancient "Rus" and the baptism of the citizens of Kiev.

By the early 1990s, anecdotal stories indicate that Russians were commenting on the *warm* winters in Siberia and the change in weather patterns (imagine it, Russians complaining about warm winters!).

By linking climate change and the fall of Soviet Communism, this author is not stating a cause-and-effect relationship. The point is merely that the two events seem to coincide, forming a plausible partial fulfillment of the prophecy in question ("ice shall flow down").

As with stories of Seraphim causing springs of water to burst forth, this account of him hearing the voice of the Lord also connects Seraphim to Doctrine and Covenants 133:26 ("their prophets shall hear his voice"). See Chapter 9 for a description of an event in which Seraphim heard the word of the Lord after praying for three days (and which holds similarities to words the Lord spoke to Joseph Smith during the First Vision).

98

Another important phrase in Doctrine and Covenants 133:26 is this: ". . . and they who are in the north countries shall *come in remembrance before the Lord*" [emphasis added]. This coming in "remembrance" may refer to more than one period of Orthodox history. There are several periods of history that could be relevant for a discussion here.

Saint Seraphim of Sarov (1754–1833) and other monks were part of a revival in Russia's monastic tradition. Catherine the Great closed many Russian monasteries in the eighteenth century (she reigned from 1762 to 1796), secularized many property holdings that had been under monastic control, and strictly regulated those monasteries that remained open. Seraphim and many other monks were practitioners of an ancient art of Christian meditation known as *Hesychasm*, which had been revived largely due to the efforts of

Saint Paisius Velichkovsky (1722–1794), as described in Chapter 4. This revival, in and of itself, constitutes an important phase of "remembrance," particularly when one keeps in mind that the labors of these monks were in great measure directed towards ministering to their countrymen, who often came to their monasteries by the hundreds or thousands daily to seek spiritual counsel and guidance for their lives.

Figure 5.5: Saint Seraphim of Sarov (1754- 1833)
Credit: Wikimedia Commons, public domain.[32]

This resurgence of Russian spirituality also coincided with a reawakened interest in Orthodox theology and the writings of earlier Greek Orthodox Church fathers. Many of the writings of these early fathers, for example, were included in the *Philokalia*.

Noted Orthodox writers from the twentieth century refer to a prolonged period of several centuries when theology in Russia was taught in Latin, using Western "theological categories and thought forms." They refer to this as a "Babylonian Captivity of Orthodox theology." This period ended in the 1840s, forming another contributor to a confluence of events that can be seen as a collective "remembrance." During this time, Russian monks and Russian Orthodoxy began a process of returning to their Greek patristic theological roots—a period of "remembrance" (not a "Reformation," in the Protestant sense).[33]

This renewal in Orthodox faith was not limited to Russia, though in other nations it seems to have been connected with nationalist movements. During the Greek War for Independence (1821–1829), Greeks sought independence from the Ottoman (Turkish) Empire. This struggle eventually led to the establishment of a Hellenic Republic and, later, a Kingdom of Greece (1832). The Greek Orthodox Church declared itself "autocephalous" (self-governing) in 1833. Other countries in Eastern Europe and the Balkans that were predominantly Eastern Orthodox also won their independence from the Ottoman Turks in the coming decades. The national churches of these countries also asserted their autocephaly (Romania, Georgia, Serbia, and Bulgaria).

This era saw a burst of creative energy in Orthodoxy in a wide range of religious activities, not just in the assertion of autocephaly by these national Orthodox churches. In the 1830s, several printed editions of important works appeared, helping standardize the daily offices (worship services) in Orthodox Churches. A new *Horologion* was printed in in 1832 and later in 1900; this work contains the hymns and psalms sung and read during the services that are fixed for particular hours of the day.[34] In 1838, the modern Greek *Typikon* was printed, with later editions in 1851 and 1868. This work is widely used in Greek-speaking Orthodox congregations and in the Balkans. It simplified in some respects the order and pattern of Church services, such as by eliminating all-night vigils that are still kept in connection with major Russian Orthodox feasts and the eves of Sundays.[35] In 1833, the famed Rila Monastery in Bulgaria was completely destroyed in a fire, later to be restored (1834–62). This monastery dates originally to the tenth century and has historically played an important role in the spiritual life of Bulgaria. Modern Latter-day Saint visitors invariably comment on the beautiful frescos and their possible theological meaning.

With the emergence of these new national Orthodox Churches, a number of renewal movements also eventually took shape, mainly in the latter years of the nineteenth century and the early twentieth century. These movements were characterized by "intensity of personal religious experience, holiness, discipline, communion, Scriptural authority, the use of vernacular languages in liturgical practice, hymn chanting, prayer, and the revival of pilgrimages and monasticism."[36]

At least in Russia, one important aspect of this renewal, or "remembrance," can be seen in a new emphasis on participating in the liturgy of the Church—specifically, by partaking of the Eucharist, or Lord's Supper (the "Sacrament" in Latter-day Saint parlance). Monks such as Seraphim encouraged the people to partake of the Eucharist as often as possible.

This emphasis is very significant, because partaking of the Sacrament is a solemn act by which the Christian believer remembers Christ (see Luke 22:19). Alexander Schmemann, an eminent Orthodox theologian (1921–1983), sees in the Eucharist a mutual remembering between God and the believers—

> "God remembers us and His remembrance, His love is the foundation of the world. In Christ, we *remember*. We become again beings open to love, and we *remember*. The Church in its separation from the "this world," on its journey to heaven, *remembers* the world, remembers all men, remembers the whole of creation, takes it in the love to God. The Eucharist is the sacrament of cosmic remembrance: it is indeed a restoration of love as the very life of the world" (original emphasis).[37]

Other Orthodox services also focus on "remembrance." During the service for Matins (a morning service), the priest calls upon God to call to remembrance the faithful:

> O Father all-holy who workest wonders, all-powerful and almighty: We all adore thee and entreat thee, calling thy mercies and thy compassion to the aid and defense of our lowliness. *Call to remembrance thy servants, O Lord*;

accept the morning prayers of us all as incense before thee; and let none of us be found reprobate, but encompass us with thy bounties. *Call to remembrance, O Lord, those who watch and sing praises to thy glory, and to the glory of thine Only-begotten Son who is our God, and of thy Holy Spirit.* Be thou their helper and their support. Receive thou their supplications upon thy most heavenly and spiritually discerning altar [emphasis added].[38]

Later, in the twentieth century, after decades of atheism, the people once again came in remembrance before the Lord. As the power of the Soviet state collapsed in 1991, people flocked back to churches, many of them remembering the great prophetic service of men of God from days past in their native land. Both of these periods of time (the nineteenth and late twentieth centuries) are times when the people of Russia "came in remembrance" before the Lord.[39]

In the narrative presented above, the people of predominantly Orthodox countries have deepened their faith and Christian devotion over the last two centuries *within* the framework of their existing churches (i.e., within Orthodoxy). It would be appropriate to refer to this process as a "remembrance."

Contrast this *remembrance* with how Latter-day Saints tell the story leading up to Joseph Smith and the Restoration. Such descriptions normally start with a narrative telling of the apostasy that took place in Christianity after the death of the original Apostles. That this event occurred is established Latter-day Saint doctrine. The next phase of this narrative takes us forward in time many centuries, to tell of men like William Tyndale (1494–1536), who translated the Bible into English. The narrative next proceeds on to speak of the great Protestant Reformers such as Martin Luther (1483–1546), then to discuss the Puritans who colonized New England, and then to the eventual adoption of the US and state constitutions with their protection for religious freedom. Citations are often made of 1 Nephi 13, which describes the colonists of North America bringing a "book," or the Holy Bible, that was "carried forth among them" (13:20).

For an understanding of how the restored Church of Jesus Christ came about in the United States of America, this narrative is *vital*.

The translation of the Bible into English, the Protestant Reformation, and the inclusion of constitutional guarantees of freedom of religion in the federal and state constitutions laid a sound foundation for the Latter-day Saint and other faiths to flourish. But talking about Tyndale or Luther, for example, in connection with religious developments in Athens or Moscow may have only limited historical relevance and even less appeal to Orthodox audiences.

This book includes the stories of men whose lives and contributions to the story of Christian faith should be considered every bit as important as those of (to name a few) Saint Patrick, Saint Augustine, Saint Thomas Aquinas, William Tyndale, Martin Luther, and other saints, Reformers and Puritans. These stories of Orthodox saints are unknown in The Church of Jesus Christ of Latter-day Saints and are virtually unknown in the United States (outside of the Orthodox churches) except in a few scholarly circles.

Doctrine and Covenants Section 7—Orthodox Missionary Labors; Appearances of John the Apostle

The Orthodox Church has played a vital role in helping Christianize Eurasia over the centuries, introducing Christianity to many different ethnic groups. Judging by sheer land mass alone, this is an impressive feat. Russia alone occupies over seventeen million square kilometers, roughly comparable to the land mass of South America. If one adds to this tally the dimensions of lands that were once part of the Russian Empire, including Alaska, one arrives at a land mass that would equal or exceed all of Latin America.

The Christianization of these lands was never complete. There are still significant numbers of Muslims, Buddhists, Jews, pagans, and adherents of other faiths, not to mention large numbers of atheists; however, Orthodox believers are by far the largest faith group in Russia.

This Christianization was accomplished in two ways primarily. It partly came about through the labors of hermit "colonist monks,"[40] who sought seclusion in the wilderness and led simple lives of prayer (many were hesychast monks who practiced the Jesus Prayer), scripture reading, and physical labors. Some of the stories in this book relate to such men, who amply fit with the term "prophets" of the "north countries"—this would include both great Orthodox missionaries from the past (many of whom were monks) and also men such as Saint Sergius of Radonezh, Saint Alexander of Svir, and Saint Seraphim of Sarov. Their wilderness dwellings often attracted others, who joined the hermit and together founded monastic communities and, eventually, built Orthodox churches, other monasteries, or convents. This activity, in turn, attracted settlers who came, built cabins, hunted, traded, and later founded villages, towns, and cities. This pattern has been referred to by historians as "monastic colonization."

This process of spreading Christianity also came about through the efforts of Orthodox missionaries, who won converts through patience, love, and other Christian virtues. Examples where Orthodoxy was imposed by fire and the sword were rare to nonexistent. On the other hand, there are indeed examples in Russian history when schismatic or non-Orthodox Christian groups were repressed, the "Old Believers" being the most well-known example.

The Orthodox missions can be seen as part of a broader process of helping the scattered remnants of Israel return spiritually to the God of Israel, to Jesus Christ.

Scholar J. M. Neale expressed precisely such a view in the nineteenth century, exultantly paraphrasing Isaiah 43:6 (quoted above) in describing the accomplishments of these missionaries, invoking Biblical prophecy related to the gathering of Israel:

> "This Church [the Russian Orthodox Church], privileged to work a conversion on the largest scale that has been seen since the days of the Apostle, namely that of Russia—that saith to the East, Give up, and to the South, Keep not back . . ."[41]

A modern example of such a missionary is Saint Innocent of Moscow (1797–1879), who took Christianity to the Aleutian Islands in the early decades of the nineteenth century. He also labored in Alaska and even visited California briefly in 1836. Innocent eventually served as the metropolitan of Moscow in the

Russian Orthodox Church. He was canonized in 1977 and given the title "Enlightener of the Aleuts, Apostle to America."

Although the story of Innocent's missionary labors is hardly known outside Russia, his service attracted the attention of J. M. Neale, who published this description of Innocent in 1857:

> What Western hears anything of the truly apostolical labours of the Archbishop of Kamchatka, Innocent, who is continually sailing over the ocean, and drives in reindeer sledges about his vast unpeopled diocese, then thousand versets in extent, everywhere baptizing the natives, for whom he has introduced the use of letters, and has translated the Gospel in the Aleoutian tongue. Some missions have been planted by him in Northern America, and its wild natives flock to the shores of their rivers, as in the first times of Christianity, seeking holy Baptism.[42]

Innocent was a gifted linguist who translated Orthodox worship materials into local languages. During the winter of 1832–33, he wrote a book on Christianity in Aleutian that was published in 1833, entitled "Directions of the Way to the Heavenly Kingdom." Later it was translated into Russian and other languages.[43]

Much of Innocent's teachings on Christ and the Gospel will resonate with Latter-day Saints, as undoubtedly with other Christians:

> Jesus Christ, the Son of God, came to this earth in order to return to us our lost capacity to spend eternity in the blissful presence of God. He revealed to people that all their evil lies in sin and that no one through their own efforts can overcome the evil within themselves and attain communion with God. Sin, ingrained in our nature since the fall, stands between us and God like a high wall. If the Son of God had not descended to us through His mercy for us, had not taken on our human nature, and had not by His death conquered sin, *all mankind would have perished forever!* Now, thanks to Him, those who wish to cleanse themselves from evil can do so and return to God and obtain eternal bliss in the Kingdom of Heaven[44] [emphasis added].

Innocent visited California in 1836 to visit Fort Ross, which was located just north of San Francisco. Reportedly, about 260 people lived in Fort Ross, about half of whom were Russians. Innocent also visited several Catholic missions in California (San Rafael, San José, Santa Clara, and San Francisco).[45]

As an interesting side note, Innocent was married and had children while engaged in his missionary labors. Only following the death of his wife in 1840 did he take monastic vows. He later served as the metropolitan of Moscow.

Figure 5.6: Ioann Veniaminov—Missionary and Enlightener (St. Innocent of Alaska aka St. Innocent of Moscow)
Coin commemorating 250 years from the discovery of Russian America (eg., Alaska)
Credit: Public Domain.[46]

The accounts of the labors of some of these missionaries are classics in Russian literature. One such account is the life story of Saint Stephen the Enlightener of Perm (ca. 1340–1396), written by Epiphanius the Wise, acclaimed as a great work of hagiographic[47] literature.[48] Stephen Christianized the Zyrians, a people that lived in the vicinity of modern-day Perm' in Russia. He also created an alphabet for the Permic language, which he used in translating religious and liturgical materials for local use. More about Saint Stephen in Part V, "April 26/May 9—Saint Stephen The Enlightener Of Perm (under D&C 50)."

Another interesting example of an early Orthodox missionary is Saint Abraham of Rostov (eleventh century). Abraham was born a pagan but later converted to Christianity and became a monk. According to Orthodox tradition, John the Theologian (i.e., John the Apostle) appeared to Abraham, gave him a rod or crucifix, and commanded him to teach the people in his region. Emboldened by the vision, Abraham used the rod to smash a stone pagan idol of a Slavic deity, Veles, that stood at the edge of town. He then built a small church, calling it the Church of the Theophany, gathered a group of monks, and built a monastery.[49] His actions were not uncontroversial. Tradition records that local pagans opposed his work, sought to harm Abraham, and attempted to destroy or burn the monastery; however, Abraham prevailed through prayer and patience, and the work continued. Many local pagans were eventually drawn to the church services and Abraham's teachings. Ultimately, the entire town accepted Christ.[50]

Figure 5.8: Abraham destroys the idol god Veles using a rod given to him by John (detail from Figure 5.7).

Credit: State Museum "Rostov – Kremlin."[51]

**Figure 5.7: Icon of the Apostle and Evangelist
John the Theologian Appearing to Abraham of Rostov.**
Church of St. John the Evangelist on the Ishnya River, near Rostov
Veliky
Credit: State Museum "Rostov- Kremilin."[52]

There are several accounts of Russian history where the smashing
of idols is associated with the adoption of Christianity. Prince
Vladimir (tenth century), who embraced Christianity and caused
his people to be baptized, also ordered the people to cut down the

idol Perun. Children swatted Perun with sticks as he was dragged down the hill and thrown into the Dnieper River. Stephen, for his part, cut down a magical tree worshiped by the people in the vicinity of Perm; eventually, the people were converted to Christianity.

This case of John's appearance to Abraham of Rostov is an instance where dialogue between Latter-day Saint and Orthodox scholars could be enriching for both sides. On June 3, 1831, Joseph Smith stated that John the Revelator was then laboring among "the Ten Tribes of Israel . . . to prepare them for their return from their long dispersion."[53] In Doctrine and Covenants 7, the Lord promised John the Beloved that he would have a special role through the ages to "prophesy before nations, kindreds, tongues and people" (D&C 7:3). In light of this prophetic role ascribed to John the Apostle, the story of Abraham of Rostov should be of interest to readers. The story shows that the fulfillment of Latter-day Saint prophetic statements is seen, in this case, in the preaching of Orthodoxy by Abraham of Rostov in the eleventh century.[54]

As mentioned above, there are at least four mentions in Seraphim of Sarov's biography of appearances of John. Similarly, Peter, John, and Mary appeared to Saint Sergius of Radonezh (fourteenth century), who is perhaps the greatest of all Russian monks. One can discover this latter fact by studying some icons that depicts scenes from his life.[55] The story is also told on the website of the Orthodox Church in America.[56] A medieval Greek saint, Peter of Argos (855–922), was warned in a dream by John the Apostle of danger to himself and his region.[57]

Doctrine and Covenants 113:10 (Isaiah 52:6–8)— Saint Symeon the New Theologian

In Doctrine and Covenants 113, some of the early Latter-day Saint elders asked Joseph Smith regarding the meaning of certain verses of Isaiah. Joseph responded to their questions in detail. In Doctrine and Covenants 113:10, Joseph Smith explains that in Isaiah 52:6–8, the "scattered remnants" of Israel are "exhorted to return to the Lord from whence they have fallen." Joseph further explains that, if they do this, "the promise of the Lord is that he will speak to them, or give them revelation."

In this verse, Joseph is interpreting Isaiah (eighth–seventh centuries BC) and is speaking of a scattered Israel. Thus, the events he speaks of could well have been in the past, perhaps even in the distant past. After all, the ten northern tribes of Israel were led away in about 721 BC. The Jews were then scattered in about 600 BC and later, after the destruction of Jerusalem in AD 70.

Isaiah 52 states:

> **6** Therefore my people shall know my name; therefore they shall know in that day that I am he that doth speak: *behold, it is I* [emphasis added].

In this verse, the Lord speaking through Isaiah expresses his intention that his people (scattered Israel) will know who he is, and they will know him because he will reveal himself to them, or give them revelations, as Joseph explained.

In this context, compare the quotation below from Saint Symeon the New Theologian (949–1022), who spent much of his life in Constantinople, with the words above from Isaiah. This is a firsthand account by Symeon of a personal meeting with God, as told to his spiritual advisor, or "father":

> The walls of my cell [i.e., his personal quarters] immediately vanished and the world disappeared, fleeing I think from before His face, and I remained alone in the presence alone of the light. And I do not know, father, if this my body was there, too. I do not know if I was outside of it. For awhile [sic] I did not know that I carry and am clothed with a body. And such great joy was in me and is with me now, great love and longing both, that I was moved to streams of tears like rivers, just as you see me now." The other [i.e., his spiritual father] then answers and says: "It is He, child." And at this word, he sees Him [God] again and, little by little, comes to be completely purified and, purified grows bold and asks that One Himself, and says: "My God, is it You?" And He answers and says: *"Yes, I am He,* God, Who for your sake became man" [compare the words in italics in the King James Version].[58]

Other Bible translations show an even stronger similarity to the words of Symeon. For example, the New International Version renders the last phrase as, "Yes, it is I"[59] (compare to the words Symeon reported that God said: "behold, it is I").

Symeon had several such encounters with God as bright light. Symeon's statement below (quoted from Meyendorff) is perhaps his best description of his encounters with God. Symeon describes meeting the Savior himself, whom he refers to as his "gentle Master":

> Then by Your grace, I was granted to contemplate a still more awesome mystery. I saw You take me with Yourself, and rise to heaven; I know not whether I was still in my body or not—You alone know, You alone who created me.

> On coming back to myself, I wept in sorrowful surprise at my abandoned state. But soon You deigned to reveal Your face to me, like the sun shining in the open heavens, without form, without appearance, still not revealing who You were. How could I have known, unless You told me, for You vanished at once from my weak sight? . . .

> Still weeping I went in search of You, the Unknown One. Crushed by sorrow and affliction, I completely forgot the world and all that is in the world, nothing of the senses remained in my mind. Then You appeared, You, the Invisible one, the Unattainable, the Intangible. I felt that You were purifying my intelligence, opening the eyes of my soul, allowing me to contemplate Your glory more fully, that You Yourself were growing in light. . . . You, the Faceless one, were taking features. . . . You shone beyond all measure, You appeared to me wholly in all things, and *I saw You clearly*. They I dared to ask You, saying: "Who are You, O Lord?"

> For the first time You allowed me, a vile sinner, to hear the sweetness of Your voice. You spoke so tenderly that I trembled and was amazed, wondering how and why I had been granted Your gifts. You said to me: "I am the God who became man for love of you. You have desired me and sought me with your whole soul, therefore henceforth

111

you shall be my brother, my friend, the co-heir of my glory
. . .'

You said this and then were silent. You departed from me,
O lovable and gentle Master, O my Lord Jesus Christ![60]

Symeon's accounts of meeting God in a cloud of bright light are
reminiscent of some passages in the Old Testament where God's
presence was visible as a cloud or pillar of fire. They also fit
closely with the account of Jesus' transfiguration, which mentions
a "bright cloud" (Matthew 17:5). Likewise, the Book of Mormon
contains such accounts.

The story of the prophet known as the "brother of Jared" in the
Book of Mormon is instructive here. From the account in the
Book of Mormon, it is evident that the brother of Jared was a great
prophet of the Lord who lived at the time of the Tower of Babel,
yet his two initial encounters with God are very much in line with
those reported in the Old Testament (and as understood in
Orthodox theology).

Consider the fact that God's first appearance to the brother of Jared
that is mentioned in the Book of Mormon occurred "in a cloud";
God did not manifest himself openly:

And it came to pass that when they had come down into
the valley of Nimrod the Lord came down and talked with
the brother of Jared; and he was in a cloud, and the brother
of Jared saw him not (Ether 2:4).

Later in the same chapter, another appearance of the Lord is
recorded, though this time the Lord was displeased:

And it came to pass at the end of four years that the Lord
came again unto the brother of Jared, and stood in a cloud
and talked with him. And for the space of three hours did
the Lord talk with the brother of Jared, and chastened him
because he remembered not to call upon the name of the
Lord (Ether 2:14).

Moroni deemed these two earlier accounts of sufficient merit that
he recorded them in the Book of Ether, even though the Lord
withheld himself from the sight of the brother of Jared.

Later, the Lord manifested himself to the brother of Jared in the body of his Spirit, appearing in the same shape and form that he would eventually be born with.

> Behold, this body, which ye now behold, is the body of my spirit; and man have I created after the body of my spirit; and even as I appear unto thee to be in the spirit will I appear unto my people in the flesh (Ether 3:7–16).

The earlier appearance of the Lord in a cloud to the brother of Jared is similar in description to the accounts of God's appearances to Moses and his people in the Old Testament, as these verses below show. Some of these verses also describe a dark cloud where God was. The cloud was thus at times associated with brightness and fire, but at other times the interior darkness is emphasized:

> And the Lord went before them by day in a pillar of a cloud . . . and by night in a pillar of fire (Exodus 13:21).

> Behold, the glory of the Lord appeared in the cloud (Exodus 16:10).

> Lo, I come unto thee in a thick cloud (Exodus 19:9).

> And the people stood afar off, and Moses drew near unto the thick darkness where God was" (Exodus 20:21).

> And Moses went up into the mount, and a cloud covered the mount. And the Glory of the Lord abode upon mount Sinai . . . and the sight of the glory of the Lord was like devouring fire (Exodus 24:15–17).

> And all the people saw the cloudy pillar stand at the tabernacle door: and all worshipped, every man in his tent door (Exodus 33:10).

> For the cloud of the Lord was upon the tabernacle by day, and fire was on it by night, in the sight of all the house of Israel, throughout all their journeys (Exodus 40:38).

> And ye came near and stood under the mountain; and the mountain burned with fire unto the midst of heaven, with darkness, clouds, and thick darkness (Deuteronomy 4:11).

And the Lord came down in the pillar of the cloud (Numbers 12:5).

Thou Lord art among this people, that thou Lord art seen face to face, and that thy cloud standeth over them, and that thou goest before them, by day time in a pillar of a cloud, and in a pillar of fire by night (Numbers 14:14).

In the daytime also he led them with a cloud, and all the night with a light of fire (Psalms 78:14).Clouds and darkness are round about him; righteousness and judgment are the habitation of his throne (Psalms 97:2).

Figure 5.9: Moses on Mount Sinai (1895-1900), Jean-Léon Gérôme (d. 1904)
Credit: Wikimedia Commons, public domain.[61]

Orthodox theologians have carefully analyzed these verses. The fact that God was inside a cloud, which was also associated (in some verses) with a darkness, points to God being ultimately an unknowable mystery, though he can partly be understood through the incarnation of his Son.[62] Nevertheless, these verses all attest to appearances of God, even if the people could not comprehend God fully.

The description of God's bright light (which might be equated with a cloud) in some of Symeon's writings is consistent with some of the verses quoted above from the Old Testament. Likewise, so are two appearances of God to the brother of Jared in a cloud, which could also be understood to be a cloud of light. What Symeon saw was consistent with Biblical accounts and even the first two appearances of God to the brother of Jared, as reported in the Book of Mormon.

Readers may note a seeming contradiction in the verses contained in the Old Testament. Some verses describe a pillar of fire, or a cloud (which we may assume is a cloud of brightness), yet others mention thick darkness. How can God appear as glorious fire or light, or a bright cloud, yet also be in thick darkness?

A set of verses from the Book of Helaman in the Book of Mormon is useful for discussion here. All in one account, both extremes were experienced by different witnesses. Helaman 5 records a miraculous occurrence (ca. 30 BC) when Nephite missionaries Nephi and Lehi were cast into prison by Lamanites. As men came to put them to death, a heavenly pillar of fire surrounded the two, preventing the Lamanites from seizing them (Helaman 5:24–25). The earth began to shake and a cloud of darkness descended upon those in the jail (5:27–28). A voice was then heard from heaven, urging these Lamanites to repent (5:29). This was the voice of God, a still voice of perfect mildness that pierced them to their souls (5:30; cf. 3 Nephi 11:3).

The Lamanites looked through the cloud and saw the faces of Nephi and Lehi, shining like those of angels, seemingly talking to a being in the cloud whom they beheld (5:36–37). The crowd was now stilled but confused. Who were Nephi and Lehi speaking with? A Nephite dissenter in the crowd explained that they were talking with angels: "[You must] repent, and cry unto the voice, even until ye shall have faith in Christ . . . and when ye shall do this, the cloud of darkness shall be removed from overshadowing you" (5:41).

Hearing this, the Lamanites pled with the voice (of God) and the cloud was removed. Following the miracle, the entire group of three hundred people was encircled by a pillar of fire (5:42–43).

115

The voice of God spoke peace to them, and angels came down to minister to the crowd (5:48).

It is worth noting that the account in Helaman 5 seemingly does not provide a first-person account of what happened from the viewpoint of either Nephi or Lehi. We only read that they were shining like angels and seemed to be talking with angels in the cloud. While the Nephite dissenter in the crowd assumed that they were speaking with angels, readers could wonder if this occurrence was actually an appearance of Jehovah himself. The indicia described in Old Testament accounts are all there – earthquakes, a cloud of darkness, a great light, and prophets shining like angels (or like Moses).

This account also shows us that what the viewers perceived depended on their spiritual state. The initial darkness was experienced by wicked men who sought to harm holy men sent by God. This fact makes an interesting context for the accounts of darkness described above in verse from the Old Testament. The people of Israel were often a rebellious group, even quickly reverting to idolatry when Moses was absent (Exodus 32:4). If an analogy is made between Helaman 5 and the Old Testament, it follows then that the Israelites (or many) might have perceived God as darkness, whereas Moses experienced a higher truth (his face shone with light, just as the faces of Nephi and Lehi, Exodus 34:29-35).

Despite the verses cited from Latter-day Saint scripture, the notion that Christians outside the Church may have seen God as bright light, or may have met the Savior, may seem difficult to accept for some readers. The assumption in the Church—that the heavens were closed until Joseph Smith's First Vision in 1820— seems widespread. Some Saints may even have assumed that miracles had ceased to occur and angels had ceased to appear (even though Moroni wrote in the fourth century that this would not necessarily be the case: see Moroni 7:29, 36).

Perhaps Latter-day Saints have unwittingly absorbed some of the attitudes of nineteenth-century Protestant clergy in the United States and abroad. The familiar dialogue between Joseph Smith and an unnamed Methodist minister comes to mind, which Joseph

Smith describes in these words in his History (see Joseph Smith— History 1:21):

> Some few days after I had this vision, I happened to be in company with one of the Methodist preachers, who was very active in the before mentioned religious excitement; and, conversing with him on the subject of religion, I took occasion to give him an account of the vision which I had had [of God the Father and his Son, Jesus Christ]. I was greatly surprised at his behavior; he treated my communication not only lightly, but with great contempt, saying it was all of the devil, that there were no such things as visions or revelations in these days; that all such things had ceased with the apostles, and that there would never be any more of them.

The preacher's views reflected the prevailing attitude among the Protestant clergy of Joseph's day. Visions, miracles, and the beholding of angels were largely viewed as things of the past: "there never would be any more of them." The Methodist minister's attitude is similar to views expressed in an 1841 book on Saint Irenaeus (AD 130–202), published in London and widely subscribed to by Church of England clerics.[63] The author, James Beavan, tends to dismiss Irenaeus's claim that Christians of his day worked miracles and enjoyed spiritual gifts. Beavan defers to an earlier work by one Dr. Kaye, bishop of Lincoln, who asserted that

> those powers [of working miracles] were conferred only by apostolical hands, and that of course they would continue till all that generation was extinct who were contemporary with St. John, the last of the Apostles. That would admit of Irenaeus having known instances; and not having any idea that the power was to be extinct, he would think that it still remained, even if he had not known any *recent* instances.[64]

The attitude expressed by Beavan is consistent with the view of the Protestant Reformers toward Catholic miracles. In the sixteenth century, several Protestant writers published works challenging the stories of miracles associated with Catholic saints. Some asserted, in fact, that the purported miracles were works of the devil and that some of the popes themselves were masters of dark magical arts

117

and were "conjurers and necromancers." One Protestant writer, John Bale, cited an example of a "Popish" (Catholic) priest who quietly pricked his finger with a needle while consecrating the Eucharist in order to create "the illusion of Christ's blood appearing on the altar."[65] Stories like this helped cement in the minds of Protestants the notion that miracles were utterly a thing of the past and that no credence whatsoever should be given to stories of Catholic miracles.

John Calvin, for example, taught of the cessation of divine healing, reasoning that such miracles were seen in the ministry of the Savior and Apostles as a way of proving the gospel in its earliest stages; Calvin further taught that the main point of the Gospel was the healing from sin, not bodily healing.[66] He referred to unction (the sacrament for blessing the sick) as a "fictitious sacrament" and stated:

> The gift of healing disappeared with the other miraculous powers which the Lord was pleased to give for a time, that it might render the new preaching of the gospel for ever [*sic*] wonderful.[67]

German Protestant Reformers also spoke out against Catholic miracles, including those associated with pilgrimages to holy shrines. Luther, for example, reportedly "denounced the miracles publicized by the clergy at particular shrines as the 'works of the devil.'"[68]

Back to the image of the "cloud," this terminology is also used repeatedly in Scripture to describe the Second Coming. The world in general will see the "Son of man coming *in* the clouds of heaven with power and great glory" (Matthew 24:30; Joseph Smith— Matthew 1:36; emphasis added). Thus, the people of the world may not perceive his bodily shape. Believers, however, will be *caught up in the cloud* and "received *into* the cloud" (1 Thessalonians 4:17; D&C 78:21; 76:102), and the righteous dead will be resurrected and caught up to "meet" the Lord *in* the cloud (D&C 45:45; 109:75; emphasis added).

Interestingly, the Doctrine and Covenants contains verses that attest to both conceptions of God—as both a light in the darkness and as a being that believers can, in fact, comprehend. In some of the earliest sections of the Doctrine and Covenants, God speaks of

118

himself in terms that may be familiar to Orthodox theologians or other Christians (relying on John 1:5): that is, as the "light which shineth in the darkness." There are at least seven sections of the Doctrine and Covenants with this wording, where Christ introduces himself in terms that are reminiscent of the Old Testament appearances of Jehovah to his people (D&C 6:21; 10:58; 11:11; 34:2; 39:2; 45:7; and 88:7, 11, 49). These sections up through Section 45 span the years 1829 to 1831. In Doctrine and Covenants 11:11, the text even repeats the wording from Isaiah 52:6, which is very similar to Symeon's account (quoted above) of God appearing to him.

This manner of speaking (i.e., that God is a light shining in the darkness) ends in Doctrine and Covenants 88, which also happens to be the section that gives the specific commandment to build the Kirtland Temple (88:119). Doctrine and Covenants 88:49 also promises that the faithful would "comprehend even God, being quickened by him." The section was revealed during the time between December 27, 1832 and January 3, 1833, a period that includes the calendar death date of Saint Seraphim of Sarov. This same time frame is also the octave of Saint John in the Traditional Catholic Calendar, which was in use during Joseph's lifetime. Saint Seraphim and Saint John both have a special connection to the doctrines expressed in Doctrine and Covenants 88.

Doctrine and Covenants 88 thus emerges as a pivotal revelation, since it contains the commandment to build the Kirtland Temple and also promises the people that they will eventually comprehend God. Before this time, God speaks in the Doctrine and Covenants in ways that would have been familiar to the people in the days of Moses or to Christian students of any denomination who have studied the Gospel of John.

---

[1] See Robert J. Matthews, "How We Got the Book of Moses," *Ensign*, January 1996.

[2] See 2019 examples under keywords "both sides of the veil" in M. Russell Ballard, "The True, Pure, and Simple Gospel of Jesus Christ," April 2019 general conference; and in Quintin L. Cook, "Great Love for our Father's Children," April 2019 general conference.

[3] Wilford Woodruff, "Intelligence Comes From God—Seek First the Kingdom of God—Great Changes to Take Place on the Earth," *Journal of Discourses* 4, February 22, 1857, p. 231.

[4] Orson Pratt, "Gathering of Israel—The Work of the Father Commenced," *Journal of Discourses* 18, April 11, 1875, p. 25.

[5] Franklin D. Richards, "Temples the Gates of Heaven—Feelings and Reflections," *Journal of* Discourses 25, May 17, 1884, p. 237.

[6] Vol. 1 of *History of the Church of Jesus Christ of Latter-day Saints,* ed. B.H. Roberts, p. 176; see ch. 15, n. 4, https://byustudies.byu.edu/content/volume-1-chapter-15#fn-3.

[7] Nick Squires, "Archeologists find evidence of St Peter's prison," *The Telegraph*, June 25, 2010, http://www.telegraph.co.uk/news/worldnews/7852507/Archeologists-find-evidence-of-St-Peters-prison.html (accessed 24/07/2019). See also Carol Glatz, "Conversion: an Ancient Prison went from Pagan to Sacred Christian Site," *Catholic News Service*, July 30, 2010, http://www.catholicnews.com/services/englishnews/2010/conversion-ancient-prison-went-from-pagan-to-sacred-christian-site.cfm (accessed 24/07/2019).

[8] See for example Boyd K. Packer, "The Twelve," *Ensign*, May 2008. "We know little of their travels and only where and how a few of them died. James was killed in Jerusalem by Herod. Peter and Paul died in Rome. Tradition holds that Philip went to the East. Much more than this we do not know." See also "Elders Bednar and Elder Rasband Testify of Jesus Christ in Rome" (The Church of Jesus Christ of Latter-Day Saints, January 16, 2019), YouTube video, https://www.youtube.com/watch?v=EAcOubokkWE.

[9] https://commons.wikimedia.org/wiki/File:Mamertine_Prison.jpg This file is licensed under the Creative Commons Attribution-Share Alike 3.0 Unported license.

[10] See for example "A Great Miracle of the Apostle Andrew in Cyprus in 1912," Mystagogy Resource Center, John Sanidopoulos, November 30, 2010, accessed July 24, 2019, http://www.johnsanidopoulos.com/2010/11/great-miracle-of-apostle-andrew-in.html.

[11] Mentioned in Seraphim Jonata, *Romania: Its Hesychast Tradition and Culture* (Wildwood, CA: St. Xenia Skete, 1992).

[12] https://commons.wikimedia.org/wiki/File:Pe%C8%99terile_Sf._Apostol_Andrei_-_detalii_01.JPG. This file is licensed under the Creative Commons Attribution-Share Alike 4.0 International license.

[13] George Poulos, *July–September*, vol. 3 of *Orthodox Saints* (Brookline MA: Holy Cross Orthodox Press, 2005), 261–3.

[14] "Venerable Sava the Sanctified," Orthodox Church in America, updated 2019, accessed July 24, 2019, http://oca.org/saints/lives/2015/12/05/103477-venerable-sava-the-sanctified.

[15]Adobe Stock photo DATEI-NR.: 265899955

[16] My sketch of Saint Amatus is taken from a short account of his life in French translation from the Latin original, found in "La Vie de saint Amé," *Notre-Dame du Scex: Une Chapelle dans la Falaise, Les Echos de Saint-Maurice* 23, special edition Fall 2011 (Saint Maurice, Switzerland: Imprimerie Saint-Augustin), 122–128. The account of his life has been by one scholar as ca. 675–690, or only fifty years after the death of Amé. Dates of his life story and life are given in *L'abbaye de –Saint-Maurice d'Agaune* 515–2015, vol. 1 of *Histoire et Archéologie*, eds. Bernard Andenmatten and Laurent Ripart, 49. See also "St. Amatus," Catholic Online, Your Catholic Voice Foundation, accessed July 24, 2019, http://www.catholic.org/saints/saint.php?saint_id=1315.

[17] "La Vie," 123.

[18] https://commons.wikimedia.org/wiki/File:St-Maurice-Kapelle.jpg. This file is licensed under the Creative Commons Attribution-Share Alike 3.0 Unported license.

[19] *St. Sergey of Radonezh* (Moscow: Panorama Publishers, 1992), 136 (bilingual Russian and English).

[20] *Zhitiye prepodobnogo Sergiya Radonezhskogo* (Izdatel'stvo "Sretenskiy stavropigial'nyy muzhskoy monastyr'", 2014) = *Житие преподобного Сергия Радонежского* (Издательство «Сретенский ставропигиальный мужской монастырь», 2014), 99–100.

[21] Mother Nectaria McLees, "Diveyevo: A Pilgrim's Chronicle 1993-2003," *A Journal of Orthodox Faith and Culture: The Road to Emaus* 4, no. 3 (14), 4–11, also republished online at: http://www.manastir-lepavina.org/vijest_en.php?id=2363.

[22] Archimandrite Lazarus (Moore), *An Extraordinary Peace: St. Seraphim, Flame of Sarov* (Port Townsend, WA: Anaphora Press, 2009), 101.

[23] Moore, *Extraordinary Peace*, index, s.v. "Appearances . . . Apostle John."

[24] McLees, "Diveyevo: A Pilgrim's Chronicle," 9. Posthumous appearances of Seraphim are reported in his printed biographies and online. For a sampling, see Moore, *Extraordinary Peace,* 353, s.v. "appearances of . . . St. S."; Maria Saradzhishvili, "St. Seraphim of Sarov in Georgia," January 15, 2017, accessed July 29, 2019 http://www.pravoslavie.ru/100142.html; A.P. Timofievich, "A Pilgrimage to Diveyevo," in Helen Kontzevitch, *St. Seraphim: Wonder Worker of Sarov and His Spiritual Inheritance* (Wildwood, CA: St. Xenia Skete, 2004), 287; and "Kratkoye zhizneopisaniye svyashchennomuchenika Mitropolita Serafima (Chichagova), Igumeniyey Serafimoy (Chernoy-Chichagovoy)" (nastoyatel'nitsey moskovskogo Novodebich'ego monastryrya) = "Краткое жизнеописание священномученика Митрополита Серафима (Чичагова) ["Short Biographical Sketch of

Holy-Martyr Metropolitan Seraphim (Chichagov)"], Игуменией Серафимой (Черной-Чичаговой)(настоятельницей московского Новодевичьего монастыря) 11/12/2012, accessed July 29, 2019, posted at: http://www.mgarsky-monastery.org/kolokol.php?id=2618. This latter article reports a posthumous appearance by Seraphim of Sarov to his biographer, Hegumen Seraphim (Chichagov) in 1902, a year prior to Seraphim's canonization. See also Moore, *Extraordinary Peace,* 135. In this passage, Saint Seraphim gives explanations to Motovilov regarding the glorious state they were in as the Holy Spirit transfigured them, citing Mark 9:1, "There are some of those standing here who shall not taste of death till they see the Kingdom of God come in power."

[25] For a short overview of his thoughts on Orthodoxy, see interview with Timothy Ware, "Becoming Orthodox," *A Journal of Orthodox Faith and Culture: The Road to Emaus* 3, no. 3 (10), 46–54, http://www.roadtoemmaus.net/back_issue_articles/RTE_10/Bishop_Kallistos_Ware_on_Personhood.pdf.

[26] See talk by Bruce R. McConkie, "Come Let Israel Build Zion," April 1977; Russell M. Nelson, "The Gathering of Scattered Israel," October 2006 general conference, The Church of Jesus Christ of Latter-day Saints, Intellectual Reserve, https://www.Latter-day Saint.org/general-conference/2006/10/the-gathering-of-scattered-israel?lang=eng.

[27] Each worthy, baptized Church member is entitled to a patriarchal blessing once in his or her life. See "Patriarchal Blessings," The Church of Jesus Christ of Latter-day Saints, Intellectual Reserve, https://www.Latter-day Saint.org/topics/patriarchal-blessings?lang=eng.

[28] See Russell M. Nelson and Wendy W. Nelson, "Hope of Israel," *Worldwide Youth Devotional*, June 3, 2018, https://www.Latter-day Saint.org/broadcasts/face-to-face/nelson?lang=eng and https://www.churchofjesuschrist.org/study/new-era/2018/08-se/hope-of-israel?lang=eng. In this same talk, Sister Nelson also reports having met a member of the tribe of Levi during her travels the following day.

[29] See James A. Miller, "That Vast Empire: The Growth of the Church in Russia," The Church of Jesus Christ of Latter-day Saints, Intellectual Reserve, February 2014, https://www.churchofjesuschrist.org/study/ensign/2014/02/that-vast-empire-the-growth-of-the-church-in-russia?lang=eng.

[30] Compare this prophecy to Psalms 147:17–18; Isaiah 64:2–3; Amos 9:5, 13. Other verses of scripture describe the melting of the elements at the time of Christ's Second Coming.

[31] Philip Shabecoff, "Global Warming has Begun, Expert Tells Senate," *New York Times,* June 24, 1988.

[32] https://commons.wikimedia.org/wiki/File:Seraphim_of_Sarov.jpg

[33] Alexander Schmemann, *For the Life of the World: Sacraments and Orthodoxy*, 2nd ed. (Crestwood, NY: St. Vladimir's Seminary Press,

1973), 136.

[34] Archimandrite Job Getcha, *The Typikon Decoded: An Explanation of Byzantine Liturgical Practice*, trans. Paul Meyendorf (Yonkers, NY: St. Vladimir's Seminary Press, 2012), 23.

[35] Getcha, *The Typikon Decoded*, 47.

[36] "Introduction: Understanding Renewal Movements in Orthodox Christianity," Aleksandra Djurić Milovanović and Radmila Radić, *Orthodox Christian Renewal Movements in Eastern Europe* (London: Palgrave Macmillan, 2017), 12.

[37] Schmemann, *Life of the World*, 36.

[38] Isabel Florence Hapgood, *Service Book of the Holy Orthodox-Catholic Apostolic Church* (1906; repr., Englewood, NJ: Antiochian Orthodox Christian Archdiocese of North America, 1996), 22.

[39] I myself was a witness to this surge in "remembering" the Lord, having served as a Latter-day Saint branch president in Moscow (1992–93). Often our meetings were thronged by so many visitors that we had in attendance as many non-Latter-day Saint friends as Latter-day Saint members.

[40] See Eugene Smirnoff, *Russian Orthodox Missions* (London: Rivingtons, 1903), 1.

[41] John Mason Neale, trans., *Voices from the East. Documents on the Present State and Working of the Oriental Church,* (London: Joseph Masters, 1850), 4, accessed August 13, 2019, available on Google Books at https://play.google.com/books/reader?id=-MsAAAAAcAAJ&hl=en&pg=GBS.PP1.

[42] John Mason Neale, trans., *Voices from the East. Documents on the Present State and Working of the Oriental Church,* (London: Joseph Masters, 1859), 45 available at https://babel.hathitrust.org/cgi/pt?id=hvd.32044005285242&view=1up&seq=65, also at http://anglicanhistory.org/neale/voices1859/01.html. Note—The two sources cited here in this note and the prior note are different editions. I was unable to find both quotations in any one edition.

[43] A copy of Innocent's book is available on the internet in Russian at http://royallib.com/book/veniaminov_innokentiy/ukazanie_puti_v_tsapctvo_nebesnoe.html.

[44] "The Way Into the Kingdom of Heaven," Orthodox Christian Information Center, Patrick Barnes, accessed July 24, 2019, http://orthodoxinfo.com/general/kingdomofheaven.aspx. Compare the italicized wording to Mosiah 15:19.

[45] See Protoiereus Dmitriy Grigor'yev, *Ot drevnego Valaama do Novogo Sveta. Rysskaya Pravoslavnaya Missiya v Severnoy Amerike* (Moscow: Izdatel'stvo PSTGU, 2007) = От древнего Валаама до Нового Света. Русская Православная Миссия в Северной Америке (Moscow:

Издательство ПСТГУ, 2007), 6.

[46] https://commons.wikimedia.org/wiki/File:RR3318-0015R.png.

[47] The term *hagiography* refers to the writing of biographies of the saints.

[48] The account by Epiphanius is considered a masterpiece of Russian hagiographic literature. It is believed to have been composed shortly after the death of Stephen. See Epifaniy Premudryy, *Slovo o zhitin svyatogo Stefana, byvsego episkopom v Permi* = Слово о житии святого Стефана, бывшего епископом в Перми (composed ca. 1396–98). A condensed Russian version is available at http://azbyka.ru/otechnik/Epifanij_Premudryj/slovo-o-zhitii-svjatogo-stefana-byvshego-episkopom-v-permi/#sel=30:13,30:29;32:104,32:117;51:103,51:112. The Institute of Russian Literature also maintains a digital version online, along with extensive footnotes translating original Slavonic phrases into Russian and giving scriptural annotations; see http://lib.pushkinskijdom.ru/Default.aspx?tabid=10091#_edn221. I am unable to locate an English translation of this important hagiographic work.

[49] In the Orthodox tradition, the term "Theophany" refers to the baptism of Christ. All three personages of the Trinity or Godhead were manifested on this occasion. Besides Christ, the voice of the Father was heard and the Holy Ghost appeared in the form of a dove.

[50] Much of this sketch is drawn from P.E. Kazanskiy, П.Е.Казанский, *Istoriya pravoslvanogo russkago monashestva ot osnovaniya Pecherskoy obitel' Prepodobnym Antoniyem do osnovaniya Pavry sv. Troitsy Prepodobnym* (Moscow: V tipografii A. Semena, 1855) = История православного русскаго монашества от основания Печерской обитель Преподобным Антонием до основания Лавры св. Троицы Преподобным (Москва: В типографии А.Семена, 1855), 169–170, https://babel.hathitrust.org/cgi/pt?id=hvd.hw6ea2&view=1up&seq=173.

[51] http://icons.pstgu.ru/icon/fragment/791

[52] http://icons.pstgu.ru/icon/3474; State Museum "Rostov – Kremlin."

[53] See *History of the Church of Jesus Chrsit of Latter-day Saints,* B.H. Roberts, ed., vol. 1:176, see notes to chapter 15, n4, available online at https://byustudies.byu.edu/content/volume-1-chapter-15#fn-3.

[54] One source from the nineteenth century reports that John the Apostle is believed in the Greek Church to have been taken to heaven, like Enoch in the Old Testament. See Charles A. Goodrich, *Religious ceremonies and customs, or, The forms of worship practised by the several nations of the known world, from the earliest records to the present time* (Hartford, CT: Hutchison and Dwier, 1834), 182, available at https://babel.hathitrust.org/cgi/pt?id=mdp.39015010776956&view=1up&seq=200.

[55] See Wikipedia Commons, s.v. "Vita Icon," at

https://commons.wikimedia.org/wiki/Category:Vita_icon, the following
file: Icon Life of Saint Sergius of Radonesh 19c.jpg
[56] "Appearance of the Mother of God to St Sergius of Radonezh," s.v.
August 24, website of the Orthodox Church in America,
https://www.oca.org/saints/lives/1999/08/24/108974-appearance-of-the-
mother-of-god-to-st-sergius-of-radonezh.
[57] A. Vasiliev, "The Life of St. Peter of Argos and its Historical
Significance," in vol. 5 of *Traditio* (Cambridge: Cambridge University
Press, 1947), 173.
[58] Saint Symeon the New Theologian, *On the Mystical Life: The Ethical
Discourses,* vol. 2 of *On Virtue & Christian Life* (Crestwood, NY: St.
Vladimir's Seminary Press, 1996), p. 54 (Fifth Ethical Discourse).
[59] New International Version available at www.biblehub.com. See
http://biblehub.com/isaiah/52-6.htm.
[60] John Meyendorff, *St. Gregory Palamas and Orthodox Spirituality*
(Crestwood, NY: St. Vladimir's Seminary Press, 1974), 47.
[61]
https://commons.wikimedia.org/wiki/File:G%C3%A9r%C3%B4me,_Jea
n-L%C3%A9on_-_Moses_on_Mount_Sinai_Jean-
L%C3%A9on_G%C3%A9r%C3%B4me_-1895-1900.jpg; uploaded
March 29, 2015, by KenjiMizoguchi.
[62] See Metropolitan Hilarion (Alfeyev), *Doctrine and Teaching of the
Orthodox Church*, vol. 2 of *Orthodox Christianity*, trans. Andrew Smith
(Yonkers, NY: St. Vladimir's Seminary Press, 2012), 57. Orthodox
author Vladimir Lossky makes this point in his classic work, *The
Mystical Theology of the Eastern Church* (Crestwood, NY: St. Vladimir's
Seminary Press, 1976).
[63] James Beavan, *An Account of the Life and Times of St. Irenaeus,
Bishop of Lyon and Martyr* (London: Rivington, 1841).
[64] Beavan, *Life and Times*, 70–71.
[65] Helen Parish, "Lying Histories Fayning False Miracles: Magic,
Miracles And Mediaeval History," *Reformation & Renaissance Review* 4,
no. 2 (Dec. 2002), 230.
[66] Pavel Hejzlar, *John Calvin and the Cessation of Miraculous Healing,*
in *Communio viatorum: A theological journal* 47, n. 1, (2007,) 31–77.
[67] Hejzlar, *John Calvin*, 33.
[68] Philip M. Soergel, "From Legends To Lies: Protestant Attacks on
Catholic Miracles in Late Reformation Germany," *Fides et Historia* 21,
no. 2 (1989), 21.

Part III

Background on the Orthodox Calendar

Could Joseph Smith Have Studied Orthodoxy?

Orthodox Worship and Sacraments

6—Calendar Correlations: Could Joseph Have Had Access to an Orthodox Calendar?

The research presented in this book describes interesting connections or parallels between the Church of Jesus Christ of Latter-day Saints and that of Eastern Orthodoxy. Other chapters in this book describe *theosis,* or deification; Orthodox teachings regarding eternal marriage; Orthodox worship and sacraments; and the lives of individual saints.

The Orthodox annual liturgical (worship) calendar forms a separate and impressive repository of correlations to Latter-day Saint teaching and experience.[1] Included under this heading are just a few of the most interesting calendar correlations that have been identified in the course of the research for this book. See Part V of this book for a more detailed discussion of these parallels.

With one exception described below, the Orthodox calendar never changes, except that some feasts are moveable, meaning that they move annually in relation to Easter. The date of the Orthodox Easter changes every year and is calculated differently than in Western Christendom.

Older Orthodox feasts are never removed; however, new commemorations are added from time to time for new saints. The feasts on this unchanging Orthodox worship calendar accumulated over the course of many centuries, with feasts and commemorations (usually simply call "feasts") going back to the earliest centuries of Christianity. Easter and the Pentecost are the earliest feasts that can be documented. In fact, adherence to this unchanging calendar is one of the chief differences between Orthodoxy and Catholicism.

The one exception to the unchangeable nature of the Orthodox calendar is that it exists in two versions: one called the *Julian,* the other called the *Revised Julian.* These different versions are described in Part V; however, for our purposes here, readers should keep in mind that the two calendars have the exact same feasts, but they are thirteen days apart. This situation came about in 1923, following a calendar reform.

Life for a Greek Christian in Byzantium or an Italian Catholic in the Middle Ages was not one where religion was relegated to Sunday only. Religion permeated daily life in the form of calendar observances (feasts, fasts, and commemorations of events in religious history and the lives of martyrs and saints), dietary or fasting guidance that varied depending on the calendar day, and myriad other traditions, guidance, or prohibitions (reportedly, even the pope once had to weigh in as to whether drinking hot chocolate constituted a break in fasting). Whether modern readers can appreciate such a lifestyle or not is not the question here. The fact is that the worship calendar, in particular, has had a very great role in the daily life of the Christian for most of the centuries since the death of the original Apostles.

Even today, devout Orthodox (and Catholic) believers will usually know on which saint's feast day they were born (this is called the "Name Day"). Some believers celebrate the Name Day like a birthday, with friends and festivities. The particular saint for that day may be considered to have a special connection to the believer, who on occasion might seek the saint's intercession in times of need. The same would hold true in Roman Catholicism.

The importance of the liturgical calendar in shaping how devout believers conceive of time can be seen in the forewords to books by leading Orthodox authors. These authors will often date their books by referring to the particular feast day on which it was completed, instead of using an ordinary calendar date.

As an illustration, Orthodox scholar Andrew Louth (cited in Chapter 7) dates his foreword simply: "Feast of the Apostle Philip." This approach is common, though nowadays both the feast and modern calendar date will usually be given. These type of date references suggest that for the Orthodox faithful even today, time is still sometimes conceived of not as a neutral series of calendar days and months that carry no particular meaning (except to mark the seasons and secular holidays), but rather as it is related to Christian history, by reference to the particular feast, commemoration, or saint of the day.

The calendar not only gives sacred meaning to each day of the year; the Orthodox calendar is linked to Orthodox doctrines. Some hymns that are sung as part of the various services constituting daily Orthodox worship are specifically tied to the feast or event being commemorated on the particular day. The hymns contain doctrine, so that believers who attend services will hear doctrines linked to the day's feast or commemoration.

Herein lies the intriguing aspect of correlations between Orthodox calendar feasts and revelations in the Latter-day Saint Doctrine and Covenants (almost all of which have precise calendar dates). Both are repositories of doctrine for their respective faiths. Both have also long served as an important vehicle for teaching doctrine to that church's faithful.

For devout believers of these traditions—and particularly for the Orthodox faithful— the worship calendar has become something so familiar and important that it is not difficult (at least for this author) to imagine that God, if he had a message for these believers, might tie it to calendar dates. With this idea in mind, this chapter includes a summary of some of the most important correlations. The rest (many more) are described in Part V.

Readers may have different reactions to the calendar research presented below and in Part V. Some will dismiss the correlations as essentially coincidental. Others may not only judge them "coincidental," but will additionally see the author's efforts to track and analyze these as *parallelomania,* or a misguided attempt to see links between events that have no historical connection whatsoever. Still other readers may (hopefully) agree with the author that the number and importance of these connections is very impressive and may indicate a providential (divine) origin.

If readers question why God would try to talk to different Christian traditions through calendar dates or the dates of revelations, one need only read some of Jesus's sermons and parables to see how he teaches. The Savior frequently used imagery that was familiar to his listeners, such as stories of sheep and shepherds, fish and fishermen, money and taxation, grapevines and vineyards, wine in bottles, and occurrences in nature, such as foxes and their holes and sparrows that fall from the sky. In short, he spoke in ways likely to be understood (see 2 Nephi 31:3).

Orthodox believers understand and love their calendar. Latter-day Saints read, study and learn from the Doctrine and Covenants.

Correlations between the two, thus, have the effect of bringing the two faiths into dialogue.

In presenting these correlations, this book's purpose is not to prove any point vis-à-vis Orthodoxy or prove the truth of Latter-day Saint doctrines, scriptures, or practices; In a sense, these correlations provide windows through which Latter-day Saint and Orthodox believers (or readers from any other Christian tradition) may view with an eye of faith events, doctrines, and commemorations that may have aspects in common or providential elements.

Included here is a summary of a few of the most significant correlations. Reference abbreviations are given to distinguish the various versions of the calendar represented by a given date; these are explained in Part V.

Annunciation of Mary and the Founding of The Church of Jesus Christ of Latter-day Saints (April 6, 1830) (**Exact Match**)

In the Orthodox faith, as in Roman Catholicism, Mary holds an especially sacred role. In Orthodoxy, Mary is known as the *Theotokos,* or Mother of God (*Bogoroditsa,* or Богородица in Russian). Her veneration forms an important part of Orthodox services, though overall, Orthodox services are infused with worship of Christ and of the Holy Trinity.

Figure 6.1: Icon of the Annunciation of the Blessed Virgin Mary
Fourteenth Century
National Museum of Serbia
Credit: Wikimedia Commons, public domain.[2]

The Orthodox calendar has twelve "great feasts" (commemorations) in the year, four of which relate to Mary and eight of which pertain to Christ. One of the four is for the Annunciation. This feast commemorates the appearance of the angel Gabriel to Mary when he announced the wonderful news that she would be the mother of the Son of the Highest (Luke 1:32).

In 1830, this feast fell on April 6 on the calendar used at the time in the United States (i.e., the Gregorian calendar). In addition to being the feast of the Annunciation, this particular date was the very day on which Joseph Smith first organized the church that was later to become known as the Church of Jesus Christ of Latter-day Saints. Section 21 of the Doctrine and Covenants was also received by Joseph Smith on this day. In this important revelation, the Lord referred to Joseph as "a seer, a translator, a prophet, an apostle of Jesus Christ" (21:1). The Lord instructed Latter-day Saints to "give heed unto all his words and commandments" (21:4).

Section 20 is believed to have been received or recorded in full about this time (a few portions may have been recorded earlier in 1829). It gives a brief doctrinal overview of the basic beliefs of the newly restored Church of Jesus Christ, establishes the basic conditions for baptism and the wording for the sacramental prayers (for the Lord's Supper), sets the duties of elders, priests, teachers, and deacons, and establishes basic regulations governing Church membership.

In discussing Orthodox feasts that are dedicated to Mary, this book is not proposing any change for how Latter-day Saints understand Mary's role in God's purposes. Latter-day Saints do not venerate

Mary, or other saints, for that matter. Prayers are only directed to God the Father, in the name of his Son, Jesus Christ; however, Mary is, and should be, held in great esteem among Latter-day Saints. Mary's future name and calling as the Savior's earthly mother were known to Book of Mormon prophets hundreds of years before Christ's birth (Mosiah 3:8; Alma 7:7).

Nephi recorded an important vision of Mary and the Christ child (see 1 Nephi 11 in the Book of Mormon). In fact, Nephi's first heavenly instructions from the angel regarding the future the Son of God *begin* with Mary and the Nativity. He sees Christ in Mary's arms as a babe.

Nephi also saw an important fact regarding Mary that is not reported in New Testament narratives—that she was carried away to heaven for a time prior to Christ's birth (1 Nephi 11:19–20).

On the topic of Mary, some readers may wonder if there is a divine role for her that hasn't been revealed yet in Latter-day Saint revelation; after all, the ninth article of faith points to future revelations of "great and important things." This book takes no position on this point. Much of the focus of this book is instead to encourage openness and the mutual sharing of readers' respective beliefs and faith. This kind of sharing presupposes that believers will not be dismissive of the theology, forms of worship, miracles, or visions held sacred by the faithful of another religious tradition.

It is also worth noting that Joseph Smith never spoke for, or against, Mary's veneration in the Roman Catholic faith and never commented on miracles attributed to her intervention. His journals mention occasional meetings with Roman Catholics (never in a negative light), yet Joseph seems to have kept a reverent silence on the topic. A few additional thoughts about Mary are presented in Chapter 14 of this book.

Diverse Angels (Doctrine and Covenants 128) and Angel Michael at Colossae (6 September) (Revised Julian)

In Doctrine and Covenants 128, Joseph Smith gives important instructions regarding baptism for the dead (mentioned also in 1 Corinthians 15:29). He also exultantly describes the visits of several angels, including Michael, Gabriel, and Raphael (D&C 128:20–21).

As it turns out, Joseph's instructions in Doctrine and Covenants 128 were recorded on the date of an Orthodox feast commemorating the angel Michael's intervention to prevent the destruction of a miraculous well of water said to have been opened in ancient times by John the Apostle. This same commemoration is also intended to honor the four great archangels: Michael, Gabriel, Raphael, and Uriel.

Joseph's inspired instructions naming three of these four angels were recorded on the date of their commemoration.

Temple Correlations and the Feast of the Prophet Elijah (July 20, August 1 and 2) (all types of calendar dates)

Figure 6.2: Icon of the Prophet Elijah in the Wilderness
Fourteenth Century
Tretyakov Gallery, Moscow
Credit: Photo by the Author

A striking set of correlations is seen in topics pertaining to the temple. Every section of the Doctrine and Covenants that refers to a specific Latter-day Saint temple, temple site, or temple ordinances contains an appropriate link to the Orthodox calendar.

As an illustration of this point, the following revelations pertaining to temples were received on the Orthodox feast of Elijah: Doctrine and Covenants 57:3; 58:57; 97:15–19. Sections 57 and 58 are the first specific mentions in the Doctrine and Covenants of future temples. To this list one can add Doctrine and Covenants 94:3–9, which pertained to a "house for the work of the presidency" that was never built; however, the promises given for his house (which was to be built next door to the Kirtland Temple) are similar to those for the temples. The dates of these revelations are, respectively, 20 July, 1 August, and 2 August.

In the restored Church of Jesus Christ, the prophet Elijah holds a special connection to ordinances that are performed in temples. Among these are baptisms for the dead, "endowment" ceremonies, and marriages. Elijah appeared to Joseph Smith and Oliver Cowdery during a Sabbath meeting on 3 April 1836 (see Doctrine and Covenants 110:1–10), just prior to the dedicatory sessions of the Kirtland Temple in 1836, and conferred sacred priesthood "sealing" keys by which these temple ordinances are performed.

Each of the sections cited above was revealed on the feast of the prophet Elijah (Sections 57, 58, 94, and 97). Readers may wonder how the feast of Elijah can fall on three separate days. While there is only *one* feast of Elijah on the Orthodox calendar, it can fall on different days, depending on the version of the calendar in question (the so-called "new" calendar, also known as the Revised Julian; the "old" or "Julian" calendar of the nineteenth century; and the Catholic calendar kept by the Carmelite Order). More information about the various versions of the calendar is provided in Part V.

The Nature of the Godhead (April 2, 1843) (**Exact Match**)

An extremely important correlation and point of contrast between the doctrines of the restored Church of Jesus Christ and Orthodoxy is seen in the feast date of Saint John the Ladder (who is also called "Saint John Climacus")[3] (AD 525–606) and the day on which Joseph Smith recorded Doctrine and Covenants 130. Joseph recorded this section on 2 April 1843, which correlated exactly to the exact day when the Orthodox world was commemorating the feast of Saint John the Ladder.

In Section 130, Joseph gave the world this succinct description of the nature of God the Father, his Son Jesus Christ, and the Holy Ghost:

> The Father has a body of flesh and bones as tangible as man's; the Son also; but the Holy Ghost has not a body of flesh and bones, but is a personage of Spirit. Were it not so, the Holy Ghost could not dwell in us [D&C 130:22].

The importance of the correlation between Saint John the Ladder and Doctrine and Covenants 130:22 is seen in a book that John wrote, entitled *The Divine Ladder of Ascent.* This work describes thirty "steps" along the path towards greater spirituality, one step for each year of the Lord's life (in Orthodoxy, it is believed that the Savior lived thirty years). John's book is one of the most influential works in the history of the Eastern Orthodox tradition. He intended his book particularly for monks, and it has been studied for centuries in monasteries. Portions of *The Divine Ladder of Ascent* are also read in Orthodox churches every year during Great Lent. Copies are widely available on the internet in many languages. This work is said to have been the first book printed in the New World (1532 in Mexico).[4]

What is remarkable for our purposes is that under step 27 ("Stillness"), John describes a conversation with an angel. During his interview with the angel, John reports having asked several questions. It is clear from his account that John was inquiring into the nature of the Holy Trinity:

> A light came to me as I was thirsting and I asked what the Lord was before He took visible form. The angel could not tell me because he was not permitted to do so. So I asked him: "In what state is He now?" and the answer was that He was in the state appropriate to Him, though not us. "What is the nature of the standing or sitting at the right hand of the Father?"[5] I asked. "Such mysteries cannot be taken in by the human ear," he replied. Then I pleaded with him right then to bring me where my heart was longing to go, but he said that the time was not yet ripe, since the fire of incorruption was not yet mighty enough within me. And whether during all this, I was in the body or out of it, I cannot rightly say.[6]

From the angel's words, one can surmise that there were truths regarding the nature of God that the angel was not permitted to tell, and which John the Ladder and mankind were not able to understand. For Latter-day Saints, important truths regarding the nature of the Godhead were revealed to Joseph Smith and learned by his own direct experience of God as described in Doctrine and Covenants 130:22.

John the Ladder's account of speaking with an angel underscores the depth of his spirituality and Christian insight. He deserves recognition from all Christians for recording this encounter, which is a dramatic illustration that angels *continued* to appear to and instruct people throughout the many centuries since the deaths of the Apostles. As Moroni wrote in the Book of Mormon, "Have angels ceased to appear to men"? He answers his own question: "Nay! Nor have miracles ceased" (Moroni 7:29–31).

Joseph Smith, Saint Alexander of Svir, and the feast of the Prophet Amos (June 27, 1844) (**Exact Match**)

The final calendar correlation that I will describe here connects Joseph Smith with Saint Alexander of Svir (1448–1533), a famed Russian Orthodox saint. Joseph was martyred on 27 June 1844, which correlates exactly to the day on the Gregorian calendar (used in the United States today and during Joseph Smith's lifetime) when the Orthodox world was observing the feast of the prophet Amos. Alexander was *born* on the feast day of Amos; in fact, his parents named him Amos in recognition of this fact. He was only named Alexander after he accepted tonsure as a monk.

One verse in the Book of Amos has been cited repeatedly by Latter-day Saint leaders to establish the proposition that the Church must be guided by a prophet. Amos 3:7 states:

> Surely the Lord God will do nothing, but he revealeth his secret unto his servants the prophets.

This verse in the Book of Amos figured so prominently in Joseph's thinking that he quoted it in the opening sentence of his article on the Church, published in a book entitled *He Pasa Ekklesia: An Original History of the Religious Denominations of the United*

*States.*⁷ This book was published shortly before Joseph's death there was no official presence of the Orthodox Church in the United States at that time); however, a lengthy chapter is devoted to Catholicism.

Figure 6.3: Appearance of the Holy Trinity to St. Alexander of Svir
Holy Trinity St. Alexander of Svir Monastery, detail of the archway above the entrance to Trinity Cloister
Credit: photo by the author

The connection between Joseph Smith and Alexander of Svir goes much deeper than their shared tie to the prophet Amos. Alexander is best known in the Russian Orthodox Church for a remarkable vision he experienced in 1508, of the Holy Trinity, making him the only Russian Orthodox saint to have had such an experience. While praying one night in his hermitage (i.e., his cabin), a great light appeared, and Svir saw three heavenly beings who neared him, each wearing "most bright garments and clothed in white, beautiful in purity, shining more than the sun and illuminated with unutterable heavenly glory, and each holding a staff in his hand."⁸

The Russian Orthodox Church understands this vision as having been an appearance of all three persons of the Holy Trinity, or of angels representing the Trinity. The words "one in essence" show that these three glorious persons were understood as ultimately being a manifestation of God in a way consistent with the Nicene Creed. The Orthodox Church also sees this experience as being similar to what Abraham experienced, as described in Genesis

18:1–2: he saw the Lord, then three men or angels. In the Orthodox understanding, this experience was a vision of the entire Godhead or Holy Trinity.

The preceding page shows an artistic rendering of this event painted above the archway leading into the Trinity Cloister of Svir's monastery. One detail that may interest readers is that while works of art and icons depicting this event show the members of the Holy Trinity as having wings, Svir's account does not mention this point; however, later in his vision, Svir did describe the Lord (i.e., Christ) has having wings.

Alexander's vision invites comparison to the First Vision of Joseph Smith, in which Joseph saw the Father and Son as separate personages. While the two men saw things that were similar, they *understood* their visions differently. Alexander understood his experience in light of the Nicene Creed and the Christian tradition that the Father, Son, and Holy Spirit were "one in essence." Joseph's understanding was based both on what he saw (as was Alexander's) and *also* on a revealed concept of God's nature, which he later succinctly expressed in Doctrine and Covenants 130:22. While the Orthodox and Latter-day Saint conceptions of God are different in important respects, the experiences of these two inspired men are extraordinary. Both serve to reinforce faith and belief in the Father, Son, and Holy Ghost.

A quotation from Joseph Smith is worth citing here, seemingly lending credibility to what Alexander saw:

> "Any person that had seen the heavens opened knows that there are three personages in the heavens who hold the keys of power, and one presides over all."[9]

The correlations described above are among approximately thirty of their kind, described in Part V and in Table 1, in detail.

These and other correlations are so numerous and doctrinally significant that they may prompt some readers to inquire if Joseph Smith may have had access to an Eastern Orthodox calendar. Judging from histories published by Orthodox sources, this does not seem likely. There were no Orthodox churches in the United States during Joseph Smith's lifetime, nor were there significant numbers of Orthodox believers in the United States. The influx of immigration from Orthodox lands did not commence until the 1860s and later.[10]   There was very little literature in English on Orthodoxy that was available during Joseph's lifetime, and none of the available literature contained Orthodox calendars.

Given the potential importance of this question—what exposure Joseph might have had to Orthodoxy—the discussion below is provided as background information for readers.

What exposure could Joseph Smith have had to Eastern Orthodoxy?

An obvious question arises: if Joseph Smith dictated revelations that show similarity to Orthodox concepts such as theosis, what influences might have contributed to his understanding of these topics?   Were books on Orthodoxy in circulation in English in Joseph's day? If so, did they treat theosis? Did they describe the prophetic ministry or miracles of Orthodox monks and holy men (which may be referenced in D&C 133:26; 113:10 [interpreting Isaiah 52:6]; and 49:8)? Did Joseph have access to an Orthodox calendar?

Another question of interest is whether Joseph had access to a Roman Catholic calendar.   This latter question takes on considerable importance in light of the range of dates during which Doctrine and Covenants 88 was received: 27 December 1832 to 3 January 1833.   This is the precise range of dates, or "octave," during which the feast of Saint John (the Apostle) could be commemorated during the nineteenth century (under the so-called "Traditional" or "Tridentine" calendar, which was adopted in the Catholic Church in the late sixteenth century).   As I describe in Part V, Saint John has a special connection to theosis as well as to some of the doctrines described in Doctrine and Covenants 88 and 93, including those related to divine light and seeing God (John 1 and 14).   Both of these doctrines are part of the Orthodox doctrine of theosis.

The short answer to the questions above is that Joseph likely had little or no access to materials on Orthodoxy. A few books on Orthodoxy were available in English; however, there is no evidence that Joseph ever read or discussed these books. Other books written more as travelogues recounting visits to Russia give descriptions of Orthodox rites and services, even describing few commemorations, such as the Great Blessing of the Waters (see below); however, none of these books contained an Orthodox calendar. None discussed deification, or *theosis,* or Saint Gregory Palamas (his writings were revived through the *Philokalia* ca. 1800, available in Greek or Church Slavonic). On the other hand, Joseph conceivably could have seen a Roman Catholic calendar. The Catholic (and Orthodox) calendar turns out to have a close connection to sections of the Doctrine and Covenants that show parallels to Orthodox teachings on theosis. Sections 88 and 93 are clear illustrations of this.

Still, in view of the possibility (however remote) that early works on Orthodoxy might have influenced Joseph, whether directly or indirectly, it is worth briefly considering their content. Some examples are presented below.

Even if these books do not contain calendars, they conceivably could have prompted Joseph to send missionaries to Russia. Joseph called Elder George J. Adams on a mission to Russia in 1843; however, for whatever the reason, Adams never actually fulfilled this mission.

In connection with this particular mission call, Joseph made this statement, explaining that the purpose of Adams's call was "to introduce the fullness of the Gospel to the people of that vast empire." Joseph also explained that to this mission was "attached some of the most important things concerning the advancement and building up of the kingdom of God in the last days, which cannot be explained at this time."[11]

- *Orthodox Catechism* by Peter Mogila (Mohyla) (originally published 1640, published in English 1762)

Philip Ludwell[12] is the translator of this important work. He was an English convert to Orthodoxy who lived much of his life in colonial Virginia. While *Orthodox Catechism* was an English translation of an interesting and influential catechism, it was written and translated in an era when Orthodox theology was under a strong Western (i.e., Catholic) influence. It does not show the more distinctive elements of Orthodoxy, like theosis and the

140

Uncreated light, which only began to be revived in monastic circles in the late 1700s and early 1800s.

- *The Rites and Ceremonies of the Greek Church* (1772)

Ten years later, in 1772, John Glen King published a book in English on the doctrine and worship of the Orthodox Church.[13] King openly declares in the first two pages of his book that the "Oriental or Greek church is incontestably the most ancient of all [C]hristian churches," that "all the fathers of the four first ages down to Jerom[e] were of Greece, Syria, and Africa," and that the rites of the Roman Catholic Church "testify even by their names that their origin was Greek."[14]

King does a competent job describing the main offices (worship services) and sacraments (ordinances) of Orthodoxy. This is where his work is most important. At this early date, no other book appears to have been available in English giving the details of Orthodox worship services, liturgies and sacraments. King makes a few interesting comments about the Greek (Orthodox) calendar that conceivably could have generated a general interest from Joseph in Orthodox or Catholic calendars; however, King does not include a calendar in his book:

> [The Orthodox] pay a secondary adoration [after Christ] to the Virgin Mary, to the twelve apostles, and to a vast number of saints, with which the Greek kalendar [*sic*] abounds.[15]

Given some obvious similarities between a few aspects of Orthodox sacraments, vestments, and worship to certain elements of Latter-day Saint temple worship, historians may want to dig further into whether this book could have been known to Joseph Smith (see Chapter 8 for a discussion of Orthodox sacraments). If so, then this may be an additional reason why the search for historical antecedents to the Latter-day Saint temple experience must look beyond freemasonry, perhaps to Orthodoxy (or Catholicism) and certainly to early Christianity and to the Jewish temple. Of course, the restored Church of Jesus Christ believes that the temple ordinances were *revealed* to Joseph Smith in their purity, thus restoring their ancient antecedents in the temples of ancient Israel (i.e., the Tabernacle of the Congregation and Solomon's Temple).[16]

141

- *The religious world displayed; or, a view of the four grand systems of religion* (1823)[17]

The author provides a short overview of Russian Orthodox theology and practice.[18] The date of the Epiphany (Theophany) or baptism of Christ is given, 6 January, as also an explanation that it is paired with the "Greater Sanctification" of the waters (Great Blessing of the Waters commemoration). This forms an important temple correlation, matching Doctrine and Covenants 124, which contains the first mention of baptism for the dead. See also below under *Domestic Scenes in Russia: In a Series of Letters* (1839).

A note underscores the religious tolerance that prevailed in Russia:

> The Russians, of all ranks, are in general free from that persecuting rancour against other religious persuasions, which has been so characteristic of the Roman Catholics; and though they adhere strictly to the doctrines and ceremonies of their own church, yet neither the laity nor the clergy believe that there is no salvation without her pale.[19]

- *The Travels of Macarius the Patriarch of Antioch* (1836)[20]

This book gives much interesting detail regarding the worship services in Russian Orthodox churches, extolling the religious devotion of both rich and poor, noble and peasant in Muscovy (Russia). Although not giving a calendar, it describes sacred boxes in the shape of books that are kept in the more important cathedrals. These boxes were called "calendars," because inside them are icons of the saints and events commemorated on each day of the year.[21]

- *Stephens's Travels in Russia* (1839)[22]

J. L. Stephens published an account of his travels in Russia and other lands in 1839. This account contains interesting material that might have caught the attention of Joseph or other Church leaders and conceivably might have directly prompted the call of Elder George J. Adams to serve a mission in Russia; however, Stephens does not provide an Orthodox calendar.

Stephens is the author whose book on travels in Central America attracted a high degree of interest in Nauvoo in 1841.[23] Excerpts of his book were published in the *Times and Seasons.*

Stephens observed a high degree of religious toleration in Russia:

> For a people so devout as the Russians, the utmost toleration prevails throughout the whole empire, and particularly in St. Petersburgh. Churches of every denomination stand but a short distance apart on the Newski Perspective [Nevskiy Prospekt]. The Russian cathedral is nearly opposite the great Catholic chapel; near them is the Armenian, then the Lutheran, two churches for Dissenters and a mosque for the Mohammedans! and on Sunday thousands are seen bending their steps to their separate churches, to worship according to the faith handed down to them by their fathers.[24]

Stephens also provides a brief sketch of how Christianity was brought to ancient Russia in "Chioff" (modern Kyiv or Kiev) in the tenth century, as well as some short comments on the Orthodox faith. He also provides this interesting account regarding pilgrims and the famous caves in Kiev that hold the bodies of scores of Orthodox saints:

> We wandered a long time in this extraordinary burial-place, everywhere strewed with the kneeling figures of praying pilgrims. At every turn we saw hundreds from the farthest parts of the immense empire of Russia; perhaps at that time more than three thousand were wandering in these sepulchral chambers.
>
> The last scene I shall never forget. More than a hundred were assembled in a little chapel, around which were arranged the bodies of men who had died in peculiar sanctity. All were kneeling on the rocky floor, an old priest, with a long white beard streaming down his breast, was in the midst of them, and all there, even to the little children, were listening with rapt attention, as if he were preaching to them matters of eternal moment. There was no hypocrisy or want of faith in that vast sepulcher; surrounded by their sainted dead, they were searching their

way to everlasting life, and in all honesty believed that they saw the way before them.[25]

According to Stephens, "Kiev" (Kyiv) is a name that is derived from a Sarmatian word, *Kiovi* or *Kii*, which means "mountains" or "hills." Upon first seeing Kiev from afar, he was struck by the beauty of the place:

> We . . . saw at a great distance the venerable city of Chioff [Kyiv or Kiev], the ancient capital of Russia. It stands at a great height, on the crest of an amphitheatre of hills, which rise abruptly in the middle of an immense plain, apparently thrown up by some wild freak of nature, at once curious, unique, and beautiful. . . . For many centuries it has been regarded as the Jerusalem of the North, the sacred and holy city of the Russians; and, long before reaching it, its numerous convents and churches, crowning the summit and hanging on the sides of the hill, with their quadrupled domes, and spires, and chains, and crosses, gilded with ducat gold and glittering in the sun, gave the whole city the appearance of golden splendor.[26]

Later, in leaving the city, Stephens describes the view and his feelings in these words:

> On the opposite bank I turned for the last time to the sacred city, and I never saw any thing [*sic*] more unique and strikingly beautiful than the high, commanding position of "this city on a hill," crowned with its golden cupolas and domes, that reflected the sun with dazzling brightness.[27]

- *Domestic Scenes in Russia: In a Series of Letters* (1839)[28]

The author was a member of the clergy, whose wife had family in Russia. He spent a year in the interior of Russia, observing and carefully noting aspects of daily life and Russian customs and beliefs. He notes the twelve-day difference between the Western (Gregorian) calendar and the older calendar used in Russia.[29] The Great Blessing of the Waters is described, a commemoration that is paired with the Theophany, or baptism of Christ. The twelve-day different in dates is again mentioned.[30] Unfortunately, the author failed to note this twin observance (the Theophany forms an important calendar correlation to Section 124 of the Doctrine and Covenants). A visit to a monastery is described, as the story of its founding—involving inspired dreams—and of a miraculous icon that appeared centuries ago in the midst of a burning bush.[31] Marriage ceremonies and the calendar rules for marriages are described.[32] A chapter is devoted to the story of a devout woman whom meticulously kept the various fasts and miraculous healings her family experienced.[33] Religious tolerance is described.[34]

- *The Church of Russia* (1842)[35]

Another early work that conceivably might have been read by Joseph Smith or other early Latter-day Saint leaders is a translation by R.W. Blackmore of a history by A.N. Mouravieff of the "Church of Russia" that was published in 1842. Mouravieff makes some interesting remarks regarding the Orthodox calendar; however, like King, he does not provide an actual calendar in his work. He notes that the Gregorian calendar was prohibited and that the Russian Orthodox Church uses the Julian calendar.[36] As did the author of *The Travels of Macarius,* he describes a special, ornate box that was present in the churches, holding inside of it the icons of many of the saints who are commemorated in daily services throughout the year.[37] Mouravieff mentions that the feelings of the people would not likely not tolerate a switch from the Julian to Gregorian calendars.[38] As interesting as Mouravieff's comments are, they came far too late to have influenced Joseph's earlier revelations that show parallels to the Orthodox calendar.

Just how rare Blackmore's skills were in translating this work was the topic of a later review of one of his books. The reviewer stated:

> It is mortifying to remember that, with so vast and so interesting a material for study as the Church annals of the Slavonic peoples, there are not, perhaps, six men in England who have the requisite acquaintance with their languages on the one hand, and with theology on the other, to labour in that inviting field. Indeed, previously to Mr. Blackmore's translation of Mouravieff's "Russian Church History" the fortunes of the largest national communion under the sun [i.e., the Russian Orthodox Church] were all but absolutely unknown in England.[39]

- *Other works*

Other works on Orthodoxy were published *after* Joseph's lifetime, but early enough that they conceivably might have formed a context for some statements by early Latter-day Saint Apostles quoted in this book. For example, Heber C. Kimball, an early member of the Quorum of the Twelve who served in the Church's First Presidency, made a statement about the prophets among the Lost Tribes in 1860.

Kimball seems to speak in the present tense in this statement:

> So it is with the lost tribes of Israel; they are not asleep. God speaks to them through their Prophets, and they are learning to be obedient and to be subject to the law of God.[40]

In Chapter 10, stories are recorded regarding the Elders of Optina that may fulfil President Kimball's prophecy. In light of his statement, a book published in London by nineteenth century scholar J. M. Neale is worth mentioning, (1859), *Voices from the East.*[41] Translator and editor J. M. Neale includes a range of materials describing some of the early saints and miracle workers of Orthodoxy, materials describing the beliefs and teachings and then-current information on the wide-ranging missions to natives and peoples across Eurasia, the Far East, and Alaska by Orthodox missionaries. Like Blackmore, Neale was praised by reviewers of his work for his work on "untrodden ground for the historian."

Of Neale, *The Morning Post* (London) wrote in 1850:

> Mr. Neale has brought to bear upon what is almost untrodden ground for the historian. For the Eastern Church (so much has this side of Europe been occupied with the questions at issue between Rome and her Protestant dissidents) has almost been overlooked as an integral part of Christianity. Her claims to veneration on the score of antiquity have been forgotten or disregarded; the purity of her doctrine has been unceremoniously and ignorantly impugned; and the pious grandeur of her Liturgies scorned as a strange worship. And yet Mr. Neale may say with no less truth than eloquence: I shall write "of prelates not less faithful, of martyrs not less constant, of confessors not less generous, than those of Europe; shall

146

show every article of the creed guarded with as much scrupulous jealousy; shall adduce a fresh crowd of witnesses to the faith once for all delivered to the saints, in the glow and splendour of Byzantine glory, in the tempests of the Oriental middle ages, in the desolation and tyranny of the Turkish empire, the testimony of the same immutable Church remains unchanged. Extending herself from the sea of Okhotsk to the palaces of Venice, from the ice-fields that grind against the Solevetsky monastery to the burning jungles of Malabar, embracing a thousand languages, and nations, and tongues, but binding them together in the golden link of the same faith, offering the tremendous sacrifice in a hundred liturgies, but offering it to the same God, and with the same rites; fixing her patriarchal thrones in the same cities as when the disciples were called Christians first at Antioch, and James, the brother of the Lord, finished his course at Jerusalem.[42]

Could Neale's books or those by other authors regarding Russian Orthodoxy have inspired statements on the "prophets" of the north countries made by Heber C. Kimball, Orson Pratt, or others?

- *Later liturgical books*

As early examples of Orthodox service books (books containing the transcriptions of actual liturgies and rites), an Anglican priest, Richard Frederic Littledale, published a translation of Eastern Orthodox service books in 1863, with both Greek and English text. His book is widely available today (including in reprint) in university libraries and even through online booksellers.[43] A more comprehensive work written by Florence Isabel Hapgood was not published until 1906[44] but is still sold in Orthodox bookstores and widely used.

The foregoing is a summary of some of the literature that touches on Russian Orthodoxy, or Orthodoxy in general, that might have been available to Joseph Smith and other early Latter-day Saint leaders. As is evident, there is no reason to believe that Joseph had access to an Eastern Orthodox calendar.

A letter written by Saint Innocent of Moscow (then metropolitan of Moscow) in 1867 seems to confirm that Russian Orthodox missionaries had not yet preached in the United States, underscoring the fact that any exposure of early Latter-day Saints to Orthodoxy was very, very limited. Innocent wrote this letter after hearing news that Alaska had been sold to the United States:

> Rumors from Moscow have reached me, to the effect that I wrote someone that I am not happy with the sale of our American colonies to the Americans; this is completely untrue; to the contrary, I see in this circumstance one of the ways of Providence, by which our Orthodoxy may penetrate the United States, where at the present time we have begun to focus serious attention.[45]

In any case, if Joseph or other early Latter-day Saint leaders were exposed to Orthodoxy or had an Orthodox calendar, the knowledge of this has escaped the Church history staff in Latter-day Saint headquarters.[46]

Even if evidence were to be discovered showing that Joseph had an Orthodox calendar, this still would not account for dates like Joseph's death. Even this date, which was totally outside Joseph's control, has a significant connection to the Orthodox calendar; as described above, Joseph died on the feast date of the Old Testament prophet Amos, a feast shared in common with Saint Alexander of Svir, who was *born* on this feast day. One would also have to account for the connections between dates in the Doctrine and Covenants and events that were only just unfolding in Russia—those related to Saint Seraphim of Sarov (1754–1833), for example. No biographical materials regarding Seraphim were even published in English until at least 1933, with biographies becoming widely available starting in the 1970s. Seraphim was only canonized in 1903, so his feast was only added to the Russian Orthodox calendar after that date.

If it turns out that somehow Joseph *knowingly* linked some of his revelations to dates on the Orthodox calendar, this will still be an important and surprising discovery. Joseph Smith's life is one of the best documented and most studied of any historical figure of nineteenth-century America. Stacks of biographical materials have been written about his life. If there were historical documents linking Joseph's revelations Eastern Orthodoxy, these should have come to light before now.

[1] For a discussion of time and feast days, see Alexander Schmemann, *Introduction to Liturgical Theology,* trans. Ashleigh E. Moorehouse (Crestwood, NY: St Vladimirs Seminary Press, 1966), 180.

[2] https://commons.wikimedia.org/wiki/File:Annunciation_Icon_Serbia_14th_c.jpg; uploaded May 31, 2012, by Dmitry Ivanov.

[3] John is considered a Saint in both the Roman Catholic and Eastern Orthodox traditions. He is also known as "John Lestvichnik," "John Scholasticus," or "John Sinaites." See his profile on the website of the Orthodox Church in America, under 30 March, https://oca.org/saints/lives/2001/03/30/100943-venerable-john-climacus-of-sinai-author-of-the-ladder. The entry gives short biographical information and confirms on the last line that his moveable feast is the fourth Sunday of Great Lent. The most recent publication in English of this book is Archimandrite Lazarus Moore, trans., *The Ladder of divine Ascent*, 4th rev. ed. (repr., Brookline, MA: The Holy Transfiguration Monastery, 2012), based on the 1959 translation by Lazarus Moore.

[4] See Raoul Smith, *The Ladder of divine Ascent—A Codex and an Icon* (Clinton, MA: Museum of Russian Icons, 2013), p. 5, n30, https://www.museumofrussianicons.org/wp-content/uploads/2016/09/LadderOfDivineAscentFINAL2013Opt.pdf, and John D. Green*, A Strange Tongue: Tradition, Language and the Appropriation of Mystical Experience in late fourteenth-century England and sixteenth-century Spain*, in *Studies in Spirituality*, Supplement 9 (Leuven: Peters, 2002), p. 50, n36.

[5] This question brings to mind the wording of the Nicene Creed, which refers to Christ having "ascended into heaven, and [sitting] at the right hand of the Father." See OrthodoxWiki, s.v. "Nicene-Constantinopolitan Creed," accessed July 25, 2019, https://orthodoxwiki.org/Nicene-Constantinopolitan_Creed

[6] Saint John Climacus, *The Ladder of Divine Ascent*, trans. Colm Luibheid and Norman Rusell, with an introduction by Kallistos Ware (Mahwah, NJ: The Paulist Press, 1982), 268.

[7] For more information on this book and Joseph's citation of Amos 3:7, see Part V under "June 27 (1844)—The Prophet Amos," note 1.

[8] See "The Life of Saint Alexander of Svir: Blessed Seer of the Holy Trinity," *The Northern Thebaid: Monastic Saints of the Russian North*, trans. Fathers Seraphim (Rose) and Herman (Podmoshnensky), with an introduction by I. M. Kontzevitch, (Platina, CA: St. Herman of Alaska Brotherhood, 1995), 123–4.

[9] Quoted in Elder Dallin H. Oaks, "The Godhead and the Plan of Salvation," April 2017 general conference.

[10] See generally, John H. Erickson, *Orthodox Christians in America* (New York, Oxford: Oxford University Press, 1999), ch. 2 and 3.

149

[11] James A. Miller, "That Vast Empire: The Growth of the Church in Russia," February 2014, The Church of Jesus Christ of Latter-day Saints, Intellectual Reserve, https://www.churchofjesuschrist.org/study/ensign/2014/02/that-vast-empire-the-growth-of-the-church-in-russia?lang=eng.

[12] Ludwell was a gentleman of considerable standing. He was personally acquainted with George Washington and other leading men of colonial Virginia. His descendants were also Orthodox and lived, at least until the 1840s, in Williamsburg, Virginia. It is believed that some of his descendants later settled in Texas, still adhering to Orthodoxy. Ludwell's life and the development of Orthodoxy in the Americas, North and South, have been the subject of research by Nicholas Chapman, an Orthodox researcher who is also the director of publications at the Holy Trinity Monastery in Jordanville, New York; see "Nicholas Chapman," Ancient Faith Ministries, https://www.ancientfaith.com/contributors/nicholas_chapman. His posts on historical topics can be found at www.orthodoxhistory.org. This monastery is under the authority of the Russian Orthodox Church Outside of Russia (ROCOR), thus answers to the Patriarch of the Russian Orthodox Church (the ROCOR website is found at https://www.synod.com/synod/indexeng.htm). Regarding Ludwell, see Nicholas Chapman, "The Righteous Shall Be in Everlasting Remembrance: Further Reflections on Colonel Philip Ludwell III," March 22, 2013, Orthodox History, The Society for Orthodox Christian History in the Americas, accessed July 25, 2019, https://orthodoxhistory.org/2013/03/22/the-righteous-shall-be-in-everlasting-remembrance-further-reflections-on-colonel-philip-ludwell-iii/. I discussed Ludwell and other evidence of early Orthodox influence in the United States with Mr. Chapman by phone in July 2017. He was unaware of any way that an Orthodox calendar that might have been available to Joseph Smith.

[13] John Glen King, *The Rites and Ceremonies of the Greek Church, in Russia; Containing an Account of its Doctrine, Worship, and Discipline* (London, 1772), eBook, https://babel.hathitrust.org/cgi/pt?id=nyp.33433000343701;view=1up;seq=1;size=125.

[14] King, *Rites and Ceremonies*, 1–2.

[15] King, *Rites and Ceremonies*, 7.

[16] While King's work was pioneering in many respects, his attitude towards Orthodoxy on some points does a disservice to this ancient faith. He sees no visual merit in icons whatsoever, referring to them as "the most wretched drawings that can be conceived" (p. 33). He dismisses as "absurdity" the legends that Andrew the Apostle preached in Kiev and "baptized the whole nation," as well as the tradition that Saint Anthony

the Great (251–357) preached as far north as Novgorod in Russia and founded a monastery outside of the city. On the other hand, after debunking these stories and other purported early miracles, King does proceed to lay out the account that is the largely accepted version for how Christianity was introduced into Russia (page 3).

[17] Robert Adam, *The religious world displayed; or, a view of the four grand systems of religion, namely Christianity, Judaism, Paganism, and Mohammedism* (L. B. Seeley, London: 1823), available at https://babel.hathitrust.org/cgi/pt?id=uc1.Sb184769&view=1up&seq=227 .

[18] Adam, *Religious world*, 197 ff.

[19] Adam, *Religious world*, 200, n.

[20] Paul of Aleppo, *The travels of Macarius, patriarch of Antioch: written by his attendant archdeacon, Paul of Aleppo, in Arabic*, trans. F.C. Belfour (London: "Printed for the Oriental translation committee, and sold by J. Murray [etc.]" 1829–36), 2 vol. (see vol. 2 in particular), available at https://catalog.hathitrust.org/Record/001854519.

[21] Paul, *Travels of Macarius*, 47–48.

[22] John Lloyd Stephens, *Incidents of travel in Greece, Turkey, Russia, and Poland / by the author of "Incidents of travel in Egypt, Arabia, Petraea, and the Holy Land"* (New York: Harper, 1839), 2 vol., available at https://catalog.hathitrust.org/Record/008643660?type%5B%5D=author&l ookfor%5B%5D=Stephens%2C%20John%20Lloyd&bool%5B%5D=AN D&type%5B%5D=year&lookfor%5B%5D=1839&bool%5B%5D=AND &type%5B%5D=title&lookfor%5B%5D=Incidents%20of%20travel%20i n%20Greece%2C%20Turkey%2C%20Russia%2C%20and%20Poland&ft =.

[23] John Lloyd Stephens, *Incidents of Travel in Central America, Chiapas and Yucatán* (London: Harper, 1841), available at https://babel.hathitrust.org/cgi/pt?id=nyp.33433081696803&view=1up&s eq=11.

[24] Stephens, vol. 2 of *Travel in Greece*, 130–31.

[25] Stephens, *Travel in Greece*, 32.

[26] Stephens, *Travel in Greece*, 21–22.

[27] Stephens, *Travel in Greece*, 36.

[28] Richard Lister Venables, *Domestic Scenes in Russia: In a Series of Letters* (London: J. Murray, 1856); note that an 1839 edition also exists— the preface to this earlier edition is included. See at https://babel.hathitrust.org/cgi/pt?id=mdp.39015020170265&view=1up& seq=232.

[29] Venables, *Domestic Scenes*, 8.

[30] Venables, *Domestic Scenes*, 34.

[31] Venables, *Domestic Scenes*, 67.

[32] Venables, *Domestic Scenes*, 116.

[33] Venables, *Domestic Scenes*, 139.

[34] Venables, *Domestic Scenes*, 208–9.

[35] A. N. Mouravieff, *The Church of Russia*, trans. Richard White Blackmore (Oxford: J. H. Parker, 1842), available at https://babel.hathitrust.org/cgi/pt?id=mdp.39015035122855&view=1up&seq=5.

[36] Mouravieff, *Church of Russia*, 136.

[37] Mouravieff, 386–7, n70.

[38] Mouravieff, 391, n12.

[39] "The Holy Places of Russia," *The Morning Chronicle,* September 17, 1852.

[40] Heber C. Kimball, "Practical Religion," *Journal of Discourses* 8, July 1, 1860, p. 107.

[41] J. M. Neale, *A History of the Holy Eastern Church: The Patriarchate of Alexandria* (London: Joseph Masters, 1859). There may have been an earlier edition, 1847.

[42] *The Morning Post,* July 11, 1850.

[43] Richard Frederick Littledale, *Offices from the Service Books of the Holy Eastern Church* (London: Williams and Norgate, 1863). Littledale's book contains extensive notes with details concerning the history of the various offices and rites of Orthodoxy, their manner of administration, and comparisons to the rites of Catholicism.

[44] See Isabel Florence Hapgood*, Service Book of the Holy Orthodox-Catholic Apostolic Church,* with a forward by Patriarch Tikhon (1906; repr., Englewood, NJ: Antiochian Orthodox Christian Archdiocese of North America, 1996), 182–97, available as an eBook, https://archive.org/details/ServiceBookOfHolyOrthodoxChurchByHapgood.

[45] Protoiereus Dmitriy Grigor'yev, *Ot drevnego Valaama do Novogo Sveta. Russkaya Pravoslavnaya Missiya v Severnoy Amerike* (Moscow: Izdatel'stvo PSTGU, 2007) = От древнего Валаама до Нового Света. Русская Православная Миссия в Северной Америке (Moscow: Издательство ПСТГУ, 2007), under "Епископское служение," n43, accessed July 25, 2019, http://www.rulit.me/books/ot-drevnego-valaama-do-novogo-sveta-russkaya-pravoslavnaya-missiya-v-severnoj-amerike-read-408614-11.html.

[46] I worked in the Church Historical Department from 1995–2000, where I frequently read and studied materials related to Joseph Smith. Nowhere have I ever encountered a reference to Joseph studying Eastern Orthodoxy. Prior to this books's publication, I confirmed this point with senior staff at the Church Historical Library. My contacts were not aware of any connection between Joseph and Eastern Orthodoxy. There are, on the other hand, a few references to Roman Catholics and Catholicism in

Joseph's papers, journals and discourses, though none of these relate to the Roman Catholic calendar.

7—Background on the Orthodox Calendar

For readers interested in the calendar correlations described in the previous chapter, detailed information on the Orthodox calendar, as well as some background on the Catholic calendar, is provided here. A more comprehensive description of individual calendar correlations is found in Part V of this book.

The Orthodox calendar differs from the Catholic calendar in several respects, most notably in its constancy through the centuries. The Orthodox calendar is transmitted from one generation to the next without change, other than the occasional addition of commemorations (often called "feasts") for new saints. The Orthodox calendar also has commemorations for Old Testament prophets, which create interesting parallels to revelations recorded in the Doctrine and Covenants.

In the Orthodox tradition, the yearly worship calendar is extremely important to how believers practice their faith. Each day on the Orthodox calendar typically contains the names of several martyrs and saints whose lives are commemorated on the particular day. Observances for numerous important events in Christian and Orthodox history are also interspersed on the calendar throughout the year, including a dozen "great feasts" marking notable events related to Christ (eight feasts) and Mary the Mother of God (four feasts). Most feasts are fixed and do not change from year to year; however, some shift in relation to Easter each year and are thus called "movable."

For each feast or event commemorated on the calendar, there are corresponding short hymns and scripture readings that are sung and read during worship services. These constitute some of the main differences from day-to-day in how the worship services are presented. Orthodox sources advise that worshippers look to the vespers (evening) services for these hymns and study them to understand the doctrines of the Orthodox Church (as with the Jewish Sabbath, the worship day begins at sundown and continues to the next day). A leading Orthodox theologian, George Florovsky, reportedly said, "if you want to understand the theology of the Church, find yourself a good chanter and stand next to him for a year."[1] Thus, by listening to the church hymns for a year, worshipers can develop an understanding for Orthodox doctrine.

With this in mind, Orthodox doctrine is linked to the worship calendar, to the particular feast being commemorated on that day. Orthodox doctrine is furthermore contained in the hymns. In this sense, the Doctrine and Covenants and the Orthodox worship calendar take on teaching roles in their respective churches that are, broadly speaking, somewhat analogous. Of course, for Latter-day Saints, the Doctrine and Covenants is the product of divine revelation. For the Orthodox, the hymnists are sometimes spoken of as having a gift comparable with that of King David, the great Psalmist.

In Part V of this book, numerous interesting correlations are described between the dates of sections in the Doctrine and Covenants and commemorations on the Orthodox calendar. The dates and themes of the respective sections in the Doctrine and Covenants and commemorations on the calendar line up in numerous cases. Some correlations also fit with Roman Catholic calendars or martyrologies.

In Orthodoxy, there are currently two sets of calendars in use. In reality, both calendars are the same, except for a thirteen-day difference between their respective dates. Both calendars commemorate the same saints and martyrs (allowing for some local variations), the same events, the same miraculous icons, the same New Testament Apostles, and the same Old Testament prophets. These two calendars are commonly referred to in the United States as the "old style" ("Julian") and the "new style" ("Revised Julian").

As an example, consider the case of the feast of Saints Peter and Paul. It is observed on June 29 in the "new-style" or "Revised Julian" calendar. This version of the calendar is used in the Orthodox churches of Constantinople, Alexandria, Antioch, Romania, Bulgaria, Cyprus, Greece, Albania, the Czech Lands and Slovakia, Estonia, and the Orthodox Church in America. In contrast, the same feast is observed on July 12 in Jerusalem, Russia, Serbia, Georgia, Poland, Sinai, Ukraine, Japan, and in most monasteries of Mount Athos in Greece. This date is the "old-style" or "Julian" calendar feast for Saints Peter and Paul.

The topic of church calendars was discussed in 1923 at an Orthodox consultative synod that was held in Constantinople (modern Istanbul). Following this synod, some Orthodox churches continued using the old Julian calendar, but in practice, the dates are now thought of as "Julian plus thirteen," giving these dates a Julian equivalent on the Gregorian calendar. In this manner, June 29 became July 12, and people started to speak of an "old-style" calendar, which is still often referred to as "Julian."[2]

Figure 7.1: Accurate Watch   **Figure 7.2: Less Accurate Watch**
Compare to Gregorian calendar   Compare to Julian calendar

At the synod, it was agreed that churches wishing to fully align with the Gregorian (i.e., the Western) calendar would move October 1, 1923 so that it actually fell on October 14. Thirteen days were dropped, as if they never existed. In this manner, the old Julian date of June 29 for the feast of Saints Peter and Paul retained the same calendar date (June 29) in churches following the "new-style" calendar, since the extra thirteen days leading to July 12 were simply dropped. Local bishops were given the discretion as to whether and when to commemorate the feasts that were dropped for that particular year. Thus, was born the "Revised Julian" or "new-style" calendar.[3]

Regardless of which calendar a particular Orthodox church chose to follow, it was intended that Easter still be commemorated based on the Julian calendar in all Orthodox churches, wherever located.[4] This requirement also meant that commemorations calculated with respect to Easter (such as Lent) would also be the same in all Orthodox churches.

A simple analogy using pocket watches will help illustrate the difference between the two versions of the Orthodox calendar. Imagine that the "accurate watch" above represents the Gregorian calendar. Its time is more precise than the other watch, which represents the Julian calendar. The accurate watch seems to be *ahead* or fast when compared to the other watch; however, in reality, it is the lack of precision in the *less* accurate watch that causes the gap in time between the two.

Readers may wonder why some Orthodox Churches would continue to use an inaccurate calendar. After all, the Julian calendar loses time each year compared to the Gregorian (which in turn is closer to true solar time than the Julian calendar): eleven minutes a year, to be precise! To answer this question, readers can imagine themselves in the place of the owner of the "slower" watch above. Imagine that it is very old and once belonged to revered ancestors. Would its inaccuracy cause you to discard it? Sell it? Put it in a museum? Or would you continue to carry the old watch, eventually passing it down to your children and grandchildren? The answer may be different for each reader; however, surely some would choose to carry the old watch and pass it down—it is, after all, a priceless family heirloom, with great sentimental importance.

For Orthodox churches that worship based on the old-style (Julian) calendar, this calendar holds far more perceived importance than does an antique watch. Beyond its historical and sentimental importance, the Julian calendar is revered because of its *religious* importance. Changing it could be viewed be by some devout Orthodox believers as tantamount to altering their religion, which they believe traces back to the original Apostles. And agreeing to even one change could open the door to further changes to "modernize" the church. To many Orthodox believers, this would be unacceptable. Much of the appeal of Orthodoxy is in the fact that it *doesn't* change.

Even the Orthodox churches that have adopted the new-style calendar (Revised Julian) have retained intact all the same feasts and commemorations that were historically observed; they have

157

merely adjusted the dates to align with the more modern (and more accurate) Gregorian calendar. In this sense, these churches *also* have refused to modify the faith received from their ancestors.

To modern minds, the notion of a sacred, liturgical calendar may seem outdated or difficult to understand. Why would a religious calendar be needed, one so full of feasts and commemorations? Why would people conceive of time with reference to religious feasts, instead of simply using ordinary calendar dates?

The simplest answer is that Orthodox and Catholic believers starting from ancient and medieval times saw the calendar as a means for giving sacred meaning to daily life. One writer describes the role of the Orthodox calendar in these terms:

> These dates [i.e., of the Orthodox calendar] are associated with many signs, events, and customs. They innerly regularize the everyday life, work and agricultural cycle of the believers. In the past the holy days determined the time for weddings, the days of remembrance of the deceased and those for merrymaking and having feasts.[5]

Even today, one can still see examples of how the sacred calendar still serves as the most important window through which devout believers conceive of time. Orthodox scholars often date their books with reference to the church calendar. For example, Andrew Louth dates the preface to one of his recent books simply as "Feast of the Apostle Philip."[6] No calendar date is given. Depending on whether Louth worships based on the old-style or new-style Orthodox calendar, the date could be either November 14 or 27. But either way, it doesn't matter. Both are the feasts of the Apostle Philip. Similarly, the Reverend Hilarion of the Russian Orthodox Church dated his foreword to a biography of Saint Seraphim of Sarov as "Great Lent, 2009."[7] By writing this forward during Great Lent, Hilarion adds dignity and seriousness of purpose to this short writing: Great Lent is a time of spiritual cleansing that leads to Easter, the holiest of all Christian holidays. In his book entitled *The Typikon Decoded,* Archimandrite Job Getcha dates his introduction using both the modern calendar and a feast date: "September 29, 2008; Feast of St Cyprian, Metropolitan of Kiev."[8] These references to Philip, Lent, and Cyprian tell us much more about the Orthodox faith and perception of time than would a simple calendar date (September 29, for example).

This gap in calendar dates was noted by early Latter-day Saint leaders who visited Russia in 1903. Joseph J. Cannon penned the observations below, which were published in the *Latter-Day Saints' Millennial Star* in August 1903. Cannon was traveling in company with Elder Francis M. Lyman of the Quorum of the Twelve that year when Lyman offered a prayer of dedication to bless Russia for the preaching of the Gospel. Cannon wrote:

> The Russians are different in many respects from other peoples. An interesting and somewhat confusing point of difference is in the reckoning of time. We entered Russia on the fifth of August, but the Russians called it the twenty-third of July. The cause of this is that while most western nations accept the Gregorian, the Russians follow the Julian, and are now thirteen days behind us in their reckoning.[9]

With this 1923 calendar reform, one can see the explanation for why some Orthodox churches celebrate Christmas on December 25 and some celebrate it on January 7. The churches that adopted the Revised Julian observe Christmas on the Western date of December 25. Those that still follow the Julian calendar celebrate Christmas on January 7, which is the Gregorian date corresponding to the old Julian date of December 25.

If one were to ask Russians on the street what the difference is between the Orthodox Church and the Roman Catholic Church, many would likely point to the calendar, perhaps even using the Christmas dates of January 7 versus December 25 as an illustration. Thus, Vladimir Khulap asks what will occur in 2100, which will be a leap year on the Julian calendar. At that point, Christmas will move to January 8, yet by then "there will already be three or four generations of believers in Russia whose parents and parish priests sincerely taught them that the Orthodox Christmas is one day earlier." Khulap observes that it "will not be easy for the Church hierarchy to explain" this change.[10]

Readers should keep in mind that these two calendar systems are sometimes referred to inconsistently. The terms "new style" and "old style" are reversed in some Russian Orthodox calendars. In the example below, Christmas (January 7) is referred to as the "new style," which is the exact opposite of how these terms are used in the United States.

If readers encounter any difficulty in discussing these two calendars among themselves or with Orthodox scholars or believers, they can always revert to simply using the terms Revised Julian and Julian. Failing this, they can simply ask on what day is the feast of Saints Peter and Paul commemorated on the calendar in question? What about Christmas? If the answers are June 29 and December 25, then the calendar is what is often called the "new style" or "Revised Julian"; if the dates are July 12 and January 7, then it is what is often referred to as the "old style" or "Julian." These respective terms are authoritative in the United States, used by OrthodoxWiki and by McGuckin in *The Encyclopedia of Orthodoxy*.[11]

Since the time of the synod in Constantinople in 1923, there have periodically been calls for calendar reform.[12] There was momentum within Orthodoxy to bring the issue of calendar reform before an important council that was held in June 2016, the "Holy and Great Council" of Orthodox churches. This event was decades in the making, with preconciliar sessions being held in Pregny-Chambésy, Switzerland in 1976, 1982, 1986, and 2009. The issue of calendar reform was dropped from the Council agenda in January 2016, because "some local Orthodox Churches have stated that they do not desire and are not ready for a calendar reform."[13]

This book uses another term for calendar correlations— "exact match"—which refers to a third category of correlations, this being for dates in the nineteenth century (i.e., Joseph Smith's lifetime) that align perfectly between the Gregorian and the Julian calendar. In the nineteenth century, the gap between the two calendar systems was twelve days. Thus, in Joseph Smith's lifetime, an exact match for the feast of Saints Peter and Paul on June 29 would have constituted July 11 on the Gregorian calendar.

A prime example of an exact match is seen in the death date of Joseph Smith, who was shot to death by a mob on June 27 1844. This date matches the Orthodox day of the feast of Amos, which was celebrated in all Orthodox countries at that time on June 15 on the Julian calendar. Thus, with a twelve-day gap, Joseph's death date of June 27 fell on this doctrinally significant date—the feast of Amos.

Because the Julian calendar loses eleven minutes per year when compared to the Gregorian calendar, the feast of the Prophet Amos today falls on June 28. By the twenty-second century, it will fall on the 29th of June (a fourteen-day gap).

A fourth set of calendar correlations is also sometimes seen in the research presented in Part V: those for the Catholic calendar. These correlations are normally for an older version of the Catholic calendar that was in use from the late sixteenth century to 1960. This variant of the calendar is referred to as the "Traditional" or "Tridentine" Roman Catholic calendar. Some citations are also given for a Roman Catholic Martyrology, which essentially is also a calendar. The Martyrology seeks to be comprehensive, showing all saints, martyrs, and events that are commemorated anywhere (locally or regionally) in Catholicism, with listings by date.

To recap, this book uses four terms to describe calendar matches: (i) Revised Julian, (ii) Julian, (iii) Exact Match, and (iv) Roman Catholic. These are also described in Part V in connection with the detailed description of date correlations.

Since this book tracks four ways for finding a calendar match (instead of just one), some readers may see a risk of numerous meaningless "hits"; however, if the author were to look for, and to present, only one type of correlation, this would essentially be favoring one calendar over another and thus one party of believers over another. The author does not wish to take sides in the long-running controversy between supporters of these different calendar systems. On the other hand, there are Christian calendar systems that have been excluded from this project, in order to keep its scope manageable. This book excludes the Coptic and Armenian calendars, for example, as well as Protestant calendars.

Even after excluding other calendar systems, finding appropriate thematic and date matches is still difficult and unlikely. This makes it all the more surprising when one sees pervasive patterns, such as those for Elijah and temples.

Tracking four sets of calendar correlations also makes sense from the *providential* perspective. For readers who are open to the notion that God might have inspired these correlations, then one could presume that the connections should cover multiple types of calendars. Otherwise, God would be favoring one party of believers over another (or one party of Orthodox believers vs. the other, i.e., those favoring the Julian vs. the Revised Julian calendar).

Correlations are also much more numerous for Orthodox feasts than for Roman Catholic commemorations. This phenomenon is due to several factors, the chief of which may simply be that it has been easier to conduct research for the Orthodox calendar: the Orthodox calendar has been preserved over time with fewer changes. There are more internet and library sources describing the variations of Orthodox calendar and Orthodox feasts and commemorations. The Orthodox calendar also has commemorations for the Old Testament prophets, which presents several additional interesting correlations, such as that of Amos and the death of Joseph Smith. In addition, the Orthodox calendar has commemorations for saints who have turned out to be important in my research, such as Gregory Palamas (1296–1359), Paisius Velichkovsky (1722–1794), and Seraphim of Sarov (1754-1833).

On the other hand, some of the most important correlations described in this book are dates on the Roman Catholic calendar, some of which also overlap with Orthodoxy—see my discussions of Doctrine and Covenants 84, 88, and 93.

Early Catholic materials provide valuable insights into how calendars developed. Prior to the adoption under church authority of the Traditional or Tridentine calendar in about 1570, there were many variations of the Roman Catholic calendar. Exploring these has been outside the scope of this project; however, these older calendars and martyrologies are quite interesting and can make for fruitful study for scholars equipped with a Latin reading ability and access to the appropriate library materials.

Martyrologies typically contain only brief information, such as the name of the martyr as well as the date and place of death, if known. Thousands of such names are included in martyrologies, with many shown for each day. In contrast, for a religious calendar, typically only a smaller number of saints are shown per day, with only the name given (and no other details).

The earliest form of respect or veneration that could be paid to martyrs was a service held on the site of the martyrdom, on the anniversary of the death of the particular individual. With this in mind, one can see how written martyrologies came about.

The oldest martyrology is attributed to Saint Jerome of the fifth century (d. AD 430); however, scholars believe the martyrology attributed to him may actually originated in the eighth century. Early variants of Jerome's martyrology (in Latin, the *Martyrologium Hieronymianum*) are described in a scholarly work, *The Name of the Saint,* by Felice Lifshitz.[14] All other Catholic martyrologies trace their origin to these works. Another important early martyrology is that of Saint Willibrord (also known as Clement, ca. 658–739), which is still extant in its original form; it also dates to the eighth century. Sometimes this document is referred to as a calendar.

In and of themselves, martyrologies are not necessarily intended for use as part of Roman Catholic Mass; however, some early versions may have been intended precisely for this purpose. The recitation of the names of martyrs and other saints was thought, at various times in the past, to be devotional practice that could invoke the intercession of these individuals and thus bring miraculous blessings.[15] Compare this to the much more widespread Catholic (and Orthodox) practice of venerating the relics of saints (i.e., venerating the graves or portions of their bodies stored for safekeeping in an ornate box called a reliquary).

The fact that martyrologies were organized by date, the same as a calendar, helped to create a sacred sense of time. Every day on the calendar was special, due to its connection to devoted believers who suffered martyrdom and due to the numerous other feast days for saints and other important religious commemorations interspersed throughout the year.

An example of how a martyrology was used to give a sacred and dignified sense to time is seen on display in the British Library. A book called the "Beaufort/Beauchamp Hours," dating to the early to mid-fifteenth century, can be seen in a glass case. It contains devotional materials, including a martyrology organized like a calendar. The book also contains handwritten notations under the appropriate day listing other important events.[16]

The Catholic Church is the custodian of much of the earliest information on Christianity; accordingly, any study of Christian calendars and martyrologies will inevitably lead to Catholic sources.[17] While such materials have rarely attracted the attention of scholars other than specialists in liturgical materials, they can serve as an important window through which believers of any denomination can understand Christian history and worship.

In Orthodoxy, the calendar is understood as a "meditative aid" that helps us have access to the "timeless moment" of God's grace. The calendar is "a cycle of recurring and elliptical reflections on the central mystery of the Word's [Christ's] redemption of his people. Easter and the Pentecost are the most important (and most ancient) events on this cycle;[18] they are seen on the calendar as "not just things of the past, [b]ut things of the present moment of God's glory, and of the church's future hope—its eschatological reality."[19] The calendar is an opportunity to "relive the whole of the life of Christ" and has "but one and the same object, Jesus Christ."[20]

The Orthodox calendar year starts on September 1 (September 14 on the "old style"), following Byzantine and Jewish practice. On this date, the entry of Christ into the synagogue is commemorated (the account of this event is given in Luke 4:16–22. The Savior quoted words of Isaiah on this occasion, mentioning preaching "deliverance to the captives,"[21] a reference that for Latter-day Saints points to baptism for the dead and Christ's ministry among the souls of the dead during the days between his death and resurrection. This date forms another interesting parallel to Doctrine and Covenants 127, which is the first in the Doctrine and Covenants to give detailed instructions on baptisms for the dead.

September 1/14 is also the feast day of Symeon the Stylite, who spent the better part of his life atop a pillar, a feat of asceticism that can scarcely be matched. One Orthodox author acknowledges that in some ways, such cases are "a scandal" and are certainly can seem a "negation of all the values honoured by 'reasonable', 'civilised', 'modern' man." Yet, such saints serve as "a voice

164

[crying] in the desert and [sending] out a strong call to renunciation and penitence."[22]

Symeon, like some of the other men of whom I write, sought to please God and find salvation by engaging in acts that might seem extreme. Readers should keep in mind that Biblical prophets also were commanded at times to engage in practices that would sound unusual (to say the least). Consider the case of the prophet Isaiah, who was commanded to go about naked for three years (Isaiah 20:2–3). Ezekiel was commanded by God to lie on his left side for 390 days for the "iniquity of the house of Israel" (Ezekiel 4:4–5), and then to lie on his right side for forty more days "for the iniquity of the house of Judah" (Ezekiel 4:6). Ezekiel was also commanded to cook his food over a fire made with human dung, while lying on his side, doing all of this in the sight of the people (Ezekiel 4:12).

By the fourth century AD, the practice of feast days for saints had taken root in Christendom. The website for the Greek Orthodox Church in America provides this information:

> The feast days and the celebrations honoring the saints had become a common practice by the fourth century. The twentieth canon of the Council of Gangra in Asia Minor (between the years 325 and 381) anathematizes those who reject the feast days of the saints. So great was the esteem in which the Apostles, prophets, and martyrs were held in the Church, that many writings appeared describing their spiritual achievements, love and devotion to God.[23]

A 2011 book by Bradshaw and Johnson (no relation to this author) traces the origins of some Christian feasts. The earliest were commemorations of Christian martyrs. Tradition holds that Peter suffered a martyr's death in Rome. Thus, the date of Peter and Paul's feast (June 29) is quite ancient and was probably commemorated before the year 250.[24] These earliest commemorations were observed on the site and day of the particular martyrdom, when possible.

Feasts such as Peter's came into being locally and were a manifestation of a "popular" side of early Christianity. Bradshaw and Johnson take the view that such feasts "must be seen as a basic, rather than peripheral, expression of Christian faith and piety in general within this period."[25] These early yearly calendars are referred to by scholars of early Christianity as "sanctoral cycles."[26]

Eastern Orthodox devotional materials include works similar to the Catholic sources described above. One such common item is sometimes called a *menalogion,* though this term has several uses. The *menalogion* is a book organized like a calendar, with daily devotional readings for noteworthy saints or Biblical figures, such as prophets and Apostles. Such items are increasingly available in digital form (just as are Latter-day Saint Conference materials, scriptures, and other items).

A related devotional work is referred to as a Synaxarion, which contains the names of saints and calendar dates, along with abbreviated biographical information.[27]

---

[1] Quoted in Frank Marangos, "Between the Flood and the Rainbow: A Study of the Great Canon of Saint Andrew," October 4, 2005, in *Internet of Orthodoxy Series*, Greek Orthodox Archdiocese of America, SoundCloud, ca. 10:00, https://www.goarch.org/-/between-the-flood-and-the-rainbow-a-study-of-the-great-canon-of-saint-andrew?inheritRedirect=true

[2] John Anthony McGuckin, "Calendar," in McGuckin, ed., *The Concise Encyclopedia of Orthodox Christianity* (Malden, MA: Wiley Blackwell, 2014), 77–78.

[3] An account of the discussions and decisions at this synod is found in Miriam Nancy Shields, "The New Calendar of the Eastern Churches," *Popular Astronomy*, August 1924, 407–11, accessed July 25, 2019, http://myweb.ecu.edu/mccartyr/orthodox-reform.html

[4] The only Orthodox churches not following the Revised Julian or Julian are those of Finland, which follow the Gregorian (Western) calendar.

[5] Vladimir Sokolovsky, with illustrations by Stanislav Kovalyov, *Circle of Holy Feasts: The Orthodox Calendar* (Moscow: Raduga Publishers, 2000), 6–7.

[6] Andrew Louth, *Introducing Eastern Orthodox Theology* (Downers Grove, IL: Intervarsity Press, 2013).

[7] See Archimandrite Lazarus (Moore), *An Extraordinary Peace: St. Seraphim, Flame of Sarov* (Port Townsend, WA: Anaphora Press, 2009).

[8] Archimandrite Job Getcha, *The Typikon Decoded: An Explanation of Byzantine Liturgical Practice*, trans. Paul Meyendorf (Yonkers, NY: St.

Vladimir's Seminary Press, 2012).

[9] Joseph J. Cannon, "President Lyman's Travels and Ministry: Praying in St. Petersburg for the Land of Russia," *Millennial Star,* Aug. 20, 1903, p. 532.

[10] Vladimir Khulap, "Pastoral Problems of a Reform of the Liturgical Calendar in Russia," *St. Vladimir's Theological Quarterly* 60, nos. 1–2 (2016), 76–77.

[11] OrthodoxWiki, sv. "Church Calendar," accessed July 25, 2019, https://orthodoxwiki.org/Church_Calendar; McGuckin, "Calendar," 78.

[12] See Pierre Sollogoub, "Why a Reform of the Established Liturgical Calendar and of the Easter Date is Necessary," *St. Vladimir's Theological Quarterly* 60, nos. 1–2 (2016), 53–64; Khulap, "Pastoral Problems," 65–77; and Thomas Pott, "The Problem of a Common Calendar: Do we Need to Reform Our Liturgical Calendar or our Understanding of the Time of Salvation," *St. Vladimir's Theological Quarterly* 60, nos. 1–2, pp. 79–89.

[13] Archbishop Job of Telmessos, "Towards the Council," point 5, "The Synaxis of the Primates of January 2016," Pentecost 2016, Holy and Great Council, accessed July 25, 2019, https://www.holycouncil.org/towards-the-council.

[14] Felice Lifshitz, *The Name of the Saint: 627–827.* See also "Holy Time: Calendars and Martyrologies Through the Ages," The Library of Trinity College Dublin, Trinity College Dublin, accessed July 25, 2019, http://www.tcd.ie/library/exhibitions/holy-time/.

[15] Lifshitz, *Name of the Saint*, 33.

[16] See "Beaufort/Beauchamp Hours," Royal MS 2 A XVIII, British Library, accessed July 25, 2019, http://www.bl.uk/manuscripts/FullDisplay.aspx?ref=Royal_MS_2_A_XVIII&index=65.

[17] The earliest martyrology is attributed to St. Jerome (d. 430). All other Western martyologies are said to trace to this document. See Lifshitz, *The Name of the Saint*, 3.

[18] Schmemann, *Introduction to Liturgical Theology*, 159.

[19] McGuckin, "Calendar," 77.

[20] *The Year of the Grace of the Lord: A Scriptural and Liturgical Commentary on the Calendar of the Orthodox Church*, trans. Deborah Cowan (Crestwood, NY: St. Vladimir's Seminary Press, 1980), 2.

[21] *Year of the Grace*, 5.

[22] *Year of the Grace*, 5.

[23] See George Brebis, "The Saints of the Orthodox Church," accessed July 25, 2019, http://www.goarch.org/resources/saints.

[24] See Paul F. Bradshaw and Maxwell E. Johnson, *The Origins of Feasts, Fasts and Seasons in Early Christianity* (Collegeville, MN: Liturgical Press, 2011), 176, table 19.1.

[25] Bradshaw and Johnson, *Origins*, 172.

[26] Bradshaw and Johnson, *Origins*, 190–95 (see other tables here).

[27] Getcha, *Typikon Decoded*, 299. See also Oxford Dictionary of Byzantium, quoted in Roger Pearse, "The differences between Menalogion, Menaion, and Synaxarion," Roger Pearse: Thoughts on Antiquity, Patristics, Information Access, and More, Roger Pearse, accessed July 25, 2019, http://www.roger-pearse.com/weblog/2017/12/01/the-differences-between-menologion-menaion-and-synaxarion/.

8—Orthodox Worship and Sacraments

Background on the Liturgy

The literature on Eastern Orthodox liturgies and other Orthodox forms of worship is vast, so much so that only a short outline can be presented below of some important aspects.

The most widely practiced form of worship in Eastern Orthodox churches is the liturgies that developed in the Eastern Roman Empire (i.e., in the Byzantine Empire). The most frequently celebrated of these is the Divine Liturgy of Saint John Chrysostom. This liturgy is the primary worship service during which the Eucharist, or Holy Communion, is consecrated in Eastern Orthodox churches. It is usually referred to simply as the "Divine Liturgy."

John Chrysostom (AD 349–407) was a famous preacher whose sermons earned him the name *chrysostomos,* or "golden mouth." As archbishop of Constantinople in the late fourth century, his efforts to reform the morals of the court and city resulted in his eventual exile. He later died when forced to travel in inclement weather.[1]

The term *liturgy* is based on two Greek words: *leitos,* meaning "people," and *ergeia,* meaning "working."[2] In pre-Christian times, this word was used for "public works," meaning an effort undertaken "for the benefit of the state or community."[3] The word thus suggests that participation in a liturgy is *work,* a service or duty that is given by the faithful (not received). Liturgy is a work of prayer.

Some helpful observations regarding the Divine Liturgy are found in a short, reader-friendly work authored by the Reverend Patrick O'Grady, an Orthodox archpriest who was raised Roman Catholic but converted to Orthodoxy in the 1990s.[4] O'Grady explains that the Liturgy is a "product of divine revelation" and "comes to us from the Lord himself and is celebrated by His apostles and their successors, the Orthodox Catholic bishops, right down to our time, in an uninterrupted, continuous expression of faith and love."[5]

O'Grady further describes the Divine Liturgy in these terms:

The Liturgy is a mosaic of Holy Scripture and prayer, all interwoven into an organic whole. Many people have attempted to enumerate how many scriptural quotations and biblical allusions are contained in the Liturgy. Such exercises are profitable, yet it is difficult to arrive at an exact accounting, since almost every word of the Liturgy is deeply scriptural in tone and content, one phrase running into and even overlapping another. By praying and, over time, memorizing the Divine Liturgy, one learns to pray and even memorize a great deal of the Bible. It has been said that while many Christians study the Bible, we Orthodox pray the Bible.[6]

Although the Divine Liturgy bears the name of Saint John Chrysostom, he is not its sole author or arranger. Rather, it is believed that John was responsible for arranging or improving some aspects of this liturgy, particularly the *anaphora,* or portion of the service during which the Eucharist is consecrated. Generations of Orthodox believers after Chrysostom recognized his contribution by continuing to attach his name to this important liturgy, even though it underwent further development.

This continuity in the Eastern Orthodox tradition holds great appeal for many believers. The beauty, depth, and constancy of Orthodox tradition, as well as its Christ-centered doctrine and practice, continue to attract converts. Some of the works cited in this book from are written by Orthodox scholars who are converts from other Christian churches.

Other liturgies are also used for the celebration of the Eucharist. The next most frequently used is the Divine Liturgy of Saint Basil the Great. This liturgy is used on Sundays during Great Lent and in connection with several specified feasts per year. There is also a still older liturgy attributed to Saint James, the brother of the Lord; this one is mainly celebrated on his feast day. Finally, there is the Liturgy of the Presanctified Gifts of Saint Gregory the Dialogist. This is a liturgy of Holy Communion, but the Communion is not consecrated; instead, the holy "gifts" (bread and wine) have been presanctified at a prior service, for use on the Wednesdays and Fridays of Great Lent.[7]

O'Grady writes that "each of these liturgies receives its name from the saint who composed the *anaphora* in it."[8] The *anaphora* is the

170

actual portion containing the blessing on the Eucharist. See more below about the anaphora. The liturgies and services that are collectively referred to as "Byzantine rite" largely took their current form by the ninth century.[9]

The most popular and widely available book containing the text of the Divine Liturgy in English is a translation by Isabel Hapgood (1906).[10] Her book also contains variations on the Divine Liturgy used on days when the Liturgy of Saint Basil the Great is used instead of that of Saint John Chrysostom, as well as the services for Vespers, Matins, Great Compline, and the services for the first hour, third hour, sixth hour, and ninth hour. Hapgood also includes the services for major feasts, for sacraments such as baptism, chrismation, and marriage, as well as other helpful explanatory material. Hapgood's book is widely available both online and in Orthodox bookstores.

Besides the Divine Liturgy and other Eucharistic liturgies (and besides Catholic Mass), there are other appointed worship services in Orthodoxy and Roman Catholicism. Both traditions have inherited worship patterns that also include services at set times of the day where the Holy Communion is *not* blessed. This tradition of prayer and worship at regular times is of ancient date. Some writers link these services even to ancient Jewish custom.

Regardless of whether these services were inspired by Judaism, the case from the New Testament is clear: early Christians prayed at set hours. Consider this quote from Robert Taft's work on this topic:

> Did the early Christians observe these Jewish hours of prayer? It is impossible to give a definitive answer to this question. But the New Testament . . . portrays Jesus as praying in the morning (Mark 1:35) and in the evening (Mark 14:23; Mark 6:46; John 6:15). Furthermore, . . . Jesus kept vigil at night (Luke 6:12). Later, in Acts, we see the disciples praying at the third (2:15) sixth (10:9), and ninth hours (3:1; 10:3, 30). The latter, at least, is referred to explicitly as "the ninth hour of prayer," and it is possible that the other two hours were also set prayer times. In addition, the disciples imitated Jesus in praying at night (Acts 16:25; 2 Corinthians 6:5).[11]

Another early source that describes worship at set hours is a letter of Saint Clement of Rome to the Corinthians, which is generally dated to AD 95 or 96. Clement was an early bishop of Rome and is thus considered by Roman Catholics as one of the popes. It is said that he was ordained by Peter himself. In this epistle, he writes:

> We should do in order (*taxei*) everything that the Master commanded us to do at set times (*kata kairous tetagmenous*). He has ordered oblations (*prosphoras*) and services (*leitourgias*) to be accomplished, and not be chance and in disorderly fashion but at the set times and hours (*ôrismenois kairois kai hôrais*).[12]

For more information on Saint Clement, see Chapter 1 in connection with the discussion of the missions of Saint Cyril and Saint Methodius.

Clement's close connection to Saint Peter is depicted in the artwork in his Basilica in Rome, as is seen in Figure 8.1.

Figure 8.1: Saint Peter (on left) and Saint Clement of Rome
From wall of the Basilica of Saint Clement of Rome.
Credit: Adobe Stock photo.[13]

Celebrating the offices or worship services of Orthodoxy requires that the priest have access to a library of various works. In a 2009 book (translated into English in 2012) on Orthodox services, Orthodox scholar Archimandrite Job Getcha comments that the

number of these works "is a daunting reality for an amateur liturgist or a neophyte." Many of my observations on the development of Orthodox worship are drawn from this book, *The Typikon Decoded.*

The *Typikon*, the subject of Getcha's book, describes the order and type of services for each day of the year (but not the wording of the actual liturgies, which was largely settled by the ninth century), as well as particulars about how the services are to be conducted. Since at least the fourteenth century, the *Typikon* was disseminated throughout the Byzantine Empire and Russia, becoming the sole regulator for worship following the Byzantine Rite (the Eastern Orthodox form of worship).

The *Typikon* that is used in Orthodoxy today is known as *The Jerusalem Typikon* or *The Sabaite Typikon* and is believed to be a product of the efforts of Saint Sabbas the Sanctified (d. 532), a Palestinian monk. Sabbas is the founder of a monastery now bearing his name, located only a few miles from Jerusalem. He is mentioned in Chapter 5 of this book in connection with a miraculous well of water.

In some cases, services not even described in the *Typikon* are commonly used in Orthodox worship; an example of this is the Russian *panakhida* (in Greek, *mnemosynon*), which is the short memorial service for the dead. Alexander Schmemann, an eminent Orthodox theologian (1921–1983),[14] comments that much of the Ordo (the pattern and order of worship) described in the *Typikon* is not being observed in full. He cites an example from the early twentieth century when the Kiev Religious Academy attempted to reconstruct the Great Vespers (evening worship) described in the *Typikon*. It took a year of research and meticulous preparation to accomplish this.[15]

This is a list of the key works that are used in Orthodox worship. The books described in items (i) – (v) are used by chanters and readers. Those described in (vi) and (vii) are used by bishops, priests, and deacons. Item (viii), the Epistle and Gospel books, contain the scriptures that are read to worshipers during services throughout the year.

> **(i)** **The Psalter or Psalms.** Since ancient times, the Psalms have always played an important role in Orthodox worship, whether read or sung. They have been organized in different patterns over the centuries, with some arrangements at least as old as the fourth century. Under the current pattern of the *Sabaite* or *Jerusalem Typikon*, the Psalms are read in their entirety in Orthodox services

each week. During Great Lent, they are read two times in a week.[16]

(ii)   The Horologion (in Russian, Chasoslov, or Часослов). This book contains the psalms and prayers for the worship services held at set hours of the day (thus, *not* for the Divine Liturgy, which has no prescribed time). This work is believed to trace back to Palestine, where it was used in monasteries such as that of Saint Sabbas outside of Jerusalem (going back to the fifth and sixth centuries). Novice monks were expected to memorize it.[17]

(iii)   The Octoechos (in Russian, Oktoikh, or *Октоих*). This book contains hymns that are sung each week, organized according to the eight musical modes or tones used in singing Orthodox hymns. The hymns are organized on an eight-week pattern, one tone per week. These are *not* all the hymns sung in Orthodox worship, just some of them, following daily themes that repeat each week. For example, the hymns in the *Octoechos* that are sung on Sunday relate to the Resurrection of Christ. On Monday, the theme is angelic powers and repentance. Like other worship materials, these hymns are very ancient. One of the "newest" hymns (dedicated to the Mother of God) dates to the tenth century![18]

(iv)   The Menaia (in Russian, Minei, or Минеи). There are multiple volumes to this work, all containing hymns that are sung on the days of the annual cycle of fixed feasts. Many of these hymns are dedicated to particular saints who have fixed feast days. In fact, most feasts on the Orthodox calendar fall on the same day each year—these are the ones included in the *Menaia*. The *Menaia* developed with regional variations over the centuries, with separate versions focused on Greek and Slavic saints, for example. The *Menaia* continues to expand as new saints are canonized. An edition published in 1978 in Russia sought to combine the hymns for all known saints of Greek, South Slavic, and Russian origin.[19]

(v)   The Triodion and Pentecostarion (in Russian, Triod', or Триодь, and Tsvetnaya Triod', or Цветная Триодь).[20] These works respectively contain the hymns and biblical readings that are used during the period of Great Lent (leading up to Easter) and the fifty-day period following Easter leading up to Pentecost. Since the date of Easter moves each year, these feasts are called "movable." These works are essential guides for conducting worship services during these two periods, which are the oldest feasts in Christendom. Hymns in the *Triodion* were composed between the fifth and fourteenth centuries.

(vi)   The   Typikon   (in   Russian,   Tipikon,   or Типикон). Described above. This work is considered the "supreme arbiter concerning all questions having to do with liturgical worship and the observance of fasts."[21]

(vii) The Euchologion and Hieratikon (in Russian, Trebnik, or Требник, and Sluzhebnik, or Служебник). These works contain the litanies and priestly prayers for all the various offices of Orthodoxy, such as (for a few examples) baptism, chrismation, penance, ordination, funerals, monastic profession, the blessing of water, and the consecration of churches. The earliest manuscript of the Euchologion that is still extant dates to the eighth century. Over the years there were many variant manuscripts, some containing services that have been lost or are not in use currently. As with the other books, the appearance of printed volumes in the sixteenth and seventeenth centuries (and later) has served to standardize these works.[22]

(viii) The Epistle and Gospel Books (in Russian, Apostol and Yevangeliye, or Апостол and Евангелие). These books contain the scriptural readings that are used for the various church services. The "Epistle" contains the Book of Acts and the Epistles; the Gospel Books include the four Gospels.[23]

The Divine Liturgy has at its core the consecration and distribution of the Eucharist, or Lord's Supper (what is called the "Sacrament" in the Church of Jesus Christ of Latter-day Saints). For the Orthodox, the Eucharist is "the centre and source of the whole life of the Church,"[24] and its spiritual "heart and soul."

While the Divine Liturgy is long, seemingly complex, and certainly much more elaborate and ornate than is seen in any service of the Latter-day Saint faith, it is a beautiful, Christ-centered religious service. Much of the service is chanted or sung, giving it a deeply spiritual feel.

The deep spirituality of Orthodox worship was the factor that attracted the ancient ruler of Kievan Rus (Russia) to this faith. According to an ancient chronicle, Prince Vladimir (then a pagan) sent messengers in the tenth century to other lands to learn of their forms of worship. His emissaries visited Jewish, Muslim, Catholic, and Orthodox services. They were impressed most of all with the Orthodox liturgy in which they participated at the church of Hagia Sophia in Constantinople. Upon returning to Kiev, they explained:

> We knew not whether we were in heaven or on earth. For on earth there is no such splendor or such beauty, and we are at a loss how to describe it. We know only that God dwells there among men, and their service is fairer than the ceremonies of other nations. For we cannot forget that beauty.[25]

The calendar, liturgy, rites, the layout of the Orthodox churches, and the icons are repositories of ancient Christian practices and beliefs. Some of these show connections to Judaism. For example, the liturgical day begins at sundown, as does the Jewish Sabbath. A menorah with seven candles sits behind the Orthodox altar table. Orthodox churches are oriented to the east, as was the ancient Tabernacle and, later, the Temple in Jerusalem.

In studying Orthodox liturgies, rites, architecture, icons, vestments, and church architecture, Latter-day Saints may discern elements that show parallels and similarity to Latter-day Saint temple worship and ordinances. Latter-day Saints believe that the temple ordinances and endowment are also of ancient origin and were revealed by God to Joseph Smith. With this in mind, it should not surprise readers if parallels may be found in Orthodox rites; the Orthodox have sought to faithfully transmit ancient forms of worship. Given that Latter-day Saint temple rites are sacred and not open to the public (as opposed to ordinary Sunday worship, which is open to the public), this book will not directly identify parallels, but some readers may see connections. Readers wishing to explore all that the Church has made public about its temple rites can study the sources indicated in this note.[26]

176

The Divine Liturgy (and the Eucharist) is celebrated only once a day (usually before noon) at a time that may vary from church to church. Thus, the Eucharist stands outside of time[27] and is believed to represent an eternal and timeless opportunity for believers to experience God's grace and the renewal of the Holy Spirit. Orthodox theologians believe that the faithful participating in the Eucharist are, in fact, in the presence of God; thus, in the Russian Orthodox church, worshippers are generally expected to stand during the entire service. In Greek Orthodox churches, there are pews on which worshippers may sit; however, they too are expected to stand during the actual consecration of the Eucharist and at other points in the service.[28]

Orthodox writers affirm that the Divine Liturgy is better experienced than explained. Orthodox theology is *experiential*: the Divine Liturgy and, indeed, God himself, are better understood through actual *experience* rather than through explanation. As one guide to the Divine Liturgy puts it, "Come and see!" (Luke 22:19)[29] This was the Lord's invitation to his early disciples.[30]

Noted Orthodox scholar Alexander Schmemann (1921–1983) has written extensively on the Orthodox liturgy. His books are standard reading for Orthodox seminary students. He compares the experience of the liturgy to a "journey or procession," one that begins as Christians "leave their homes and their beds" to gather together as the Church in one place. The liturgy invites the believers to separate themselves from the world, enter into the joy of the Lord, and ascend into heaven. Orthodox worship focuses on "the joyful character of the Eucharistic gathering," rather than solely on the "medieval emphasis on the cross."[31]

Schmemann writes that the joyful aspect of Orthodox worship is seen in the "singing, and ritual, in vestments and in censing and the whole 'beauty' of the liturgy which has so often been denounced as unnecessary and even sinful."[32]

Defending this role for beauty in Orthodox worship, Schmemann explains:

> Unnecessary it is indeed, for we are beyond the categories of the "necessary." Beauty is never "necessary," "functional," or "useful." And when, expecting someone whom we love, we put a beautiful tablecloth on the table and decorate it with candles and flowers, we do all this not

out of necessity, but out of love. And the Church is love, expectation and joy. It is heaven on earth, according to our Orthodox tradition.[33]

The Orthodox worship experience is one involving all the physical senses. Worshippers see the beauty of icons and candles. They use their voices to participate in the Liturgy. They hear the chanting and singing. They bow at various points from the waist or in prostration from the ground, make the sign of the cross, bow their heads, place hands over the heart and lift their hands; and worshippers engage their physical senses of smell and touch by experiencing the aroma of incense and by kissing icons.

Schmemann further describes the liturgy as the time to "offer to God the totality of all our lives, of ourselves, of the world in which we live."[34] As believers give thanks to the Lord during the liturgy, they experience great joy:

> When man stands before the throne of God, when he has fulfilled all that God has given him to fulfill, when all sins are forgiven, all joy restored, then there is nothing else for him to do but give thanks. Eucharist (thanksgiving) is the state of perfect man.[35]

According to Schmemann, Christ is the ultimate focus of the Eucharistic experience:

> But as we stand before God, remembering all that He has done for us, and offer to Him our thanksgiving for all His benefits, we inescapably discover that the content of all this thanksgiving and remembrance is Christ. All remembrance is ultimately the remembrance of Christ, all thanksgiving is finally thanksgiving for Christ. . . . There is nothing else to remember, nothing else to be thankful for, because in Him everything finds its being, its life, its end.[36]

This great joy that believers receive through the Eucharist prompts them to "*remember* the world and pray for it." As the believers are sent home, they are "witnesses of this Light" with a duty to continue the "never-ending mission of the Church." For these, the "Eucharist was the end of the journey, the end of time," yet is also the "beginning and things that were impossible are again revealed to us as possible."[37]

The Eucharist is considered the point to which all other sacraments of Orthodoxy point. According to M. C. Steenberg, the "Eucharist is considered by the Orthodox to be the chief of the church's mysteries, effecting the true communion of God and humankind."[38] Since Christ took on a human nature, it is through repentance of our sins and access to his body and blood (i.e., through the Eucharist) that the faithful can receive forgiveness and put on his divine nature.

The Orthodox also take literally the Savior's words that the bread and water are his body and blood (Matthew 26:26–28; Mark 14:22–24; and Luke 22:19–20).[39] This is close to the Catholic teaching of transubstantiation; however, unlike in the Catholic tradition, the Orthodox belief has not occasioned elaborate doctrinal justifications by Orthodox theologians. The bread and wine simply are the body and blood of the Savior—no explanations are needed.

Schmemann points to an earlier era in centuries past when Western theology sought to answer questions of precisely *when* and *how* the Eucharist becomes the body and blood of Christ. He refers to this as a "consecratory formula" for the Eucharist. For Schmemann, the act of consecrating the bread and wine cannot be separated from the Liturgy. The gathering of the church faithful to the temple (church), together to ascend to "table of the Lord, in his Kingdom,"[40] and the participation of the faithful are essential parts of the Eucharistic Liturgy. In the Liturgy, the faithful not only witness the consecration of the Eucharist; they also participate. The church faithful, in Orthodox understanding, are (together with the ordained clergy) the "royal priesthood," spoken of in 1 Peter 2:9.[41] The Eucharistic Liturgy should thus be seen as the act of the whole church.

Schmemann also sees a second flaw in this Western "consecratory formula" to understanding the Eucharist: this mode of thinking reduces the Eucharist to a mere *illustrative symbol.* For Schmemann, the Eucharist is indeed a symbol, but the symbol is *actual reality,* not an illustrative symbol.[42] Schmemann further explains that "the true and original symbol is inseparable from faith, for "faith is the 'evidence of things unseen.'"[43]

In a similar vein, Kallistos Ware comments that the Orthodox Church accepts a change to indeed take place—that is, that the bread and wine do indeed become the body and blood of Christ—however, the Orthodox Church has never sought to answer the question of how exactly *how* this happens and *when*. Ware cites several sources for this point, including an 1839 catechism of the Russian Orthodox Church:

> The word transubstantiation is not to be taken to define the manner in which the bread and wine are changed into the

> Body and Blood of the Lord; for this none can understand but God; but only thus much is signified, that the bread truly, really, and substantially becomes the very true Body of the Lord, and the wine the very Blood of the Lord.[44]

Orthodox writers see the Eucharist as an important part of the believer's path to union with God, or theosis. In his entry on the "Eucharist" in *The Concise Encyclopedia of Orthodox Christianity,* Steenberg writes:

> The Eucharist, then, serves as the perfection and fulfillment of confession: the sinner who has offered up his transgressions and received absolution, is united in flesh and blood to the Son who is the true Redeemer of the fallen creature. . . . The Eucharist serves as the height of human persons' union with, and communion in, his or her Maker. In the remission of sins, the fallen person is drawn into renewed communion with the Lord, which leads to their deeper union in the Lord's person. In this way, the Eucharist is inextricably connected to the Orthodox understanding of deification, whereby the human creature participates in God's glory, the divine energies, being transfigured thereby into "god by participation."[45]

Orthodox theologians and saints have emphasized the importance of the Eucharist in helping man experience theosis. The sacredness of the Eucharist is attested by accounts of glorious visions of Christ and angels that Orthodox saints have experienced while serving at the Eucharist altar. Among these are Saint Symeon the New Theologian (949–1022), Saint Sergius of Radonezh (1319–1392), Saint Paisius Velichkovsky (1724–1794), Saint Seraphim of Sarov (1754–1833), and Saint John of Kronstadt (1829–1909).

The Divine Liturgy consists of three portions. These three are described below under three headings.

Note that some sources only consider the second and third portions as actually being part of the Divine Liturgy.

LATTER-DAY SAINT CONTEXT: For Orthodox and other readers wishing to study the Sacrament (Lord's Supper) in The Church of Jesus Christ of Latter-day Saints, the following verses of scripture will be helpful: Doctrine and Covenants Section 20:75-79.

While these verses mention *wine,* today's practice is to use water in the administration of the Sacrament. The Sacrament is the most sacred portion of Sunday Services.

The Sacrament is normally prepared, blessed and administered by young men between the ages of 12-18 years who have been found worthy to hold the offices of the Aaronic Priesthood (i.e., Deacon, Teacher or Priest).

The sacredness of this ordinance is reflected in New Testament accounts reporting Jesus' institution of this holy ordinance. The Book of Mormon also records a visit of Christ to the Ancient peoples of the Americas during which he also instituted the Sacrament (3 Nephi 18:1-11).

Additional information is available under "Topics" of

The first involves the private preparation of the priest for the services. He first says introductory prayers, then enters the holy altar of the church, puts on his priestly vestments, and washes his hands, thus demonstrating "his rejection of all sin, any grudges, and all impurity."[46]

The elaborate vestments worn by the clergy during services have been interpreted differently. Modern scholarship seems inclined to see in these the influences of secular clothing worn in Byzantium. In contrast, Neale in his 1870 work sees origins in the clothing worn by the Jewish priests, as described in the Old Testament.[47]

This quotation from Hapgood's service book gives a sense for the reverence and solemnity exhibited by the deacons as they prepare for the Divine Liturgy:

> When they enter the Sanctuary, they make three lowly reverences of adoration before the Holy Altar, and kiss the book of the Holy Gospels, and the Holy Altar, saying:
>
> > O God, cleanse thou me, a sinner, and have mercy on me.
>
> Then the Deacon approacheth the Priest, holding in his right hand his dalmatic, his stole, and his gauntlets; and bowing his head before the Priest, he saith:
>
> > Bless, Master, the dalmatic and the stole.
> >
> > Priest: Blessed is our God always, now, and ever, and unto ages of ages. Amen.
>
> The Deacon then retireth, kisseth the cross on his dalmatic, and putteth it on, praying thus:
>
> > My soul shall exult in the Lord. For he hath endued me with the robe of salvation, and with the garment of joy hath he clothed me. He hath set a crown upon my head, like unto a bridegroom, and as a bride hath he adorned me with comeliness.
>
> Then, having kissed his stole, he layeth it on his right shoulder. And when he putteth the cuffs on his wrists, he saith, as he putteth that on the right:
>
> > The right hand, O Lord, is glorified in strength. The right hand, O Lord, hath shattered the enemy, and though the multitude of thy glory hast thou crushed the adversaries.

Notwithstanding Hapgood's mention of the deacon wearing the stole on his right shoulder, most sources mention or depict the deacon as wearing it on the left.[48]   Figure 8.2 is one such illustration.

Figure 8.2: Russian Orthodox Deacon

Credit: J. M. Neale.[49]

The priest clothes himself in similar fashion with similar prayers, though his vestments are different. Under his vestments, he wears a simple cassock (in Russian, *podriznik*, or подризник) that, at least in the Russian use, is white. This is worn when the priest serves the Divine Liturgy. The priest's stole is more substantial than the deacon's: unlike the deacon's stole, the priest's passes around his neck, being joined in the middle.

No deacon or priest may celebrate the Eucharist without a stole. It represents the consecrating grace of the priesthood. For the priest, the stole (called an *epitrachelion*) hangs low upon the cassock and is bound by a girdle that the priest wears around his waist. He also wears a chasuble over his cassock and stole, which is an "ample garment without sleeves, short in the front with an opening for the head, which is put on over the other vestments."[50]

The priest's stole is symbolic of his anointing. Before putting on the stole, he says this prayer:

> Blessed is God, who poureth out upon his priests his grace, like unto the precious ointment on the head, which ran down upon the beard, even upon the beard of Aaron; which ran down to the skirts of his garment (Psalms 133:2).[51]

Shmemann provides these observations regarding ritual clothing:

> The white garment—the *podriznik* or *stikharion* (alb)—is first of all the same white baptismal robe that each of us received at baptism. It is the garment of all the baptized, the garment of the Church herself, and in putting it on the priest manifests the oneness of the assembly, uniting all of us with himself. The *epitrakhiliion* (stole) is the image of the Savior taking on of our nature for its salvation and theosis, a sign of the priesthood of Christ himself. Such is also the case with the *epimanikia* (cuffs): the priest's hands, with which he blesses and performs the service, are no longer his own but the hands of Christ. The belt or girdle has always been a sign of obedience, preparedness, brotherhood and service. The priest does not take himself to the "high places" on his own authority; he "is not greater than his master." Rather, he is sent to this ministry by his master, whom he follows and by whose grace he serves. Finally, the *phenolion* or *riza* (chausable)

184

represents the glory of the Church as the new creation, the joy, truth and beauty of the new life, the prefiguration of the kingdom of God and the King who forever "reigns; he is robed in majesty" (Psalms 93:1).[52]

Next, the priest and deacons (all of whom are dressed in ritual clothing) engage in the *proskomide*, or the preparation of the actual bread and wine for the Eucharist. The bread is referred to as *prosphora,* a term which sometimes is applied to the whole Eucharistic liturgy. The *prosphora* bread is ordinarily baked by lay members, who consider it a great honor to prepare it for the Eucharist service. It is baked with only water, flour, salt and yeast. In the Greek use, one large loaf is used. In the Slavic use, five loaves are used. Loaves usually have an imprint baked into them with a cross-shaped cipher reading, "IC XC NIKA," meaning "Jesus Christ conquers." The priest uses a ceremonial lance or knife to cut portions of the bread out representing the "Lamb" (Christ), the Mother of God, the orders of saints (angels, prophets, Apostles, hierarchs, ascetics, and martyrs), the saint who composed the particular liturgy being used that day (normally the Divine Liturgy of Saint John Chrysostom) as well as particles representing the ruling bishop, civil authorities, the founders of the church, and living and dead Orthodox faithful who are specifically being remembered.

All of these pieces of the *prosphora* bread are arranged in a prescribed order upon a sacrament plate called the *diskos*. On the *diskos* are also placed the names of living and dead Orthodox Christians for "whom prayers are desired." The Eucharist thus brings the faithful and priest in "communion with our beloved departed."[53] In fact, the priest keeps a book with the names of the persons he prays for, both living and dead.[54] A chalice with wine is also placed on the *diskos*, which is then covered with small veils.

O'Grady includes an appendix in his work dedicated to guiding the faithful in their preparation for the Eucharist.

Among his points of advice, worshippers are reminded that they should "have no ill will, unforgiveness, or rancor toward anyone." O'Grady cites Matthew 5:23–24 in support of this advice. He also advises readers to ensure that recent confession should have taken place, meaning that confession occurs *more often* than during the annual Great Lent (which is a common time for even occasional worshippers to make confession). Worshippers are also reminded to arrive on time; partaking of the Holy Communion when one is late does not show respect for the Lord. Worshippers are also instructed to abstain from all food and water from the previous evening, at least from midnight for a morning Liturgy. He also reminds readers of the importance of pre-Communion prayers.[55]

The Divine Liturgy is too detailed, rich and lengthy to describe every detail here. Part of its beauty (and complexity) is heard in what at times are simultaneous prayers by the priest and singing by the choir (or chanting by a deacon). For those who wish to listen in Church Slavonic to a lovely recording of a Divine Liturgy, a 2009 CD is available for purchase online. The music was composed by Metropolitan Hilarion (Alfeyev); his voice is also heard in the background as celebrant (i.e., the officiating priest).[56] Other online sources, such as YouTube, contain video recordings of actual Divine Liturgy services in various languages.

Below is a list of some highlights from the second and third portions of the Liturgy, that of the Liturgy of the Word and the Liturgy of the Faithful.

Second Part: Liturgy of the Word

- **The Opening of the Royal Doors.** These ornate doors are located in the center of the *iconostasis,* or partition on the east end of the Church that separates the altar and sanctuary from the nave, or main hall of the church. The *iconostasis* is not considered a wall—it is merely a stand on which icons are displayed. The opening of these doors symbolizes that the path to God is open to man, just as the veil of the ancient temple of Jerusalem was rent in two at the time of Christ's resurrection.[57]

- **Prayers and responses from worshippers.** The Liturgy begins with the declaration, "Blessed is the Kingdom," meaning the Kingdom of God, to which the worshippers respond with a rousing "Amen." The Eucharist is the "sacrament of the Kingdom," which unites the body of the Church to Christ.

The Liturgy contains a series of prayers and litanies that draw united responses from the worshippers, such as "Amen," or "Lord have mercy." Ancient writers tell of these same prayers and responses being offered at the Church of the Holy Sepulcher in Jerusalem, the site that is widely accepted in Christendom as the place of Jesus's resurrection (though the Church of Jesus Christ of Latter-day Saints and some other denominations favor the nearby Garden Tomb as the sacred site).[58] According to Jerome (fifth century), worshippers at this holy site pronounced the *Amen* with the force of a thunderclap. Much of the Liturgy derives from the ancient form of worship practiced at the Church of the Holy Sepulcher.

- **The Litany of Peace, or the Great Litany.** The Litany of Peace, or the Great Litany, encompasses "the whole world and everyone in it in the loving and merciful embrace of the Lord," invoking God's blessings on holy temple (the church structure) and worshippers, the clergy, government leaders and armed forces, the country and its cities, the weather and natural elements, the land (to be fruitful), travelers, the sick and suffering, for deliverance from affliction and danger, and so on.

- **The antiphons.** Following this litany, worshippers chant a series of *antiphons,* or short refrains to Mary the Mother of God and to the Son of God, followed by one called the *apolytikion,* a short hymn reflecting the theme of the day (such as commemorating the life of a particular saint). Traditionally, the antiphons are sung by two choirs when possible, each singing antiphonally (in response) to the other.

- **The Little Entrance.** Then begins what is known as the Little Entrance, or procession of a deacon and the presiding priest, while the deacon carries in the Gospel Book and the cry is heard, "Wisdom! Let us attend!" O'Grady calls for worshippers to now "be aware of Christ, the 'Wisdom of God' (see Prov. 8), along with the ministering of angels in our midst."[59] Another Entrance also occurs later in the Liturgy. The reading of the four Gospels, the Epistles, and other excerpts from the Holy

187

Bible has always played an important role in Orthodox worship.

- **Troparia and kontaktia (hymns).** Following this entrance, a series of hymns, the *troparia* and *kontaktia*, are chanted by the faithful. These also pertain to the feast of the particular saint for the day. These hymns are linked to the Orthodox liturgical calendar and embody Orthodox doctrine. Worshippers who consistently attend Orthodox services over the course of the liturgical year (which goes from September to August) and listen to the hymns will hear a beautiful exposition on church doctrines and the worthy deeds of saints.

As an example of these kinds of hymns, included here are the words for two such hymns. The first is the *troparion* for Elijah.

> *Troparion*
> An angel in the flesh and the cornerstone of the prophets,
> the second forerunner of the coming of Christ,
> Glorious Elijah sent grace from on high to Elisha,
> to dispel diseases and to cleanse lepers.
> Therefore, he pours forth healings on those who honor him.[60]

The faithful also participate in singing a simple prayer, the Trisagion: "Holy God, Holy Mighty, Holy Immortal: have mercy on us."

Frederica Mathewes-Green relates an interesting story or tradition associated with this prayer. It is said that in Constantinople in AD 434, an earthquake shook the city violently. While the people fled to the land outside the city and prayed, a young boy was somehow thrown into the air or into heaven by the shaking of the earth. He heard the angels singing these very words; soon all the people took up the same words.[61]

- **Readings of the Holy Scriptures and the Homily.** The choir begins this portion of the Liturgy by singing portions of a psalm. This singing is referred to as the *prokeimenon,* meaning that it prepares worshippers for another text. The reading of the Word is the central portion of this part of the Liturgy.

The "Liturgy of the Word," also called "the Liturgy of the Catechumens," was intended in centuries past particularly for individuals who were preparing for baptism; this preparation could take up to three years. This portion of the Liturgy also includes a homily, or sermon, which is delivered by the bishop, priest, or deacon. The homily is based on the designated scripture readings and may also include material related to the saint being commemorated that day.

This pattern of listening to scripture readings has always been followed in Orthodoxy, done in a language understood by the people. This practice is seen in the writings of early Christian writers. For example, Justin Martyr wrote the following description of a worship service in the second century AD:

> On the day called Sunday there is a meeting in one place of those who live in the cities or the country, and the memoirs of the apostles or the writings of the prophets are read as long as time permits. When the reader has finished, the president in a discourse urges and invites [us] to the imitation of these noble things. Then we all stand up together and offer prayers . . . and when we have finished the prayer, bread is brought, and wine and water.

While the scriptures have always been read to worshippers, Orthodox services have not always included sermons or preaching. Neale wrote in 1873:

> Preaching is but little resorted to except during Lent. In the seventeenth century it was forbidden in Russia. The last Patriarch of Moscow procured the banishment of several Priests to Siberia for preaching sermons, on the pretext that the Lord had always operated through His mere word, and had thus founded His Church without further

explaining it, wherefore it was not needful for His clergy to do so.[62]

Orthodoxy services have always placed emphasis on reading the Word of God to parishioners in a language they understand, though in recent centuries, readings and services in Church Slavonic have become more and more distant from the modern Russian and other languages (more about Church Slavonic and its origin is described in Chapter 1). Each daily Divine Liturgy contains a selection of readings from the four Gospels, Acts, the Epistles, Psalms, or Old Testament prophets. The current "Lectionary," or daily and weekly reading lists, traces its origins to the ninth century, to the reading schedule of the Great Church of Constantinople (Hagia Sophia, which is now a mosque). Such readings were intended for the church as a whole, for the general body of believers, not just for monks or the clergy. The reading lists for Saturdays and Sundays are believed to be the most ancient; some scholars believe these readings can be traced to the second century AD.[63]

While in ancient times this system helped promote an understanding of scripture, at least for those who could attend services, Schmemann sees in this an explanation for why the majority of modern Orthodox believers have a "striking ignorance of the scriptures." The lectionary was originally constructed on an assumption of daily attendance at church. If worshippers only attend services infrequently, or once a week, they miss much of the reading.[64]

The *catechumens* (people studying for baptism) were historically dismissed at this point; not so today in most churches.

- **Fervent Litany.** This litany and three others are said before the bread and wine are transferred to the Holy Table at the altar.

Third Part: The Liturgy of the Faithful

Now begins the part of the Divine Liturgy leading up to the blessing of the Eucharist, or body and blood of Christ. The *antimension*, or sacramental cloth, is unfolded on the altar.[65]

- **Cherubic Hymn, Cherubic Prayer.** The choir sings the Cherubic Hymn and the priest offers a prayer simultaneously by the same name, invoking God's assistance, "beseeching God for the grace to serve Him without offense during the coming Eucharist."[66]

- **Great Entrance.** The deacon and priest carry in the *diskos* with the bread and the chalice with the wine. They enter the main hall of the church, or nave, through the north doors. These are carried to the Holy Table at the altar and placed on a rectangular cloth called the *antimension* (in Russian, *antimins*, or антиминс). This cloth has an image of the entombment of Christ embroidered on it, with the signature of the bishop who consecrated it. The Eucharist cannot be served without the authorization of the bishop, so this cloth constitutes the proper authorization. A small relic of a saint or martyr is usually sewn into it.[67]

- **Augmented litany; The Doors.** A prayer and litany are offered that the faithful "have a good defense before the fearful judgment seat (*bema*) of Christ." O'Grady explains the significance of this phrase: the bread and wine are actually on the *bema*, which is also one of the names for the altar. Thus, partaking of the Eucharist is also, in a sense, meeting the Lord in judgment.[68]

Before the choir sings the Symbol of the Faith (described below), the deacon cries out, "The Doors! The Doors!" Hapgood gives this explanation for this curious feature of the Divine Liturgy:

> In the early Church the Deacons, Sub-Deacons and Sacristans were wont to guard the doors, that no heathen or unworthy person might enter in, and that no one should go out during the solemn celebration of the Holy Sacrament. At the present time, the words, "The Doors!" warn us to guard

the doors of our souls against all evil thoughts, as we prepare to confess our faith by the Creed, and to give heed to the Holy Mysteries.[69]

- **The Symbol[70] of the Faith.** The choir sings the Nicene Creed. This Creed was first written in AD 325 and updated at the Council of Constantinople in 381 (Second Ecumenical Council). According to *The Concise Encyclopedia of Orthodox Christianity,* no manuscript with the original creed exists; however, the text is known through the records of the Fourth Ecumenical Council, that of Chalcedon (451). This Creed has become widely accepted in Christian churches around the world, even though few if any representatives of the Western Church attended the Council at Nicaea.[71]

Latter-day Saints do not accept the creeds of Christendom (see Joseph Smith History—1:19). Fundamental truths regarding God's nature derive from revelation as well as the firsthand experience of Joseph Smith; however, much of the wording of the different creeds surely would resonate with Latter-day Saints, to the extent these embody references to the Bible.[72]

This is the Nicene Creed as translated by Hapgood in her *Service Book.*[73]

THE SYMBOL OF THE FAITH

I believe in one God the Father Almighty, Maker of heaven and earth, And of all things visible and invisible;

And in one Lord Jesus Christ, Son of God, the only-begotten. Begotten of his Father before all worlds; Light of Light, Very God of very God, Begotten, not made; Being of one Essence with the Father; By whom all things were made;

Who, for us men, and for our salvation, came down from heaven, And was incarnate by the Holy Ghost of the Virgin Mary, And was made man.

And was crucified also for us under Pontius Pilate, and suffered and was buried.

And the third day he rose again, according to the Scriptures.

And ascended into heaven, And sitteth on the right hand of the Father.

And he shall come again with glory to judge both the quick and the dead; Whose kingdom shall have no end.

And in the Holy Ghost, the Lord, Giver of Life, Who proceedeth from the Father, Who with the Father and the Son together is worshipped and glorified, Who spake by the Prophets.

In one Holy Catholic and Apostolic Church.

I acknowledge one Baptism for the remission of sins.

I look for the Resurrection of the dead,

And the Life of the world to come. Amen.[74]

- **The Anaphora.** This prayer is the actual Eucharistic blessing, the "highpoint of the Liturgy, and the embodiment of the apostolic tradition."[75] It culminates in the actual consecration of the bread and wine and their transfiguration into the body and blood of the Lord.

- **Holy Communion.** After a series of prayers offered by the priest and simultaneous singing by the choir, the faithful recite the Lord's Prayer. The consecrated bread (the "Lamb") is separated into four pieces. The piece with the letters "IC" is put into a chalice with a cut of hot water, symbolizing "the living character of the Risen Christ whose body and soul are reunited and filled with the Holy Spirit in the glorified life of the Kingdom of God." The clergy receive the portion stamped "XC" and partake of the consecrated wine.[76]

- **The faithful line up to receive the Holy Communion.** As each communicant approaches the stand before the priest, he or she states: "The servant of God, [baptismal name]." The Communion is always received with the name given at Holy Baptism, whether it is the name the communicant uses in daily life or not.[77] The faithful receive the portion of the bread stamped "NIKA" along with consecrated wine from a spoon.

Figure 8.3: Boy receiving the Eucharist
Credit: Adobe Stock photo[78]

- **Post-Communion hymn, litany, and dismissal.** Worshipers are encouraged to remain for the rest of the service. This shows respect and thanks to the Lord, like the one leper of ten who returned to give thanks to the Lord for his healing blessing (Luke 17:11-19). The priest emerges through the Royal Doors to stand behind a platform in the nave and pray. The faithful pray with the priest for "peace to Thy world, to all of the churches." The priest then pronounces a formal dismissal, invoking the Lord, the Lord's most holy Mother, all the saints and, in particular, the saint of the day.[79]

Other Sacraments

What follows is a short summary of other sacraments of the Eastern Orthodox faith, or what Latter-day Saint members would refer to as "ordinances" of the Gospel. The first three sacraments are administered for infants (generally aged four to twelve months) and normally occur at the same time (Baptism, Chrismation, and taking the Holy Communion). The Orthodox Church recognizes seven major sacraments: Baptism, Chrismation (Confirmation), Repentance and Confession, Eucharist (or Holy Communion), Marriage, Holy Orders, and Anointing of the Sick.

- **Baptism.** Baptism is the "door" that leads to the Christian church. The newly baptized person is a member of the people of God (the "Royal Priesthood"—see 1 Peter 2:9). In the Orthodox Church, as in many other Christian faiths, infants and children (and converts) are baptized; the Council of Carthage recommended this practice in AD 253, though baptism of adults was common in the following century. In the fourth century, Church Fathers encouraged people not to delay baptism until their deathbed.[80]

Figure 8.4: Orthodox Baptism
Credit: Adobe Stock photo[81]

Orthodox writers marshal other evidence to support the practice of baptizing infants. Baptism in the Orthodox Church for adult converts is by immersion; for infants, the child is submerged only partly, then water is poured over the head. The person is immersed three times, once each for the Father, Son, and Holy Spirit. The three-fold immersion also represents the three days that Christ's body lay in the tomb. Orthodox writers point to Christ's invitation for children to come unto Him as a doctrinal justification (Matthew 19:14). In its commentary for this verse, *The Orthodox Study Bible* explains: "Therefore, children are invited (even as an example to adults) to participate in the Kingdom through prayer, worship, baptism, chrismation, and Communion."[82] Only baptism by immersion can serve as a symbol of the grave and new life in Christ.[83]

Ware explains that Orthodox theologians generally do not accept the concept of "original guilt" as understood in the Roman Catholic Church. "Humans automatically inherit Adam's corruption and mortality, but not his guilt."[84] People are only responsible for what they do of their own free will. The fall brought disease and death, as well as

196

separation from God. Verses from the Bible are also cited where one reads of entire households and families that were baptized (Acts 11:14; 16:15, 33; 18:8; 1 Corinthians 1:16).

> **LATTER-DAY SAINT CONTEXT:** For readers wishing to study how baptisms are performed in The Church of Jesus Christ of Latter-day Saints, the following verses of scripture will be helpful: Doctrine and Covenants Section 20:37; and 3 Nephi 11:23-28.
>
> Baptisms may be performed by young men having the office of a Priest in the Aaronic Priesthood, or by men holding one of the offices of the Melchizedek Priesthood. Normally, children are baptized at age eight (see Doctrine and Covenants 68:25 and 27).
>
> Additional information is available under "Topics" cf. "Baptism" on the Church's website at this link.

- **Chrismation.** In this sacrament, infants, children, and converts are anointed with oil and blessed for the reception of the Holy Spirit. Ware explains that through this Chrismation, "every member of the Church becomes a prophet, and receives a share in the royal priesthood of Christ"; by virtue of it, all "are called to act as conscious witnesses to the Truth."[85] This sacrament is similar to Confirmation in the Roman Catholic faith.

The Concise Encyclopedia of Orthodox Christianity gives this explanation for how Orthodox Chrismation is administered:

> After baptism, the initiate stands in the church dressed in white robes and with bare feet. The gateways of the human senses are marked with chrism in the form of the cross: forehead, eyes, nostrils, lips, ears, breast, hands back and front, and the feet.[86]

197

Hapgood describes the purpose of Chrismation in these terms:

> Anointment with the holy Chrism (Chrismation) is a Sacrament whereby the recipient, through the anointing of various parts of the body in the name of the Holy Spirit, receives the gifts of the Holy Spirit, to rear and strengthen him in the spiritual life, and to render him strong, firm and invincible in faith, in love and hope; in boldness, that without fear he may confess before all men the name of Christ: that he may grow in all virtues, free himself from the Evil One and all his guile, and preserve his soul in purity and righteousness. After anointing with the Holy Chrism the child is a member of the Church of Christ and receives the holy Communion, without preliminary confession, until he reaches the age of seven years. Beginning with that age confession is obligatory.[87]

> **LATTER-DAY SAINT CONTEXT:** Latter-day Saints receive the laying on of hands for the receipt of the gift of the Holy Ghost. This is called "Confirmation." It is performed following baptism.
>
> For readers wishing to learn more about Confirmation, the information under "Topics" cf. "Holy Ghost" and "Laying on of Hands" on the Church's website will be helpful.

- **Repentance and Confession.** Much of Orthodox worship is focused on repentance. The faithful are encouraged to confess often, more often that just during the season of Great Lent, which leads up to Easter. Children starting at age six or seven (as soon as they know right from wrong) are also encouraged to participate in Confession.
Confession is usually made standing, with the penitent person facing a table with an icon of the Savior or a Book

198

of the Gospels. Usually the priest is standing slightly to the side. Thus, confession is made to God, not to the priest, who is witness and may offer words of encouragement or advice.

While the penitent person faces the table, the priest pronounces these words (with slight differences between the Greek and Slavic use):

> Behold, my child, Christ stands here invisibly and receives your confession. Therefore do not be ashamed or afraid; conceal nothing from me, but tell me without hesitation everything that you have done, and so you shall have pardon from Our Lord Jesus Christ. See, His holy icon is before us: and *I am merely a witness,* bearing testimony before Him of all the things which you have to say to me. But if you conceal anything from me, you shall have greater sin. Take care, therefore, lest having come to a physician's you depart unhealed.[88]

At this point, the priest puts his stole on the head of the penitent and pronounces an absolution.

Confession also includes an expected element of private prayer, spoken or silent.[89]

The full Sacrament of Confession also includes prayers, the recitation of Psalm 11, and hymns.[90]

> **LATTER-DAY SAINT CONTEXT:** For readers wishing to study repentance and confession in The Church of Jesus Christ of Latter-day Saints, the information under "Topics" cf. "Repentance" on the Church's website will be helpful.

- **Eucharist.** Children are given the Holy Communion at the time of their Baptism and Chrismation. Of the Eucharist and children, Ware writes:

A child's earliest memories of the Church will centre on the act of receiving the Holy Gifts of Christ's Body and Blood . . . not something to which infants come at the age of six or seven (as in the Roman Catholic Church) or in adolescence (as in Anglicanism), but something from which they have never been excluded.[91]

See above in this chapter for a description of the Holy Eucharist.

- **Marriage.** There are several aspects of Orthodox teaching on marriage that are interesting and are close in some aspects to Latter-day Saint views on marriage. Orthodox marriage is intended to be eternal in nature, as is abundantly attested to in my following writing in this section. Given that this topic may be of considerable interest to readers, it covers several pages.

Orthodox marriage includes a ceremony of crowning and the removal of the crowns. These crowns embody at least two doctrinal concepts. They invite the couple to devote themselves fully to each other and to Christ, and to make sacrifices for each other and the family. As they do this, they exemplify the dedication of Christian martyrs, who all wear a crown in heaven (Revelation 2:10). In wearing the marriage crowns, the couple are also reminded that in creating a family, they become kings and queens over their family.

On the intended eternal nature of Orthodox marriage, these lines from the article on "Marriage" in *The Concise Encyclopedia of Orthodox Christianity* are informative:

> Through marriage, man and woman become "one flesh" (Eph. 5:31) and belong to each other eternally ("into the Kingdom"). Orthodox marriage is not seen as being only "Until death doth you part."

The same entry also states:

> This mystery of Christian marital love is everlasting because it flows out from Christ and

200

makes the person eternal (deified by grace) though their partaking in the communion of the chosen one.[92]

The writings of other Orthodox scholars support the paragraphs cited above regarding the intended *eternal* nature of marriage. Recent examples of this scholarship are seen in an outstanding collection of articles and essays on Orthodox marriage by a wide range of Orthodox writers, entitled *Glory and Honor: Orthodox Christian Resources on Marriage*.[93] One of the editors of this work, David C. Ford, devotes several pages to this theme under the heading, "The eternality of marriage." He writes:

> Another especially glorious aspect of Christ-centered marriage is that it is meant to last forever—indeed, for all those who enter into the heavenly kingdom, every relationship formed in this life will continue in the next life, in a deeply healed and purified way. Just as Christ will be married to his Church eternally in an unbroken continuity, with each believer experiencing the unity of his or her marriage with Christ more and more in the timeless eternity of the life in Heaven, so too a Christian marriage is meant to last forever.[94]

Thoughts such as these are not of recent origin. Ford cites the quotation below from none other than Saint John Chrysostom himself (fourth century), whose name, readers will remember, is attached to the Divine Liturgy. Using the imaginary words of a hypothetical bridegroom speaking to his new wife, Chrysostom wrote:

> I fell in love with you for the excellence of your soul, which I value above all gold. For a young woman who is discreet and ingenuous, and whose heart is set on piety, is worth the whole world. For these reasons, then, I courted you, and I love you, and prefer you to my own soul . . . . For our time here is brief and fleeting. But if we shall be counted worthy by having pleased God to exchange this life for that one, *then shall we ever*

be both with Christ and with each other, with more abundant pleasure [emphasis added].[95]

Other writers cite Chrysostom on the eternal nature of marriage. Frederica Mathewes-Green affirms the importance of being a wife because it is an eternal call, and cites the words of Chrysostom to a young widow:

> You shall depart to join the same company with him, not for twenty or one-hundred and twenty years, nor for a thousand or twice that number, but for infinite and endless ages. . . . Then you will receive him back again no longer in that corporeal beauty which he had when he departed, but in luster of another kind, and splendor outshining the rays of the sun.[96]

Orthodox teachings on the eternal aspect of marriage rest in large measure on the *sacramental* nature of marriage as understood in Orthodoxy and its connection to the Kingdom of God. As explained above in connection with the discussion of the Divine Liturgy, the sacrament of the Eucharist represents a timeless moment during which the faithful and the church are united to Christ in his Kingdom, becoming part of his body.

The sacred and timeless nature of sacraments, including the marriage sacrament, are discussed in a recent guide to Orthodox marriage by Bishop John Abdalah and Nicholas G. Mamey. The authors mention the Greek word *kairos* in connection with the eternal nature of Orthodox marriage. This term is Greek for a "special or opportune time," which for the Orthodox Church means "God's time, which is outside of historical time and is in eternity."[97] The authors further explain that marriage and other sacraments "cannot be reduced to momentary acts in history," because they are "God acting with us and impact our lives before and after the gift."[98] The authors further underscore this thought in these words:

> The idea that marriage is dynamic and extends from the wedding service in both directions, both

202

before and after, is expressed liturgically by the resistance of the Church to pronounce a couple "*now* husband and wife" [emphasis added].[99]

Ford makes the same point, explaining that "in the Orthodox wedding service there are no vows spoken. Hence, the familiar words of the Western marriage service— 'until death doth us part'—do not appear in the Orthodox service." Interestingly, Ford also observes that these words were not in the early marriage ceremonies used in France and England, having only been added around 1400.[100]

Orthodox writers invariably cite verses in Ephesians 5 when discussing Christian marriage. In Ephesians 5:25, we read:

Husbands, love your wives, even as Christ also loved the church, and gave himself for it.

In Ephesians 5:30, we read:

For we are members of his [Christ's] body, of his flesh, and of his bones.

In the Orthodox understanding, these two verses are more than an exhortation for husbands to be loving and Christlike; this wording invokes the imagery commonly used to describe theosis, the so-called exchange formula as articulated (in the wording given here) by Saint Athanasius of Alexandria (see Chapter 2): "God became man so that man may become God." Christ gave himself, or lowered himself, for the church, so that he might raise the church and unite it to himself. Under Orthodox teaching, the Eucharist is the key means by which Christ unites the church unto himself, making believers the faithful "members of his body."

When this same thinking is applied to the relationship between Christian husband and wife, the husband should likewise give himself in love and sacrifice to his wife, seeking to unite both her and himself (and their family) to the Lord through the sacrament of marriage.

The sacramental nature of marriage is also seen in Ephesians 5:32:

> This [i.e., Christian marriage] is a great mystery; but I speak concerning Christ and the church.

According to theologian John Meyendorff, the comparison of Christian marriage to the union between Christ and the Church as discussed by Paul in Ephesians 5:30–32 is "the basis for the entire theology of marriage in the Orthodox tradition."[101] Meyendorff also explains that in calling Christian marriage a "mystery," Paul "affirms that marriage also has a place in the eternal Kingdom."[102] As used in Orthodoxy, the term *mystery* is equivalent to the term *sacrament.* King points this out in his work published in 1772, explaining that in the Greek faith, a mystery is a "ceremony or act appointed by God, in which God giveth or signifieth to us his grace."[103]

Meyendorff explains that the "true meaning of marriage as a sacrament becomes understandable in the framework of the Eucharistic Divine Liturgy."[104]

In their guide on Orthodox marriage, Abdalah and Mamey cite a Greek Orthodox Dictionary to explain the origin of the word *mystery*, or sacrament, explaining that it derives from the Greek word *mystērion* and its root verb *myō*, meaning to "close the eyes for the purpose of protecting them from . . . a vision of deity." The authors comment on this meaning in these words:

> This definition of 'sacrament' paints an icon of dwelling in the presence of God, where the extreme brilliance of God is revealed to the participant(s) for the intention of change.[105]

In Russian, the term for mystery or sacrament is *tainstvo* (таинство); this term is also used in Latter-day Saint translations of the scriptures for the term "ordinance" (as in *Gospel ordinances*).

For many centuries, the sacrament of Holy Matrimony has been connected with the Eucharist, at least in doctrine, if not in actual practice. Meyendorff explains that until the fifteenth century, married couples partook of reserved Communion in connection with their marriage (i.e., Holy Communion that had been consecrated during a prior Divine Liturgy services and reserved for the couple's wedding). Thus, they shared an eternal moment together, in the presence of God, connecting them both to Christ. In earlier Christian times, baptisms, ordinations, and marriages were always celebrated in connection with the Eucharist; priesthood ordinations in the Orthodox church continue this pattern today. Strictly speaking, Orthodox marriages are still supposed to be conducted while the priest is at the Eucharist altar, during a short break in the Divine Liturgy; however, this practice no longer occurs. Meyendorff has called for Orthodox clergy to return to this tradition, or at least so that the crowning portion of the Orthodox marriage rite could take place during the Eucharist; this would serve to strengthen the Eucharistic connection to marriage.[106]

In addition, from the earliest times, Christian marriage always involved the bishop. During this early era, there was no specific Christian ceremony of marriage; instead, marriages were contracted under the authority of Roman law. The couple, however, later partook together of the Eucharist (after their civil marriage), and this was deemed to assure God's blessing, providing an eternal expectation for the marriage.

Meyendorff cites Tertullian (second century) on this point:

> [Marriage] "is arranged by the church, confirmed by the oblation (the Eucharist), sealed by the blessing, and inscribed in heaven by the angels."

Myendorff further explains:

> Every Christian couple desirous of marriage went through the formalities of civil registration, which

gave it recognition in secular society; and then through their joint participation in the regular Sunday liturgy, in the presence of the entire local Christian community, they received the Bishop's blessing. It was then that their civil agreement became also a "sacrament" with eternal value, transcending their earthly lives because it was then "inscribed in heaven."[107]

Early Christian bishop-martyr Ignatius of Antioch wrote (ca. AD 100):

> Those who get married must unite with the knowledge of the bishop, so that the marriage may be according to the Lord, and not by human desire.[108]

Current Russian language materials, both in print and on the internet, support this requirement as well.[109]

> With the coming of Christ, marriage no longer had as its primary goal the reproduction of human beings and the perpetuation of a family line, although procreation was still regarded as an important part of marriage. But Christ had come to the world and brought with Him the proof and guarantee of the resurrection of the dead, therefore giving to Christian marriage a new primary goal— the attainment of eternal life by husband, wife, and all children.[110]

Orthodox writers emphasize the joy and completeness that marriage in Christ can bring to the husband and wife. Ford quotes Saint Tikhon of Moscow, who retold the story of Adam and Eve in these moving terms at a wedding in San Francisco (1902):

> It is not good that the man should be alone; I will make a helper for him" (Gen 2:18), said God himself when our forefather Adam was still in Paradise. Without a helpmate, the very bliss of Paradise was not complete for Adam. Endowed with the ability to think, speak, and love, the first

206

man in his thoughts is seeking another being who is able to think. His speech sounds sorrowfully in the air, and only a lifeless echo serves as an answer to him. And his heart, full of love, is looking for another heart that is close and equal to his. . . . Then the All-Merciful God, who cares about the bliss of man, fulfills his need and creates for him a helpmate appropriate for him—a wife.[111]

Ford cites Church Fathers, including Saint John Chrysostom, who taught that sexual relations between husband and wife are inherently good.[112] Another writer in Ford's volume comments that the "Orthodox teaching is clear that the purpose of sexual intimacy is to help the partners bring each other closer to Christ, and not primarily the procreation of children."[113] On the other hand, an Orthodox priest is expected to refuse to solemnize a marriage if the partners are unalterably opposed to conceiving a child.[114]

The enduring aspect of Orthodox marriage is seen on a Russian Orthodox website that presents several question-and-answer scenarios related to marriage and family. This one is right on point with the Orthodox view of marriage in the afterlife:

[Question:] There is an opinion of the Church that all partners will meet at the Last Judgment as spouses. Is that so?

[Answer:] Partners? No. The church never said that sexual partners would be together in eternity, but, on the contrary, it was said that loving spouses would meet in eternity, because love is an indestructible feeling of the soul, it is an eternal value.

We can recall a number of gospel expressions that tell us that there are some values that will come with us into eternity.[115]

A 2015 Russian-language pamphlet for couples preparing for Orthodox marriage provides a range of practical and theological guidance. The publication information on the second page indicates that is has been officially approved by the Russian Orthodox Church. This work devotes two pages to describing the eternal significance of the couple's coming marriage, including these words:

> The Savior himself gave direct instruction that marriage is a Godly unification of two individuals, which must not be destroyed by man. In other words, we see here the beginning of the Christian teaching on marriage: marriage is an eternal ontological union of two individuals, having existed before the fall and afterward. Some of the holy fathers, continuing this line of thought, state that even after physical and bodily death, the souls of the departed can commune in the Kingdom of God, thus making their love in a classical sense immortal.[116]

The writer continues:

> "Church marriage is a unique union of people who can overcome the limitations of their own human nature and be united in marriage not only in this life, but in eternity."[117]

Under Orthodox teaching, the relations between spouses in the afterlife will not be sexual in nature; however, in all other respects, the faithful can anticipate a joyous physical resurrection of their bodies, which will be deified by the very energies of God (i.e., by the light called the "Tabor" or "Uncreated" light—see Chapter 2, "Theosis").

This point is made by Meyendorff, who discusses the dialogue between Jesus and the Pharisees on the "Levirate" obligation of a brother to marry the wife of his deceased brother (Matthew 22:30). According to Meyendorff, this verse is often cited "to imply that marriage is only an earthly institution and that its reality is dissolved by death." To such reasoning, he points out that this interpretation is a "clear contradiction to the teaching of St. Paul and to the very consistent canonical practice of the Orthodox Church throughout the centuries."[118] Meyendorff explains that in this dialogue, the Savior was "not rejecting marriage, but ridding their minds of the expectation that in the resurrection there will be carnal desire." The Savior's answer is thus "strictly limited by the meaning of [the Pharisees'] question."[119]

The wording "unto ages and ages" is found in the marriage ceremony and is equivalent to a reference to "eternity." There are at least eighteen uses of this wording in the Orthodox rite of Holy Matrimony, which includes an initial betrothal and crowning and (traditionally) a second ceremony that historically occurred eight days later, when the crowns are removed (the crowning and removal of the crowns now occur during the marriage ceremony). This reference to "ages and ages" is also used in other Orthodox sacraments; however, the wording of the rite of Matrimony contains other elements that suggest an intended eternal duration. The rite contains this verse, "For thou wilt give them thy blessing forever and ever: thou will make them to rejoice with gladness through thy presence."[120] The priest also prays, "receive their crowns into thy kingdom, preserving them spotless, blameless, and without reproach, unto ages of ages."[121]

The rite also contains numerous references to the covenant God made with Abraham and Sarah and confirmed upon Isaac and Rebecca. The priest prays that the couple may "shine like the stars of heaven" and be "exalted like the cedars of Lebanon." References are made also to Jacob and Rachel, as well as to Mary and noted Biblical prophets and patriarchs, as well as to Christian martyrs. Christ's first recorded miracle is also mentioned, the miracle of water and wine at the marriage feast at Cana in Galilee. This setting for the miracle (at a marriage) is cited by Orthodox writers to underscore the importance of marriage. The transformation of water to wine is furthermore seen as an allusion to the Eucharist.

Figure 8.5: Orthodox Marriage
Credit: Adobe Stock photo[122]

> **LATTER-DAY SAINT CONTEXT:** Latter-day Saints are encouraged to marry in a Holy Temple, of which there are approximately 160 functioning around the world. The temple marriage ("sealing") binds the couple and their children eternally.
>
> The sealing "keys" of authority were bestowed upon Joseph Smith and Oliver Cowdery in the Kirtland Temple in 1836, by the Prophet Elijah, whose return was prophesied (Malachi 4:5-6). Temple "Sealers" act under delegated authority from the President of the Church in performing sealings in temples around the world.
>
> For more information, see under the "Topics" cf. "Marriage," "Temple," and "Sealing" on the Church's website will be helpful.

- **Holy Orders.** The Orthodox Church recognizes three "major orders" of the clergy: deacons, priests, and bishops. These are believed to be the same offices found in the church of the New Testament. There are also "minor orders," including subdeacons, chanters, and readers.

The consecration or ordination of members of the clergy follows prescribed ritual. The particular orders for each ordination or setting apart are too detailed to describe here; however, a few excerpts are included below from the order of electing and consecrating a bishop.

In the case of the Russian Orthodox Church, the ordination of a bishop for a vacant episcopal (bishop's) seat is approved by the Holy Synod, or governing body of the church. During the meeting of the Synod, specific hymns are sung and the presiding bishop recites a litany (series of blessings).   The assembly is then closed with a benediction.

The hymns and benediction are given here:

Troparion Hymn
> Blessed art thou, O Christ our God, who has revealed the fishers most wise, sending down upon them thy Holy Spirit, and thereby catching the universe in a net. Glory to thee, O thou who lovest mankind.
>
> Glory to the Father, and to the Son, and to the Holy Spirit, now, and ever, unto ages of ages. Amen.

Kontakion Hymn
> When the Most High confounded the tongues, he dispersed abroad all the nations: but when he distributed the tongues of fire, he called all men unto unity.   Wherefore, with one accord, we glorify the all-holy Spirit.

Benediction
> May he who, in the form of tongues of fire, sends down from heaven the Holy Spirit upon his Disciples the Apostles, Christ our true God; through the prayers of his all-pure Mother, of the honourable, glorious Prophet, the Forerunner and Baptist, John, and Saint N (whose day it is), and of all Saints, have mercy upon us and save us, for he is good and loveth man.[123]

Prior to the actual consecration ceremony, an all-night vigil (worship service) is held, accompanied by the ringing of bells. The bishops and other clergy assemble with the bishop-elect (who is a monk, such as an archimandrite or hieropriest) at the cathedral. The bishop-elect is invited to stand upon the Orletz, which is a round rug that depicts an eagle with outstretched wings. The eagle is depicted with one head only, distinguishing it from the imperial symbol of Russia (an eagle with two heads). At first, the bishop-elect stands upon the tail of the eagle. During the consecration, he moves forward at prescribed increments to the middle and then the head of the eagle. Hapgood's notes for the ordination of a bishop explain that the bishop's teaching should be pure and upright in imitation of "that eagle which is depicted with St. John the divine."[124]

The bishop-elect also reads the "Symbol of the Faith" (Nicene Creed) and other confessions of faith, indicating his adherence to church doctrines and canons of governance.

The actual ordination then takes place by the laying on of the bishops' hands, with the presiding bishop saying the following prayer:

> O Master, Lord our God, who through thine all-laudable Apostle Paul has established for us an ordinance of degrees and ranks, unto the service and divine celebration of thine august and all-spotless Mysteries upon thy holy Altar; first, Apostles, secondly, Prophets, thirdly, teachers: Do thou, the same Lord of all, who also has graciously enabled this chosen person to come under the yoke of the Gospel and the dignity of a Bishop through the laying-on of hands of us, his fellow Bishops here present, strengthen him by the inspiration and power and grace of thy Holy Spirit, as thou didst strengthen thy holy Apostles and Prophets; as thou didst anoint Kings; as thou has consecrated Bishops: And make his Bishopric to be blameless; and adorning him with all dignity, present thou him holy, that he may be worthy to ask those things which are for the salvation of the people, and that thou mayest give ear unto him. For blessed is thy Name, and glorified thy Kingdom, of the Father, and of the Son, and of the Holy Spirit, now, and ever, and unto ages of ages. Amen.[125]

One of the assembled bishops then quietly recites a series of petitions as part of a prayer, invoking the Lord's blessings upon the world, the church, the new bishop, the rulers of the land, the Army and Navy, the city and upon all who call upon God for aid. Following this, the presiding bishop lays his hand one more time upon the bishop and blesses him that he be like the true Shepherd (Christ), a teacher and light for the people in his care. The bishop's prayer states that "it is impossible for the nature of man to endure the Essence of the Godhead," so God calls men as teachers and to keep his altar for the people (i.e., to serve at the Eucharist table).

Those present then exclaim "Axios!" three times, meaning, "He is worthy!" This exclamation is also made in connection with the ordination of deacons and priests and serves, in a sense, as an expression of support for the ordination by the congregation.

The new bishop then receives his staff, or crosier, which has two snake heads facing each other, reminiscent of the brass pole with serpent that Moses made and raised in the wilderness (Numbers 21:8–9; John 3:14; cf. Helaman 8:14, 15; for Latter-day Saints, the serpent was a figurative representation of Christ).

The new bishop is then given this exhortation:

> Receive thou the pastoral staff, that thou mayest feed the flock of Christ entrusted unto thee: and be thou a staff and support unto those who are obedient. But lead thou the disobedient and the wayward unto correction, unto gentleness, and unto obedience: and they shall continue in due submission.[126]

- **Anointing of the Sick.** This sacrament is not reserved for the dying but can be administered to any with spiritual or physical ailments. It is also associated with the forgiveness of sins, so it is normally preceded by confession. This office can be celebrated at church in a public ceremony or in a home. It is commonly celebrated on the Wednesday of Holy Week. It is administered to the sick who are capable of participating in prayer (but it can also be performed for children). Orthodox sources cite James 5:14–15 as scriptural support for the practice.

The office itself requires the participation of seven priests, one or more deacons, and a choir. A small table is also prepared in the church or room where the office will be celebrated. On the table is a bowl of wheat and seven candles, as well as a cup of wine. A cross and book of the Gospels is also placed on the table. The candles represent the gifts of the Holy Spirit, the wine symbolizes divine healing, and the wheat represents newness of life and resurrection.

The office includes the singing or reading of Psalms 143 and 51 and a series of litanies and hymns, including a canon composed of several "canticles" (short hymns) known as "The Prayer of the Oil, A Song of Arsenius." Gospel readings are also included, among which are Matthew 7:14–24; 9:9–14; 10:1, 5–9; 14:21–29; 25:1–14; Luke 10:25–38; 19:1–11; Romans 15:1–8; 1 Corinthians 12:27; 13:1–8; 2 Corinthians 1:8–12; Galatians 5:22; 6:1–2; 1 Thessalonians 5:14–24.[127]

LATTER-DAY SAINT CONTEXT: The anointing and blessing of the sick is also practiced in The Church of Jesus Christ of Latter-day Saints, as prescribed in James 5:14-15. The ordinance is practiced by two holders of the Melchizedek Priesthood, one of whom first anoints the person who is ill using ordinary olive oil that has been consecrated by prayer for the blessing of the sick. The second Melchizedek Priesthood holder then joins the first and pronounces a blessing to seal the anointing.

For more information, see under "Topics" cf. "Priesthood Blessings" on the Church's website will be helpful.

[1] *The Blackwell Dictionary of Eastern Christianity*, ed. Ken Parry et al., s.v. "John Chrysostom," (Malden, MA: Blackwell Publishers, 2001), 268.

[2] V. Rev. Patrick B. O'Grady, *Come, Let Us Worship: A Practical Guid to the divine Liturgy for Orthodox Laity* (Chesterton, IN: Ancient Faith Publishing, 2016), 30.

[3] John Anthony McGuckin, "Divine Liturgy, Orthodox," John Anthony McGuckin, ed., *The Concise Encyclopedia of Orthodox Christianity* (Malden, Massachusetts: Wiley Blackwell, 2014), 153.

[4] O'Grady, *Come, Let Us Worship*. See also "Meet our Clergy," St Peter Antiochian Orthodox Church, , accessed July 25, 2018, http://www.stpeterantiochian.org/about.html.

[5] O'Grady, *Come, Let Us Worship*, 24.

[6] O'Grady, *Come, Let Us Worship*, 31.

[7] Regarding the other liturgies, see generally Isabel Florence Hapgood, ed. and trans., *Service Book of the Holy Orthodox-Catholic Apostolic Church,* forward by Patriarch Tikhon (1906; repr., Englewood, NJ: Antiochian Orthodox Christian Archdiocese of North America, 1996), 64, eBook, tps://archive.org/details/ServiceBookOfHolyOrthodoxChurchByHapgood

.

[8] O'Grady, *Come, Let Us Worship*, 81.

[9] McGuckin, "divine Liturgy, Orthodox," John Anthony McGuckin, ed., *Encyclopedia of Orthodox Christianity*, 154–5.

[10] Hapgood, *Service Book.*

[11] Robert Taft, *The Liturgy of the Hours in East and West: The Origins of the divine Office and its Meaning for Today*, 2nd ed. (Collegeville, MN: The Liturgical Press, 1993), 9.

[12] Taft, *Liturgy of the Hours*, 14.

[13] DATEI-NR.: 41032950

[14] Schmemann's books on the liturgy are said to be standard reading for Orthodox seminarians.

[15] Alexander Schmemann, *Introduction to Liturgical Theology,* trans. Ashleigh E. Moorehouse (Crestwood, NY: St Vladimir's Seminary Press, 1966), 34, 36.

[16]Archimandrite Job Getcha, *The Typikon Decoded: An Explanation of Byzantine Liturgical Practice*, trans. Paul Meyendorf (Yonkers, NY: St. Vladimir's Seminary Press, 2012), 18.

[17] Getcha, *Typikon Decoded*, 21–22.

[18] Getcha, *Typikon Decoded*, 24–30.

[19] Getcha, *Typikon Decoded*, 32–34.

[20] Getcha, *Typikon Decoded*, 35–39; see also Mother Mary and Archimandrite Kallistos Ware, *The Lenten Triodion* (1978; repr., South Canaan, PA: St. Tikhon's Seminary Press, 2002).

[21] Getcha, *Typikon Decoded*, 39–47.

[22] Getcha, *Typikon Decoded*, 47–52.

[23] Getcha, *Typikon Decoded*, 53–66.

[24] Schmemann, *Introduction to Liturgical Theology,* 24.

[25] Nestor the Chronicler, *Povest' vremennykh let* (*The Russian Primary Chronicle*), ca. 1113, quoted in Getcha, *Typikon Decoded*, 9.

[26] See under "Gospel Topics," s.v. "Temples" at ChurchofJesusChrist.org; "Preparing to Enter the Temple," accessed July 26, 2019, at https://www.churchofjesuschrist.org/study/manual/preparing-to-enter-the-holy-temple/preparing-to-enter-the-holy-temple?lang=eng; *Temples of the Church of Jesus Christ of Latter-day Saints,* LDS Distribution item LDS-09339000, available at https://deseretbook.com/products?keywords=temples+of+the+church+of+jesus+christ+of+latter-day+saints ; and Boyd K. Packer, *The Holy Temple* (Salt Lake City: Deseret Book, 1980).

[27] O'Grady, *Come Let Us Worship*, 28.

[28] Cf. Doctrine and Covenants 45:32; 101:22.

[29] O'Grady, *Come Let Us Worship*, 12.

[30] A theme, by the way, that two current Latter-day Saint leaders have emphasized in their talks. See David A. Bednar, "Come and See," October 2014 general conference; and Russell M. Nelson, under "Member Missionaries," "Be Thou and Example of the Believers," October 2010 general conference.

[31] Alexander Schmemann, *For the Life of the World: Sacraments and Orthodoxy*, 2nd ed. (Crestwood, NY: St. Vladimir's Seminary Press, 1973), 27–29.

[32] Schmemann, *For the Life*, 29–30.

[33] Schmemann, *For the Life*, 30.

[34] Schmemann, *For the Life*, 34.

[35] Schmemann, *For the Life*, 37.

[36] Schmemann, *For the Life*, 40.

[37] Schmemann, *For the Life*, 45–46.

[38] M. C. Steenberg, "Eucharist," in McGuckin, *Encyclopedia of Orthodox Christianity*, 185.

[39] For Latter-day Saints, the Sacrament is a very sacred remembrance of Christ, by which Church members renew their baptismal covenants, thus

assuring continued enjoyment of the Holy Ghost in their lives. In 3 Nephi 18, the Savior refers to this sacrament both as a "remembrance" of his body and blood *and also* as his body and blood (3 Nephi 18:7, 11, 28, 29). The Gospel of Luke also references this remembrance aspect (Luke 22:19). Schmemann refers to the Eucharist as "the sacrament of the kingdom, the Church's ascent to the 'table of the Lord, in his kingdom'"; see Alexander Schmemann, *The Eucharist: The Sacrament of the Kingdom*, trans. Paul Kachur (Crestwood, NY: St. Vladimir's Seminary Press, 1987), 37. Doctrine and Covenants 27 makes for interesting comparison to Schmemann's words and the title of his book. In it, the Lord refers to the kingdom twice, promising personally to partake of the Sacrament on the earth with the faithful from all dispensations (D&C 27:4, 5, 13).

[40] Schmemann, *Eucharist*, 27.

[41] Schmemann, *Eucharist*, 92–93.

[42] Schmemann, *Eucharist*, 27–28, 37, 38.

[43] Schmemann, *Eucharist*, 39.

[44] Timothy Ware (Bishop Kallistos of Kokleia), *The Orthodox Church* (London: Penguin Books, 1997), 285; see also 283–284.

[45] Steenberg, "Eucharist," 188.

[46] O'Grady, *Come Let Us Worship*, 33–34.

[47] John Mason Neale, *The History of the Eastern Church: A Popular Outline of its History, Doctrines, Liturgy and Vestments,* 2nd ed., with a preface by Rev. Dr. Littledale (London: J. T. Hayes, 1873), 71.

[48] Hapgood describes the placement as being on the right shoulder. Other sources and images on the internet seem to depict placement on the left shoulder for deacons. See Neale, *History*, following p. 16; a search on Google images using the terms "Orthodox deacon stole" shows all stoles on the left shoulder.

[49] John Mason Neale, *The History of the Eastern Church: A Popular Outline of its History, Doctrines, Liturgy and Vestments,* 2nd ed., with a preface by Rev. Dr. Littledale (London: J. T. Hayes, 1873), following page 16.

[50] Hapgood, *Service Book*, xxxvii, xxxviii.

[51] Hapgood, *Service Book*, 69–70.

[52] Schmemann, *Eucharist,* 25–26.

[53] O'Grady, *Come Let Us Worship*, 37.

[54] Compare this book mentioned by O'Grady with Doctrine and Covenants 128:24, which concerns baptism for the dead ("a book containing the records of our dead, which shall be worthy of all acceptation").

[55] O'Grady, *Come Let Us Worship*, appendix A, 105–9.

[56] Bishop Hilarion (Alfeyev), *The Divine Liturgy*, November 1, 2009, audio CD, Amazon.com.

[57] Hapgood, *Service Book*, 65.

[58] Some Latter-day Saint leaders have expressed a view that the Garden Tomb in Jerusalem was the actual site of Christ's Resurrection. Church President Harold B. Lee (1899–1973) was the first President to state this. See John A. Tvedtnes, "The Garden Tomb," *Ensign* (April 1982), 4–11, https://www.Latter-day Saint.org/ensign/1983/04/the-garden-tomb?lang=eng. See also the website "The Garden Tomb," https://gardentomb.com/.

[59] O'Grady, *Come Let Us Worship*, 56.

[60] "Holy, Glorious Prophet Elijah - Troparion & Kontakion," Orthodox Church in America, accessed June 7, 2019, https://oca.org/saints/troparia/2000/07/20/102060-holy-glorious-prophet-elijah.

[61] Frederica Mathewes-Green, *Welcome to the Orthodox Church: An Introduction to Eastern Christianity* (Brewster, MA: Paraclete Press, 2015), 208.

[62] Neale, *History of the Eastern Church*, 94.

[63] Getcha, *Typikon Decoded*, 53.

[64] Schmemann, *The Eucharist*, 74.

[65] Schmemann, *The Eucharist*, 94.

[66] O'Grady, *Come Let Us Worship*, 70.

[67] John A. McGuckin, "Antimentions," in McGuckin, *Encyclopedia of Orthodox Christianity*, 28.

[68] O'Grady, *Come Let Us Worship*, 74. See also Hapgood, *Service Book*, 98–99.

[69] Hapgood, *Service Book*, 599, para. 18.

[70] This term is translated as "Article of Faith" in Russian-language materials of the restored Church of Jesus Christ.

[71] Tarmo Toom, "Council of Constantinople," in McGuckin, *Encyclopedia of Orthodox Christianity*, 129.

[72] The Latter-day Saint understanding of Christ is defined in a document entitled "The Living Christ: The Testimony of the Apostles." The opening lines state: "He was the Great Jehovah of the Old Testament, the Messiah of the New. Under the direction of His Father, He was the creator of the earth. 'All things were made by him; and without him was not any thing made that was made (John 1:3).'" See "The Living Christ: The Testimony of the Apostles," Jesus Christ, The Son of God, Intellectual Reserve, Inc., http://jesuschrist.lds.org/testimonies-of-him/articles/the-living-christ-the-testimony-of-the-apostles-of-the-church-of-jesus-christ-of-latter-day-saints?lang=eng&_r=1.

[73] There are slight differences compared to other translations found online, chiefly in the use of "we" vs. "I" in the professions included in the creed.

[74] There are twelve articles in the Nicene-Constantinopolitan Creed.

[75] O'Grady, *Come Let Us Worship*, 81.

[76] "Communion," Orthodox Church in America, accessed July 26, 2019,

https://oca.org/orthodoxy/the-orthodox-faith/worship/the-divine-liturgy/communion.

[77] O'Grady, *Come Let Us Worship*, 96.

[78] DATEI-NR.: 55283883

[79] O'Grady, *Come Let Us Worship*, 100–2.

[80] Sergey Trostyanskiy, "Baptism," in McGuckin, *Encyclopedia of Orthodox Christianity*, 55.

[81] DATEI-NR.: 255386669

[82] See note under Matthew 19:14, *The Orthodox Study Bible,* ed. Fr. Jack Norman Sparks (Thomas Nelson, 1993).

[83] Ware, *Orthodox Church*, 277–8.

[84] Ware, *Orthodox Church*, 224.

[85] Ware, *Orthodox Church*, 278–9.

[86] Sergey Trostyanskiy, "Christmation," in McGuckin, *Encyclopedia of Orthodox Christianity*, 94; see also Schmemann, *Life of the World*, 75.

[87] Hapgood, *Service Book*, 603.

[88] Ware, *Orthodox Church*, 289.

[89] For more about confession, see Tenny Thomas, "Confession," in McGuckin, *Encyclopedia of Orthodox Christianity*, 109.

[90] Hapgood, [286]–290.

[91] Ware, *Orthodox Church*, 279.

[92] Dan Sandu, "Marriage," in McGuckin, *Encyclopedia of Orthodox Christianity,* 307–8.

[93] David C. Ford, Mary S. Ford, and Alfred Ketigern Siewers, eds., *Glory and Honor: Orthodox Christian Resources on Marriage* (Yonkers, NY: St. Vladimir's Seminary Press, 2016).

[94] David C. Ford, "The Glory of Marriage," in Ford, Ford, and Sieweres, *Glory and Honor,* 38.

[95] David C. Ford, "Glory of Marriage," 38–39.

[96] Frederica Mathewes-Green, "The High and Holy Calling of Being a Wife," in Ford, Ford, and Siewers, *Glory and Honor*, 97–98.

[97] Bishop John Abdalah and Nicholas G. Mamey, *Building an Orthodox Marriage: A Practical Commentary on the Eastern Orthodox Marriage Rite* (Yonkers, NY: St. Vladimir's Seminary Press, 2017), 29, including n1.

[98] Abdalah and Mamey, *Building an Orthodox Marriage*, 29.

[99] Abdalah and Mamey, *Building an Orthodox Marriage*, 30; cf. the endless mirror-reflections that Latter-day Saint couples being married see from both directions as they kneel over the Temple altar.

[100] David C. Ford, "Glory of Marriage," 40.

[101] John Meyendorff, *Marriage: An Orthodox Perspective*, 3rd ed. (Yonkers, NY: St. Vladimir's Seminary Press, 1975), 15.

[102] Meyendorff, *Marriage*, 19.

[103] John Glen King, *The Rites and Ceremonies of the Greek Church, in Russia; Containing an Account of its Doctrine, Worship, and Discipline*

(London, 1772),10, eBook,
https://babel.hathitrust.org/cgi/pt?id=nyp.33433000343701;view=1up;seq
=1;size=125.

[104] Meyendorff, *Marriage,* 10.

[105] Abdalah and Mamey, *Building an Orthodox Marriage*, 34.

[106] Meyendorff, *Marriage*, 42–43.

[107] Meyendorff, *Marriage*, 21–22.

[108] Quoted in Meyendorff, *Marriage*, 22.

[109] "Pravoslavnyy brak" = "Православный брак," Holy Transfiguration
Church, Transfiguration of Our Lord Russian Orthodox Church,
"Vzglyady na brak v Vetkhom i Novom Zavete" = "Взгляды на брак в
Ветхом и Новом Завете," accessed July 26, 2019, http://www.holy-
transfiguration.org/ru/library_ru/fam_orthodox_ru.html.

[110] "The Orthodox Christian Marriage," Transfiguration of Our Lord,
Transfiguration of Our Lord Russian Orthodox Church, accessed July 26,
2019, www.holy-transfiguration.org/library_en/sacr_marriage.html.

[111] David C. Ford, "Glory of Marriage," 25.

[112] David C. Ford, "Glory of Marriage," 31–35.

[113] Philip Mamalakis, "The High and Holy Calling of Being a Husband,"
in Ford, Ford, and Siewers, *Glory and Honor,* 112.

[114] Alexander F. C. Webster, "Icons of the 'Nuclear' Family," in Ford,
Ford, and Siewers, *Glory and Honor*, 175.

[115] Priest Konstantin Parkhomenko, "Budet li brak v vechsnoti?" =
"Будет ли брак в вечности?," Orthodox Site: Family and Faith for the
Whole Family, Sem'ya i Vera = Семья и Вера, August 4, 2014, accessed
July 26, 2019, http://semyaivera.ru/2014/08/04/budet-li-brak-v-
vechnosti/.

[116] Antoniy Skrynnikov, *Tainstvo Venchaniya* (Slovo i Delo, 2015) =
Антоний Скрынников, Таинство Венчания (Слово и Дело, 2015), 68.

[117] Skrynnikov, *Taintsvo Venchaniya*, 69.

[118] Meyendorff, *Marriage*, 13.

[119] Meyendorff, *Marriage*, 14.

[120] Hapgood, *Service Book*, 297.

[121] Hapgood, *Service Book*, 301.

[122] DATEI-NR.: 59393981

[123] Hapgood, *Service Book*, 324.

[124] Hapgood, *Service Book*, 606–7. In fact, the eagle is used in Orthodox
iconography and in Catholic art to represent John the Apostle (often
referred to as John the Theologian in the Orthodox Church). Compare to
the Latter-day Saint belief that John is still alive, having been promised
by the Lord that he would "tarry" till the Lord came again, in order "to
bring souls to [Christ]" (see John 21:22–23; D&C 7). Readers may also
want to review the Joseph Smith Translation, Revelation 12:4, 5, 7, 14.
Under Latter-day Saint theology, the "woman" represents the Church of
God. The inspired changes by Joseph show that the time period in

question is one of many centuries.

125 Hapgood, *Service Book*, 329–30.
126 Hapgood, *Service Book*, 331.
127 Hapgood, *Service Book*, 332–59.

Part IV

Background Information on the Monks Described in This Book

9–Saint Seraphim of Sarov (1754-1833)

The single most intriguing figure in nineteenth-century Russian monasticism is Saint Seraphim of Sarov, a Russian Orthodox saint whose stature in the eyes of his countrymen can hardly be overstated.[1] He was a monk who spent much of his life in seclusion, reading his New Testament and engaging in prayer and physical labor in one of two wilderness "hermitages" near his monastery in Sarov, Russia. From 1825 on, he began to receive visitors, who often lined up to see him by the hundreds and even thousands. The well-documented stories of miracles he worked, such as healings, and of his prophetic statements regarding future tribulations to come in Russia and the country's eventual spiritual rebirth, serve as the basis for his veneration and fame in his native land to this day. It is said that when Russian Orthodox authorities reviewed the facts of his life in 1903 prior to his canonization, opposition to his canonization arose within the ranks of the church, precisely because Seraphim had worked *so many* miracles.

Seraphim is an outstanding example of a Russian *starets*, or elder. Unlike in the Latter-day Saint faith, the term "elder" is not an office of the priesthood; in fact, some Orthodox elders are never ordained to the priesthood (but some are, allowing them to officiate at the Eucharist altar in the churches of the monastery). Such elders are always monks and are generally older. Their recognition and authority stem purely from the saintliness of their lives, their ability to give spiritual counsel, and the respect or esteem of others. Elders invariably have monastic disciples whom they tutor: being subject to an elder's advice and leadership is an important aspect of Orthodox monasticism. More about eldership below in Chapter 10.

Seraphim was also a *hesychast,* meaning that he practiced continual silent prayer focused on Christ. The hesychasts practiced the "Jesus Prayer," usually in these words:

"Lord Jesus Christ, Son of God, have mercy upon me, a sinner."

Hesychast monks have served in Russia as early as the fourteenth century; Saint Sergius of Radonezh (ca. 1319–1392) was a hesychast and is also considered the greatest of Russian monks. Hesychasm should not be confused with Eastern, non-Christian religions; the spiritual power of hesychasm was not just in the meditation or in breathing techniques, but in the effort to totally focus on Christ in all their thoughts.

Seraphim's life also presents a modern, well-documented example of a believer who experienced theosis. Several witnesses describe the Tabor light, or Uncreated light, shining from Seraphim. This chapter discussed a remarkable account of a transfiguring experience involving Seraphim and a lay disciple, Nikolay Motovilov. This event occurred in November 1831 (referred to hereafter as the "Conversation of St. Seraphim"). It describes a glorious transfiguring light that enveloped and shone from both Seraphim and Motovilov.

Accounts differ as to the year of Seraphim's birth; however, it is generally given as July 19, 1759, though recent scholarship gives it as 1754.[2] His life has been the subject of multiple biographies, including several written in or translated into English. The most detailed of the biographies in the English language was written by Archimandrite Lazarus Moore, an Orthodox monk who was English by birth and who died in 1992. This book is entitled, *An Extraordinary Peace: St. Seraphim, Flame of Sarov,* with the most recent edition having been published in 2009.

At birth, Seraphim was given the name of Prokhor.[3] He was born on the feast day of the prophet Elijah.[4] Prokhor was born into the Moshnin family, a prosperous merchant family of Kursk, Russia.

As a boy, Prokhor exhibited a "bright mind, strong memory [and] impressionable heart." At age seven, he took an unexpected fall from the top of a church bell tower, but his life was miraculously spared; he suffered no harm and in fact was standing on his feet when his mother reached him, she having herself seen his fall from the tower.

On this occasion and others when his life was spared following accidents or illness, Orthodox tradition ascribes the miracle to the intervention of Mary. In fact, like some of the other saints profiled in this book, Seraphim is said to have had visions and dreams of Mary the Mother of God, or Theotokos, as she is known in Greek. In one such dream, Mary came to him with Saint Clement of Rome[5] and Saint Peter of Alexandria. This appearance occurred on November 25, 1825, which happens to be the feast date of Saint Peter of Alexandria. As a result of this dream, Seraphim understood that he should give up his seclusion; from this point, Seraphim began to more actively receive visitors. There is also at least one story of John the Apostle appearing to him. Seraphim's leading biography describes at least four appearances of John the Apostle, all involving other early church leaders as well as Mary.[6]

The last of Seraphim's visions of Mary occurred on March 24, 1831,[7] about eight months prior to the remarkable transfiguring event that he experienced with his disciple Nikolay Motovilov. This vision occurred about three months prior to Joseph Smith's statement that John the Beloved was then laboring among the lost tribes of Israel.

As a seventeen-year-old, Prokhor felt a call to serve as a monk and decided, accompanied by like-minded young men, to take a pilgrimage to the Kiev Cave Monastery (Kievo-Pecherskaya Lavra). This monastery was founded in 1051 and is the most famed of all the lands once part of ancient "Rus," or Russia. To this day, it remains one of the great spiritual centers for the Eastern Orthodox Church.

While Prokhor was visiting the monastery, he was told of a monk named Dositheus, who was known for his clairvoyance and lived in the Kitaev Monastery, located not far from Kiev. Prokhor went to find Dositheus, who, upon seeing in Prokhor "the grace of God," spoke prophetic words to him, urging him to go to the Monastery at Sarov, located not far from the young man's home in Kursk. Dositheus gave this counsel to Prokhor:

> Go, child of God, and stay there. That place will be to thee for salvation, with the Lord's help. There thou shalt finish thy earthly pilgrimage. Only try to acquire unceasing remembrance of God through the constant invocation of the name of God. . . . With it thou shalt find rest, thou shalt obtain spiritual and bodily purity and the Holy Spirit Who is the source of all blessings will dwell in

thee and will direct thy life in holiness and all piety and
purity.[8]

These prophetic words pointed Prokhor not only to the monastic
vocation and to Sarov:[9] the reference to "spiritual and bodily
purity" seems to prefigure the astonishing spiritual heights that
Seraphim was later to attain.

Prokhor heeded Dositheus's advice, later entering the Monastery at
Sarov as a novice and taking his monastic vows in 1786. At the
time of his tonsure, Prokhor was given the name of "Seraphim,"
referring to the heavenly creatures with six wings described in the
Bible.[10] The very fact that Prokhor was given this name seems
prophetic in light of the many miraculous events later associated
with him; in Orthodox theology, the seraphim are among the
highest classes or orders of beings in heaven, standing close to
God.[11] Not long after, Seraphim was ordained a deacon and
subsequently a priest. Seraphim often assisted with church
services, attaching particularly great significance to the Holy
Eucharist (the Holy Communion). He once was asked how often
people should partake of the Eurcharist; to this he answered, "the
oftener, the better."[12]

Seraphim is said to have often spent entire nights in prayer before
Sunday services, later lingering in the church for hours into the
night on Sunday to reverently care for liturgical vessels and to tidy
up.[13] He reportedly saw holy angels more than once during church
services, describing their garments as being "white as snow or
woven with gold." Seraphim not only saw the angels—he heard
their wondrous singing, commenting that nothing "can compare to
this heavenly music," and describing his service at the altar as
"bliss which nothing could disturb" that caused his heart to "melt
like wax."[14]

During one such church service, Seraphim had a remarkable vision
of the Savior and holy angels. He reported seeing

> our Lord and God Jesus Christ, in the image of the Son of
> Man in glory, shining brighter than the sun with an
> ineffable light and surrounded by the Heavenly Powers:
> Angels, Archangels, Cherubim and Seraphim. He
> proceeded through the air from the western doors of the
> church. On reaching the ambon, He raised His hands and
> blessed the clergy and the congregation. Then He stepped

into His local image to the right of the royal gates and was transfigured, surrounded by choirs of angels whose unearthly light shone all through the church.[15]

Moore describes what happened next:

St. Seraphim's appearance changed and, struck by the divine vision, he could not even move from his place by the royal gates. When Fr. Pachomius [the Monastery's leader] noticed this, he sent two other hierodeacons, who took him under their arms and led him into the sanctuary. But he continued to stand there motionless for about three hours in ecstasy. And only his face constantly changed; now it would become white as snow, now a flush would spread all over it.[16]After several years of monastic service, Seraphim received permission to leave the monastery in order to live in seclusion in a nearby forest located on the river Sarovka, returning to the monastery only on Sundays to attend worship services and to obtain bread. There, in the solitude of the forest, Seraphim lived

a simple life for many years, engaged in gardening, prayer, reading the Bible and the *Philokalia*, and other spiritual pursuits. The *Philokalia* is a multivolume set of the writings of earlier Greek Church Fathers, including excerpts from the writings of Saint Symeon the New Theologian (949–1022). More about the *Philokalia* below, in Chapter 10, "The Elders of Optina."

Seraphim was particularly devoted to reading the New Testament. "The soul must be fed on the Word of God," he said. "The Word of God is the bread of angels, and souls that are hungry for God are nourished by it. Above all spiritual exercises the reading of the New Testament and Psalter [Psalms] must occupy the first place."[17]

Figure 9.1: Saint Seraphim and the Bear
Credit: Wikimedia Commons, public domain.[18]

Seraphim's residence was a simple cabin, or "hermitage," as he called it. In fact, Seraphim lived in two hermitages during his life in the wilderness; one was his "distant hermitage," the other his "near hermitage." In these dwellings, Seraphim had no bed and only minimal furnishings, such as a stove, an icon of the Mother of God, and a stump that he used as both table and chair, as well as a pot where he kept bread.

Seraphim is said to have befriended a bear while living in the wilderness; the bear even brought him food at times. In this, Seraphim's experiences were similar to those told of other great monks from centuries past, such as: Saint Sergius of Radonezh who also befriended wild animals (fourteenth century), and Saints Jerome (third - fourth centuries) and Gerasimus who befriended lions (fifth century)(compare to Moses 7:13, regarding lions and the Prophet Enoch).

Although he was a devout Orthodox believer in every respect,[19] Seraphim was unconventional in a few ways. Instead of the black robes usually worn by monks, he wore a white smock.[20] Instead of the somber countenance that monks and nuns sometimes showed, Seraphim once commented that "cheerfulness is not a sin . . . but to say a kind or friendly or cheering word, in order that everyone might be cheerful in the presence of God, and not in a despondent mood, is not sinful at all."[21] He advised monks not to overdo their fasting, saying that even on fasting days "food should be taken once a day, and the angel of the Lord will stick close to you." For the Diveyevo sisters (near his monastery), he encouraged them to eat whenever needed based on the view that women were less capable of enduring "severe labors" in their temperance (fasting).[22]

Seraphim served as the spiritual advisor for the Diveyevo Convent, but only visited once. The sisters came to him for advice, when needed. This fact that Seraphim only visited Diveyevo once underscores the Elder's strict chastity, a point raised by More.[23] Seraphim advised aspiring young monks (called "novices") not to overdo their physical labors and ascetic efforts, referring to his body as "his friend the flesh."

The most famous event involving Seraphim occurred when he and a young lay disciple, Nikolay Motovilov, were transfigured in a blaze of heavenly light in November 1831. This event is well documented and taken seriously by Orthodox scholars. Of significance also is the fact that this event involved a lay person, Motovilov. Seraphim told him that this event was "for the whole world."[24] The account of this remarkable event was written in the first person, presumably by Motovilov himself. Motovilov later became a conciliation judge, school inspector, and court counselor, so he was an educated and credible person, though later in life, some accounts report that he exhibited signs of mental illness.

This amazing transfiguration of Seraphim and Motovilov also took place during the same month (November 1831) when Latter-day Saint elders on the other side of the world, in Kirtland, Ohio, were meeting to discuss plans to publish the Book of Commandments, the precursor to the modern Doctrine and Covenants. There are numerous interesting parallels between dates involving Seraphim and dates of great significance to Latter-day Saints. Here are several of these:

Death: Seraphim died on January 2, 1833. (Julian date; corresponding to 14 January on the Gregorian calendar in the nineteenth century). Doctrine and Covenants 88 was revealed between December 27, 1832 and January 3, 1833. This section contains numerous similarities to Orthodox teachings on theosis or deification. See Part V, under "January 2/15, Saint Seraphim of Sarov."

Canonization: Seraphim of Sarov was glorified (canonized) by the Russian Orthodox Church on July 19, 1903 (Julian date; corresponding to August 1, 1903 on the Gregorian calendar). Richard L. Lyman of the Quorum of the Twelve Apostles dedicated Russia for the preaching of the gospel a week later (August 6–9, 1903 on the Gregorian calendar).[25]

Relics (Body) of Saint Seraphim Talen to Diveyevo: On June 25, 1991, Patriarch Aleksii graciously met with Elders Russell M. Nelson and Dallin H. Oaks of the Quorum of the Twelve. That same day,[26] the two Apostles offered a prayer of recommitment near the Kremlin walls, blessing Russia once again for the preaching of the gospel by Latter-day Saint missionaries.

In July 1991, Patriarch Aleksii II and other Orthodox clergy set out from Moscow with the newly-rediscoverd relics (body) of Saint Seraphim to bring them to the Diveyevo Convent near Sarov, their final resting place. Dates differ as to when the Patriarch actually set out from Moscow for Diveyevo, with dates given variously as "early July" or July 23.[27] On August 1, an all-night vigil was held inside the Diveyevo Cathedral.[28] Outside, the Patriarch and other hierarchs held a service and a then a holy procession brought brought Seraphim's body to its final resting place near the Cathedral.

The account of the transfiguration of Seraphim and Motovilov was first published in the United States in 1953, under the name *A Wonderful Revelation to the World: Conversation of St. Seraphim with N.A. Motovilov*.[29] English-language biographies of Seraphim followed in the 1970s and later, with the most complete having been published in 1994 and reprinted as recently as 2009. All of the English-language biographies of Seraphim in English discuss the *Conversation of St. Seraphim* and quote from it extensively.[30] The Blackwell Dictionary of Eastern Christianity refers to it uncritically.[31] The account is also widely available online.[32]

The famous discussion between Seraphim and Motovilov began with Seraphim explaining that the real aim of Christian life is to receive and enjoy the Holy Spirit. His remarks to Motovilov exhibit clairvoyance, or the gift of discerning the very thoughts of his disciple:

> The Lord has revealed to me," said the great elder [Seraphim], "that in your childhood you had a great desire to know the aim of our Christian life, and that you have continually asked many great spiritual persons about it."

To this Motovilov observed:

> I must admit, that from the age of twelve this thought had constantly troubled me. In fact, I had approached many clergy about it, however their answers had not satisfied me. This could not have been known to the elder.

Seraphim continued:

> But no one," continued St. Seraphim, "has given you a precise answer. They have said to you: 'Go to church, pray to God, do the commandments of God, do good—that is the aim of the Christian life.' Some were even indignant with you for being occupied with such profane curiosity and said to you, 'Do not seek things which are beyond you.' But they did not speak as they should. Now humble Seraphim will explain to you of what this aim really consists.
>
> However [good] prayer, fasting, vigil and all the other Christian practices may be, they do not constitute the aim of our Christian life. Although it is true that they serve as the indispensable means of reaching this end, the true aim of our Christian life consists of the **acquisition of the Holy Spirit of God**[33] (original emphasis).

A key portion of the dialogue between Motovilov and Seraphim begins when Motovilov inquires how he can recognize the Spirit of God:

"Nevertheless," I [Motovilov] replied, "I do not understand how I can be certain that I am in the Spirit of God. How can discern for myself His true manifestation within me?"

Fr. Seraphim replied: "I have already told you, your Godliness,[34] that it is very simple and I have related in detail how people come to be in the Spirit of God and how we can recognize His presence in us. So what do you want, my son?"

"I want to understand it very well," I said.

Then Fr. Seraphim took me very firmly by the shoulders and said: "We are both in the Spirit of God now, my son. Why don't you look at me?"

I replied: "I cannot look, Father, I replied, because your eyes are flashing like lightning. Your face has become brighter than the sun, and my eyes ache with pain."

Fr. Seraphim said: "Don't be alarmed, your Godliness! Now you yourself have become as bright as I am. You are now in the fullness of the Spirit of God yourself; otherwise you would not be able to see me as I am."

Then, bending his head towards me, he whispered softly in my ear: "Thank the Lord God for His unutterable mercy to us! You saw that I did not even cross myself; and only in my heart I prayed mentally to the Lord God and said within myself; 'Lord, grant him to see clearly with his bodily eyes that descent of Thy Spirit which Thou grantest to Thy servants when Thou art pleased to appear in the light of Thy magnificent glory.' And you see, my son, the Lord instantly fulfilled the humble prayer of poor Seraphim."[35]

At this point in their conversation, Seraphim begins to pose questions to Motovilov regarding what he is experiencing, with the evident goal of teaching him how to recognize the Holy Spirit. The dialogue that ensued could almost have been taken as a page out of Latter-day Saint missionary lessons:

"How do you feel now?" Fr. Seraphim asked me.

"Extraordinarily well," I said.

"But in what way? How exactly do you feel well?"

I answered: "I feel such calmness and peace in my soul that no words can express it."

"This, your Godliness," said Fr. Seraphim, "is the peace of soul of which the Lord said to his disciples: My peace I give unto you; not as the world gives, give I unto you. [John 14:27] . . .

"What else do you feel?"

"An extraordinary joy in all my heart."

And Fr. Seraphim continued: "When the Spirit of God comes down to man and overshadows him with the fullness of His inspiration, then the human soul overflows with unspeakable joy, for the Spirit of God fills with joy whatever He touches."[36]

Other portions of the *Conversation of St. Seraphim* may interest Latter-day Saint readers. He describes Adam and Eve in glorious terms:

Adam was made so wise by this breath of life, which was breathed into his face from the creative lips of God, the Creator and Ruler of all, that there has never been a man on earth wiser or more intelligent, and it is unlikely that there ever will be. . . . The Lord God also gave Eve the same wisdom, strength, unlimited power, and all the other good and holy qualities.[37]

Seraphim describes the fall of Adam and Eve as "premature and contrary to the commandments of God." He states that even after the fall, "many mysteries in connection with the future salvation of the human race were revealed to Adam as well as to Eve."[38]

During this famous conversation, Seraphim also explained that people can really meet God and speak with him. His comments here are similar to the teachings of Saint Symeon the New Theologian who taught the very same thing. Seraphim stated:

"At the present time," the elder replied, "Owing to our almost universal coldness to our holy faith in our Lord

Jesus Christ, and our inattention to the working of His divine Providence in us, and to the communion of man with God, we have gone so far that, one may say, we have almost abandoned the true Christian life. The testimonies of Holy Scripture now seem strange to us; when, for instance, by the lips of Moses the Holy Spirit says: 'And Adam saw the Lord walking in Paradise' (cf. Gen. 3:10), or when we read the words of the Apostle Paul: 'We went to Achaia, and the Spirit of God went not with us; we returned to Macedonia, and the Spirit of God came with us.' More than once in other passages of Holy Scripture the appearance of God to men is mentioned.

"That is why some people say: **'These passages are incomprehensible. Is it really possible for people to see God so openly**?' But there is nothing incomprehensible here. This failure to understand has come about because we have departed from the simplicity of the original Christian knowledge. Under the pretext of education, we have reached such a darkness of ignorance, that the things the ancients understood so clearly, seem to us almost inconceivable. Even in ordinary conversation, the idea of God's appearance among men did not seem strange to them. Thus, when his friends rebuked him for blaspheming God, Job answered them: 'How can that be when I feel the Spirit of God in my nostrils?' (cf. Job 27:3). That is, 'How can I blaspheme God when the Holy Spirit abides with me? If I had blasphemed God, the Holy Spirit would have withdrawn from me; but look! I feel His breath in my nostrils.'

"It is said that Abraham and Jacob saw the Lord and conversed with Him in exactly the same way, and that Jacob even wrestled with Him. Moses and all the people with him saw God, when he received the tablets of the law on Mount Sinai from God. A pillar of cloud and a pillar of fire, or in other words, the evident grace of the Holy Spirit, served as guides to God's people in the desert. People saw God and the grace of His Holy Spirit not during sleep, in dreams, or in the excitement of a disordered imagination, but truly and openly.

"We have become so inattentive to the work of our salvation, that we misinterpret many other words in Holy Scripture as well, all because we do not seek the grace of God and in the pride of our minds, do not allow it to dwell in our souls. That is why we are without true enlightenment from the Lord, which He sends into the hearts of men who hunger and thirst wholeheartedly for God's righteousness or holiness [emphasis added].

Seraphim's teachings show similarities to what Joseph Smith on the nature of God in the King Follett discourse. Granted, there is a broad gap between the Trinitarian and Latter-day Saint concepts of God (for Latter-day Saints, both the Father and Son have glorified, physical bodies). Still, important aspects of the teachings of these two men are similar (almost word-for-word). Consider this quote from Joseph's famous King Follet discourse:

> "**These ideas are incomprehensible to some,** but they are simple. It is the first principle of the gospel to know for a certainty the character of God, and to know that **we may converse with Him as one man converses with another**, . . ." (emphasis added in bold; compare to the bolded words for Seraphim above).

Seraphim's teachings also show similarity to Joseph's Teaching on the "other Comforter," also called the "Second Comforter." The quotation below is from an official New Testament Student manual of the restored Church of Jesus Christ:

> The Prophet Joseph Smith spoke of the two Comforters in this way:
>
> "There are two Comforters spoken of. One is the Holy Ghost, the same as given on the day of Pentecost, and that all Saints receive after faith, repentance, and baptism. This first Comforter [is the] Holy Ghost. ...
>
> "The other Comforter spoken of is a subject of great interest, and perhaps understood by few of this generation. After a person has faith in Christ, repents of his sins, and is baptized for the remission of his sins and receives the Holy Ghost, (by the laying on of hands), which is the first Comforter, then let him continue to humble himself before God, hungering and thirsting after righteousness, and

living by every word of God, and the Lord will soon say unto him, Son, thou shalt be exalted. When the Lord has thoroughly proved him, and finds that the man is determined to serve Him at all hazards, then the man will find his calling and his election made sure, then it will be his privilege to receive the other Comforter, which the Lord hath promised the Saints, as is recorded in the testimony of St. John, in the 14th chapter, from the 12th to the 27th verses.

"Note the 16, 17, 18, 21, 23 verses. ...

"Now what is this other Comforter? It is no more nor less than the Lord Jesus Christ Himself; and this is the sum and substance of the whole matter; that when any man obtains this last Comforter, he will have the personage of Jesus Christ to attend him, or appear unto him from time to time, and even He will manifest the Father unto him, and they will take up their abode with him, and the visions of the heavens will be opened unto him, and the Lord will teach him face to face, and he may have a perfect knowledge of the mysteries of the Kingdom of God" (in *History of the Church,* 3:380–81).[39]

Readers can compare the teachings above with similar instruction given by Saint Syme on the New Theologian in Chapter 12.

Lest future readers think that Motovilov exaggerated this account, or mistook the rays of the sun reflecting off the snow for a heavenly light, he starts his narrative specifically commenting on the weather conditions: It was a "gloomy" day; the sun was not shining.

"It was Thursday," writes Motovilov. "The day was gloomy. The snow lay eight inches deep on the ground; and dry, crisp snowflakes were falling thickly from the sky when St. Seraphim began his conversation with me in a field near his hermitage, opposite the river Sarovka, at the foot of the hill which slopes down to the river bank. He sat me on the stump of a tree which he had just felled, and squatted opposite me.[40]

Motovilov concludes his account with these words:

And during the whole of this time, from the moment when Fr. Seraphim's face became radiant, this illumination continued; and all that he told me from the beginning of the narrative till now, he said while remaining in one and the same position. The ineffable glow of the light which emanated from him I myself saw with my own eyes. And I am ready to vouch for it with an oath.[41]

The *Conversation of St. Seraphim* has its sceptics. The account reportedly lay unread for nearly seventy years, to be discovered and printed not long before Seraphim's canonization in 1903. In its initial edition, the *Conversation of St. Seraphim* was printed and bound together with another work, *The Great in the Small*.[42] It was also published in the Moscow News in 1903.[43]

The conditions under which *The Conversation of St. Seraphim* was found were unusual, to say the least. Publisher Sergey Nilus reportedly was given the document, in a jumbled, deplorable state, covered with "pigeon feathers and bird droppings."[44] Nilus received them from the widow of Motovilov, who was then a nun at the Diveyevo Convent, which is located near the monastery in Sarov where Seraphim served. Seraphim had in fact served as the spiritual advisor to the Diveyevo Convent. Motovilov's widow personally knew Seraphim.

To some, it might be hard to believe that such a valuable manuscript could lay undiscovered and neglected for so long. To these doubts, one has to consider as well that Nilus himself is a controversial figure, having later published an infamous anti-Semitic piece in 1905 that turned out to have been an earlier forgery.[45] One well-documented book links the publication in 1905 of this later anti-Semitic work to a possible czarist, anti-Semitic, anti-revolutionary plot hatched by the Tsar's security service in Paris.[46]

Author Richard Price takes the position that Motovilov "composed the text many years later," though he allows that Motovilov may actually have beheld the face of Seraphim shining like light. Overall, however, Price views Motovilov as "a maker of myths."[47]

In contrast, a 2005 work by scholar Ann Shukman reviews the various versions of the *Conversation of St. Seraphim* that have been published and reaches a different conclusion.[48] She states that it is "beyond doubt" that the miraculous event in question actually took place and "that the vision did indeed occur." In support of this, Shukman points to multiple other sources that mention the event, including letters from Motovilov and records kept at the Diveyevo Convent. These records contain references to the *Conversation of St. Seraphim* and a miraculous healing Seraphim performed for Motovilov in September 1831. Still, Shukman acknowledges that there are questions regarding who the real author of the *Conversation* is.

Other Orthodox writers take the published account of the *Conversation of St. Seraphim* even more seriously. Father Lazarus Moore, the author of the most complete English-language biography of Saint Seraphim, expresses the view the discovery of this manuscript as a "great miracle."[49]

Figure 9.2: Saint Seraphim Praying with Upraised Arms
Korennaya Monastery Kursk Region
Credit: Adobe Stock photo[50]

The *Conversation of St. Seraphim* is extremely popular with the Orthodox faithful, being perhaps the most widely read tract on Russian spirituality in the world (with the possible exception of the *Way of the Pilgrim,* mentioned above in Chapter 1). It is posted on numerous websites maintained by various Orthodox churches, in many countries and languages.[51]

Motovilov wasn't the only witness to have seen Seraphim's face shine with heavenly light. Another was a monastic novice, John Tikhonov. His account is notable not only for the description of the heavenly light that shone from Seraphim's face (described in the second paragraph below) but also for the account of a glorious vision that Seraphim experienced, in which he saw heaven and experienced its joys. Latter-day Saint readers will note similarities to Joseph Smith's vision of the celestial kingdom that is recorded in Doctrine and Covenants 137.[52]

Seraphim's vision of heaven is described in these words, included in Moore's biography of Seraphim:

> [W]hile I was reading in the Gospel of St. John the words of the Saviour: "In My Father's house are many mansions," (14:2) I, poor creature as I am, stayed my thought on them and desired to see those heavenly dwellings. Five days and nights I spent in vigil and prayer, asking the Lord for the grace of that vision. And indeed the Lord, in His great mercy, did not deprive me of consolation according to my faith; for He showed me those eternal mansions where I, poor earthly pilgrim, was caught up for a moment (whether in the body or out of the body, I do not know) and saw the unutterable heavenly beauty and those who dwell there: the Lord's Great Forerunner and Baptist John, the Apostles, holy hierarchs, martyrs and our Holy Fathers—Anthony the Great, Paul of Thebes, St. Sabbas, Onuphrius the Great, Mark of Thrace and all the saints shining with unspeakable glory and joy, which eye has not seen nor ear heard, neither has entered into the heart of man, (Is. 64:4; 1 Cor. 2:9) but which God has prepared for them that love him.

Tikhonov continues his account:

> With these words, Fr. Seraphim became silent. At the same time he leaned forward a little, his head (with closed eyes) bent down, and with the extended palm of his right hand he evenly (rhythmically) and gently stroked over his heart. His face gradually changed and gave out a wonderful light, and at the last it became so radiant that it was impossible to look at him.[53]

Recent scholarship suggests that this vision was included in the manuscript for the first published account in Russian of Seraphim's life and sayings, but was removed from the published account. This first work was published in 1841, after two years of review by church censors.[54]

Like Seraphim, Joseph Smith saw biblical figures in his vision, beholding Adam and Abraham in the celestial kingdom, as well as his father, mother, and brother, Alvin. Similarly, Seraphim saw prophets and Apostles from ages past, as well as many of the great spiritual fathers who are saints in the Catholic and Orthodox traditions, all shining with "unspeakable glory and joy."[55]

Regardless of any differences between the visions experienced by Joseph and Seraphim, both visions are remarkable in making both men eyewitnesses to the glory of heaven. The witness that both men left has served to inspire generations of faithful Latter-day Saints and Russian Orthodox believers, respectively.

Another highly interesting correlation to Joseph Smith's life is seen in an experience in which Seraphim heard the voice of the Lord speaking to him after a long period of prayer, which I reproduce here in the original Russian and in translation:

> Я, убогий Серафим, три дня и три ночи молил Господа, чтобы он лучше лишил меня Царствия Небесного, а их бы помиловал. Но Господь ответил: "Не помилую их, ибо они учат учениям человеческим и языком чтут Меня, а сердце их далеко отстоит от Меня.[56]

> I, humble Seraphim, for three days and three nights prayed to the Lord, that it would be preferable that he deprive me of the Kingdom of God, and spare them. But the Lord answered: "I will not have mercy on them, for they teach the doctrines of men and with their words honor me, but their heart is far from me."

Latter-day Saint readers will immediately see the similarity to words the Lord spoke to Joseph Smith during his First Vision (Joseph Smith—History 1:19); however, the context for Seraphim's revelation is different. Seraphim's words seem to have been understood in Russia as a prophecy that Orthodox bishops would someday become so ungodly that they would deny even the most important dogma of Christianity— namely, the Resurrection of Christ.[57]

To put these words in context, this is not an obscure statement. There are thousands of hits for this quotation on the internet. It has been reprinted in numerous books on Russian Orthodox topics. In substantially identical form, this quotation is also given in a modern English-language biography of Seraphim, in its reprint of excerpts from the memoirs of a nun who personally knew Seraphim in the early nineteenth century.[58]

[1] Biographies include Archimandrite Lazarus (Moore), *An Extraordinary Peace: St. Seraphim, Flame of Sarov* (Port Townsend, WA: Anaphora Press, 2009); Valentine Zander, *St. Seraphim of Sarov*, trans. Sister Gabriel Anne, with introduction by Father Boris Bobrinskoy (Crestwood, NY: St. Vladimir's Seminary Press, 1975); Constantine Cavarnos and Mary-Barbara Zeldin, *St. Seraphim of Sarov*, vol. 5 of *Modern Orthodox Saints* (Belmont, MA: Institute for Byzantine and Modern Greek Studies, 1993); and Helen Kontzevitch, *Saint Seraphim: Wonderworker of Sarov and his Spiritual Inheritance* (Wildwood, CA: St. Xenia Skete, 2004). I have generally taken this sketch from Moore's biography, referenced above.

[2] Recent research on Seraphim that examined archival sources supports a birth year of 1754. See V. A. Stepashkin, "Biografiya prepodobnogo Serafima Sarovskogo v svete arkhivnykh dokumentov," chap. 2 of *Prepodobnyy Serafim Sarvoskiy v istoriko-kul'turom i khudozestvennom nasledii Rossii*, in the series *Svyatyye Rossii* (Moscow: Leto, 2015) = В. А. Степашкин, Глава 2 "Биография преподобного Серафима Саровского в свете архивных документов," Преподобный Серафим Саровский в историко-культурном и художественном наследии России, Серия "Святые России" (Москва: Лето, 2015), 88–89.

[3] Based on tradition, Prokhoros was a nephew of Saint Stephen, later a bishop. Orthodox iconography depicts Prokhoros as the scribe of the Apostle John.

[4] Moore, *Extraordinary Peace*, 12. Elijah's day on the Julian calendar of the day was July 20, but the feast day is deemed to begin at sundown the day previous, thus the nineteenth.

[5] Interestingly, it is beneath Saint Clement's Basilica in Rome that Saint Cyril is buried; Cyril and his brother Methodius are responsible for creating the first written Slavic language and alphabet, which opened the way for Christianity to be preached in Central and Eastern Europe beginning in the ninth century. See Part I, Chapter 2.

[6] Moore, *Extraordinary Peace*, 353, s.v. "appearances of . . . Apostle John."

[7] Moore, *Extraordinary Peace*, 262; see also Michael D. Peterson,

"Seraphim of Sarov, St.", in William M. Johnson and Christopher Kleinhenz, eds., *The Encyclopedia of Monasticism*, vol. 2 (Paris: Routledge, 2000), 1146.

[8] Moore, *Extraordinary Peace*, 19. Dositheus instructed Prochorus to repeat what is known as the "Jesus Prayer," which I discuss below in connection with Hesychasm (see Chapter 4).

[9] The Monastery at Sarov was built starting in 1654 at the site of an old fort and had been the scene of miraculous occurrences, including the occasional appearance of bright, heavenly light that illuminated the location. The monks who led the Monastery at Sarov were at times subjected to imprisonment, despite their faithful service (or because of it). For example, the second leader of the monastery, one Father John, was imprisoned as a result of his efforts to labor among Old Believers, a Russian Orthodox group that rejected changes introduced into Orthodox practice in the seventeenth century. John died in prison. His successor, Father Ephraim, spent sixteen years in prison but later returned to the monastery.

[10] Mentioned in Isaiah 6:2, 6. According to *The Orthodox Study Bible,* Isaiah's vision that is reported here "has strongly influenced the development of Orthodox worship. For the Church, like heaven, has an altar, a throne, smoke from the incense, and believers singing 'Holy, holy, holy, the Thrice-Holy Hymn.'" See under Isaiah 6:1–6 in *The Orthodox Study Bible,* ed. Fr. Jack Norman Sparks (Thomas Nelson, 1993).

[11] "The Church's Teaching Concerning Angels," Orthodox Christian Information Center, Patrick Barnes, accessed July 28, 2019 http://orthodoxinfo.com/death/angels2.aspx.

[12] Moore, *Extraordinary Peace,* 43.

[13] Moore, *Extraordinary Peace*, 41.

[14] Moore, *Extraordinary Peace,* 42.

[15] Moore, *Extraordinary Peace*, 43.

[16] Moore, *Extraordinary Peace,* 42–43.

[17] Moore, *Extraordinary Peace*, 82.

[18] https://en.m.wikipedia.org/wiki/File:Serafim_and_a_bear.jpg: uploaded July 29, 2006, by Alex Bakharev.

[19] Some sources assert that Seraphim had close ties to Old Believer groups, the Russian Orthodox Christians who split with the main church after liturgical reforms were introduced in the seventeenth century. The point is disputed by mainstream Russian Orthodox sources.

[20] Numerous paintings of Seraphim confirm this point.

[21] Moore, *Extraordinary Peace,* 33.

[22] Moore, *Extraordinary Peace*, 29. Wednesdays and Fridays are designated as fasting days; however, these are partial fasts involving abstinence from specified foods. Some seasons of the year may involve entire days of complete fasting. The first three days following "Bright Monday" of Great Lent are days that, based on monastic practice, require

complete fasting until Wednesday night.

23 Moore, *Extraordinary Peace* , 33–34, 49.

24 Cited in many of the accounts of this event. See "Saint Seraphim of Sarov: On The Acquisition of the Holy Spirit," Orthodox Christianity, OrthoChristian.com, posted July 31, 2011, accessed July 29, 2019, http://www.pravoslavie.ru/english/47866.htm

25 See Joseph J. Cannon, "President Lyman's Travels and Ministry: Praying in St. Petersburg for the Land of Russia," *Millennial Star,* Aug. 20, 1903, 532.

26 Gary Browning, *Russia and the Restored Gospel* (Salt Lake City: Deseret Book, 1997), xix

27 For the early July date, see John Garrard and Carol Garrard, *Russian Orthodoxy Resurgent: Faith and Power in the New Russia* (Princeton, NJ: Princeton Universtiy Press, 2008), 61. For the date of July 23, see A. Viktorov, *Pereneseniye moshchey prepodobnogo Serafima Sarovskogo iz Moskvy v Diveyevo* (23 *iyuliya–1 avgusta 1991 g.*) А.Викторов, Перенесение мощей преподобного Серафима Саровского из Москвы в Дивеево (23 июля – 1 августа 1991 г.), January 15, 2008, accessed July 29, 2019, https://www.sedmitza.ru/text/753137.html.

28 August 1 is one of two feast days on the calendar for Saint Seraphim of Sarov. The other is January 2/15. August 2 was the feast of Elijah.

29 Some publications call it: "St. Seraphim of Sarov's Conversation With Nicholas Motovilov" or "Saint Seraphim of Sarov: On The Acquisition of the Holy Spirit."

30 The most detailed Russian-language biography of Seraphim, written by Saint Seraphim Chichagov, does not mention the *Conversation of St. Seraphim.* Orthodox scholar Ann Shukman quotes materials suggesting that Chichagov lacked confidence in Motovilov due to mental instability that he exhibited later in life; however, Shukman also points out that in his younger years (thus, when he knew Seraphim of Sarov), Motovilov was an educated man who held important posts, including as a conciliation judge, school inspector and later as a court councilor. See Ann Shukman, "The Conversation between St Seraphim and Motovilov: the author, the texts and the publishers," *Sobornost: Incorporating Eastern Churches Review* 27*,* no.1, 50. Chichagov was also the Orthodox bishop with jurisdiction over the Optina Monastery, where Nilus reportedly lived for a time with a woman he was not married to; this may have influenced Chichagov's view of the *Conversation of St. Seraphim.*

31 *The Blackwell Dictionary of Eastern Christianity*, Ken Parry, et al. (Malden, MA: Blackwell Publishers, 2001), s.v. "John Chrysostom," 441–2.

32 For internet versions of this account, see "Saint Seraphim of Sarov: On The Acquisition of the Holy Spirit," Orthodox Christianity, OrthoChristian.com, July 31, 2011, accessed July 29, 2019, http://www.pravoslavie.ru/english/47866.htm; "St. Seraphim's

Transfiguration in the Holy Spirit," Orthodox Christianity, OrthoChristian.com, August 1, 2017, accessed July 29, 2019 http://www.pravoslavie.ru/english/47867.htm; and "St. Seraphim of Sarov's Conversation With Nicholas Motovilov," Orthodox Christian Information Center, Patrick Barnes, accessed July 29, 2019 http://orthodoxinfo.com/praxis/wonderful.aspx.

[33] "Saint Seraphim of Sarov: On The Acquisition of the Holy Spirit," Orthodox Christianity, OrthoChristian.com, posted July 31, 2011, http://www.pravoslavie.ru/english/47866.htm.

[34] Seraphim often referred to people as "your godliness."

[35] See "St. Seraphim's Transfiguration in the Holy Spirit," Orthodox Christianity, OrthoChristian.com, posted August 1, 2017, accessed July 29, 2019 http://www.pravoslavie.ru/english/47867.htm.

[36] "St. Seraphim's Transfiguration."

[37] "Saint Seraphim of Sarov: On The Acquisition of the Holy Spirit," Orthodox Christianity, OrthoChristian.com, posted July 31, 2011, accessed July 29, 2019, http://www.pravoslavie.ru/english/47866.htm.

[38] "Saint Seraphim of Sarov."

[39] *New Testament Student Manual*, s.v. "John 14–16," accessed July 30, 2019, https://www.churchofjesuschrist.org/study/manual/new-testament-student-manual/introduction-to-the-gospel-according-to-st-john/chapter-26-john-14-16?lang=eng.

[40] *New Testament Student Manual*, s.v. "John 14–16."

[41] See "St. Seraphim's Transfiguration in the Holy Spirit," Orthodox Christianity, OrthoChristian.com, posted August 1, 2017, accessed July 29, 2019 http://www.pravoslavie.ru/english/47867.htm.

[42] Garrard and Garrard, *Russian Orthodoxy Resurgent*, 109–10.

[43] Moore, *Extraordinary Peace,* 111, n1.

[44] Moore, *Extraordinary Peace*, 109.

[45] John and Carol Garrard, *Russian Orthodoxy Resurgent*, 111–13. Unfortuantely, in 1905, *The Conversation of St. Seraphim* was bound and printed along with the anti-semitic work. This second work, *Protocols of the Elders of Zion,* has subsequently been shown to be a forgery. Author's Note: In all my research for this book (*Unexpected Parallels*), I have not encountered any information that connected Saint Seraphim of Sarov (1754–1833) with anti-Semitic views. In fact, in the famous Conversatuion of Saint Seraphim, he referred to the Jews (all Israelites) as "the holy Hebrew people, a people beloved by God" (See "Saint Seraphim of Sarov: On The Acquisition of the Holy Spirit," Orthodox Christianity, OrthoChristian.com, posted July 31, 2011, http://www.pravoslavie.ru/english/47866.htm. Seraphim's global esteem is seen in a 1994 publication in which Pope John Paul II made a favourable reference to him as an example of the power of prayer, citing him as the sole named, non-Catholic example among several noted Roman Catholic saints. This same publication discusses Judaism

extensively and unequivocally condemns anti-Semitism and the Holocaust of the Jewish people. See Pope John Paul II, *Crossing the Threshold of Hope*, Kindle (New York: Alfred Knopf, 1994 and 2005; translation 1994), Kindle locations 256 and 1077.

[46] John Paul II, *Crossing the Threshold*, locations 256 and 1077.

[47] Richard Price, "The Canonization of Seraphim of Sarov: Piety, Prophecy and Politics in Late Imperial Russia," Peter Clarke et al., eds., *Saints and Sanctity* (Woodbridge, United Kingdom: Boydell Press, 2011), 346–64.

[48] Shukman, "Conversation," 47–57.

[49] Moore, *Extraordinary Peace,* 111, n1. Moore's manuscript was itself lost for decades and rediscovered just prior to his death in 1992. Its rediscovery is something of a miracle in and of itself. See Moore, *Extraordinary Peace,* "The Manuscript," 322.

[50] DATEI-NR.: 259731341

[51] According to the *Conversation of St. Seraphim*, Seraphim told Motovilov that he would be able to retain the conversation in his memory forever; see Moore, *Extraordinary Peace*, 135. Latter-day Saint history presents a similar situation. Wilford Woodruff was blessed with the gift to remember Joseph Smith's sermons until he could write them down. *"I could write a sermon of Joseph's a week after it was delivered almost word for word, and after it was written, it was taken from me or from my mind. This was a gift from God unto me."* *Teachings of Presidents of the Church: Wilford Woodruff,* (2011), p. 125; available at: https://www.churchofjesuschrist.org/study/manual/teachings-wilford-woodruff/chapter-13?lang=eng&_r=1 [emphasis added].

[52] Joseph's vision is broader, revealing new or amplified truth regarding the afterlife; however, the visions of both men are remarkable and confirm basic Christian truths regarding the afterlife.

[53] Moore, *Extraordinary Peace*, 84–85.

[54] See L.I. Alekhina, "Istoriya publikatsiy pervykh zhizneopisaniy prepodbnogo Serafima Saranska," in Podarochi, *Prepodobnyy Serafim Sarovskiy* = "История публикаций первых жизнеописаний преподобного Серафима Саранска," Podarochi, Преподобный Серафим Саровский, 111–12. This source is a 2015 publication that contains chapters and sections authored by several historians. Beautifully illustrated, with detailed endnotes, the work seems to reflect careful scholarship.

[55] Moore, *Extraordinary Peace,* 84–85.

[56] This quote is found on thousands of websites in Russia. The original source seems to be a memoir of Elena Motovilova, the wife of Motovilov, as reported by Sergei Nilus. Motovilova later served as a nun in the Diveyevo Convent. See "Appendix—Elena Ivanovna Motovilova," in Helen Kontzevitch, *St. Seraphim: Wonder Worker of Sarov and His Spiritual Inheritance* (Wildwood, CA: St. Xenia Skete, 2004), p. 346.

[57] Moore's biography of Seraphim mentions a prophecy that was unpublished, "in order that it may not give offense," regarding the "fall of the members of the episcopate and their lack of zeal for the glory of God." It seems the monasteries were also within scope of this prophecy. The author then refers to the trials that the bishops and priests have borne under communism, and the fact that some "betrayed the holy Orthodox Church into the hands of their enemies." In context, I believe the prophecy Moore refers to is likely the one now found on many websites in Russia, which I cite. See Moore, *Extraordinary Peace,* 176, including n2. See also Kontzevitch, *Saint Seraphim*, "Appendix: Elena Ivanovna Motovilova," 346.

[58] Kontzevitch, *Saint Seraphim*, "Appendix: Elena Ivanovna Motovilova," 346.

10—The Elders of Optina and Others

The Optina monastery is located some four hours south of Moscow, near the town of Kozel'sk. As with other Orthodox monasteries and places of worship, Optina is a lovely place, composed of churches, monastic residences, and other structures. People who visit Optina are mainly pilgrims who come to pray and worship.

While Optina today is off the beaten path, in the nineteenth century it was the spiritual heart of Russia. For a century (1829–1923), a series of remarkable monastic elders (*startsy*, or старцы) served in Optina, engaging in a spiritual ministry that blessed the entire nation. The service of these monks so marked Russian society in their day that people great and small came to them for spiritual advice, including the famed novelists Tolstoy, Dostoevsky, and Gogol. Fourteen of the Elders of Optina have since been canonized by the Russian Orthodox Church.

Many of the Optina Elders were particularly reputed for "clairvoyance" (*prozorlivost'*, or прозорливость), which is also sometimes translated as "discernment"; this term refers to an elder's ability to perceive the very thoughts and spiritual needs of his visitors.

The photo on the left below (**Figure 10.1**) is of the angel standing atop the original "beautiful gate," or principal entry gate to the Optina Monastery (traffic today passes through a different gate). The photo in the middle (**Figure 10.2**) is a close-up of the Optina angel. The photo at right (**Figure 10.3**) is the angel Moroni, whose statue is found atop the spire of almost all Latter-day Saint temples (all photos by the author).

Figure 10.1   **Figure 10.2**

Figure 10.3

In connection with this discussion of the Optina Elders, it is worth considering a statement made by President Heber C. Kimball of the Church's First Presidency in 1860. In the quote below, he refers to the prophets of the lost tribes of Israel. Kimball seems to speak in the present tense in this quotation:

> So it is with the lost tribes of Israel; they are not asleep. God speaks to them through their Prophets, and *they are*

248

learning to be obedient and to be subject to the law of God[1] [emphasis added].

President Kimball is known in Latter-day Saint history for his prophetic gift.[2] His statement may fit nicely with the ministry of the Elders of Optina.

Consider this quotation from 1862. It was written by a Russian Orthodox novice monk from the Optina Monastery who described a miraculous event associated with his Elder, one Father Anthony:

> On November 8th, 1862, on the commemoration of the Archangel Michael, before Matins I heard in a dream an unknown voice telling me, "Your Elder, Fr. Anthony, lives a holy life and is a great Elder of God." Right after that the bell rang, and therefore all the words said by the mysterious voice became clearly imprinted in my memory. Meditating upon what I heard, I went to Matins. I passed by close to the building where the Elder lived and saw the cell where Fr. Anthony prayed. Out of nowhere there appeared a bright white, fiery cloud nearly eight feet long and about five feet wide; quietly and slowly it began to rise from the roof and disappeared in the heavenly region of the sky. This appearance startled me, and returning from Matins I wrote it down for remembrance. I didn't dare tell the Elders about it, but considered the vision as teaching me, the unworthy one, to have faith, devotion and *obedience to my Elder*, and as clear evidence of his pure, flaming and God-pleasing prayers[3] [emphasis added].

Monks such as the novice who penned this statement were taught *obedience*—to an Elder, to the commandments of God, and to the rules of the Orthodox Church; however, the ministry of the Elders of Optina was directed not just at fellow monks. Their ministry involved providing service and counsel for all who came to them for spiritual direction. This kind of eldership and mentoring presupposes that the listener is willing to follow the counsel of the Elder (and obey the commandments as well). The Elders of Optina also carried on extensive correspondence with people all over Russia who were seeking spiritual advice. The biographies of the Elders, as well as the website for the monastery at Optina contain abundant citations to these letters.

The literature regarding these elders is voluminous, so the lives of all these elders cannot all be described here. Elder Anthony (1795–1865) is mentioned in the story quoted above. The life of Anthony was marked by almost constant illness, yet despite this he lived to a ripe old age. Anthony had a gift for counseling others and reportedly healed many individuals of illness.[4] His biographer recounts many stories of Anthony's wise, inspired counsel given to people of all ages who came to him for advice.

Unlike monks of earlier eras, several photographs of Anthony as an older man exist. His joyous countenance seems to attest to the happiness and peace with which God blessed him, despite his lifelong battle with debilitating illnesses.

As another interesting quotation, consider the words below regarding another of the fourteen great Optina Elders—Elder Ambrose—who sat transfigured in heavenly light as a newly married couple came to him for advice. Recall that experiences involving transfiguring light are understood in Orthodoxy as part of deification and attest to the saintliness of those who shine with this light:

> They entered his cell (room). The Elder sat on his bed in a white monastic tunic and cap. In his hand was a prayer rope. His face was transfigured. It was somehow especially illuminated, and everything in his cell had taken on a solemn appearance. The visitors trembled and were seized with an inexpressible happiness. They could not utter a word and stood for a long time in a reverie, pondering the Elder's countenance. All around was quiet. Batiushka [the Elder] was silent. They came up to receive his blessing. He wordlessly made the sign of the cross over them. They glanced once more at this scene, so that they might forever preserve it in their hearts. The Elder still sat with the same transfigured face, immersed in contemplation of the heavenly world.[5]

This photo shows part of the wall in the gateway leading into the Optina Monastery. The murals depict fourteen Optina Elders who have been canonized by the Russian Orthodox Church. Saint Anthony is shown at right. On November 8, 1862, a pillar of heavenly fire about eight feet long and five feet wide was seen rising from the cell (room) where he was praying (photo by the author).

This same Ambrose was particularly noted for his ability to comfort people and give wise counsel, as is evident from this description of him on the Optina website:

> Discernment (*prozorlivost'*, прозорливость) and foresight were combined in Elder Ambrose with amazing, purely maternal tenderness of the heart, through which he was able to alleviate the most difficult sorrow and comfort the most mournful soul. Love and wisdom—these are the qualities that attracted people to the Elder. The old man's word was spoken with authority based on closeness to God, which gave him knowledge. It was a prophetic ministry.[6]

Ambrose is possibly the best known of the Elders of Optina. Like many monks who achieved great spirituality, Ambrose (born Aleksandr Grenkov) exhibited an early devotion to God. As a boy, he studied at a theological school in Tambov, Russia. His biographer relates an experience that occurred later, in 1838, when Ambrose (before becoming a monk) was teaching in a theological school. While walking in the forest one day, contemplating the things of God, Ambrose passed by a lovely waterfall. In its bubbling waters, Ambrose "clearly began to hear the words, 'Praise God, hold on to God!'"[7]

Later, during the summer vacation period, Ambrose visited a friend whose father was a priest. This friend urged Ambrose to seek advice for his future life from a hermit, one Father Hilarion, who was locally much sought after for counsel. This recluse was unequivocal in his advice, urging Ambrose to go to the monastery at Optina: "You are needed at Optina!"[8] Interestingly, Hilarion knew of the great reputation of the monastery at Sarov, where Saint Seraphim (1754–1833) had served; however, he commented, "They do not have the same kind of elders as they once did" (Seraphim had died only a few years before). Ambrose heeded this advice and later served for thirty years as the principal Elder, or *starets*, of the monastery at Optina.

Ambrose's biography contains many accounts attesting to his love, compassion, and spiritual gifts he employed in counseling others. His deep humility gave him a "prayerful state of being." It is said

251

that he often shed tears during prayer. Like other Elders of Optina, he was noted for his clairvoyance, having exhibited a frequent ability to discern the very thoughts of others and to perceive in each the inner state of their souls.

The Elders of Optina were immensely influential in Russian society, so much so that people small and great came to them for advice. The website for Optina currently has a list of notable people who came there for advice. It is a long list.[9]

Among the great writers who came to Optina, Tolstoy, Dostoyevsky, and Gogol top the list. Gogol penned an enthusiastic description of the Elders of Optina in a letter to Tolstoy, dated July 10, 1850, declaring that he had "never seen such monks anywhere . . . their faces tell everything."[10]

One author quotes the famous Russian-American playwright and actor Mikhail Chekhov (not to be confused with the more famous playwright *Anton Chekhov*), describing how an Elder named Nektary came to him in dreams, following that elder's death:

> "Two or three times following the Elder's death, I dreamt about him, and each time he gave me advice that delivered me from emotional difficulties which I, alone, did not have the strength to remove myself."[11]

Nektary was the last of the Elders of Optina and died in 1928, five years after Soviet authorities closed the monastery. The statement above attests to the influence of Elder Nektary on Chekhov. Nektary was himself a very learned man. In fact, in addition to studying spiritual texts, Nektary regularly studied works on philosophy, literature, mathematics, science, and art. He reportedly made the following statement while his face grew unusually bright, so much so that it was difficult to look upon him:

> "God not only allows, He demands that a man grow in knowledge. There is no stopping place in God's creation; everything moves; and even the angels do not remain in one rank, but ascend from step to step, receiving new revelations. And even if a man has studied for a hundred years, he must still go on to ever new knowledge. . . . You must work—years pass unnoticed while you work."[12]

Nektary's reading habits form another illustration of how each monastery, and even each monk, had an ability to prescribe or

252

follow a different routine. The key here is that any rule followed (i.e., a daily schedule or pattern for life and worship), or any individual routine observed by a monk, was invariably prescribed, or blessed by a mentoring elder.

Saint Sergius of Radonezh (Russia)

No work concerning Orthodoxy would be complete without mentioning another early *hesychast* monk, Saint Sergius of Radonezh (ca. 1319–1392), who came on the scene in Russia long before the Optina Monastery achieved its fame in the nineteenth century. Sergius is one of the greatest, if not the single greatest, spiritual figure in the history of the Russian Orthodox Church. The monastery he founded outside of Moscow in Sergiyev Posad, the Trinity Lavra, remains to this day one of the most important of the Russian Orthodox Church. In addition to being a spiritual center, its proximity to Moscow makes it an easy day-trip destination: tens of thousands of tourists and pilgrims make their way to the Trinity Lavra every year.

Sergius began his service as a monk by seeking solitude in the forest and there developing great spirituality. Later, other monks joined him, and a monastic community grew around him. Sergius reportedly sent his disciples out to found monasteries and preach the gospel widely in a process that has been referred to as "monastic colonization." Sergius thus set a pattern that resulted in the settlement and Christianization of a wide region in Russia:

> For the sake of the salvation of his soul a monk fled from the world to the woods across the Volga, and a layman clutched to him and with the former's help set up in that wood a new Russian secular community. Thus Great Russia of the upper reaches of the Volga was created through a joint effort of a monk and a lay Christian brought up in the spirit breathed into the Russian society by St. Sergey [Sergius].[13]

Sergius, too, experienced visions of light. For example, late at night on one occasion while he was praying, the monk saw an unusual light from heaven and heard a voice: "Sergius, the Lord has heard your prayers about your [spiritual] children!" Sergius then saw a flock of wondrous white birds. The voice continued to speak, telling him that the number of his disciples would multiply like the birds he was seeing, and his disciples would be adorned with great virtues should they follow in his footsteps.[14]   Indeed, his disciples—"whole legions of ascetics"—spread Russian culture and Christianity over a vast expanse of land to the north and east.[15]

Sergius is revered in Russia not just for his leadership in matters of faith, but also for his statesmanship. He was in a great measure responsible for bringing the warring princes of Russia to peace. Later, he gave his blessing to troops under the command of Prince Dmitriy of Moscow, who subsequently won a historic victory over Mongol-Tatar forces at Kulikovo. This battle marked the first time that Russian forces had defeated the Mongol-Tatars, who had ruled the region since at least 1240, when they destroyed Kiev.

At the time of Sergius's death in 1392, it is said that "an indescribable fragrance issued from his body, while his face shone with heavenly rapture" and was "as white as snow." [16]

Euthymius of Tarnovo (Bulgaria)

Saint Euthymius of Tarnovo (ca. 1327–1402), also known as Sai Evtimii, Patriarch Tarnovski, is an important figure in the history of Bulgaria. He was born about 1327 in the former Bulgarian capital of Veliko Trnovo and served as the patriarch of the Bulgarian Orthodox Church from 1375 to 1393.

Saint Euthymius of Tarnovo was a hesychast. He entered monastic life as a young man in the Kilifare Monastery, which was an important learning center at the time. He later served on Mount Athos and in Constantinople. Saint Euthymius also founded a theological academy and was a gifted scholar. He was the author of numerous religious and hagiographical works, including the life story of Saint John of Rila (see below). He retranslated older church works from the original Slavic language created by Cyril and Methodius (then five hundred years old) and is credited with reviving and updating Old Church Slavonic, inspiring similar reforms throughout Eastern Europe.

Saint Euthymius became a patriarch in times that were very difficult for Bulgaria. When Ottoman forces besieged the capital, Veliko Trnovo, Patriarch Euthymius personally led the defense of the city. In the end, the capital fell and Saint Euthymius of Tarnovo was sentenced to death. According to tradition, the executioner's hand turned to stone, or became motionless, at the very instant he attempted strike the fatal blow. Saint Euthymius spent the rest of his life in the Bachkovo Monastery, and after his death he was almost immediately proclaimed a saint.

The memory of Saint Eutychius continues to live in Bulgaria. His monument, on which flowers are always located, is located in the center of Sofia. His feast day is January 20.[17]

John of Rila (Bulgaria)

Saint John of Rila (876–946) was born in the village of Skrini near Sofia. A monastery with his name is the spiritual center in Bulgaria today. The monastery website has a short biography of John in English.[18] It gives this account for how God called him to monastic service:

> Long after his parents had died, some jealous and indolent people reproved him as a hypocrite utterly unfit for worldly life. Wearied and disturbed, John resolved to give all his possessions to the poor and "render unto Caesar that which is Caesar's" so that he might unhindered "render unto God that which its God's." And God "who called light to shine out of darkness" and "Who ordered Abraham: 'Get out of thy country and from thy kindred and go to the land that I will show thee,'" appeared to John in a dream speaking the very same words and pointed out the place where John might please Him. Awakening, he reflected upon the meaning of the vision and his heart burned with zeal "like a stag for the water springs." Like another David, he armed himself against the spiritual Goliath, and taking three stones - faith, hope and love-he put on the armor of righteousness and over his head the divine cover as a helmet of salvation. He entered the monastery of St. Dimitry, near Skrino, and was tonsured a monk, casting off with his hair all lust and carnal desire. Here he received his education, learned to read and write, and grew spiritually by studying the Holy Gospel.

After a period of service in the Monastery of St. Dmitry, John became a hermit, retreating into a wild mountain, living for many years in a cave. Later, he settled in a parched tree on Rila Mountain. He lived for years without any human contact (other than with a group of roving bandits), being ultimately discovered only when a heard of sheep mysteriously bolted in his direction, running a good distance before arriving at John's dwelling place.

After the shepherds arrived to retrieve the sheep, word began to spread of his miracles. Eventually, John's fame came to the attention of King Peter I of Bulgaria, who dispatched a team of experienced hunters with instructions that they not return until they located John in the wilderness. When they finally found John, they were exhausted and hungry. John fed them miraculously with a small loaf of bread, just as the Savior himself had done anciently. Later, King Peter himself travelled to the mountain where John lived, to receive his blessing. John declined to descend the mountain, but rather bowed to the King from a distance by command of God. John later turned away gifts of gold that were proffered by the King, giving this explanation:

> "'Wealth is proper to a king's state,' it is to be used for his arms and his army, not for his own pleasure, but most of all it is for the disabled and the poor, for the naked and the homeless. Therefore, if you wish to inherit the kingdom of heaven, be generous as our heavenly Father is generous. Flee injustice and plundering. Be meek, calm and accessible, and let your eyes be opened for all. 'Let the oil of your mercy run over all, but let not your left hand know what your right hand is doing! Let the poor be happy when they leave your palace! Your princes curry praises on their lips! Your purple robe shine with the light of virtue! Your sighs and tears be your offspring! The remembrance of death be always on your mind! Your thoughts be unceasingly centered upon longing for the Kingdom! Prostrate yourself at the feet of your mother the church. Diligently kneel and bend your neck before those who rule her, so that the King of kings and Lord of lords, when He sees your diligence, will give you the reward which 'eye has not seen, nor ear heard neither has entered into the heart of man - that which God has prepared for those who love Him.'" The king read the message and held the saint's words in high esteem. Kissing the message with

256

love, he carried it close to his heart like a precious treasure. He read it often, for it helped to drive away the spiritual darkness of worldly confusion.

Saint John of Rila's disciples founded a church in a cave as well as a monastery during his lifetime, with John serving as its abbot. The number of monks serving with him eventually reached 66. John left a last testament with his spiritual admonitions that is a classic of Bulgarian literature.[19] Pictured here are photos from the monastery he founded.

Figure 10.4: Rila Monastery, Bulgaria.
Credit: Adobe Stock photo.[20]

Figure 10.5: One of many murals in the Rila Monastery.
Credit: Adobe Stock photo.[21]
Explanation for Figure 10.5: The three great patriarchs, Abraham, Isaac, and Jacob are seated, with Christ to their right. Saint Peter in blue is seen holding the key to the Kingdom of God. The four great rivers described in the Bible that flow from Eden are pictured (Pison, Gihon, Tigris, and the Euphrates—see Genesis Chapter 2).

Nicodemus of Tismana (also called Nicodème de Tismana, Nikodim de la Tismana or Nikodim Grcic)

Nicodemus of Tismana was born in the early fourteenth century ca. 1420. He is believed to be a native of Macedonia, or possibly of Kosovo. As his father was a Greek, he is often called *Nikodim Grcic*. Saint Nicodemus learned to read the Bible as a child and had a gift from his youth of working miracles that has not weakened even after his death.

Although he was born into a family with wealth and rank, Nicodemus chose to serve as a monk on Mount Athos as a young man. Like many other monks profiled in this work, Nicodemus was a hesychast. On Athos, he quickly proved a gifted student, learning Greek and Slavic languages, excelling at theology, oratory and even miniature painting and calligraphy.

Later he returned to Serbia where he founded monasteries and churches. Nicodemus had a great deal of support in influential circles which was helpful in raising funds for the monasteries he founded. When he settled in Wallachia (located in modern Romania) in 1378, St. Nichodemus founded the monastery of Tisman. He was dedicated to Christ with his disciples, and he was a great organizer of monastic life. At the end of his life Nikodemus lived as a hesychast, in a cave near the Tisman monastery.

Because of the many miracles he has done during his life, St. Nicodemus was proclaimed a saint soon after his death. Although originally buried in the Tisman Monastery, it is unknown today where his remains are. In the monastery there is only one finger that is stored in a golden suitcase. The Orthodox Church celebrates St. Nicodeme on December 26th.[22]

Davit Garejeli (Georgian)[23]

Davit Garejeli (sixth century) is one of thirteen Georgian fathers who arrived from Mesopatamia as missionaries to support Christianity in Georgia. Davit was born Syria (or Assyria, depending on the source). He was an ascetic monk and an influential Georgian enlightener. In Georgia, Saint Davit and his spiritual son Lucian settled near Kartli, whose people were then being attacked by Persian fire-worshipers. Saint Davit spent his days in prayer for the salvation of the souls of those in the city, and once a week visited the city to preach. Nevertheless, during his mission, he encountered resistance from fire-worshipers who tried in various ways to discredit him.

After a time, Saint Davit and Lucian moved to a cave in the desert where their days were spent in prayer. Their meals were taken only from nearby plants and from the bark of trees. At one point the plants died out because of the heat, and God sent them deer, whose milk was miraculously transformed into cheese. There were many people in the desert of Garea who wanted to learn of Christ. A monastery was founded in this location that grew in size and prominence, becoming today one of the best-known landmarks in Georgia. Its importance to world heritage has been recognized by UNESCO.[24]

Saint Davit went to Jerusalem late in life on a pilgrimage, but he did not enter the city, considering himself unworthy to walk the footsteps of Jesus. He decided to only observe Jerusalem from the city gates. His arrival near Jerusalem prompted an angel to appear to the Patriarch of Jerusalem, who gave instructions to the Patriarch regarding stones that Davit was carrying back to Georgia. Davit was persuaded by messengers to leave two behind. He eventually returned to Georgia, still retaining one marvelous stone from Jerusalem. This stone is still believed to have miraculous powers.

George the Hagiorite (Georgia)

One of the most influential Georgian saints (1009–1065). He was prepared to devote his life to God from his childhood. David was born to a pious and reputable Georgian family, studied in Constantinople and was a religious writer, translator and calligrapher.

During his lifetime, George worked towards intercultural cooperation between Georgia and Byzantium. He translated many works from the Greek language that did not yet exist in Georgian. In addition to being distinguished by his valuable work, Saint George the Hagiorite also is remembered as one of only a few Eastern churchmen who supported his separated Western brethren. Although Saint George was completely Orthodox, he did not exclude the possibility of various liturgical practices. He lived at a time when the church split into Eastern and Western halves (1054), but believed that the same Christian faith could have various forms of worship.

St. George traveled to the Holy Land during his lifetime and stayed on Mount Athos. In 1056, he withdrew to the monastery of the Black Mountain near Antioch, but continued to translate and write books. He died in Constantinople, but his remains were later transferred to Holy Mountain.

The accomplishments of Saint George the Hagiorite were extremely important for Georgia. He improved the translations of the Gospels, as well as the writings of John of Damascus, Basil of Caesarea and others, and his overall work established the foundations of the principles of Christian and monastic life in Georgia.[25]

Daniil Sihastrul (also Daniel the Hesychast)(Romanian/Moldovan)[26]

Daniil Sihastrul or Daniel the Hesychast (d. 1496) was a great Romanian spiritual guide, hermit, and advisor to Stephen the Great, a Moldovan prince. He was born at the beginning of the fifteenth century as Demetrius in a small village in the north of Moldova (a territory now divided between Romania and Moldova)

260

in a modest family. Although he did not receive more than a rudimentary education, his life's work was of such importance that he is still remembered in Romania where he is known as Saint Daniil.

Demetrius as a child became an apprentice to the bishop in Rădăuți, and at age of 16 became a monk in the Monastery of Saint Nicholas, receiving the name David. By nature, Daniil preferred peace and quiet for which he took the vows of the so-called "great Skim" (Great Schema), and on that occasion he was named Daniel, or Daniil. The monastic tradition of "great Skim" is reserved for monks who have attained great spirituality. Many of these monks prefer to alone in the forests and caves. Accordingly, Daniil retired to a remote area near the village of Putna where he lived as a hermit. In that forest, a small chapel was carved in stone and there was a small prayer room underneath in which Daniel lived. This place attracts many pilgrims today.

Daniil served as the spiritual guide for Stephen the Great, a Moldovan prince (or *voivode*) who enjoyed great success in defending his realm from the encroachments of the Ottoman Turks. After his father (Bogdan II) was assassinated, Stephen consulted with Daniel, who prophesied that he would one day become ruler.

Stephen also consulted with Daniil in connection with his military campaigns. Following Stephen's defeat by the Turk's in 1476 at Războieni, Stephen went to see Daniil. The saint was in the process of praying inside his cave at the time, and simply gave Daniel instructions, or "orders" through the door that Stephen must not yield the land to the Turks. That Stephen could hold on to this region seemed impossible at the time, but several years later, Stephen's forces prevailed. In commemoration of this victory, Stephen built the Monastery of Voroneț, dedicated to Saint George. When this monastery was completed, Daniel moved his residence there and served as the monastery's abbot until his death in 1496.

Saint Daniil devoted his life to reflecting on spiritual and religious issues. He was one of the founders of the Hesychast movement in northern Moldova, and his influence spread to his disciples in the forests, monasteries and deserts around Voronet.

[1] Heber C. Kimball, "Practical Religion," in *Journal of Discourses* 8, July 1, 1860, 107.

[2] For example, in 1848, at a time when newly arrived Latter-day Saint pioneers in Utah were short of needed goods, Kimball prophesied that merchandise would soon be "sold in the streets of Great Salt Lake City cheaper than in New York." This seemingly implausible prophecy came true the next year in 1849, as hundreds of wagons loaded with goods arrived in Salt Lake City on their way to the California gold mines. Some of their owners sold the goods off at bargain prices, in order to lighten their loads before the dangerous crossing through the desert and Sierra Nevada mountains on the way to California. See also "Heber C. Kimball," BYU Religious Studies Center, accessed July 30, 2019, https://rsc.byu.edu/archived/prophets-and-apostles-last-dispensation/first-counselors-first-presidency/3-heber-chase.

[3] Clement Sederholm, *Elder Anthony of Optina*, vol. 2 of *Optina Elders Series* (Platina, CA: St. Herman of Alaska Brotherhood, 1994), 97–98.

[4] See "Rev. Ambrose of Optina" (in Russian; translation by the author), Optina Pustyn' = Оптина Пустынь, accessed July 30, 2019, http://www.optina.ru/starets/amvrosiy_life_short/.

[5] Sergius Chetverikov, *Elder Ambrose of Optina* (Platina, CA: St. Herman Press, 1997), 224.

[6] "Rev. Ambrose of Optina."

[7] Sederholm, *Elder Ambrose*, 56; and Stephen Fanning, *Mystics of the Christian Tradition* (London, 2001), 63.

[8] Sederholm, *Elder Ambrose*, 54; and Fanning, *Mystics,* 63.

[9] "The Optina Monastery and Russian Culture" (in Russian), Optina Pustyn' = Оптина Пустынь, accessed July 30, 2019, http://www.optina.ru/history/optina/.

[10] "Blessed Optina" (in Russian), Optina Pustyn' = Оптина Пустынь, accessed July 31, 2019, http://www.optina.ru/history/optina/.

[11] R. Andrew White, "Embodying the Disembodied: *Hesychasm*, Meditation and Michael Chekhov's Higher Ego," in Lance Gharavi, *Religion, Theater, and Performance: Acts of Faith,* (London: Routledge, 2011), 67.

[12] Cf. Doctrine and Covenants 130:18–19; quoted on the website of the Optina Monaster, accessed July 31, 2019 https://www.optina.ru/nektariy_pavlovich/3. The full quote in Russian reads: Однажды старец сказал: "Бог не только разрешает, но и требует от человека, чтобы тот возрастал в познании. В Божественном творчестве нет остановки, все движется, и Ангелы не пребывают в одном чине, но восходят со ступени на ступень, получая новые откровения. И хотя бы человек учился сто лет, он должен идти к новым и новым познаниям... И ты работай. В работе незаметно пройдут годы". В это время лицо его было необыкновенно светлым, таким, что трудно было смотреть на него."

[13] *St. Sergey of Radonezh* (Moscow: Panorama Publishers, 1992), 136 (bilingual Russian and English).

[14] M. V. Tolstoy, *Historiya russkoy Tserkvi: Rasskazy iz istorii russkoy tserkvi* (Saint Petersburg: Izdaniye Spaso-Preobrazhenskogo Valaamskogo monastirya, 1991) = М. В., Толстой, История русской Церкви: Рассказы из истории русской церкви (Санкт-Петербург: Издание Спасо-Преображенского Валаамского монастыря, 1991), 183. See also "St. Sergius: Wonderworker of Radonezh," October 8, 2008, accessed July 31, 2019, http://www.pravmir.com/article_386.html.

[15] Eugene Smirnoff, *Russian Orthodox Missions* (London: Rivingtons, 1903), 4.

[16] "Saint Sergius, wonderworker of Radonezh," Orthodoxy and the World, Pravmir.com, http://www.pravmir.com/article_386.html; and "Athlete Of Virtues—St. Sergius Of Radonezh, Commerated July 5/18; September 25/October 8," Pravoslaviye, http://www.pravoslavie.ru/47628.html, both sites accessed July 30, 2019.

[17] See generally Encyclopedia Brittanica, s.v. "Euthymius Of Tŭrnovo Orthodox Patriarch," https://www.britannica.com/biography/Euthymius-of-Turnovo; and "We honor the memory of St. Evtimii – Patriarch Tarnovski – Society," January 20, 2019, accessed July 31, 2019 https://tech2.org/bulgaria/we-honor-the-memory-of-st-evtimii-patriarch-tarnovski-society/.

[18] See generally "The Life of st. John of Rila," accessed July 31, 2019, https://rilskimanastir.org/en/st-john-of-rila/zhitie-na-sv-ioan-rilski/ (quotations are taken from this source); "Repose of the Venerable John the Abbot of Rila," under August 18, accessed July 31, 2019, https://oca.org/saints/lives/2019/08/18/102336-repose-of-the-venerable-john-the-abbot-of-rila; and *The Encyclopedia of Monasticism,* eds. William Johnston and Christopher Kleinhentz (London and New York: Routledge, 2000), p. 226, s.v. "Bulgaria."

[19] See the English translation, "Testament of St. John of Rila," Pravoslaviye accessed July 31, 2019, http://www.pravoslavieto.com/docs/eng/Testament_of_John_of_Rila.htm

.

[20] DATEI-NR.: 240196165

[21] DATEI-NR.: 30150953

[22] See generally, "St Nicodemus The Sanctified Of Tismana," Basilica News Agency, December 26, 2016, accessed July 31, 2019 http://orthochristian.com/99752.html; "Nicodème De Tismana," accessed July 31, 2019 https://fracademic.com/dic.nsf/frwiki/1231714; his labors in what now is Romania are described s.v. "Romania," in *The Encyclopedia of Monasticism,* 1079–80.

[23] See "St. David of Gareji," accessed July 31, 2019 https://www.holytrinityorthodox.com/calendar/los/May/07-08.htm and "St. David Gareji, and Ven. Lucian, spiritual son of St. David," accessed

July 31, 2019 https://oca.org/saints/lives/2007/06/09/502-st-david-gareji-and-ven-lucian-spiritual-son-of-st-david.

[24] See "David Gareji Monasteries and Hermitage," accessed July 31, 2019 http://whc.unesco.org/en/tentativelists/5224/.

[25] See generally, "George the Hagiorite," Oxford Reference, accessed July 31, 2019 https://www.oxfordreference.com/view/10.1093/oi/authority.20110803095848935; and Saint George the Hagiorite, Mystagogy Resource Center, accessed July 31, 2019 https://www.johnsanidopoulos.com/2018/06/saint-george-hagiorite-1065.html (drawn from Lives of Georgian Saints (Platina, CA: Saint Herman of Alaska Brotherhood, 2006), 237-241.

[26] See generally, "Venerable Daniel the Hesychast," commemorated December 18, accessed August 1, 2019 https://oca.org/saints/lives/2014/12/18/149006-venerable-daniel-the-hesychast; "Saint Daniel the Hermit," accessed August 1, 2019, http://theodialogia.blogspot.com/2011/12/saint-daniil-hermit.html; "15th Century Monk Built This Stone House to Find Solitude," Ancient Origins, accessed August 1, 2019, https://www.ancient-origins.net/history-famous-people/15th-century-monk-built-stone-house-find-solitude-009470.

11—Saint Alexander of Svir (1448-1553)

Over the last five hundred years, Saint Alexander of Svir has been one of the best-known Russian saints. He is the only Russian Orthodox saint to have experienced a vision of the entire Holy Trinity (1508). According to Alexander's biography, this heavenly manifestation was a glorious occurrence. The three persons of the Trinity appeared "in most bright garments and clothed in white, beautiful in purity, shining more than the sun and illuminated with unutterable heavenly glory, and each holding a staff in his hand."[1]

Much of this overview of Alexander's life has been taken from his official biography that was written only twelve years following his death. The author was one Irodion, a disciple who succeeded Svir as abbot of the monastery he founded.[2] In addition, some facts are cited from a modern tribute entitled *St. Alexander; Karelian Miracle Worker*, published in Finland in 1996 in connection with an exhibit held in Alexander's honor in Helsinki. This latter work refers to Alexander as "the most significant figure in Karelia[3] of late medieval and early modern times."[4]

Besides the above, this sketch of Alexander's life and of his monastery has been supplemented with other sources, including materials provided by the staff of Alexander's monastery.[5] All of these sources underscore the important role the monastery played for centuries in the spiritual life of the northwest of Russia. Over the centuries, Alexander's monastery has sometimes been informally referred to as the as the "Lavra of the North." The term "Lavra" (or Laura) is reserved for only a few of the most important Orthodox monasteries. Only two Russian Orthodox monasteries have been designated as Lavras: the Trinity Lavra of St. Sergius, just outside Moscow, and the Alexander Nevsky Lavra in Saint Petersburg.

Alexander was born in the village of Mandera near the Oyat' River in the Novgorod Republic, east of Lake Ladoga. Events leading to Alexander's birth pointed toward an important destiny. His

265

parents already had children, but after several years of being unable to conceive another child, they prayed and visited a nearby monastery dedicated to the "Entrance of the Most Holy Mother of God."[6] There they fasted and prayed to Mary for a child, later receiving a divine manifestation in which they heard a voice that said:

> "Rejoice, blessed couple; for the Lord has heard your prayer, and you shall give birth to a son with the name of consolation: for God shall grant in his birth consolation to His churches."[7]

Alexander of Svir was given the name "Amos" at birth, having been born on the feast day of this Old Testament prophet on June 15, 1449.[8] He was given the name "Alexander" later, when he was tonsured a monk at age 26.

Alexander's path to monastic life seems to have been charted early in life. His parents arranged for him to study the holy scriptures as a boy, but he initially had no gift for learning. After fervent prayer, however, Alexander received greatly enhanced abilities, soon excelling and surpassing his classmates. His biography describes him as a serious-minded child, not inclined to games, yet one who was meek, loved the poor, and had great esteem for monasticism.

As an adult, Alexander prayed for an opportunity to lead a monastic life, desiring specifically to enter the Monastery of the Lord's Transfiguration on Valaam Island in the northern reaches of Lake Ladoga. He had heard of the fame of this place, which indeed has long been one of the most noted Russian monasteries; however, its northerly location also makes it one of the most remote. Valaam is subject to harsh, long winters and was accessible only by boat.

Later, several monks from Valaam visited the village near Alexander's home, and he had the opportunity to question one of the elders regarding life at their monastery. The elder perceived the young man's earnest desire to embark on a monastic life and described the way to the monastery, which was a long journey from Alexander's home. This elder visited Alexander's parents and spoke of a great future for him, telling them, "Your son will be great before the Lord and a servant of the Holy Trinity."[9]

Alexander later left for Valaam without informing his parents, indicating only that he was headed to a nearby village for a "certain business." After receiving his parents' blessing for this stated purpose, Alexander actually started out to Valaam, taking nothing but his clothing and a little bread; it was three years before his parents actually learned where he had gone.

Alexander's journey to reach Valaam took him perhaps two-hundred kilometers, through remote and inhospitable country as he journeyed west towards Lake Ladoga and Valaam Island. His biography says nothing about what he ate on this journey (since he only had a little bread when he set out); however, a fair assumption is that Alexander lived off the land as he travelled. Locals living near the monastery today confirm that Alexander was an ethnic Vepsian. The Vepsians were a Finnic people who were skilled outdoorsmen. This fact may account for how Alexander was able to travel and live in such harsh conditions.

After a time, Alexander reached the river Svir', which he then crossed, traversing a landscape that was "very desolate, and forested, and inaccessible." As it grew dark, Alexander walked toward a nearby lake, looking for a resting spot for the night. This lake is shown as "Roshchinskoye Lake" or "Рощинское Озеро" on modern maps (meaning "Grove Lake"). It is a small, picturesque body of water, perhaps only covering a few hundred acres.

Figure 11.1: Roshchinskoye Lake and the Transfiguration Cloister of the Holy Trinity St. Alexander of Svir Monastery. Credit: Photo by the author.

Alexander prayed to the Lord Jesus Christ after arriving at this spot, asking that he be "directed on the path of salvation," and then fell asleep. Soon, he heard a voice, which said:

> O youth, the path is straight for you to go where you wish to go, to the monastery of the All-merciful Savior at Valaam; go in peace, and labor there unto the Lord for a sufficient time, and then you will be in this place and build a monastery, and many will be saved by you.[10]

After hearing these words, Alexander's biography recounts that "a great light also appeared" with "a certain bright ray resting upon him." Overcome first with fear, then with joy, Alexander shed "fountains of tears" and set off toward Valaam.

During part of his journey to Valaam, Alexander was guided by a mysterious traveler, or monk, who helped show him the way, walking with him for a number of days. Together, the two made rapid progress in their travels, where others would only make it in a longer time. As they approached Valaam, Alexander stopped to pray, then looked for his companion, but could not find him. Alexander concluded that this man was in reality an angel of God who had been sent to assist him.[11]

Upon arrival at the monastery on Valaam, Alexander met the abbot and bowed down in front of him, begging in tears that he be made a monk. The abbot duly cautioned the young man regarding the rigors and sorrows of monastic life and, upon Alexander's continued entreaty, gave his assent and tonsured the young man, giving him the monastic name by which he is still known: Alexander.

During part of his time on Valaam, Alexander lived in a cave in primitive conditions. Patriarch Kirill of the Russian Orthodox Church commented in 2016, that if someone in our day had managed to live even one winter in such conditions, people would be writing and talking about it.[12]

While Alexander was at Valaam, his father came to visit and begged his son to return home. Alexander, of course, refused and, in fact, persuaded his father to become a monk. Before long, both parents embarked (separately) on a monastic life, being given the names Sergius and Barbara. Both have also been canonized and are considered saints in the Russian Orthodox tradition.

In 1485, seven years after arriving at Valaam, Alexander heard a voice while praying that instructed him to return to the place that had previously been shown to him. Along with the voice, there was a great light that pointed towards the east and south— Roshchinskoye Lake—where Alexander eventually built his monastery.

Alexander returned to this location, taking nothing with him but his clothing. Arriving at the place and finding it once again illuminated by light, he built a small cabin and made up his mind to remain at that spot and repose there (in death) for "ages of ages." This was a spot where no man had ever lived, so truly an unspoiled, remote location.[13]

While living in this remote location, Alexander one day heard a voice from heaven, which said:

> Alexander, as you have kept My commandments from your youth, you have frequently passed through a narrow and most sorrowful path; wherefore, I have prepared for you a countless multitude of people, as before I told you. Do not refuse them, but receive them with outstretched arms, and you shall be their instructor unto salvation.[14]

Subsequent to this experience, Alexander's remote dwelling place was discovered by a passing nobleman, Prince Andrey Zavalishin, who was hunting and by chance had pursued a deer that led him to Alexander's location. Zavalishin explained to Alexander that he had observed several miraculous occurrences on this very spot:

> And I believe that it was not a deer which I was pursuing, but a certain power of God that brought me to your holiness, that I might receive your holy blessing and prayer. For I should inform you that previously when I have gone out hunting in this wilderness, many times I have seen right on this spot, sometimes as it were a fiery pillar standing, and sometimes a certain divine ray shining,

and sometimes a bright smoke ascending from the earth to the heights.[15]

Alexander and Zavalishin formed a lasting bond; Zavalishin himself was eventually tonsured a monk. He founded his own monastery and has been canonized as well. He is known as Saint Adrian of Ondrusov.

From this point on, Alexander could no longer remain undiscovered in the wilderness. Many men came to him, wishing to join him in monastic life. These included one of his own brothers, John. His monastery began to take shape as the men labored under his leadership and began to till the ground and provide for their own needs, benefited on occasion by Zavalishin's generosity and donations.

During this time, Alexander still maintained his own hut as a hermitage where he lived. On one particular evening, as Alexander walked towards this hermitage, he had an encounter with "a countless multitude of demons, as it were a great army, leaping at him with great rage and gnashing their teeth."[16] According to his biography, Alexander was not afraid, but rather "like a good warrior of Jesus Christ, being armed with prayer" he repulsed the demons as "a fiery flame came out of his mouth."

Alexander soon arrived at his hut, when an angel appeared:

> I am an Angel of the Lord, sent by God to preserve you from all the deceptions of the cunning devil and to remind you of the divine visions which came to you before in this place where you have settled, that His command may be executed: for the Lord has chosen you to be a guide for many to salvation. I declare to you that it is God's will that you build a church in this place to the name of the Holy Trinity, and that you gather brethren and establish a monastery.[17]

Alexander's biography records numerous instances when Alexander was given heavenly instructions, all essentially bearing the same message: he was to build a monastery, gather disciples, and help lead people to salvation.[18] The last such message was delivered to him by the Lord himself.

The angel's promise that Alexander would be a "guide for many to salvation" is consistent with the service performed by other

270

"colonist monks" throughout Russian history. Alexander's labors in particular helped to implant Christianity among Finnish tribes in the upper northwestern region of Russia.

In addition, labors by monks such as Alexander served not only a spiritual mission but also ultimately formed part of a great nation-building process that helped peacefully integrate various tribes into the great-Russian nationality. As one Orthodox cleric wrote in 1903, through these missionary efforts, the "native learned the living, colloquial Russian language, love for the Church and her services, ceremonies and fasts, a moral form of family and social life, the habit of work, etc.; and at the same time he learned to recognize himself as a Russian and a member of the Russian State."[19] From today's vantage point, such sentiments may seem quaint (teaching the natives the habit of work, etc.) and one may find the loss of native culture a lamentable development; however, the overall point regarding nation-building and the role of monk-colonists is undeniable.

In 1508, Alexander had the vision of the Holy Trinity, or Godhead, for which he is best known. While praying one night in his hermitage, a great light appeared, and he saw three heavenly beings approach him, each wearing "most bright garments and

clothed in white, beautiful in purity, shining more than the sun and illuminated with unutterable heavenly glory, and each holding a staff in his hand."[20]

Figure 11.2: Small chapel (часовня) marking the spot where the Holy Trinity Appeared to Saint Alexander Svir in 1508.
Credit: Photo by the author.

During this vision, Alexander was commanded, once again, to build a monastery and gather brethren. He was uncertain at this point of one thing:

> My Lord, be not angry at me, that I have dared to speak before Thee; inform me by what name this church shall be called which Thy love of mankind desires to build on this spot."[21]

Alexander was commanded at that point to build his church in the name of the "Father and the Son and the Holy Spirit, the Trinity One in essence."

The Russian Orthodox Church understands this vision as having been an appearance of all three persons of the Holy Trinity, or of angels representing the Trinity. The words "one in essence" shows that these three glorious persons were understood as ultimately being a manifestation of God in a way consistent with the Nicene Creed.

This vision is taken seriously by the Russian Orthodox Church. On April 17, 2016, Patriarch Kirill—the head of the Russian Orthodox Church—visited the monastery that Alexander built and blessed a small chapel that stands on the exact spot where Alexander of Svir saw the Father, Son and Holy Spirit of the Holy Trinity (see Figure 11.2). Kirill delivered a fine sermon praising Alexander, describing Alexander's spiritual accomplishments, explaining that no man could have achieved what Alexander did without help from above (i.e., from God). The Patriarch explained that God was present in the life of Saint Alexander, and that Alexander sought to be closer to God, understanding that the further one is from crowds, the closer one can become to God. Patriarch Kirill further explained, "thus, to see God, one must live quietly and protect himself from the vanity of the world."[22]

Sometime later, Alexander and the brethren were attempting to channel water from another lake in the vicinity toward the larger Roshchinskoye Lake, which was located at a lower elevation. Their efforts triggered an unexpected result, causing a large volume of water to gush out of the upper lake and descend toward the monastery as a wall of water. Fearing imminent damage to the monastery, Alexander began to pray to "God the Father of our Lord Jesus Christ," asking that he restrain the waters as he did "in Colossae through the Archangel Michael by Thy powerful right arm."[23] Alexander made the sign of the cross with his righthand, and immediately the flood stopped.

The miracles and visions described in this sketch helped assure Alexander's speedy glorification after his death in 1533. He was canonized by a church synod in 1547, only fourteen years after his death.[24] Compare to other Russian monks of legendary renown, like Saint Sergius of Radonezh (died 1392, canonized in 1452) or Saint Seraphim of Sarov (died 1833, canonized in 1903).

Following his canonization, Alexander was named one of the twelve great saints whose lives were to be commemorated throughout the Russian Orthodox Church. His life was written into the *Great Minea*, a comprehensive service book with (among other things) information on the lives of great saints; this volume is the oldest surviving account of his life. It was donated in 1552 to the Cathedral of the Dormition (Uspenskiy Sobor) in the Moscow Kremlin. In 1560, one of the altars in that Cathedral was consecrated to Alexander. Alexander's rapid canonization and the writing of his life story has been attributed to the support Metropolitan Makarius, a leading religious figure in Russia at the time. The influence and wealth of Alexander's monastery is also attributed in significant measure to the intervention of Makarius.[25]

The Russian Orthodox Church sees a comparison between Alexander's vision of the Trinity and that of Abraham on the plains of Mamre (as described in Genesis 18:1–2). In fact, the Russian Orthodox Church believes that only twice in human history has the full Trinity appeared to mankind—once to Abraham and once to Saint Alexander of Svir (in 1508).

Genesis 18:1–2 states:[26]

> **1** And the Lord appeared unto him [i.e., Abraham] in the plains of Mamre: and he sat in the tent door in the heat of the day,
>
> **2** And he [Abraham] lift up his eyes and looked, and, lo, three men stood by him: and when he saw them, he ran to meet *them* from the tent door, and bowed himself toward the ground.

Alexander subsequently built a church and monastery on the site, named after the Holy Trinity, as commanded in his vision. His monastery consists of two cloisters, one named for the Holy Trinity and the other named for the Transfiguration. His relics (body) today are found in the Transfiguration cloister, in the

Cathedral of the Lord's Transfiguration, which was built in 1641–44. They are in a remarkable state of preservation, a fact seen by Orthodox believers as evidence of his saintly life. His casket is covered with glass, allowing visitors to see his clothed body, including his hands; the face is covered and is exposed for special services, such as on Trinity Sunday (the Pentecost).

A few historical facts will provide some context that may possible help readers better understand Alexander's life and experiences. When he entered monastic service in 1478, some believers were expecting the end of the world in 1492. This date was based on the Orthodox calculations for the presumed date of the Fall of Adam, which was calculated as 5508 BC. It was assumed that the world would end seven thousand years later. Histories describing this era attest to apprehension about what would come in 1492.[27]

Events of decades prior to 1492 helped give impetus to the dire expectations. In 1439, the Council of Florence convened, seeking a reunification of the Roman Catholic and Eastern Orthodox Churches. Metropolitan Isidore, the Russian representative at this Council, signed the document, later returning to Russia only to be arrested, imprisoned and labeled an apostate. He eventually went to Rome, where he died in 1463. Moscow burnt to the ground in 1445. In 1453, Constantinople fell to the Ottoman Turks. Due to its historic role as the capital of the Byzantine Empire, which was the most important stronghold of Eastern Orthodoxy, the fall of Constantinople was viewed as a devastating blow to Orthodoxy and to Christianity in general.

To the list above, one would also have to add one other historical development, that of the "heresy of the Judaizers."[28] This group of Orthodox believers and clergy were influenced by the views of one "Skhariya the Jew."[29] According to official accounts of their trials for heresy, the Judaizers denied the Holy Trinity, called into question the divinity of Jesus, opposed monasticism, and questioned other fundamental tenets and practices of Orthodoxy. The heresy originated in Alexander's home region of Novgorod; however, he likely was not aware of its initial phases, because he lived in total wilderness isolation from 1485–1493. There were executions of Judaizers during these years. More executions came in subsequent years after Alexander emerged from isolation; conceivably, Alexander may have known of these latter events.

The timing of Alexander's vision in 1508 fits in an interesting sequence that seems to align well with the prophetic destiny his parents would have anticipated for him. As the heavenly voice declared to his parents, Alexander's visions and ministry indeed have given "consolation to His churches," in Russia and throughout Orthodoxy. At a time when Skhariya's teachings were causing some to doubt the divinity of Christ, or the existence of the Godhead (or Holy Trinity), Saint Alexander's firsthand witness surely came as a great comfort to Orthodox believers. The oppression and execution of the Judaizers forms a stark contrast to Saint Alexander's ministry based on a personal witness of God, monastic labors, and Christian virtues.

Events in the decades following Alexander's death also seem to underscore how important his spiritual ministry may have been in offering consolation to the people of Russia, especially in his own region. During 1565–1572, troops loyal to Tsar Ivan, who were known as the "Oprichniki," oppressed many prominent citizens in Russia, particularly from Alexander's home region of Novgorod. Often dressed in black, these henchmen of the Tsar are believed responsible for torturing and killing thousands. Further woes afflicted Russia from 1598 to 1613, during a period known as the "Time of Troubles." These years saw famine, extreme weather, lawlessness, political intrigue, popular uprisings, and outside intervention—all of which sorely tried the Russian people.

Saint Alexander's monastery was located at the south end of the Olonetskiy Krai (region), which at the time included the land between the lakes Ladoga on the west and Onega on the east and extended northward to the Kola Peninsula. According to a nineteenth-century book on the monastery, this region was "unenlightened": though Christian in a formal sense, Christianity in the Krai was not firmly implanted in the lives of local people, making them potentially susceptible to heresies and the schism with "Old Believers" in the mid-seventeenth century. The monastery at various times had responsibility for the spiritual welfare of the entire region.[30]

Figure 11.3: Iconostasis or screen of icons that separates the altar from worshipers.
Trinity Church in the Trinity Cloister of the Alexander of Svir Monastery.
Credit: Photo by the author.

During the reign of Tsar Ivan the Terrible, the monastery does not seem to have experienced any of the difficulties attributed to the Tsar's "Oprichniki" in Novgorod and elsewhere. Elsewhere at this time, the Tsar chided some of the noblemen of Moscow who were accepting tonsure as monks (presumably at the Tsar's insistence) but chose to serve in monasteries not known for the ascetic rigor and discipline of Alexander's monastery.[31] Monastery records indicate that Tsar Ivan gave precious gifts to the monastery, as well as a silver cross in which they were housed. Some of these gifts are said to have included a burial cloth of Christ, stones believed to come from Christ's tomb and from the place where the Apostles heard Christ pray "Our Father," wood from the Sea of Tiberias where Christ and the Apostles fished, and a stone from the Jordan where Christ was baptized. The case for the cross that houses these items is stamped with the date 7084/1576.[32]

Alexander's monastery eventually had jurisdiction over twenty-seven other monasteries in the region. By the beginning of the seventeenth century, the monastery was the richest of the entire Novgorod oblast. Among the patrons and visitors of the monastery were the Tsar Mikhail Fëdorovich (Mikhail I, r. 1613–1645), and Peter I, the Great (r. 1682–1725).[33] In the eighteenth century, the Trinity Church was designated a cathedral, or seat of the local bishop (though this bishopric was later attached to that of Arkhangel'sk), and a seminary was opened in the monastery.[34] During the nineteenth century, the monastery's influence saw a period of relative decline, though once again in 1827, there was a bishop seated in the monastery.[35]

Interestingly, there is a connection between the monastery that Saint Alexander of Svir founded and the monastery at Optina. Elder Leonid of Optina (1768-1841, the first Elder of Optina) was a disciple of Elders Theodore of Svir and Cleopas of Valaam, both of whom were direct disciples of Saint Paisius Velichkovsky. The revival of *hesychasm* and the translation of the *Philokalia* into Slavonic were the great accomplishments of Saint Paisius (see Chapter 4).

The monastery and its monks endured several periods of great difficulty over the centuries. The monastery's prominence, wealth, and spiritual importance—not to mention its location near the Swedish border— made it a target for armed assault. During the Time of Troubles, roving bands of Polish robbers sacked the monastery after the monks refused to hand over the monastery's treasures, resulting in the death of fifty-nine monks and workers, among whom was the abbot.[36] A later project resulted in the construction of a stone wall around the monastery in 1677.[37]

One of the most famous features of Alexander's monastery is the casket with his body, which through the centuries has remained in a remarkable state of preservation. When Alexander died in 1533, he was buried on a spot that later became the location for the Transfiguration Cathedral in the Transfiguration cloister. His body was relocated when excavations were being made in 1641 for the foundations of the current Transfiguration Cathedral. His body was said (and is still said) to be in a remarkable state of preservation which, depending on one's point of view, was either a result of a "natural mummification process" or evidence of a miracle.

When the author visited Alexander's monastery, the staff shared an electronic copy of a manuscript describing the history of his relics. It is a well-reasoned document, with several references to published books and numerous references to government records tracing the history of Alexander's relics. Unfortunately, it is not dated, nor is the author's name given. Summarized below are some of the facts that this document recounts.

Included is a quotation from Abbot Abraham, describing in detail the perfect state in which Alexander's body was found in 1641, 107 years after his burial.[38] According to the same source, Tsar Mikhail I ordered a thorough inquiry to identify the remains. A careful examination was conducted, using even the oldest icon of Alexander for comparison. The examining commission concluded that the relics were indeed the remains of Alexander of Svir. The Tsar rejoiced at this news and ordered that a fine casket be made for Alexander's relics. It was duly constructed, then pulled to the monastery by eleven horses.[39]

In October 1918, after the Soviets came to power, a Chekist (i.e., secret police) officer came to the monastery with orders to seize a "wax doll" (Alexander's body).[40] As it turned out, what the officer found was not a wax doll, but an actual body – Svir's remains. Earlier that year, in April 1918, several of the monks were forced to dig their own graves by Bolsheviks, then were shot while singing "Christ Is Risen."

The basis for this search reportedly was a request from a priest in Novgorod (over four hundred kilometers away), which stated:

> In our place, information was received from newspapers and verbally that it was alleged that instead of the holy relics of Alexander of Svirsky, a wax doll was found. This information is creating great excitement among the people. And for that I ask in the name of duty and an honest word to tell the truth about the holy relics.

From this point, the document analyzes and refutes the various stories and rumors that arose during the Soviet era regarding Alexander's relics. Ultimately, the narrative traces their whereabouts to an anatomical museum, where they were kept uncatalogued for decades.

The body was returned to the Orthodox Church in 1998, but not before a number of modern analyses were made attesting to the authenticity of the remains. Experts have considered all potential possibilities, including whether that the body was really that of a political prisoner who died in a local Soviet prison camp. This latter hypothesis was dismissed, because the remains showed no signs of the diseases that usually afflicted the prisoners due to harsh conditions and poor diet. An anthropologist also noted that the body was *not* that of an ethnic Russian, due to its thin beard and facial features, and concluded it was that of an ethnic Vepsian (Alexander's actual ethnicity). As in the 1640s, the oldest icons were also studied and compared to the face. Similarly, the position of the legs was studied and compared to descriptions from centuries past.

Stories of perfectly preserved dead bodies may strike non-Orthodox readers as strange or even dubious; however, under Orthodox tradition, the bodies of saints have often been found "incorrupt" after their death. This is one of the usual points that Church authorities consider when determining whether a particular believer should be canonized (though the body of Saint Seraphim of Sarov was reportedly *not* incorrupt when examined prior to his canonization). One can trace this tradition in Russia back a thousand years to the early days of ancient Rus (Russia), when the dead bodies of the princes Gleb and Boris were found incorrupt some five years after their murders. Traditional accounts attribute their deaths to their scheming of their elder brother, Prince Sviatopolk, who sought to ascend the throne in place of their deceased father, Saint Vladimir (the "Baptizer of Russia"). Gleb and Boris were subsequently glorified and were the first saints to be canonized in Russia.

Miraculous stories are associated with the bodies of monks in other ways. For example, at the Kiev Cave Monastery, a sign tells a story about the mummified bodies of monks that had lain undisturbed underground in a tunnel below the monastery for centuries. The cool, dry air was perfect for ensuring their preservation. During World War II, German troops loaded the mummies onto a truck and tried to take them away, intending to throw them in the river, but their trucks would not start. After repeated efforts to start the trucks, the drivers returned the mummies to their previous resting spot. Whether this was an actual miracle, a coincidence, or even an embellished story, it certainly fits in an Orthodox context, where relics and the bodies of saints are visible reminders of God's grace.

Alexander's relics (in a casket) are carried each year on Holy Trinity Sunday (Pentecost Sunday) from the Transfiguration Cathedral to the Trinity Cathedral for services.

---

[1] See "The Life of Saint Alexander of Svir: Blessed Seer of the Holy Trinity," *The Northern Thebaid: Monastic Saints of the Russian North*, trans. Fathers Seraphim (Rose) and Herman (Podmoshnensky), with an introduction by I. M. Kontzevitch, (Platina, CA: St. Herman of Alaska Brotherhood, 1995), 123–124. The biography was later printed in Slavonic in Saint Petersburg in 1843. My sketch of Alexander's life and visions is mainly taken from a 1995 English-language translation and abridgment of his biography (originally published in 1975). This translation includes accounts of the lives of several other well-known Russian saints. It was published by one of the leading Orthodox publishers in the United States, the St. Herman of Alaska Brotherhood.

[2] "Life of Saint Alexander," 123-124.

[3] The northwestern region of Russia, bordering Finland.

[4] See Aune Jääskinen, "Homage to a Great Man," *St Alexander: Karelian Miracle Worker* (Helsinki, 1996), Publications of the Museum of Foreign Art Sinebrychoff, no. 8.

[5] Monastery staff gave me electronic copies of helpful materials. These are referenced below in the discussion of the analysis of Saint Alexander's relics after they were returned to the Orthodox Church in 1998.

[6] That is, it was dedicated to Mary's entrance into the Temple as a child. Under Orthodox tradition, she was raised in the Temple in Jerusalem.

[7] "Life of Saint Alexander," 113.

[8] Joseph Smith died on the feast day of Amos, on June 27, 1844. The twelve-day gap between June 15 and June 27 is due to the difference in the nineteenth century between the Gregorian calendar, used at the time in the United States and Western Europe, and the Julian calendar.

[9] "Life of Saint Alexander ," 114.

[10] "Life of Saint Alexander," 115.

[11] "Life of Saint Alexander," 115. Tales of mysterious, helpful strangers are a staple of Latter-day Saint folklore and also have a basis in Latter-day Saint scripture (see generally, 3 Nephi 28; and D&C 7). In connection with a story of this magnitude, the story of this stranger may lend added authenticity for some Latter-day Saint readers.

[12] Remarks given when Patriarch Kirill visited Alexander Svir's monastery on April 17, 2016, on the 375th anniversary of the recovery of

Svir's relics (body) in 1641. See the official website of the Moscow Patriarchate of the Russian Orthodox Church, under the date 17 April 2016, accessed August 2, 2019 at http://www.patriarchia.ru/db/text/4436674.html   A twenty-minute recording of the Patriarch's sermon is included on the page linked above.

[13] "Life of Saint Alexander," 119.

[14] "Life of Saint Alexander," 120.

[15] "Life of Saint Alexander," 120.

[16] "Life of Saint Alexander," 123. In Latter-day Saint scripture, assaults by demons sometimes precede revelations of great magnitude. See Joseph Smith—History 1:15; Moses 1:12–22. The arrival of the first Latter-day Saint missionaries in Great Britain in 1837 also saw one such occurrence, subsequent to which the missionaries enjoyed immense success in that land. See Christopher James Blythe, "Heber C. Kimball and Orson Hyde's 1837 Vision of the Infernal World," BYU Religious Studies Center, Brigham Young University, June 8, 2019, https://rsc.byu.edu/archived/eye-faith/heber-c-kimball-and-orson-hyde-s-1837-vision-infernal-world.

[17] "Life of Saint Alexander," 123. This same message in different words was repeated to Alexander on multiple occasions. See "Life of Saint Alexander," 123–124. Compare to the appearance of the angel to Joseph Smith on September 21 and 22, 1823: the angel appeared four times in less than twenty-four hours, each time repeating the same message. See Joseph Smith—History, verses 27-49. Important messages from God are sometimes repeated multiple times—consider the story of Peter and Cornelius, Acts 10.

[18] "Life of Saint Alexander," 115, 120, 123.

[19] Eugene Smirnoff, *Russian Orthodox Missions* (London: Rivingtons, 1903), 2–3.

[20] "Life of Saint Alexander," 123.

[21] "Life of Saint Alexander," 124. Alexander's question and manner of addressing the Lord bring to mind 3 Nephi 27:3 and Ether 3:2.

[22] Patriarch Kirill visited the Monastery on April 17, 2016, on the 375th anniversary of the recovery of Svir's relics (body) in 1641. See the official website of the Moscow Patriarchate of the Russian Orthodox Church, under the date 17 April 2016, at http://www.patriarchia.ru/db/text/4436674.html   A twenty-minute recording of the Patriarch's sermon is included on the page linked above.

[23] For information about the miracle of Saint Michael at Colossae, see Part V, under "September 6/19—Angel Michael At Colossae," regarding Doctrine and Covenants 128.

[24] From my research, it appears that this may have been one of the most rapid canonizations in the history of the Russian Orthodox Church.

[25] Jääskinen, "Homage to a Great Man," 9.

[26] See the King James edition of the Old Testament published by the

Church of Jesus Christ of Latter-day Saints; cf. Genesis 18:22 with the Joseph Smith translation and its mention of three angels or holy men.

[27]James H. Billington, *The Icon and the Axe: An Interpretive History of Russian Culture* (New York: Vintage Books, 1970), 81–82.

[28] For background on the Judaizers, see Jana Howlett, "The heresy of the Judaizers and the problem of the Russian reformation," (PhD diss., University of Oxford, 1979), PDF, https://ora.ox.ac.uk/objects/uuid:e4a48eeb-6eee-4585-8a29-6ccbc7f7cc48.

[29] Also spelled "Skhary" or "Zechariah."

[30] A. H., *Svirskiy Aleksandrovskiy monastyr': Istoricheskiy ocherk po dokumentam monastyrskogo arkhiva* (Saint Petersburg: *v sinodar'noy tipografii*, 1874) = А.Н., Свирский Александровский монастырь: Исторический очерк по документам монастырского архива (Санкт-петербург: в синодальной типографии, 1874), 4–6.

[31] A. H., *Svirskiy Aleksandrovskiy monastyr'*, 17.

[32] A. H., *Svirskiy Aleksandrovskiy monastyr'*, 22. The date 7084 is based on the Orthodox calendar used at the time, which counted from the date of the presumed fall of Adam.

[33] A. H., *Svirskiy Aleksandrovskiy monastyr'*, 3–4.

[34] A. H., *Svirskiy Aleksandrovskiy monastyr'*, 57–58.

[35] A. H., *Svirskiy Aleksandrovskiy monastyr'*, 63–64.

[36] A. H., *Svirskiy Aleksandrovskiy monastyr'*, 26, 27.

[37] A. H., *Svirskiy Aleksandrovskiy monastyr'*, 41.

[38] *Prepodobnogo Bogonosnogo ottsa nashego Aleksandra, Svirskogo chudotvortsa, ZHITIYE, CHUDESA i SLUZHBA*, 2nd ed. (Moscow: V Sinodal'noy Tipografii, 1859) = Преподобного Богоносного отца нашего Александра, Свирского чудотворца, ЖИТИЕ, ЧУДЕСА и СЛУЖБА (Москва: В Синодальной Типографии, 1859), второе издание, 84.

[39] *Prepodobnogo Bogonosnog*, 34.

[40] The fuss over a purported "wax doll" is ironic and tragic, given the eventual closure of Alexander's monastery and the death of a number of the monks there who were killed by Bolsheviks. Vladimir Lenin's body has been housed in a mausoleum on Red Square for decades, as if "incorrupt." Rumors I heard as a student in Moscow during the 1980s suggested that the body is made of wax, except the head. For information on the cult of Lenin, see generally Nina Tumarkin, *Lenin Lives! The Lenin Cult in Soviet Russia* (Cambridge: Harvard University Press, 1997), enlarged ed.

12–Saint Symeon the New Theologian (949-1022)

 Saint Symeon the New Theologian is perhaps the greatest of all Orthodox monks. He is also a saint in the Roman Catholic tradition. Symeon not only had sacred or mystical experiences; he wrote of them in the first person. These visions gave him an independent basis for speaking and writing of God; thus, his writings reveal few connections to earlier Greek Church Fathers who wrote of mystical theology. He was attracted by the accounts of people in the scriptures who had visions of God (such as Paul and Stephen).[1] His writings also reveal a devotion to and great grasp of the Bible, with close to five thousand references and allusions to both the Old and New Testaments.[2]

Symeon's descriptions of his encounters with God are touching and compelling. His insistence on writing and describing encounters with God was controversial. He had many disciples as well as many enemies, the latter of whom ultimately brought about his exile from Constantinople in old age. Symeon's works have long been read in monastic circles, but only in the later decades of the twentieth century have they achieved wider recognition.[3]

Symeon was raised in a noble family. As a boy, his parents sent him to live with an uncle who held an important post in the imperial court. Symeon himself rose in the imperial service, achieving a rank some historians believe was reserved for eunuchs, though this point is disputed.[4] Some sources indicate that he served as chamberlain of the bodyguard and in the state senate; however, he eventually left imperial service, found a spiritual father,[5] and became associated with the famed Studion monastery. At this early phase of his life, he had not yet accepted tonsure as a monk, so was a layman seeking spiritual guidance.

It is not clear what prompted Symeon to leave imperial service; however, some of his writings hint at a feeling of being unloved and a dissatisfaction with a life seeking to acquire wealth. The words of one of the hymns he wrote describe these feelings:

My parents did not harbour natural love for me,
My brothers and all my friends laughed at me . . .
Relatives, acquaintances from outside and powerful people
in the world
Turned away from me and could not bear to see me,
And even more strove to ruin me through their dishonour.
Often I desired glory without sin,
But I did not find it in this present life . . .
How many times I wanted people to love me,
Desired to have closeness and openness with them,
But nobody among upright people could bear me;
Others wanted to see me and to be more closely acquainted
with me
But I ran away from them . . .
Good people avoided me on account of my external
appearance,
While evil people I myself avoided from my own volition.[6]

For several years, Symeon kept regular contact with his spiritual father in the Studion Monastery while managing the household of a patrician. After a period of prayers one evening, Symeon had his first visionary experience, when a flood of divine light filled his room and seems to have transfigured Symeon with light.[7]

After this vision, however, Symeon seems to have slipped in his spiritual devotion for a time, "falling into more evils than had before befallen [him]."[8] Years later, he composed a hymn describing the many sins he engaged in, though his disciple Niketas (who kept Symeon's writings and was responsible for transmitting his legacy) expressed the view that this list was an "example of modesty," and that Symeon had actually kept his baptism "pure and undefiled."[9]

As a young man, Symeon developed a deep respect for the Eucharist, or Holy Communion. He heeded his elder's advice to never "partake of the Communion without tears." Symeon followed this advice for the rest of his life, even though it drew hostility at times from others. At twenty-nine, Symeon was tonsured a monk and formally entered the Studion monastery. He subsequently served in Saint Mamas monastery in Constantinople, where he held the position of abbot for twenty-two years.

Symeon may be the fulfillment of a prophecy in Isaiah, which Joseph Smith himself referred to in the Doctrine and Covenants. In Doctrine and Covenants 113, some of the early Latter-day Saint elders asked Joseph regarding the meaning of certain scriptures in the Bible. He responded to their questions in detail.

In Doctrine and Covenants 113:10, Joseph explains that in Isaiah 52, the "scattered remnants" of Israel are "exhorted to return to the Lord from whence they have fallen." Joseph further explains that if they do this, "the promise of the Lord is that he will speak to them, or give them revelation."

Keep in mind that in this verse, Joseph is interpreting Isaiah (eighth century AD) and is speaking of a scattered Israel. Thus, the events he speaks of could well have been in the past, perhaps even in the distant past. After all, the ten northern tribes of Israel were led away about 721 BC. The Jews were scattered first in about 600 BC and later, after the destruction of Jerusalem in AD 70.

Isaiah 52:6 states:

> Therefore my people shall know my name; therefore they shall know in that day that I am he that doth speak: *behold, it is I* [emphasis added].

In this verse, the Lord speaking through Isaiah expresses his intention that his people (scattered Israel) will know who he is. They will know God because he will reveal himself to them, or give them revelations, as Joseph explained.

In this context, compare this quotation of Symeon's writings, recorded over one thousand years ago, with the words above from Isaiah. This is a firsthand account by Symeon of a personal meeting with God, as told to his spiritual advisor, or "father":

> The walls of my cell [i.e., his personal quarters] immediately vanished and the world disappeared, fleeing I think from before His [God's] face, and I remained alone in the presence alone of the light. And I do not know, father, if this my body was there, too. I do not know if I was outside of it. For awhile [*sic*] I did not know that I carry and am clothed with a body. And such great joy was in me and is with me now, great love and longing both, that I was moved to streams of tears like rivers, just like

285

now as you see." The other [i.e., his spiritual father] then answers and says: "It is He, child." And at this word, he sees Him [God] again and, little by little, comes to be completely purified and, purified grows bold and asks that One Himself, and says: "My God, is it You?" And He answers and says: "*Yes, I am He*, God, Who for your sake became man; and behold, I have made you, as you see, and shall make you, god" [emphasis added].[10]

The phrase "shall make you, god" could also presumably be translated "shall make of you, a god."

Other Bible translations of Isaiah show an even stronger similarity to Symeon's words. For example, the New International Version renders the last phrase of Isaiah 52:6 as: "Yes, it is I."[11] Compare to the words recorded in the King James edition for this verse: "Behold, it is I."

Symeon's vision of God is thus strikingly similar to what Isaiah predicted in Isaiah 52:6. Interestingly, one of Joseph's own revelations contains this same wording (D&C 11:11)

Symeon had other encounters with deity. In the quotation below, he describes meeting the Savior himself, calling him his "gentle Master":

> I was granted to contemplate a still more awesome mystery. I saw You take me with Yourself, and rise to heaven; I know not whether I was still in my body or not—You alone know, You alone who created me.
>
> On coming back to myself, I wept in sorrowful surprise at my abandoned state. But soon You deigned to reveal Your face to me, like the sun shining in the open heavens, without form, without appearance, still not revealing who You were. How could I have known, unless You told me, for You vanished at once from my weak sight? . . .
>
> Still weeping I went in search of You, the Unknown One. Crushed by sorrow and affliction, I completely forgot the world and all that is in the world, nothing of the senses remained in my mind. Then Thou appeared, You, the Invisible one, the Unattainable, the Intangible. I felt that You were purifying my intelligence, opening the eyes of my soul, allowing me to contemplate Your glory more

286

fully, that You Yourself were growing in light. . . . You shone beyond all measure, You appeared to me wholly in all things, and I saw You clearly. Then I dared to ask You, saying: "Who are You, O Lord?"

For the first time You allowed me, a vile sinner, to hear the sweetness of Your voice. You spoke so tenderly that I trembled and was amazed, wondering how and why I had been granted Your gifts. You said to me: "I am the God who became man for love of you. You have desired me and sought me with your whole soul, therefore henceforth you shall be my brother, my friend, the co-heir of my glory." . . .

You said this and then were silent. Slowly You departed from me, O lovable and gentle Master, O my Lord Jesus Christ! [12]

Though Symeon's inspired witness for God was recorded long ago, his writings have had continuing relevance over the centuries, at least in monastic circles. Excerpts from his accounts of meeting God were included in the *Philokalia* (and in the Slavonic Dobrotolyubie) in the late eighteenth century. The *Philokalia* in turn helped inspire men like Saint Seraphim of Sarov (1754–1833) and the great Elders of Optina (1829–1923) to great levels of faith, devotion and spirituality, and their example and teachings, in turn, inspired Orthodox Christians in the Soviet era. It is not too much of a stretch to say that Symeon is indirectly responsible, in part, for the survival of Christianity in Russia.

Even though Symeon's words have long been accessible in the Orthodox world, such as through the *Philokalia,* they have only been readily available in English since recent times. The full set of his writings in English was only published in the 1990s. An earlier volume was available in 1980, with yet another in 1982. [13]

Besides Doctrine and Covenants 113:10, other writings of Joseph Smith can perhaps be better understood by having Symeon's writings in mind.

Symeon devotes several pages to proving that the believers in heaven will still retain their individuality. The context for his remarks is not provided; however, one can surmise that this must have been a point of theological debate in his day. As in many of his discourses, Symeon reproves those who advocate foolish theology:

> It therefore follows that they who say that the saints will not see or even know one another when they are come to the contemplation of God are in fact simply whistling in the dark. Since they themselves have not arrived at participation in, nor contemplation nor knowledge of God, they are still chattering about, and giving testimony to matters which they neither understand nor have ever seen. It is as if they were saying that the saints on that day, even as it occurs now, will enter into ecstasy, and so forget both themselves and those who are with them. It seems to me that their knowledge of the Holy Scriptures is very weak.[14]

His words recall instruction that Joseph Smith provided in Doctrine and Covenants 130:2, on April 2, 1843:

> And that same sociality which exists among us here will exist among us there, only it will be coupled with eternal glory, which glory we do not now enjoy.

In the Church and in other Christian faiths, it is widely assumed that believers will retain their individual identity and enjoy sociality one with another in heaven. The very fact of the universal Resurrection, taught clearly in the New Testament and in Latter-day Saint scripture, seems to establish this point; if we rise as individuals, we will have interactions with others. Thus, to modern readers, Joseph's instruction could seem like an obvious confirmation of a truth that no Christian ever doubted.

Why then did Joseph give this instruction? His many revelations, statements, and teachings are so loaded with truth, insight, and beauty that this point seems almost mundane in comparison.

In considering this question, readers should consider Doctrine and Covenants 130:2 in its context:

> **1** When the Savior shall appear we shall see him as he is. We shall see that he is a man like ourselves.
>
> **2** And that same sociality which exists among us here will exist among us there, only it will be coupled with eternal glory, which glory we do not now enjoy.

3 John 14:23—The appearing of the Father and the Son, in that verse, is a personal appearance; and the idea that the Father and the Son dwell in a man's heart is an old sectarian notion, and is false.

All three of these verses reflect themes seen in Symeon's writings. Consider this remarkable quote from Symeon's writings, which conveys doctrine very similar to Joseph's words in verses 1 and 3:

> That it is possible for us to look upon God, insofar as men are able to see at all, listen once more to Christ, the Son of God Himself, when He says: "Blessed are the pure in heart, for they shall see God." So what do you have to say to that? I am aware, however, that the man who does not believe in the good things which he has in his very hands and makes no attempt to seize them will take refuge in the future, and so will reply: "Yes, certainly the pure in heart will see God, but this will happen only in the future, not in the present age." My dear friend, just why or how will this happen? If He said that God will be seen by purity of heart, then clearly when this purity comes to pass the vision will follow in consequence. And if you had ever purified your heart, you would know that what is said is true, but, since you have not taken this to heart nor believed that it was true, you have accordingly also despised that purity and completely failed to obtain the vision. For if the purification takes place in this life, then so does the vision. On the other hand, if you should say that the seeing is for after death, then you certainly posit the purification as also after death, and thus it will turn out that you will never see God since after death there will be no work for you to do by which you might find purification.

> However, what else does the Lord say? "He who loves Me will keep My commandments, and I will love him and manifest Myself to Him" [John 14:21]. So when will this manifestation occur? In this life or the future one? It is clear that He means the present life. For wherever the commandments are kept exactly, there, too, is the manifestation of the Savior, and it is after the manifestation that perfect love comes to pass in us.[15]

Joseph's words in Doctrine and Covenants 130:2 regarding sociality are part of an overall context of meeting Jesus Christ, which finds support in the words of Symeon. Is this reference to "sociality" here providential or coincidental? Either way, Joseph's words in Doctrine and Covenants 130:1–3 put him in dialogue with one of the greatest saints of the ages, Saint Symeon the New Theologian. What is more, Symeon's words would not be widely available in English for a century and a half after Joseph died.

While Symeon's comments are similar in substance to Joseph Smith's, the tone of his remarks seems to suggest that they were directed at a skeptical audience. Symeon's remarks may have been intended as reproof for the clergy and monks of his day, men who professed a knowledge of spiritual things, but who perhaps did not grasp a truth that Symeon thought was core to Christ's message: that believers can be purified and meet God, even in this life.

Symeon directed other comments at the clergy of his day, employing a seemingly harsh tone. In an epistle attributed to Symeon that is included among his published writings, Symeon expresses the view that unordained monks who exhibit spiritual gifts and lead virtuous lives can receive confessions in place of priests and bishops.

Symeon's reasoning was thus:

> . . . only the bishops had that authority to bind and loose which they received in succession to the Apostles. But, when time had passed and the bishops had become useless, this dread authority passed on to priests of blameless life and worthy of divine grace. Then, when the latter in their turn had become polluted, both priests and bishops becoming like the rest of the people with many—just as today—tripped up by spirits of deceit and by vain and empty titles and all perishing together, it was transferred, as we said above, to Gods elect people, I mean to the monks. It was not that it had been taken away from the priests and the bishops, but rather that they had made themselves strangers to it . . .[16]

Some monks believed that the principles of faith and prayer by which they lived applied to all, including laymen. Any believer could draw near to God and experience the divine light.

Symeon was the most emphatic of all in emphasizing this point. In seemingly autobiographical remarks on faith, he described a twenty-year-old man (himself, presumably) who was good-looking, well dressed, and well mannered, and who had a meaningful job during the day. In the evenings, the young man spent considerable periods of time in prayer. After reading the story of the blind man in Luke 18:42, who received his sight by faith in the Lord and then beheld the Lord with his newly healed eyes, the young man himself began to desire to see the Lord. One evening, he prayed the words: "God, have mercy upon me, a sinner" (Luke 18:13), and suddenly a glorious heavenly vision unfolded.[17] Symeon's "first vision" thus occurred even before he became a monk.

From this experience, Symeon reminds readers that anyone can meet God, whether layman or monk. He explains that "the heart of the city cannot prevent us from practicing God's commandments, so long as we are diligent and watchful.[18] Symeon explains that anyone who lives "a worthy life" can "achieve salvation," regardless of whether they live "in the midst of the noise and hubbub of the city, or dwell in monasteries, mountains and caves."[19]

---

[1] Hilarion Alfeyev, *St. Symeon the New Theologian and Orthodox Tradition*, in Oxford Early Christian Studies (Oxford: Oxford University Press, 2005), 69–70.

[2] Alfeyev, *St. Symeon*, 52.

[3] Alfeyev, *St. Symeon*, Introduction, 2.

[4] Saint Symeon the New Theologian, *Life, Times, and Theology*, vol. 3 of *On the Mystical Life: The Ethical Discourses*, author, ed. and trans. Alexander Golitzin, Popular Patristics Series no. 16 (Crestwood, NY: St. Vladimir's Seminary Press, 1996), 22–24; Hilarion Alfeyev, *St. Symeon*, 29–30.

[5] Symeon the Studite, to whom the younger Symeon remained loyal throughout his life, though the elder Symeon reportedly engaged in odd behavior, which would cause some to characterize him as a "fool for Christ." See Symeon, *Life, Times, and Theology*, 25.

[6] Alfeyev, *St. Symeon*, 30.

[7] Symeon, *Life, Times and Theology*, 26.

[8] Symeon, *Life, Times and Theology*, 26.

[9] Symeon, *Life, Times and Theology*, 27. Hilarion Alfeyev writes that Symeon led a "dissipated life" during these years; see Alfeyev, *St. Symeon*, 32.

[10] Saint Symeon the New Theologian, *On the Mystical Life: The Ethical Discourses,* vol. 2 *On Virtue & Christian Life,* Popular Patristics Series

no. 15 (Crestwood, NY: St. Vladimir's Seminary Press, 1997), intro. and trans. Alexander Golitzin, 54. See also Alfeyev, *St. Symeon*, 37. Note, these words could be translated either "shall make you god" or "shall make you a god."

[11] New International Version, www.biblehub.com. See http://biblehub.com/isaiah/52-6.htm

[12] John Meyendorff, *St. Gregory Palamas and Orthodox Spirituality* (Crestwood, NY: St. Vladimir's Seminary Press, 1974), 47.

[13] Saint Symeon the New Theologian, *On the Mystical Life: The Ethical Discourses*, 3 vols, intro. and trans. Alexander Golitzin (Crestwood, NY: St. Vladimir's Seminary Press, 1995–1997): *The Church and the Last Things*, vol. 1 (1995), *On Virtue and Christian Life*, vol. 2 (1996), and *Life, Times, and Theology*, vol. 3 (1997); *Symeon the New Theologian: the Practical and Theological Discourses* (Kalamazoo, Michigan: Cistercian Studies, 1982), trans. and intro. by P. McGuckin; *Symeon the New Theologian: The Discourses*, trans. C. J. deCatanzaro, with a preface by Basil Krivoshein and an introduction by George Maloney, S.J., in Classics of Western Spirituality (Mahwah, NJ: Paulist Press, 1980).

[14] Symeon, *The Church and the Last Things,* vol. 1, 74.

[15] Symeon, *On Virtue and Christian Life,* vol. 2, 47–48.

[16] Symeon, *Life, Times, and Theology,* vol. 3, 41–42.

[17] *The Philokalia: The Complete Text Complied by St. Nikodimos of the Holy Mountain and St. Makarious of Corinth,* ed. and trans. G. E. H. Palmer, Philip Sharrard, and Kallistos Ware (London: Faber & Faber, 1995), vol. 4, 18.

[18] *Philokalia,* vol. 4, 19.

[19] *Philokalia,* vol. 4, 20.

13—More Orthodox Holy Men

The annals of more recent Orthodox history contain stories of noted holy men whose lives also serve as illustrations of saintliness and faith. This chapter describes three such men. The first is an unnamed *hesychast* monk—a practitioner of the Jesus Prayer (described in Chapter 4, in connection with the discussion of the *Philokalia*) who wrote a manuscript describing his own personal spiritual journey in 1851. This record was kept in the archives of the Sacred Monastery of Saint Xenophon on Mount Athos in Greece. It was subsequently forgotten for many decades, then rediscovered in 1978. It was published in English translation by the St. Vladimir's Seminary Press in 2014.[1]

The work describes the unnamed monk's intensely personal spiritual struggle as well as some beautiful revelations. The writer, in fact, also describes not only his own experiences, but also those of men he served with. While some visions and experiences must be understood through the lens of the ecclesiastical and monastic culture in which he lived, others speak for themselves.

The final section of the book recounts a beautiful, lengthy vision in which the author sees the Savior both officiating and offering himself at the Eucharist altar. The glorious scene includes worshippers whose faces shine with the grace of God, golden rays radiating from them. The author weeps continuously for joy and describes a personal encounter with Christ in these terms:

> Seeing my sweet Jesus in front of me, him who is beyond and better than all sweetness, I wept out of joy and wonder, for I was deemed worthy to enjoy my sweet vision and the appearance of my Jesus, my master and my God, the vision that my soul had desired to enjoy for a long while, and my heart burned with in me as I meditated on the vision with streaming tears.

> When I kissed his all-immaculate and all-pure chest, I felt the Holy Spirit deep within me ("and renew a right spirit in the depths of me," says David), who warmed both my spirit and my heart more and more in the eros of my Jesus and caused me to melt like wax at that moment on account of my great compunction.[2]

The author then asks Christ regarding the "simple book" he has written, and whether it was written by His grace. The Savior replies in these terms: "When you were writing and were filled with compunction and wept, then it was my Holy Spirit speaking in you." The Savior describes situations where the author struggled with the right words and even stopped writing in some instances, because the Lord's grace was taken from him. The Savior also speaks of "spiritual conceptions" that he "did not want written down."[3]

The experience quoted above brings to mind a description that Elder Melvin J. Ballard (1873-1939) gave of meeting the Savior in a dream. Elder Ballard served in the Quorum of the Twelve (1919-39).

Elder Ballard describes this sacred event in these terms:

> He took me into His arms and kissed me, pressed me to His bosom, and blessed me, until the marrow of my bones seemed to melt! When He had finished, I fell at His feet, and, as I bathed them with my tears and kisses, I saw the prints of the nails in the feet of the Redeemer of the world. The feeling that I had in the presence of Him who hath all things in His hands, to have His love, His affection, and His blessing was such that if I can receive that of which I had but a foretaste, I would give all that I am, all that I ever hope to be, to feel what I then felt![4]

The unnamed monastic author also provides helpful spiritual guidance. For example, he gives insightful advice to those who experience visions but are not sure if they are from the Lord:

> God wants you to become good, loving, merciful, compassionate, longsuffering, patient, pure, and have pure love for your neighbor. But the devil is completely wicked and evil, and since he is such, he wants you to imitate his wickedness and evil.
>
> After you see the vision, beloved, if you notice that your soul suddenly rejoices in God's attributes and your heart is filled with compunction and extreme calm from God's attributes, know that your vision is from God. Since it is from God, your spirit is gladdened by God's attributes and you are filled with a longing from heaven to imitate, as

much as you can, your heavenly God and Father's attributes. All you want to do are those things that please and gladden your heavenly God and Father.

But if after you see the vision your soul does not rejoice in God's attributes, and your heart is not filled with compunction from then and you experience no spiritual desire to imitate your heavenly God and Father's attributes, know that your vision is from the demons.[5]

The writer's words contain themes seen in verses of the Book of Mormon that address a similar question: how may one tell if a thing is from God, or from the devil? Consider these words from Moroni 7:

15 For behold, my brethren, it is given unto you to judge, that ye may know good from evil; and the way to judge is as plain, that ye may know with a perfect knowledge, as the daylight is from the dark night.

16 For behold, the Spirit of Christ is given to every man, that he may know good from evil; wherefore, I show unto you the way to judge; for every thing which inviteth to do good, and to persuade to believe in Christ, is sent forth by the power and gift of Christ; wherefore ye may know with a perfect knowledge it is of God.

17 But whatsoever thing persuadeth men to do evil, and believe not in Christ, and deny him, and serve not God, then ye may know with a perfect knowledge it is of the devil; for after this manner doth the devil work, for he persuadeth no man to do good, no, not one; neither do his angels; neither do they who subject themselves unto him.

18 And now, my brethren, seeing that ye know the light by which ye may judge, which light is the light of Christ, see that ye do not judge wrongfully; for with that same judgment which ye judge ye shall also be judged.

The anonymous monk-author promises rich spiritual blessings for those who truly love Christ:

[Christ] richly bestows divine gifts upon the person who sincerely loves him and who joyfully and gladly takes on his good yoke of his light burden. To such a person he reveals various visions and mysteries, according to the purity of his heart, and he reveals his divine glory to him, sometimes more and sometimes less, in accordance with his struggle and the extent of his asceticism. His good Spirit rests in the person because he keeps his divine commandments perfectly and because of the extreme humility of his heart, and so he endows him with his grace.[6]

The principles expressed in this quotation also make for interesting comparison to verses in the Book of Mormon. Alma 12:9–11 states:

9 And now Alma began to expound these things unto him, saying: It is given unto many to know the mysteries of God; nevertheless they are laid under a strict command that they shall not impart only according to the portion of his word which he doth grant unto the children of men, according to the heed and diligence which they give unto him.

10 And therefore, he that will harden his heart, the same receiveth the lesser portion of the word; and he that will not harden his heart, to him is given the greater portion of the word, until it is given unto him to know the mysteries of God until he know them in full.

11 And they that will harden their hearts, to them is given the lesser portion of the word until they know nothing concerning his mysteries; and then they are taken captive by the devil, and led by his will down to destruction. Now this is what is meant by the chains of hell.

Alma 26:22 states:

22 Yea, he that repenteth and exerciseth faith, and bringeth forth good works, and prayeth continually without ceasing—unto such it is given to know the mysteries of God; yea, unto such it shall be given to reveal things which

never have been revealed; yea, and it shall be given unto such to bring thousands of souls to repentance, even as it has been given unto us to bring these our brethren to repentance.

The anonymous monk describes the feeling of the Holy Spirit in these terms:

When someone feels the grace of the Holy Spirit dwelling in his heart, then he also feels a certain divine joy and spiritual comfort at his core, that is, in his bowels. When the heart is comforted, then it is warmed by immaterial and heavenly warmth from the grace of the Holy Spirit.[7]

As is the case with all the holy men described in this book, the unnamed monk had great love for the Eucharist, or Lord's Supper. He recounts the story of one priest who officiated during the Eucharist and experienced such "compunction" (a sense of spiritual duty) that he wept tears of joy all through the service. The parishioners were so moved in the experience that many also wept with him.[8]

Another holy man whose story makes for inspiring reading is Saint Silouan the Athonite (1866–1938). Born in Russia as Simeon, Silouan is the subject of a short but interesting biography that has been translated into English.[9] In 1892, Silouan went to Mount Athos to begin life as a monk. He remained on Athos in the Russian monastery of Saint Panteleimon until his death.

Silouan's biography was written by his disciple, Archimandrite Sophrony, who treats readers to a modern example of a hesychast monk who humbly sought God and experienced glorious manifestations. Like Saint Seraphim of Sarov (1754–1833) before him, Silouan on occasion was reportedly "transformed out of all recognition," having his countenance illuminated "by an expression so striking that one thought of the glory of the face of Moses, which shone so that the Israelites were afraid to look upon it."

Once, after a prolonged period of darkness and despair in which he experienced deep despondency and a "black hell," Silouan had a remarkable vision during vespers. This occurred while he was still a novice monk (still named Simeon). His biographer describes this event as "a personal meeting" with Christ that subsequently transformed his prayers into something deeply personal.[10] Sophrony writes:

> That same day, during vespers in the Church of the Holy Prophet Elijah (adjoining the mill), to the right of the royal gates, by the ikon of the Savior, *he saw the living Christ.*
>
> In a manner passing all understanding the Lord appeared to the young novice whose whole being filled with the fire of the grace of the Holy Spirit—that fire which the Lord brought down to earth with His coming.
>
> There is no describing how it was with Brother Simeon [Silouan]. From his words and from his writings we know that a great divine Light shone about him, that he was taken out of this world and transported in spirit to heaven, where he heard ineffable words; that he received, as it were, a new birth from on high.
>
> The gentle gaze of the joyous, all-forgiving boundlessly-loving Christ drew Simeon's [Silouan's] entire being to Himself, and then, departing, by the sweetness of God's love lifted his spirit to contemplation of a divinity beyond all earthly vision" [emphasis added].[11]

Silouan's experience with darkness was neither the first nor the last trial of darkness that he was to endure; however, he eventually grew to feel the grace of God, which "no longer left him. . . . He felt the living presence of God and was filled with wonder at the divine compassion." His biographer writes that Silouan's prayers increasingly focused on those in the world who were ignorant of God. He prayed for all, as "he could not bear to think that anyone would languish in 'outer darkness.'" He prayed for people "for generations to come," with prayers reaching "beyond the bounds of time" for the "living and the dead, for friend and foe, for all men." Silouan once explained that his soul seemed to know "better without the newspapers how the whole earth is afflicted and what people's needs are."[12]

The fact that Silouan "could not bear to think that anyone would languish in 'outer darkness'" brings to mind the following verse from the Book of Mormon regarding the sons of King Mosiah who underwent a profound spiritual conversion. Compare the account quoted above from Silouan to Mosiah 28:

> **3** Now they were desirous that salvation should be declared to every creature, for they could not bear that any human souls should perish; *yea, even the very thoughts that any soul should endure endless torment did cause them to quake and tremble* [emphasis added].

According to his biography, Silouan gave this advice for believers and religious leaders seeking to understand how to recognize guidance from God:

> In practice, the process is as follows: every Christian, and in particular every bishop or priest, when faced with the necessity of finding a solution consonant with the will of God, makes an inner rejection of all his own knowledge, his preconceived thoughts, desires and plans. Freed from everything "of his own," he then turns his heart to God in prayer and attention, and the *first thought* that finds birth in his soul after such prayer he accepts as a sign from on high. Such search for the knowledge of God's will through direct invocation in prayer leads man, especially in need and distress, "to hear God answering him in his heart," as the Staretz [Elder] said, "and he learns to understand God's guidance" [emphasis added].[13]

Silouan's advice about "the first thought" is similar to advice given by Elder Ronald A. Rasband of the Quorum of the Twelve at April 2017 general conference. He provided the following counsel on how Church members can recognize promptings from the Holy Ghost:

> We must be confident in our *first promptings*. Sometimes we rationalize; we wonder if we are feeling a spiritual impression or if it is just our own thoughts. When we begin to second-guess, even third-guess, our feelings—and we all have—we are dismissing the Spirit; we are questioning divine counsel. The Prophet Joseph Smith taught that if you will listen to the first promptings, you will get it right nine times out of ten. . . .
>
> *First promptings* are pure inspiration from heaven. When they confirm or testify to us, we need to recognize them

for what they are and never let them slip past" [emphasis added].[14]

Silouan served as a monk at a time when his countrymen in Russia were living through great calamities, so there is little doubt that millions of stood to benefit from his prayers. The years of his service on Mount Athos (1892–1938) spanned the Russo-Japanese War (1904–1905), World War I (1914–1918), the Russian Civil War (1917–1923), the Soviet famine of 1932–1933, and Soviet oppression of Orthodox monks, nuns, priests, and believers. He died on the very eve of World War II, which the Russians to this day refer to as the "Great Fatherland War," a conflict in which the civilian and military casualties exceeded twenty million people.

Another story of a visionary monk mentioned in the introduction to this book is Saint Paisios (1924–1994), who served as a monk on Mount Athos and was canonized in 2015. Paisios is a modern example of an Eastern Orthodox monk who is reported to have achieved great spirituality.[15] His biography recounts an interesting story from his youth of a vision he had of the Savior before entering the monastery. At age fifteen, a friend of his brother, named Costen, spoke with the young Paisios (then named Arsenios) to convince him to abandon his Christian faith. The friend was determined to "make him give up all this stuff" regarding Christianity, speaking of Charles Darwin and the theory of evolution. Young Paisios was a bit shaken by this talk, but still maintained his faith in the Lord. This is his account of what he told the other boy and of what he did next:

> "I'll go and pray, and, if Christ is God, He'll appear to me so that I'll believe. A shadow, a voice—He'll show me something." That's all I could come up with.

> "So, I went and began to pray and make prostrations, which I did for hours, but—nothing happened. Finally, I stopped in a state of exhaustion. Then something Costen had said came to mind: 'I can accept that Christ is an important man,' he had told me, 'righteous and virtuous, Who was hated out of envy for His virtue and condemned by His countrymen.' I said to myself, 'Since that's how Christ was, even if He was only a man, He deserves my love, obedience, and self-sacrifice. I don't want

paradise—I don't want anything. It is worth making every sacrifice for the sake of His holiness and kindness.'

"God was waiting to see how I would deal with this temptation. And after this Christ Himself appeared to me in a great light. He was visible from the waist up. He looked on me with tremendous love and said to me, 'I am the resurrection, and the life: he that believeth in Me, though he were dead, yet shall he live.' He was holding open the Gospel in His left hand, where the same words were written."[16]

Paisios prayed for confirmation of his Christian faith, at a time when the young people of his era were questioning the relevance of Christianity in an age of science. Paisios's faith led to a wondrous vision that confirmed the most basic of Christian tenets: that Christ did rise from the dead and is "the Resurrection and the life."

Latter-day Saint readers will see some broad similarities between the vision of young Paisios and Joseph Smith's First Vision, which he experienced at age fourteen. Whatever meaning Latter-day Saints will attach to the life of Paisios, he is well-known and much beloved in his native Greece.

One correlation of dates should be mentioned here: the feast date for Saint Paisios is that of his repose date (death date): July 12. This is the date for the commemoration of Peter and Paul on the Orthodox calendar. It is also the date on which Doctrine and Covenants 132 was revealed.

It seems that Paisios's service to his countrymen and indeed the traditions of the Orthodox Church have helped maintain strong family values in Greece. Data from the Euronews show that Greece has the lowest out-of-wedlock birthrate in the European Union.[17]

---

[1] *The Watchful Mind: Teachings on the Prayer of the Heart,* trans. George Dokos (Yonkers, NY: St. Vladimir's Seminary Press, 2014).
[2] *The Watchful Mind,* 231–2.
[3] *The Watchful Mind,* 232–3.
[4] Elder Melvin J. Ballard, "I Know that He Lives," *Ensign Magazine* Dec. 2014, available at
https://www.churchofjesuschrist.org/study/ensign/2014/12/i-know-that-

he-lives?lang=eng, taken from Bryant S. Hinckley, *Sermons and Missionary Services of Melvin Joseph Ballard* (1949), 147–57, as reprinted in "Classic Discourses from the General Authorities: The Sacramental Covenant," *New Era,* Jan. 1976, 7–11.

[5] *The Watchful Mind*, 160.

[6] *The Watchful Mind*, 138.

[7] *The Watchful Mind*, 119.

[8] *The Watchful Mind*, 114.

[9] Archimandrite Sophrony, *The Monk of Mount Athos: Staretz Silouan 1866–1938* (Crestwood, NY: St. Vladimir's Seminary Press, 1989).

[10] Sophrony, *Monk of Mount Athos,* 80

[11] Sophrony, *Monk of Mount Athos ,* 19

[12] Sophrony, *Monk of Mount Athos ,* 48. Cf. Mosiah 28:3; Moses 7:41.

[13] Sophrony, *Monk of Mount Athos*, 52.

[14] Ronald A. Rasband, "Let the Holy Spirit Guide," The Church of Jesus Christ of Latter-day Saints, Intellectual Reserve, April 2017, https://www.lds.org/general-conference/2017/04/let-the-holy-spirit-guide?lang=eng.

[15] See Hieromonk Isaac, *Elder Paisios of Mount Athos*, trans. Hieromonk Alexis and Fr. Peter Heers, eds. Hieromonk Alexis (Trader), Fr. Evdokimos (Gorantis), and Philip Navarro (Chalkidiki, Greece: Holy Monastery Saint Arsenios the Cappadocian, 2012).

[16] Isaac, *Elder Paisios of Mount Athos,* 23–24.

[17] See Alice Tidey, "Number of births outside marriage rise in EU," April 16, 2018, accessed August 2, 2019, https://www.euronews.com/2018/04/16/number-of-births-outside-marriage-rise-in-european-union.

14—Conclusions and Summary

The main purpose of this book is to identify commonalities in the teachings, practices, experience, and history of The Church of Jesus Christ of Latter-day Saints and the Eastern Orthodox Church. Some of the most interesting parallels are seen in the doctrines of the respective churches on seeing God, divine light, and the potential for believers to become gods in the afterlife. Both churches teach that marriage between believers is intended to have an eternal duration. The elders, leaders, monks, and saints of both faiths have had mystical or sacred visions and revelations that show similarities and can be seen as mutually validating in important respects, even if the understanding of God differs in the respective churches.

Of the saints who are profiled in this book, Saint Seraphim of Sarov (1754–1833) deserves particular attention. He was a contemporary of Joseph Smith and, as seen in Chapter 9, there are several parallels in experiences, dates and teachings between Seraphim and Joseph Smith. Many of the other saints profiled in this book were selected because they constitute, in a sense, Seraphim's spiritual pedigree. This applies in particular to Saint Symeon the New Theologian (949–1022), Saint Gregory Palamas (1296–1359), Saint Alexander of Svir (1448–1533), and Saint Paisius Velichkovsky (1722–1794).

The Orthodox calendar and the Latter-day Saint Doctrine and Covenants both exhibit fascinating parallels in date and theme. For those readers interested in exploring these parallels, Part V of this book contains a comprehensive exploration of these connections.

Although I am a devout Latter-day Saint in every respect, it is my conviction that the Orthodox (and Catholic) saints profiled in this book were servants of God whose lives and teachings are worthy of study and emulation in many ways. The men profiled in this book deserve to be better known outside of the Eastern Orthodox Church. Their stories attest to the vitality and strength of the Orthodox tradition.

The work of Orthodox missionaries and monks in preaching Christianity in the native tongues of peoples over an immense swathe of the earth's surface has done tremendous good in advancing the "knowledge of a Savior" among mankind (see D&C 3:16; Mosiah 3:20; Isaiah 11:9). This preaching was accomplished among non-Christian peoples, largely without force and compulsion, though Orthodox *dissenters* were sometimes repressed, such as the Old Believers in Russia. This peaceful spread of Christianity is seen in the fact that large numbers of Muslims, Buddhists, and adherents of other faiths still remain in Russia and among peoples once part of the Russian Empire: they were not forced to convert to Orthodoxy.

In focusing on Orthodoxy, I do not intend to imply that other Christian traditions are not worthy of such comparisons. Mysticism (sacred experiences) has a long history in Christianity. Men and women through the ages have experienced visions and miracles that have inspired other Christians; however, exploring the full range of this literature is outside of the scope of this work. Readers interested in a concise overview of Christian mysticism will appreciate Steven Fanning's book, *Mystics of the Christian Tradition*.[1] Incidentally, Fanning includes several pages in his book on Joseph Smith.

Eastern Orthodox mysticism is unique in that it can involve not only visions of light or miracles but, more specifically, the actual transfiguration of the human body with divine light. Some Orthodox monks have reported visions of the risen Christ and of Deity. Orthodox mysticism is also unique in that it seems to plausibly fulfill prophetic statements contained in the Latter-day Saint Doctrine and Covenants.

In Orthodox theology, the resurrection of the body at the last day is fully anticipated, as is the deification, or transfiguration, of the body with divine light. These points find strong parallels in Latter-day Saint scripture.

Doctrine and Covenants Section 88 states:

> **49** The light shineth in darkness, and the darkness comprehendeth it not; nevertheless, the day shall come

when you shall comprehend even God, being quickened in him and by him.

50 Then shall ye know that ye have seen me, that I am, and that I am the *true light that is in you*, and that you are in me; otherwise ye could not abound. . . .

67 And if your eye be single to my glory, *your whole bodies shall be filled with light*, and there shall be no darkness in you; and that body which is filled with light comprehendeth all things.

68 Therefore, sanctify yourselves that your minds become single to God, and the days will come that you shall see him; for *he will unveil his face unto you*, and it shall be in his own time, and in his own way, and according to his own will [emphasis added].

Section 93 contains similar promises, also combining the promise that believers can see the Lord with mention of divine light.

1 Verily, thus saith the Lord: It shall come to pass that every soul who forsaketh his sins and cometh unto me, and calleth on my name, and obeyeth my voice, and keepeth my commandments, shall *see my face* and know that I am;

2 And that I am the *true light that lighteth every man* that cometh into the world [emphasis added].

This book's focus on these mystical aspects of Latter-day Saint and Orthodox doctrine should not be misunderstood. This book is not suggesting that they should occupy a place that is front and center in pastoral ministering and teaching. These experiences in proper perspective—they *can* occur in this life, but more often, believers should look for God's blessings in their lives in less visible and miraculous ways.

The Book of Mormon teaches that all who are baptized, receive the Holy Ghost, exercise faith in Christ, and live so as to enjoy its companionship are on the path that leads to eternal life.

This principle is taught in 2 Nephi 31:

19 And now, my beloved brethren, after ye have gotten into this strait and narrow path, I would ask if all is done? Behold, I say unto you, Nay; for ye have not come thus far save it were by the word of Christ with unshaken faith in him, relying wholly upon the merits of him who is mighty to save.

20 Wherefore, ye must press forward with a steadfastness in Christ, having a perfect brightness of hope, and a love of God and of all men. Wherefore, if ye shall press forward, feasting upon the word of Christ, and endure to the end, behold, thus saith the Father: Ye shall have eternal life.

Orthodox Metropolitan Ware presents an important perspective in discussing deification. While glorious transfiguring events can occur in this life, these are the exception rather than the rule. Yet, these are experiences that all the righteous can anticipate in the Resurrection day:

> The full deification of the body must wait, however, until the Last Day, for in this present life the glory of the saints is as a rule an inward splendor, a splendor of the soul alone; but when the righteous rise from the dead and are clothed with a spiritual body, then their sanctity will be outwardly manifest. "At the day of Resurrection the glory of the Holy Spirit comes out from within, decking and covering the bodies of the saints—the glory which they had before, but hidden within their souls. What a person has now, the same then comes forth externally in the body." The bodies of the saints will be outwardly transfigured by divine light, as Christ's body was transfigured on Mount Tabor. "We must look forward also to the springtime of the body."

> But even in this present life some saints have experienced the firstfruits of this visible bodily glorification. St. Seraphim is the best known, but by no means the only, instance of this.[2]

Readers will note the absence of women in this story; however, there absolutely *are* inspiring accounts of nuns and devout women in many Christian traditions, including the Eastern Orthodox faith; however, to my knowledge, none of their published experiences fit squarely within this book's focus.

A few examples here may serve to whet the appetite of those who wish to study the lives of female Orthodox saints.[3] One of the best known is Saint Nino (Nina), Enlightener of Georgia (ca. AD 296–ca. 338). According to tradition, Nino experienced a vision in which the Theotokos (Mary) instructed her to preach the Gospel in Georgia. Nino's uncle was then the patriarch of Jerusalem, and she sought his blessing to undertake this mission. After hearing of her vision, the patriarch led her to the royal (central) doors of his church and placed his hands on her head, blessing her as follows:

> O Lord, God of Eternity, I beseech Thee on behalf of my orphaned niece: Grant that, according to Thy will, she may go to preach and proclaim Thy Holy Resurrection. O Christ God, be Thou to her a guide, a refuge, and a spiritual father. And as Thou didst enlighten the Apostles and all those who feared Thy name, do Thou also enlighten her with the wisdom to proclaim Thy glad tidings.

Nino's preaching and ministry in Georgia led to the establishment of Christianity in that land. The Georgian Orthodox Church is now counted among the fifteen autocephalous, or independent, churches in Eastern Orthodoxy.[4]

A modern example of an Orthodox woman who has been canonized is Saint Matrona (Matrona Dimitrievna Nikonova). She was born blind in 1881 and lost the ability to walk by age sixteen. Despite her infirmities, she lived until 1952. Early in life, Matrona exhibited a gift of spiritual vision, being able to see in her mind what her natural eyes could not. By age seven or eight, she had a gift for healing and for prophecy.

Her prophetic statements are legendary. Once, she warned of a coming fire, telling a woman named Natalia the following:

> "I'm leaving now. Tomorrow there'll be a fire, but your house won't suffer." As she said, fire broke out in the morning, nearly the whole village burned down. But then the wind changed and Natalia's house remained untouched.[5]

During the difficult years under Soviet communism and World War II, Matrona was often in hiding, avoiding arrest by the authorities. People often came to her for advice, and her replies often turned out to be inspired, even miraculous.

On one occasion in 1946, an architecture student came to her and asked for advice. He was concerned that he would fail his exam the next day; in fact, he believed that his that his supervisor would *intentionally* fail him. Without a diploma, the student would not obtain good employment and this would cause family hardship. He describes what happened next:

> My father was in prison and Mother was my dependent. My only hope was to get the diploma and start working. Matushka [Matrona] listened to me and said: "Come, you'll do it. We'll have tea in the evening and talk." I could hardly wait till evening. Matrona [who was a blind woman] said: "We're now going to Italy, to Florence, to Rome, we'll have a look at the works of great masters. . . ." And she started naming the streets and buildings! Then she made a pause: "Here is Pitti Palazzo, and here's another palace with arches. You should copy this: the first three levels with big bricks and two arches for entrance." I was struck by her knowledge. In the morning I rushed to the Institute. I quickly did the necessary corrections and at 10 a.m. the committee came. They looked at my project and said: "It looks great! Congratulations!"[6]

Orthodox readers may wonder why this book says nothing about the veneration of relics. In Orthodoxy, the relics (remains) of saints—particularly their graves—are venerated, and many miracles have been reported through this practice. Under Orthodox teaching, the grace of God can remain in the body of a departed saint, or even in an object touched or used by a saint or by Christ.

The simple fact is that this is *not* a Latter-day Saint practice, so no parallels are seen here; however, the lack of parallel should not imply any condemnation on the part of one faith toward the other. In the case of relics, there is in fact a scriptural basis for the idea that visiting the graves of holy men can produce miracles. The book of 2 Kings, Chapter 13 gives this interesting story regarding the bones of the prophet Elisha. Mere contact with his bones brought another dead man back to life:

> **20** And Elisha died, and they buried him. And the bands of the Moabites invaded the land at the coming in of the year.

> **21** And it came to pass, as they were burying a man, that, behold, they spied a band of men; and they cast the man into the sepulcher of Elisha: and when the man was let down, and touched the bones of Elisha, he revived, and stood up on his feet.

Similarly, the mere fact of touching the hem of Christ's garment resulted in miraculous healings, as reported in the book of Matthew Chapter 14:

> **35** And when the men of that place had knowledge of him, they sent out into all that country round about, and brought unto him all that were diseased;

> **36** And besought him that they might only touch the hem of his garment: and as many as touched were made perfectly whole.

The same held true for fabric that had merely been in contact with Paul's body—people who touched handkerchiefs and aprons that he handled were healed of diseases (Acts 19:12).

Likewise, some readers may wonder what place the Theotokos or Virgin Mary has in Latter-day Saint theology. The answer is that she is held in great esteem among Latter-day Saints. Mary's name and future calling as the Savior's earthly mother were known to Book of Mormon prophets hundreds of years before Christ's birth. For example, Nephi saw Mary in a vision with the Christ child; he also saw that she was carried to heaven for a time prior to Christ's birth (1 Nephi 11:19–20), an important detail not recounted in New Testament narratives. Other prophets even prophesied that her name would be *Mary* (Mosiah 3:8; Alma 7:7).

On the other hand, Latter-day Saints do not venerate saints, so Mary is not venerated. Prayers are only offered to God the Father in the name of Jesus Christ.

Two stories are worth citing here. One concerns the common garden insect called the *ladybug* in the United States. According to Catholic tradition, during the Middle Ages, a plague of pests (likely aphids) was devouring crops, threatening the food supply. The people prayed, petitioning Mary to save them. In response to the prayers of the people, God sent massive swarms of the bugs now called ladybugs, meaning "Our Lady's Bug" (i.e., Mary's Bug). The bugs devoured the pests and the crops were saved. An analysis of the bug's name in numerous languages reportedly confirms that there is an association between this insect and Mary, as well as with God.[7]

The second story is similar in some respects. After Latter-day Saint pioneers arrived in the Great Salt Lake Valley in 1847, they planted crops for the coming season, anticipating an influx of additional emigrants. By the spring of 1848, as the pioneers' crops started to grow, insects began arriving in vast numbers, devouring the young crops. This insect is often called a "Mormon cricket," though it was wingless and is more closely related to katydids.

This plague of insects threatened the survival of the emigrants, who soon took to prayer, petitioning God for help. Their prayers were answered in early June 1848, when flocks of California seagulls flew in and began devouring the pests. After filling themselves, the seagulls would fly to the nearby Salt Lake, regurgitate, and return to the crop fields to devour more insects.

In these two stories, readers can see two instances where God's miraculous help was experienced by people in dire need. In the earlier example, the miracle is attributed to Mary's intervention. In the latter, it is attributed to God the Father (*in the name of Christ,* the usual manner of prayer for Latter-day Saints). Yet in both situations, the *experiences* of the faithful believers were similar: God helped in a time of need.

Even if the doctrinal underpinnings in the two situations are somewhat different, the two stories are mutually supportive. Both stories point towards the reality and love of God for all, regardless of doctrinal understanding. Surely, both accounts also involve faith in Jesus Christ, regardless of whether this faith is implicit or actually articulated in the prayer of the believer. Faith in Christ can bring miracles (Moroni 7:33; Mormon 9:24; Mark 16:17).

Latter-day Saint readers should particularly note that numerous appearances of John and other Apostles are reported in Orthodox tradition; however, these often involve appearances of Mary as well. These appearances are mentioned in Chapter 5.

With or without Mary, any reported ministration of John the Beloved in the centuries after his assumed death in about AD 100 can be seen as a fulfilment of Latter-day Saint prophecy (see D&C 7).

A scriptural basis for the many appearances of Mary may be inferred from John 19, which reports these words that were spoken by Christ while he was on the cross:

> **26** When Jesus therefore saw his mother, and the disciple standing by, whom he loved, he saith unto his mother, *Woman, behold thy son*!
>
> **27** Then saith he to the disciple, *Behold thy mother*! And from that hour that disciple took her unto his own home [emphasis added].

Under Orthodox tradition, John is said to have traveled with Mary on at least one occasion. Mary visited Mount Athos in Greece with him, when both were traveling from Joppa to Cyprus to see Lazarus. They were blown off course, landing near the present site of some of the monasteries on Athos. Besides this occasion, one may presume they were often together, given the Savior's charge to John as quoted above.

In the centuries following the ministry of the original Apostles, the joint appearances and ministry of Mary, John, and other Apostles have been recorded in at several times in history.

Returning to the topic of Mary, is there a divine role for her that hasn't been revealed yet in Latter-day Saint revelation? This book takes no position on this. Much of the focus of this book is instead to encourage openness and the mutual sharing of readers' respective beliefs and faith. This kind of sharing presupposes that believers will not be dismissive of the theology, forms of worship, miracles, or visions held sacred by the faithful of another religious tradition.

In any case, Joseph Smith never commented on miracles attributed to Mary; he seems to have kept a respectful silence on the topic. Readers (of any tradition) who might otherwise be skeptical would do well to follow his example on this point.

If readers agree with this author and see a measure of divine providence in the connections between the two churches presented in this book, then perhaps the most important point is that all Christian groups now have a little more to talk about and a little more in common. With more connection points, the collective Christian story of faith should ring truer, not less true. This may be a very important consideration in a world where traditional church attendance is declining in many countries.

The Book of Mormon affirms that God manifests himself among all nations, by the power of the Holy Ghost, according to the faith of the people (2 Nephi 26:13):

> He manifesteth himself unto all those who believe in him, by the power of the Holy Ghost; yea, unto every nation, kindred, tongue, and people, working mighty miracles, signs, and wonders, among the children of men according to their faith.

Latter-day Saint leaders from the early nineteenth century have taught that the restored gospel of Christ embraces *all truth* wherever found. Consider these words from Elder Howard W. Hunter in October 1991. Hunter was the President of the Quorum of the Twelve at the time he made this statement and later served briefly as the President of the Church until his death in 1995. His words came at a time when the restored Church of Jesus Chrsit was expanding its activities into regions and nations once closed to Latter-day Saint missionaries:

> The gospel of Jesus Christ, which gospel we teach and the ordinances of which we perform, is a global faith with an all-embracing message. It is neither confined nor partial nor subject to history or fashion. Its essence is universally and eternally true. Its message is for all the world, restored in these latter days to meet the fundamental needs of every nation, kindred, tongue, and people on the earth. It has been established again as it was in the beginning—to build brotherhood, to preserve truth, and to save souls.

> Brigham Young once said about such a broad and stimulating concept of religion: "For me, the plan of salvation must . . . circumscribe [all] the knowledge that is upon the face of the earth, or it is not from God. Such a plan incorporates every system of true doctrine on the

earth, whether it be ecclesiastical, moral, philosophical, or civil. . . . (Journal of Discourses, 7:148.)

As members of the Church of Jesus Christ, we seek to bring all truth together.

Hunter continued:

Mormonism, so-called, is a world religion, not simply because its members are now found throughout the world, but chiefly because it has a comprehensive and inclusive message based upon the acceptance of all truth, restored to meet the needs of all mankind.

This book may shed new light on the meaning of these statements quoted above from Elder Hunter and Brigham Young. They spoke of a religion (Mormonism, or the Latter-day Saint faith) that embraces *all truth, wherever found.*

The truth of the statements given above is suggested by my research. It is now evident that the Doctrine and Covenants, for example, *already* embraces (and refines) teachings on theosis and divine light that show interesting parallels to the writings of Saint Gregory Palamas. The Doctrine and Covenants also contains revelations from God that were delivered on the exact feast days on the Orthodox and Catholic calendars that hold appropriate themes. Joseph Smith taught of the possibility that believers could actually meet the Lord, in this life. His ideas would have sounded utterly fanciful and implausible in the nineteenth century United States which, at the time, was predominantly Protestant. Yet, in Russia at almost the same time, Saint Seraphim of Sarov was teaching the same thing, using words similar to Joseph's. Moreover, Seraphim's teachings were not an aberration; in the Orthodox monastic tradition, saints going back at least to Symeon the New Theologian had taught the same thing.

Similarly, Joseph taught of eternal marriage and salvation for the dead. Similar concepts are contained in Orthodoxy. In Chapter 8, I describe Orthodox teachings on eternal marriage, quoting from early Church Fathers whose teachings form a doctrinal basis. Orthodoxy has several Saturday's per year that are known as Saturdays of Souls or Memorial Saturdays, where the names of deceased Orthodox believers can be placed on the Eucharist altar for prayers.

Ultimately, my hope is that this book will give impetus to new avenues for scholarship and open opportunities for dialogue between the scholars and leaders of restored Church of Jesus Christ and Eastern Orthodoxy—two Christian churches that both assert claims of divine or apostolic authority and yet that are very different in their doctrines, modes of worship and governance. I would also hope that readers from all faith traditions will be inspired by this book, giving glory to Jesus Christ, who "manifests himself to all nations" (Title Page of the Book of Mormon) and is the source of all good things (Moroni 7:24).

---

[1] Stephen Fanning, *Mystics of the Christian Tradition* (London: Routledge, 2001).

[2] Timothy Ware (Bishop Kallistos of Kokleia), *The Orthodox Church* (London: Penguin Books, 1997), 233.

[3] Materials on woman saints in the Eastern Orthodox tradition can be found at "Orthodox Women Saints," Antiochian Orthodox Christian Archdiocese of North America, accessed March 21, 2019, at http://ww1.antiochian.org/women/orthodox-women-saints.

[4] Archpriest Zakaria Machitadze, "Saint Nino, Equal-to-the-Apostles and Enlightener of Georgia (†335 AD)," Orthodox Christianity, accessed March 21, 2019, http://orthochristian.com/7215.html.

[5] "The Life of Blessed Matrona Of Moscow," trans. Liudmila and Evgeny Selensky, Pravoslaviye, May 1, 2015, accessed March 22, 2019, http://pravoslavie.ru/79033.html.

[6] "Life of Blessed Matrona." Online booksellers feature several publications about Matrona.

[7] "Our Lady's Bug," Catholicism.org, Saint Benedict Center, October 30, 2004, accessed March 22, 2019, https://catholicism.org/our-ladys-bug.html; Elaine Jordan, "Our Lady's Bug: Symbol of divine Protection," June 20, 2018, accessed July 29, 2019, https://www.traditioninaction.org/religious/f040_Ladybug.htm.

Part V:

Calendars and Date Correlations

Introduction to Part V—Calendars and Date Correlations

"All Things Are Created And Made To Bear Record Of Me." (Moses 6:63)

This Part V describes in detail many correlations between feast dates on the Eastern Orthodox and (in a few cases) Roman Catholic liturgical calendars and the Doctrine and Covenants. Twenty of these are presented below, following the order of the Orthodox liturgical year, which begins in September. Additional correlations relating to Latter-day Saint temples and temple ordinances are given in Table 1.

These date correlations connect important revelations in the Doctrine and Covenants with appropriate feasts and themes on the Orthodox and Catholic calendars. These are not random, trivial correlations. They run all through the Doctrine and Covenants, with approximately thirty sections showing meaningful ties to dates and themes on these ancient calendar systems. Moreover, the themes pertain to some of the deepest and most significant doctrines of the Restoration: seeing God, temples and temple ordinances, Joseph's prophetic call, the Priesthood, the founding of the Church of Jesus Christ of Latter-day Saints, the appearance of the Angel Moroni to Joseph Smith, the inspired nature of the Doctrine and Covenants, and even the Word of Wisdom.

This author is not the first writer to observe date correlations that may be providential. Other authors have noted interesting calendar connections. A posting in 2016 on Book of Mormon Central describes connections between important Jewish feasts and the date on which the angel Moroni appeared to Joseph Smith.[1] It turns out that the precise day on which the angel Moroni delivered the plates to Joseph was the Jewish feast of Rosh Hashanah, also known as the Feast of Trumpets (September 22, 1827).

This posting on Book of Mormon Central shows that the theme of this feast is a good match for Moroni's delivery of the gold plates to Joseph. It explains that this ancient feast signified "admonitions and warnings, covenant making, remembrance, sacrifice, prophecy, a new beginning, and God's involvement in history." The post also quotes writer Lenet Hadley Read for the following explanation:

The Feast of Trumpets signifies the time of Israel's final harvest; the Day of Remembrance of God's covenants with Israel; the announcement of revelation or truth; and preparation for God's holiest times, including the Messianic Age.

In 2015, John W. Welch wrote in *BYU Studies Quarterly* regarding the statues of Christ and the twelve Apostles by Danish sculptor Bertel Thorvaldsen.[2] Thorvaldsen's important work was commissioned in 1820, which happens to be the year when Joseph Smith experienced his First Vision. The work was completed in 1829, the year when Joseph translated the Book of Mormon. The artist died in 1844, which was also the year of Joseph Smith's death. Thorvaldsen's statue of Christ (the "Christus") has been reproduced by the Church and is on display at several temples and chapels around the world.

As another illustration, the final events of Jesus's life, his resurrection, and the appearance of Elijah in the Kirtland Temple in 1836 have been shown to have significant date-connections to the Jewish calendar. Author John Pratt[3] wrote of these coincidences in 1985:

> As an astronomer who has studied the lunisolar calendar, I was intrigued by Elijah's return occurring not only during Passover week, as anticipated by the Jews, but also on an Easter Sunday that was calendrically similar to the proposed date of the Savior's resurrection, being both April 3 on the Julian and 16 Nisan on the Hebrew calendar.
>
> Was that merely a calendrical coincidence? Or could the timing of Elijah's return have been purposely chosen to correspond to some special Passover in accordance with Jewish tradition? Pursuing these types of questions led me to discover an interval of time that is so remarkable in an astronomical sense that it seems to constitute evidence that the timing of Elijah's return was carefully chosen.[4]

While some readers will be impressed with the correlations described in this book, or those given above from The Book of Mormon Central, John W. Welch and John Pratt, other readers may find any attempt to see date parallels as meaningless or even misguided.

Scholars sometimes refer to efforts to find correlations in dates as *parallelomania*. This term applies when there is no historical basis for linking the two events. For example, it is safe to assume that Saint Alexander of Svir's vision of the Holy Trinity (1508) had no bearing whatsoever in shaping Joseph's account of his First Vision (1820). Joseph would have had very little access—if any at all—to materials on Russian Orthodoxy. Accordingly, undue attention to the date connection may be meaningless from a strictly historical point of view.

Similarly, the correlation between Alexander's date of birth and Joseph's date of death (both fell on the feast of Amos) may also be unimpressive from a statistical point of view. What are the chances that Alexander and Joseph Smith would share a connection to Amos's feast? Not more than 1 in 365. Less in fact, since the discussion here centers on a death date *and* a birth date.

Still, the fact remains that these correlations run all through The Doctrine and Covenants; moreover, some of Joseph's revelations show traces of Orthodox theology and teachings that go back many centuries, yet there is seemingly no human way that Joseph could have known this.

The fundamental question that readers should examine is whether the calendar correlations presented in this book form patterns that seem (1) likely coincidental and thus meaningless, (2) intentional, or (3) providential (i.e., inspired by God).

I invite readers to focus on the latter two possible hypotheses (numbers 2 and 3) for how these date and thematic parallels came about:

> **The "intentional" hypothesis:** *The question to explore under this approach is whether Joseph Smith had access to Orthodox and Catholic calendars and intentionally aligned some of his revelations with these (and perhaps some date-parallels are also purely coincidental).*
>
> Accepting this hypothesis would require that we also assume that Joseph wished this fact not to be easily discovered, or only discovered in a future century. Based on evidence currently available, neither Joseph nor his scribes or associates are known to have left any records attesting to an influence of Eastern Orthodoxy or Roman

Catholicism on his revelations. See Part III, Chapter 6 for a discussion of whether Joseph could have access to Orthodox or Catholic materials.

Even if writings were to be discovered showing that Joseph had access to an Orthodox and Catholic calendar, this would still be a very significant find. Until now, no historian has advanced such a claim.

The "providential" hypothesis: *In this assumption, readers would accept that some or all of the correlations that are identified in this book are providential, or inspired by God.*

Even from this perspective, there could be many interpretations for what these correlations mean. This author believes that these correlations should be seen as attesting to Joseph's inspiration and that through these correlations, God is seeking to draw believers of very different Christian traditions into closer dialogue.

If these date parallels are of interest to Latter-day Saint, Orthodox, or other readers at all, it will likely be under one or both hypotheses described above. Historians and readers who are intrigued by the first hypothesis may wish to conduct their own research. What Orthodox or Catholic materials (other than those described in Part III, Chapter 6) might Joseph have been exposed to? Could these have influenced the content or timing of his revelations in some way? This could be an interesting avenue for further study.

Readers who can accept that God may have inspired some of the calendar connections described in this book should consider Moses 6:63: "All things are created and made to bear record of me."

Perhaps we could rephrase this verse in the following words: Anything created or inspired by God will ultimately contain elements that testify of Him, directly or indirectly.

With this in mind, should it be surprising if unexplainable links are found between the history and teachings of various Christian faith traditions? Some might particularly expect to see connections between faiths purporting to have apostolic origins (i.e., Orthodoxy, Catholicism and others) and those claiming to be founded on divine revelation (i.e., the restored Church of Jesus Christ).

Readers who can at least accept as a *possibility* that these parallels in dates and themes are providential are already navigating the waters of faith. Statistical methodology will be of little help here. Are readers sailing toward an insignificant, isolated island— toward meaningless, random correlations? Or will readers make landfall on a much larger landmass that holds promise for many future theological explorations and discoveries? Only time will tell.

Note: Readers wishing to consult online calendars in order to conduct their own research can consult the references given in this endnote.[5]

A summary of the main date correlations is presented below, beginning from September 1, which is the first day of the new liturgical (worship) year.

The date correlations are of four types. *These four types (given in bold below) are used to describe the twenty correlations presented in this Part V, and others given in Table 1.*

1.   **The Revised Julian**: This calendar has been in use <u>only</u> since 1923, for Orthodox worship in a number of countries. It was formed by moving October 1, 1923 (Julian) to October 14, 1923 (Gregorian), dropping thirteen days. This resulted in feasts that kept their original dates on the Julian calendar, but which were aligned with the same date on the Gregorian calendar. The Gregorian is the modern calendar used virtually all over the world today. It is the calendar that was used in the United States during Joseph Smith's lifetime (and today).

The new calendar was called the "Revised Julian." It is used today by the Greek Orthodox Church and several other branches of Orthodoxy. In contrast, the Russian Orthodox Church and others continue to use the Julian calendar (see point 2 below).

As an example, in Joseph Smith's day (in the nineteenth century), Christmas fell on December 25 on both the Julian and Gregorian calendars; however, the Julian calendar was thirteen days behind the Gregorian in 1923; thus, Christmas was actually falling on January 7 on the Gregorian calendar. After the calendar reform of October 1923, Christmas is December 25 on both the Revised Julian and the Gregorian calendar.

In the United States, the Revised Julian calendar is often referred to as the "new-style" calendar and the Julian is referred to as the "old-style" (unfortunately, Russian sources generally seem to use the opposite terms, reversing the terms "old-style" and "new-style").

2.   **The Julian**: Until 1923, this was the calendar used by all Orthodox churches. It was in use in much of the world since Roman times, but gradually, countries in Europe and elsewhere began to adopt the Gregorian calendar starting in the late sixteenth century. The Gregorian is more accurate than the Julian. The Julian calendar looses eleven minutes a year compared to the Gregorian. Due to this, in the twenty-second century, the gap between the Gregorian dates and those of the Julian calendar will be fourteen days.

After the calendar reform in 1923, this calendar remains in use by several Orthodox churches for worship purposes, the largest of which is the Russian Orthodox Church. These churches *still* follow the Julian calendar, but in practice, dates are now thought of as "Julian plus thirteen," giving these dates a Julian-equivalent date on the Gregorian calendar. In this manner, Peter and Paul's feast of June 29 became July 12."[6] This type of calendar is called the "old style" in the United States.

Several matches to today's Julian calendar are shown below. Two examples are Peter and Paul's day (July 12) and the Theophany (Christ's baptism) (19 January). These feasts two match the dates Doctrine and Covenants Sections 132 and 124, respectively. In the nineteenth century, these feasts would have fallen on July 11-12 and January 18-19, due to the fact that the Orthodox worship day begins at sunset and carries over to the next day's sunset, as in Judaism. Today, these feast dates fall on July 12-13.

3.   **Exact Matches (for the nineteenth century):** This term refers to a date on the Gregorian calendar in the 1800s (during Joseph Smith's lifetime) that exactly matched the day of a corresponding Orthodox feast on the Julian calendar.

One example below in Part V, is the feast of the Prophet Amos, which was June 15 on the Julian calendar used in Russia but fell on June 27 on the Gregorian calendar during Joseph's lifetime (twelve-day difference). Joseph Smith was martyred at Carthage Jail on June 27, thus on the day of Amos's feast.

Due to the fact that the Julian calendar looses eleven minutes a year compared to the Gregorian, the feast of the Prophet Amos now falls thirteen days later, on June 28.

4.   **Roman Catholic:** My references to the Catholic calendar are to the so-called "Traditional" or "Tridentine" calendar, unless indicated otherwise. This calendar was used from the late sixteenth century to 1960. I also make reference to a Roman Catholic martyrology, which also has date listings with the names of saints, martyrs, and events that are commemorated.

An important example of a Catholic feast is the feast of Elijah (July 20), which is commemorated by the Carmelite order of Catholic monks and nuns on the same day as on the Revised Julian calendar (also July 20).

---

[1] See "Why Did Moroni Deliver the Plates on September 22?, Know Why # 193," September 22, 2016, at Book of Mormon Central, https://knowhy.bookofmormoncentral.org/knowhy/why-did-moroni-deliver-the-plates-on-september-22.

[2] John W. Welch, "The Christus in Context," *BYU Studies Quarterly* 54, no. 2 (2015), 148–161.

[3] Pratt has degrees in math, physics, and astronomy. He introduces himself at this page: http://www.johnpratt.com/jpp.html. He gives background on the Julian and Gregorian calendars here: http://www.johnpratt.com/items/calendar/cal_intro.html. At this page, he

provides links to other calendars and calendar correlations: http://www.johnpratt.com/items/calendar/. All accessed by the author August 2, 2019.

[4] John P. Pratt, "The Restoration of Priesthood Keys on Easter 1836, Part 2: Symbolism of Passover and of Elijah's Return," *Ensign* 15, no. 7 (July 1985), https://www.churchofjesuschrist.org/study/ensign/1985/07/the-restoration-of-priesthood-keys-on-easter-1836-part-2-symbolism-of-passover-and-of-elijahs-return?lang=eng.

[5] See Stephen P. Morse, "Converting between Julian and Gregorian Calendar in One Step," at https://stevemorse.org/jcal/julian.html; Petko Yotov, "Side-by-side Easter calendar reference for the 19th century," http://5ko.free.fr/en/easter.php?y=19 (some feasts are calculated with reference to Easter); Holy Trinity Russian Orthodox Church, "Orthodox Calendar," Baltimore, MD, Patriarchate of Moscow, at https://www.holytrinityorthodox.com/calendar/index.htm; Greek Orthodox Archdiocese of America, "Calendar Of Saints, Feasts, And Readings In The Orthodox Church," at https://www.goarch.org/chapel/calendar; "Tridentine Calendar," [Catholic, prior to 1962], at https://en.wikipedia.org/wiki/Tridentine_Calendar#The_Tridentine_Calendar; "Traditional Liturgical Calendar Following the Rubrics of Pope St. Pius X, For the Universal Calendar (Roman Rite) of the Church," at http://www.traditio.com/cal.htm; https://www.catholic.org/saints/; for a complete Roman Catholic martyrology, see the following resource (which is set for the month of May; scroll to the bottom to select another month), See "Roman Martyrology (Martyrologium Romanum)," Boston Catholic Journal, Boston Catholic Journal, s.v. "May 6," accessed August 2, 2019 http://www.boston-catholic-journal.com/roman-martyrology-in-english/roman-martyrology-may-in-english.htm#May_6th).

[6] John A. McGuckin, "Calendar," *The Concise Encyclopedia of Orthodox Christianity*, ed. John A. McGuckin (Malden, MA: Wiley Blackwell, 2014), 77–78.

September 1/14—Christ's Entry into the Synagogue
CORRELATES TO DOCTRINE AND COVENANTS SECTION 127

On the Orthodox calendar, the liturgical (worship) year begins on September 1 on the Revised Julian Calendar (Greek) and September 14 on the Julian Calendar (Russian).

In Orthodoxy (September 1, Revised Julian):

- This date on the Revised Julian calendar commemorates the entry of Christ into the synagogue (see Luke 4:16–22), in addition to marking the beginning of the church year.
- On this occasion, the Savior quoted Isaiah 61:1–2.[1] Verse 1 states, in part:

> The Spirit of the Lord is upon Me, because of which He anointed Me . . . to heal the brokenhearted, *to preach liberty to the captives* and recovery of sight to the blind [emphasis added].

- Verses 1–9 are read in church on the Great and Holy Saturday, the day before Easter.
- A Russian Orthodox website provides this commentary about Christ's descent into Hades on Holy Saturday:

> The traditional icon used by the Church on the feast of Easter is an icon of Holy Saturday: the descent of Christ into Hades. It is a painting of theology, for no one has ever seen this event. It depicts Christ, radiant in hues of white and blue, standing on the shattered gates of Hades. *With arms outstretched He is joining hands with Adam and all the other Old Testament righteous whom He has found there. He leads them from the kingdom of death. By His death He tramples death* [emphasis added][2]

In the Restored Church of Jesus Christ (September 1):

- In the Latter-day Saint understanding, the term "captives" as used here is a reference to the spirits of the dead in the spirit world.
- Following his death, Christ appeared in the spirit world, taught his Gospel, and organized ministers to proclaim "liberty to the captives who were bound." These authorized messengers taught "vicarious baptism," meaning baptism for the dead. See Doctrine and Covenants 138:33.
- Baptism for the dead is also mentioned in 1 Corinthians 15:29.
- The first specific instructions on how baptisms for the dead should be conducted were given by Joseph Smith on September 1, 1842, in what now is known as Doctrine and Covenants Section 127.

---

[1] See s.v. Isaiah 61:1-2, *The Orthodox Study Bible,* ed. Fr. Jack Norman Sparks (Thomas Nelson, 1993

[2] Quoted from Fr. Alexander Schmemann, "The Orthodox Celebration of Great and Holy Saturday, at https://pravoslavie.ru/61230.html (accessed 18 July 2019)

September 6/19—Angel Michael at Colossae
CORRELATES TO DOCTRINE AND COVENANTS SECTION 128

This ancient feast honors the archangel Michael; however, Orthodox sources indicate that it is intended also to honor the other archangels besides Michael, including Raphael, Uriel, and Gabriel.

In Orthodoxy (September 6; Revised Julian):

- Orthodox tradition tells of a prophecy by Saint John the Apostle that he made while laboring in the vicinity of Hierapolis and Colossae (in modern-day Turkey), that "the community would soon be blessed with a miraculous well to which the ailing could go for cure." [1]
- The prophecy came true and the people attributed the miraculous appearance of water to Saint Michael the Archangel.
- Subsequent to this time, local pagans sought to destroy the well by diverting the nearby Chryssos River, but the well was rescued by the appearance of Michael, who descended from heaven with a flaming sword.
- This miracle is commemorated on the Revised Julian Calendar (Greek Orthodox) on September 6.

In the Restored Church of Jesus Christ (September 6):

- In Doctrine and Covenants 128:20–21, Joseph mentions the angels Michael, Raphael, and Gabriel.
- These verses state, in part:

20 And again, what do we hear? . . . *The voice of Michael* on the banks of the Susquehanna, detecting the devil when he appeared as an angel of light!
21 . . . And *the voice of Michael, the archangel; the voice of Gabriel, and of Raphael,* and of divers angels, from Michael or Adam down to the present time, all declaring their dispensation, their rights, their keys, their honors, their majesty and glory, and the power of their priesthood; giving line upon line, precept upon precept; here a little, and there a little; giving us consolation by holding forth that which is to come, confirming our hope [emphasis added]!

September 8/21—Nativity of the Theotokos (Mary)

CORRELATES TO DOCTRINE AND COVENANTS SECTION 2 AND JOSEPH SMITH—HISTORY 1:27–54

This very important Orthodox feast commemorates the birth of the Virgin Mary, or the Theotokos, as she is known in Greek Orthodoxy. On the evening of September 21, the angel Moroni appeared to Joseph Smith to tell him of an ancient book of scripture known now as *The Book of Mormon.* The book was hidden not far from Joseph's home in a hill that subsequently became known as the Hill Cumorah.

In Orthodoxy (September 21; Julian):

- This feast is one of the most important in Orthodoxy, being one of twelve "Great Feasts" for the year and one of only four specifically dedicated to Mary.
- It commemorates the birth of Mary, the Mother of God, or Theotokos.
- The date correlates to September 21 -22 on today's Julian Calendar (Russian Orthodox).

In the Restored Church of Jesus Christ (September 21):

- The Book of Mormon contains the fullness of Christ's everlasting Gospel as taught by Christ to the ancient inhabitants of the Americas following his resurrection and ascension to heaven (see Joseph Smith—History 1:27–54).
- Feast days in Orthodoxy are deemed to begin at sundown and continue until sundown of the next day. This feast would have covered parts of September 20 and 21 on the Gregorian calendar in Joseph Smith's day; today's feast would be September 21-22.
- If one were to construct a list of the most important dates in the history of the Restored Church of Jesus Christ, this date, September 21, would be one of the most important.

---

[1] George Poulos, *July–September,* vol. 3 of *Orthodox Saints,* (Brookline, MA: Holy Cross Orthodox Press, 2005), 262. For the mention of Michael, Raphael, Uriel and Gabriel, see p. 261 in the same source.

September 9/22 and September 10/23—Multiple Correlations

CORRELATES TO DOCTRINE AND COVENANTS SECTION 84

Doctrine and Covenants Section 84 has three interesting correlations to Orthodox or Catholic feasts. The first two commemorate (i) the Third Ecumenical Council (AD 431) and (ii) the Conception of John the Baptist. These correlations invite readers to consider the different ways in which the dogmas and doctrines of the restored Church of Jesus Christ and Eastern Orthodox Churches came into being.

The third correlation pertains to famous early Christian martyrs, Saint Maurice and his fellows. These men were soldiers in a Roman legion composed of Christians. Many men of this legion were put to death for refusing to obey unjust orders to kill Christians or (depending on the version of the story) for refusing to sacrifice to pagan gods.

Section 84 of the Doctrine and Covenants mentions a "new song" that will be sung on the Millennial Day (D&C 84:98–102). The reference to a *new song* raises an obvious question: what was the *old song*? An answer is seen in the story of Maurice and an ancient abbey that bears his name, founded on September 22 in the year 515.

Third Ecumenical Council

In Orthodoxy (September 22; Julian):

- The first seven Ecumenical Councils (up until 781) set in place the core, fundamental beliefs of the Christian faith relating to the Holy Trinity and the person of Jesus Christ.
- The Third Ecumenical Council condemned the teaching of Nestorius, who taught that Christ was born as an ordinary man, but "and afterwards because of sanctity of life that he was conjoined with the Divinity."
- The Third Ecumenical Council confirmed the teachings of the first two councils that established the Nicene Creed (also called the Nicene Constantinopolitan Creed). The date correlates to September 22 in today's Julian Calendar (Russian Orthodox).

328

In the Restored Church of Jesus Christ (September 22):

- This feast would have fallen on September 21-22 on the Gregorian calendar in the nineteenth century.
- For Latter-day Saints, basic doctrines are found in the Holy Bible and in modern scripture received through Joseph Smith and other modern prophets holding the Melchizedek Priesthood.
- Doctrine and Covenants 84 is one of the most important revelations defining the role of the Melchizedek Priesthood, which holds the key to the knowledge of God (see D&C 84:18–25).

The Conception of John the Baptist

In Orthodoxy (September 23; Revised Julian)

- This is one of several feasts on the Orthodox calendar honoring John the Baptist.
- It honors the *conception of John*, which was foretold by the angel Gabriel to John's father Zacharias (Luke 1:13).
- John's importance in Orthodoxy is seen in the placement of his icon on the *iconostasis* (the screen with icons separating worshipers from the Eucharist altar). The Holy Doors leading to the altar where the Eucharist is placed are in the middle, with Christ just to the right of these doors. John is just to the right of Christ. The date of September 23 is John's feast on the Revised Julian Calendar (Greek Orthodox).

In the Restored Church of Jesus Christ (September 22–23):

- Doctrine and Covenants Section 84:27–28 gives details regarding the prophetic role of John the Baptist, especially pertaining his infancy.
- According to verse 27, he was *"filled with the Holy Ghost from his mother's womb."* This is a direct match for the name of this feast, the *Conception* of John the Baptist.
- Verse 28 states:

For he was baptized while he was yet in his childhood, and was ordained by the angel of God at the time he was eight days old unto this power . . . to make straight the way of the Lord.

Feast of Saint Maurice

Catholicism (September 22; <u>Roman Catholic</u>*)[1]:*

- Saint Maurice was the commander in the late third century AD of a Roman legion from North Africa that was composed of Christians.
- His legion was ordered north into Europe for service.
- He and his men (or a significant number) were put to death for refusing to kill other Christians (or to sacrifice to pagan gods).
- The feast day of Saint Maurice and his companions is September 22.
- On this day in AD 515, an abbey was founded to preserve the memory of these remarkable men who paid the ultimate sacrifice for their faith. The abbey is located in Switzerland, near the spot of the martyrdom.
- The monastery has never missed a day of worship since that time.
- For the first three centuries, the worship was a musical liturgy brought from Constantinople. Even today, the worship involves the participation of singing monks, or *chanoines,* as they are known.
- The abbey commemorates the memory of not only Saint Maurice and his men but also of all Christian martyrs around the world.

In the Restored Church of Jesus Christ (September 22):

- Doctrine and Covenants 84:98–102 gives the words for a future song that will be sung on the Millennial Day.
- This "new song" will celebrate the redemption of God's people, the victory over Satan, the emergence of a new Zion, or the Pure in Heart (<u>D&C 97:21</u>), the establishment of truth, the clothing of the Earth in glory, and the personal reign of the Lord.
- The term new song implicitly raises the question: what was the *old song*?

- Given that Doctrine and Covenants 84 was revealed, in part, on September 22, which is the feast day of Saint Maurice, the answer may be seen in the tragic but vital role that martyrdom has played over the centuries in preserving Christianity. The story of Maurice and his men, as well as of many other martyrs, is told at the Abbey of Saint Maurice in Switzerland.
- The musical worship of this abbey has been dedicated from its inception to the memory of the martyrdom of Maurice and his men.
- Thus, the *old song* can be understood as an implicit reference to the sacrifices of martyrs through the centuries—men and women whose devotion to Christ has helped ensure the survival of Christian faith.[2]

---

[1] On the current Catholic calendar, and older versions. See at https://www.catholic.org/saints/saint.php?saint_id=368.

[2]Foxe's Book of Martyrs (1830) tells the story of these men and gives the date of their martyrdom (September 22), however, the details of the St. Maurice Abbey and its musical heritage are not described. See Rev. John A. Fox, *Book of Martyrs: or History of the Lives, Sufferings and Triumphant Deaths* (Hartford: Philemon Canfield, 1830) ed. Rev. Charles A. Goodrich, 50–51. Joseph Smith is only known to have read Fox's book in 1834. D&C 84 was recorded before he read Fox's book. See under "Foxe's Book of Martyrs" at https://josephsmithfoundation.org/foxes-book-of-martyrs-2/.

October 19/ November 1—The Prophet Joel

Joel's best-known prophecy is this one: "And it shall come to pass afterward, that *I will pour out my spirit upon all flesh*" (Joel 2:28; emphasis added). The promise points to a time when prophetic gifts will be widely enjoyed among the people of the world.

In Orthodoxy (November 1, Revised Julian):

- Orthodox icons depict Joel holding a scroll with the words of his famous prophecy:

   "I will pour out my spirit upon all flesh."

- In another possible correlation, in November 1831 (exact date unknown), Saint Seraphim of Sarov (1754–1833) had a famous discussion on the Holy Spirit with his disciple Nikolay Motovilov. Both were transfigured in glorious light. Seraphim said that the knowledge of this event was *"for the whole world."*
- Several other correlations to feasts in the month of November are a good fit with the *Conversation of St. Seraphim with Motovilov.* November has the feasts of both Saint Paisius Velichkovsky (November 15/ 28) and Saint Gregory Palamas (November 14/27).
- Palamas is a match due to his writings on heavenly light. It is also a match to Paisius because he included some of Palamas's writings in the *Philokalia,* which was edited by Pasisius Velichkovsky (in Slavonic) and inspired monks in the nineteenth century to seek greater spiritual devotion and imitate great Orthodox monks of centuries past.
- The feast of the prophet Joel falls on November 1 on the Julian Calendar.

In the Restored Church of Jesus Christ (November 1):

- On November 1, 1831, Latter-day Saint elders met in conference to approve the publication of compiled revelations given to the Church by the Lord. This book was first known as *The Book of Commandments* and is now known (in an expanded form) as the *Doctrine and Covenants.*

332

- Section 1 is the Lord's preface to this book. Other revelations were given in November 1831—see sections 67–70; 107:60–100; and 133.
- Section 1 of the Doctrine and Covenants articulates a theme similar to Joel's prophecy among the reasons why the Lord restored the fullness of his Gospel through Joseph Smith in the latter days:

"**that *every man* might speak in the name of God the Lord,**
even the Savior of the world (1:20; emphasis added).

- The phrase "speak in the name of the Lord" implies great spiritual gifts and the receipt of divine revelation.
- Other sections describe how revelation is received (D&C 6:22-23; 8:2; 9:8-9); the right of elders to speak the mind and will of the Lord (D&C 68:4); the promise of revelations to individuals who serve the Lord faithfully (D&C 76:7); the role of the First Presidency and Quorum of the Twelve as prophets, seers, and revelators; and the principle that revelations for the whole Church come through the appointed channel (i.e., through the President; see D&C 28:2–8; 100:11; 107:91–92).

December 27/January 3–Saint John, Apostle and Evangelist

COMPARE TO DOCTRINE AND COVENANTS SECTION 88

On the Traditional Roman Catholic calendar, the feast of Saint John can be observed anytime in an "octave" from December 27 to January 3. Section 88 of the Doctrine and Covenants was revealed by the Lord to Joseph Smith precisely in this range of dates. Joseph Smith called this revelation the "Olive Leaf . . . the Lord's message of peace to us" (*History of the Church*, 1:316).

John's Gospel account contains teachings on divine light and on the ability of believers to meet Christ that find strong parallels to similar concepts taught in Doctrine and Covenants Section 88. These themes of heavenly light and meeting God are important in Eastern Orthodoxy.

In Catholicism and Orthodoxy:

- Saint John's feast day is December 27 on the traditional Roman Catholic calendar.
- The Catholic calendar was updated in 1962. The prior calendar, the *Traditional* (also called *Tridentine),* was the one in use in Joseph Smith's lifetime. It dates back to the late sixteenth century.
- Under the Traditional calendar, this feast could be commemorated on any day in the "octave," or eight-day range, from December 27 to January 3, which is the precise date range during which this revelation was received.
- On the Orthodox calendar (Revised Julian), December 27 is the feast of Saint Stephen the Protomartyr (First Martyr) who saw Christ on the right hand of God the Father.
- January 2 is the day Saint Seraphim's repose (death) is commemorated on the Orthodox calendar (Revised Julian).
- December 3 is the feast of Malachi (Revised Julian). Malachi prophesied that Elijah would come to turn the hearts of the fathers to the children, etc.

In the Restored Church of Jesus Christ:

- This revelation was given precisely on the dates covered by the octave of St. John.
- The combination of John, Stephen, Seraphim, and Malachi fits the doctrines articulated in Doctrine and Covenants 88.
- John taught of divine light and that believers can meet Christ (John 1:4, 5, 7–9; and John 14:18, 21, and 23). Stephen saw Christ on the "right hand of God" (Acts 7:55–56). Seraphim was personally transfigured by heavenly light (see Chapter 9 of this book). Malachi taught of a future temple to which the Lord would come (Malachi 3:1).
- Doctrine and Covenants 88 also teaches that people can meet the Lord (88:49–50, 68–69).
- This section also teaches of divine light, the "light of Christ" (88:7-13).
- Doctrine and Covenants 88:119 contains the first commandment to build the Kirtland Temple, which was the first Latter-day Saint temple actually completed. Verse 49 promises that the Saints will someday comprehend God.
- This section has more parallels of date and theme to the Orthodox or Catholic calendars than any seen in the research for this book. Doctrine and Covenants 88:44 even references timekeeping, mentioning minutes, hours, days, months, and years.

January 2/15—Saint Seraphim of Sarov
CORRELATES TO DOCTRINE AND COVENANTS SECTION 38
ALSO CORRELATES TO DOCTRINE AND COVENANTS SECTION 88

Saint Seraphim of Sarov (1754–1833) is the greatest Russian saint of recent centuries. His prophecies of Russia's future trials and spiritual rebirth inspired many Orthodox Christians during the difficult years of Soviet Communism (1917–1991). Numerous parallels are seen in his life and teachings to the Prophet Joseph Smith, yet the two could never have met and would not even have known of each other's teachings and ministry.

In Orthodoxy (January 2; Revised Julian for both Section 38 and 88):

- In his famous discussion with Nikolay Motovilov, Seraphim taught that people can meet God in this life.
- Both men were transfigured by heavenly light, the "Uncreated" or "Tabor" light.
- Saint Seraphim died on January 2, 1833, while praying before an icon of the Theotokos, or Virgin Mary.
- Seraphim died in 1833 and was canonized in 1903. His body was recovered and returned to Diveyevo (the town nearest his monastery) in 1991.

In the Restored Church of Jesus Christ (January 2):

- On January 2, the Lord revealed to Joseph Smith Doctrine and Covenants Section 38, which contains the first revealed statement pointing towards a future spiritual endowment for the restored Church of Jesus Christ:

32 Wherefore, for this cause I gave unto you the commandment that ye should go to the Ohio; and there I will give unto you my law; and there you shall be *endowed with power from on high. . .*

38 See that all things are preserved; and when men are endowed with power from on high and sent forth, all these things shall be gathered unto the bosom of this church.

- The promise of a spiritual endowment was fulfilled in the outpouring of heavenly light and manifestations that accompanied the dedication of the Kirtland Temple in 1836.
- The outpourings of divine light that were seen in Kirtland bring to mind the transfiguration of Seraphim and Motovilov in 1831, and the accounts of monks in the centuries before Seraphim who likewise experienced heavenly light.
- Section 38:1 mentions *seraphs*, a variation on the word *seraphim*, the heavenly beings described in the Bible (Isaiah 6:2); Saint Seraphim was named after these beings. The dedicatory prayer for the Kirtland Temple also mentions seraphs (see D&C 109:79).
- Saint Seraphim died during the date range when D&C 88 was revealed. This section shows numerous similarities to Orthodox teachings on *theosis* or deification (on divine light and seeing God, see verses 6-13 and 67-68). The commandment to build the Kirtland Temple was given in this revelation (verse 119). This was the first Latter-day Saint temple actually constructed. Its dedication was accompanied with visions and outpourings of heavenly light.

January 6/19 The Holy Theophany of the Lord (Baptism of Christ)

CORRELATES TO DOCTRINE AND COVENANTS 124

The feast of Theophany is the day when the baptism of Jesus by John the Baptist is commemorated on the Orthodox calendar. This event is remarkable for the manifestation of the entire Godhead, or Holy Trinity, on the occasion; the Father's voice was heard and the Holy Ghost descended "like a dove" on the occasion of Christ's baptism (Matthew 3:16–17). This event also suggests the universal need for baptism, since Christ himself requested baptism at the hands of John the Baptist.

In Orthodoxy (January 19; Julian):

- Orthodox sources offer interesting insights into the theological meaning of the theophany. For example, the descent of the Holy Ghost in the form of a dove over Jesus, John, and the Jordan River is compared to the Spirit of God hovering over the waters at the first creation (Genesis 1:2). The ministry of Christ is a "new creation" for the world, suggested by the descent of the Holy Ghost at the time of Christ's baptism.
- Of the baptism of Christ, The Orthodox Study Bible explains (see s.v. Luke 3:22):

  "The Son is revealed by the descent of the Holy Spirit and by the voice of the Father. This is the greatest and clearest public manifestation of God as Trinity in human history, as we sing, 'The Trinity was made manifest.'"

- Since Christ himself does not need purification by baptism, this event is seen as his purification of humanity. One Greek church father wrote: "Jesus enters the filthy, sinful waters of the world and when He comes out, brings up and purifies the entire world with Him" (see *The Orthodox Study Bible,* s.v. Matthew 3:15).
- The Theophany is paired with another feast, the Great Blessing of the Waters, which occurs on the same day.

In the Restored Church of Jesus Christ (January 19):

- The baptism of Jesus shows that all people everywhere need baptism. Consider these verses from the Book of Mormon regarding Christ's baptism:

> 7 Know ye not that he was holy? But notwithstanding he being holy, he showeth unto the children of men that, according to the flesh he humbleth himself before the Father, and witnesseth unto the Father that he would be obedient unto him in keeping his commandments. . . .
>
> 9 And again, it showeth unto the children of men the straitness of the path, and the narrowness of the gate, by which they should enter, he having set the example before them (2 Nephi 31:7, 9).

- In the teachings of the restored Church of Jesus Christ, everyone must be baptized. Vicarious baptisms are available in Latter-day Saint temples for the dead, assuring that all will eventually have this opportunity.
- The first mention of baptism for the dead in modern scripture is given in Doctrine and Covenants 124 (see verses 29, 32, 36, and 39).
- This section of the Doctrine and Covenants was revealed on January 19, 1841.
- It contains the Lord's commandment for the Latter-day Saints to build the Nauvoo Temple (D&C 124:31, 42–43).
- The Lord also commands Joseph Smith to "make a solemn proclamation of the gospel" to the kings, rulers and nations of the world, giving this revelation a clear global dimension (D&C 124:1–14).

February 27—First Meal after Bright Monday
CORRELATES TO DOCTRINE AND COVENANTS SECTION 89

The period of Great Lent is one of the most sacred seasons on the Orthodox calendar. During the weeks of Great Lent, the Orthodox faithful keep a series of fasts and other observances intended to deepen their devotion and promote a spirit of repentance in preparation for Easter, which is the single most important event on the Orthodox calendar.

The Word of Wisdom was received on the day when Orthodox monks and other faithful believers were enjoying their first meal following two days of total fasting at the start of Great Lent. The Word of Wisdom provides dietary guidance that, if adhered to, brings promised blessings. The dietary guidance given in the Word of Wisdom is similar to that prescribed for the Wednesday and Friday meals of Great Lent.

In Orthodoxy (February 27, 1833; exact match):

- Orthodox monks and other Orthodox believers who are physically able are encouraged to keep a total fast from the first Monday of Great Lent to Wednesday evening.
- The permitted foods for meals on Wednesday and Friday are described in this quotation from the website of the Orthodox Church in America:

  At the meals on Wednesday and Friday xerophagy is prescribed. Literally this means 'dry eating'. Strictly interpreted, it signifies that we may eat only vegetables cooked with water and salt, and also such things as fruit, nuts, bread and honey. In practice, octopus and shell-fish are also allowed on days of xerophagy; likewise vegetable margarine and corn or other vegetable oil, not made from olives.[1]

- The purpose of fasting is aptly described by Saint Symeon the New Theologian:

  Fasting gradually disperses and drives away spiritual darkness and the veil of sin that lies on the soul, just as the sun dispels the mist. Fasting enables us spiritually to see that spiritual air in which Christ, the Sun who knows no setting, does not rise, but shines without ceasing.[2]

In the Restored Church of Jesus Christ (February 27, 1833; exact match):

- The Word of Wisdom provides dietary guidance, including prohibitions or strong cautions against tobacco, alcohol, and hot drinks, which are understood as coffee and tea.
- Church members are encouraged to include in their diet "all wholesome herbs," "fruits in the season thereof," and grain, which is to be the staff of life.
- Latter-day Saints who keep the Word of Wisdom are promised spiritual and physical blessings (D&C 89:18–21).
- In addition to keeping the Word of Wisdom, Latter-day Saints are encouraged to fast once a month. For those who are physically able, the fast is kept by skipping two meals during a 24-hour period.

For Latter-day Saints, fasting is also seen as a joyous exercise that should be accompanied with prayer (see D&C 59:14).

---

[1] "Fasting & Fast-Free Seasons of the Church," Orthodox Church in America, Orthodox Church in America, under "Concerning Fasting," accessed April 7, 2019, https://oca.org/liturgics/outlines/fasting-fast-free-seasons-of-the-church.

[2] *Symeon the New Theologian: The Discourses*, trans. C. J. deCatanzaro, with a preface by Basil Krivoshein and an introduction by George Maloney, S.J., in Classics of Western Spirituality (Mahwah, NJ: Paulist Press, 1980), 168.

March 12/25–Saint Symeon the New Theologian
February 27/March 11–Saint Symeon the New Theologian

CORRELATES TO DOCTRINE AND COVENANTS SECTION 113

Saint Symeon the New Theologian (949–1022) left touching accounts of his encounters with God in the form of brilliant light, reminiscent of some Old Testament accounts of appearances of Jehovah.

In Doctrine and Covenants 113:10, Joseph Smith gives an interpretation of Isaiah 52:6 and other verses. Joseph Smith's interpretation of Isaiah 52:6 seems a close fit for Symeon's experience in meeting God. This revelation was received in Missouri. It was likely received in the latter half of March since his journal records that he arrived in Missouri on March 13, 1838.

In Orthodoxy (March 1838):

- Symeon's writings describe encounters with God, as seen in this quotation where he speaks of himself in the third person:

  And at this word, he [Symeon] sees Him [God] again and, little by little, comes to be completely purified and, purified grows bold and asks that One Himself, and says: "My God, is it You?" And He answers and says: *"Yes, I am He, God,* Who for your sake became man." [emphasis added; quoted in Chapter 12].

- Symeon's writings on meeting God were included in the *Philokalia,* a late-eighteenth compilation of the writings of earlier Greek Church Fathers. The Slavonic version of the *Philokalia* was studied by monks and clergy in Russia, Ukraine, Bulgaria, Romania, and other countries in the nineteenth century.
- Symeon's writings are taken seriously today by Orthodox scholars; however, his writings stirred up opposition in his day. He was exiled from Constantinople in 1009 for claiming to have met God.
- His feast day is September 12 (Revised Julian and Roman Catholic) and September 25 (Julian).

- In Doctrine and Covenants 113:10, Joseph interpreted Isaiah 52:6, which states:

  Therefore my people shall know my name: therefore they shall know in that day that I am he that doth speak: *behold, it is I* [emphasis added].

- Joseph explained the meaning of Isaiah 52:6–8 as being that the Lord would speak to the scattered remnants of Israel or give them revelation as they return to him.
- It seems that the prophecy in Isaiah 52:6 has a partial fulfilment in Symeon the New Theologian.
- Doctrine and Covenants Section 130, verses 1–3, also show parallels to the teachings of Saint Symeon the New Theologian. See Chapter 12 of this book for more.

April 2 (1843)—Saint John the Ladder, Fourth Sunday of Great Lent

CORRELATES TO DOCTRINE AND COVENANTS SECTION 130

John is also called Saint John *Climacus* and Saint John *Lestvichnik* (both terms mean *ladder*). He wrote a book in the sixth century AD that is entitled *The Divine Ladder of Ascent*. Portions of *The Divine Ladder of Ascent* are read in Orthodox churches every year during Great Lent.

In his book, John describes a conversation he had with an angel regarding the Holy Trinity. This feast day is determined with reference to Easter, thus its date moves every year. It always falls on a Sunday.

In Orthodoxy (April 2, 1843; exact match):

- John gave many points of wise counsel to his readers, who mainly were other monks.
- One of the best-known passages in his book gives this account of a meeting with an angel:

    A light came to me as I was thirsting and I asked what the Lord was before He took visible form. The angel could not tell me because he was not permitted to do so. So I asked him: "In what state is He now?" and the answer was that He was in the state appropriate to Him, though not us. "What is the nature of the standing or sitting at the right hand of the Father?" I asked. "Such mysteries cannot be taken in by the human ear," he replied. Then I pleaded with him right then to bring me where my heart was longing to go, but he said that the time was not yet ripe, since the fire of incorruption was not yet mighty enough within me. And whether during all this, I was in the body or out of it, I cannot rightly say.[1]

- From these questions, one sees that John was asking questions about the nature of the Holy Trinity.
- In 1843, this particular feast day fell on April 14 on the Julian calendar,

---

[1] See St. John Climacus, *The Ladder of divine Ascent*, trans. Colm Luibheid and Norman Russell, with an introduction by Kallistos Ware (Mahwah, New Jersey: The Paulist Press, 1982), 268

corresponding to April 2, 1843 in the United States.

- This work was the first book printed in the New World (1532 in Mexico).[2]

In the Restored Church of Jesus Christ:

- On this same day (April 2, 1843), Joseph Smith recorded Section 130 of the Doctrine and Covenants. This section gives this succinct description of the members of the Godhead:

  The Father has a body of flesh and bones as tangible as man's; the Son also; but the Holy Ghost has not a body of flesh and bones, but is a personage of Spirit. Were it not so, the Holy Ghost could not dwell in us (D&C 130:22).

- Latter-day Saints could conclude that the answers to John's questions came centuries later, in the revelations given by God to the Prophet Joseph Smith.

---

[2] See Raoul Smith, The Ladder of divine Ascent—A Codex and an Icon (Clinton, MA: Museum of Russian Icons, 2013), 5, note 30, accessed July 25, 2019, https://www.museumofrussianicons.org/wp-content/uploads/2016/09/LadderOfDivineAscentFINAL2013Opt.pdf, and John D. Green, *A Strange Tongue: Tradition, Language and the Appropriation of Mystical Experience in late fourteenth-century England and sixteenth-century Spain,* in Studies in Spirituality, Supplement 9 (Leuven, Paris, and Dudley: Peters, 2002), 50, note 36

April 6 (1830)—The Annunciation of Mary

In the Orthodox faith, as in Roman Catholicism, Mary holds an especially sacred role. In Orthodoxy, Mary is known as the Theotokos, or Mother of God (Bogoroditsa, or *Богородица* in Russian). Her veneration forms an important part of Orthodox worship services, though Orthodox services are overall infused with worship of Christ and of the Holy Trinity, or Godhead.

In Orthodoxy (April 6, 1830; exact match):

- The Orthodox calendar has twelve "great feasts" (commemorations) in the year, four of which relate to Mary and eight of which pertain to Christ. One of the four is for the Annunciation of Mary.
- This feast commemorates the appearance of the Angel Gabriel to Mary, announcing the wonderful news that she would be the mother of the Son of the Highest (Luke 1:32).
- On today's Orthodox calendar, this feast falls on March 25/April 7.

In the Restored Church of Jesus Christ (April 6):

- In the nineteenth century, this feast fell on April 6 in the United States.
- In addition to being the feast of the Annunciation of Mary, this particular date was the very day on which Joseph Smith first organized the church that was later to become known as The Church of Jesus Christ of Latter-day Saints.
- Section 21 of the Doctrine and Covenants was also received by Joseph Smith on this day.
- In this important revelation, the Lord referred to Joseph as "a seer, a translator, a prophet, an apostle of Jesus Christ" (D&C 21:1). The Lord instructed Latter-day Saints to "give heed unto all his words and commandments" (D&C 21:4).

- Passages in the Book of Mormon show that Mary's name was known to holy prophets centuries before the birth of Christ. Nephi saw in a vision that Mary was caught up to heaven for a time, prior to the birth of Jesus (1 Nephi 11).
- See the discussion in Chapter 6 of this book under "Annunciation of Mary."

April 26/May 9—Saint Stephen the Enlightener of Perm
CORRELATION TO DOCTRINE AND COVENANTS SECTION 50

The date on which Section 50 was revealed correlates to the feast of Saint Stephen the Enlightener of Perm (born ca. 1340) on the Julian calendar. Stephen converted the Zyrian people to Orthodoxy. The Zyrians were a pagan people who worshiped idols, particularly a birch tree referred to in an Orthodox account as the "magic-mischief birch tree."

In Orthodoxy (May 9; Julian):

- Stephen preached Orthodox Christianity among the Zyrian people in the region of modern Perm', Russia. He was opposed by a local magician, Pan, who was described by Stephen as a "gloomy child of dark darkness," "a magician," an "evil soothsayer," and an "elder witch doctor."[1]
- Stephen's biography states that demons had "filled the whole country and the land with idolatrous deceit."
- Pan and Stephen engaged in lengthy and famous debate over the merits of their respective religions before a crowd of Zyrians.
- During this encounter, the two agreed that the matter should be put to a test of fire and water.
- They would pass through a hot fire, then plunge into the freezing water of a nearby river through a hole in the ice. He whose faith was correct would emerge whole and unharmed.
- Stephen then addressed the crowd, asked for their prayers and expressed a willingness to die for his faith; however, Pan ultimately refused to participate.
- With Pan's refusal, the people sided with Stephan and Pan was exiled.
- The account of Stephen's life is considered a classic of medieval Russian hagiographic literature (biographies of the saints). It was written shortly after Stephen's death. The story describes courageous efforts of a Christian missionary to turn people away from superstition and darkness to the light of Christianity.

- The website for one Russian Orthodox church describes how Stephen went about accomplishing this great work:

This great deed was accomplished by his strength of faith and Christian love. The life of the saint was a victory of faith over unbelief, of love and meekness over malice and impiety.[2]

In the Restored Church of Jesus Christ (May 9):

- Doctrine and Covenants Section 50 was revealed at an early time when some members of the restored Church of Jesus Christ were experiencing strange spiritual phenomena.
- In response to Joseph Smith's inquiries, the Lord gave a revelation cautioning against false spirits, the influence of Satan, and "abominations" in the Church among people who professed the name of the Savior.
- No other revelation given to the Latter-day Saints so clearly delineates the difference between light and darkness in spiritual matters.
- Verses 23 and 24 explain:

23 That which doth not edify is not of God, and is darkness.
24 That which is of God is light; and he that receiveth light, and continueth in God, receiveth more light; and that light growth brighter and brighter until the perfect day.

---

[1] Epifaniy Premudryy, "Slovo o zhiti svyatogo Stefana, byvshego episkopom v Permi" = "Слово о житии святого Стефана, бывшего епископом в Перми," accessed August 2, 2019, http://azbyka.ru/otechnik/Epifanij_Premudryj/slovo-o-zhitii-svjatogo-stefana-byvshego-episkopom-v-permi/#sel=30:13,30:29;32:104,32:117;51:103,51:112;54:1,54:28.
[2] For this quote and others in this heading, see information regarding Stephen under 9 May at http://www.holytrinityorthodox.com/calendar/. Additional information at "St. Stephen the Bishop of Perm," Orthodox Church in America, Orthodox Church in America, https://oca.org/saints/lives/2015/04/26/101208-st-stephen-the-bishop-of-perm.

May 2/15—Saint Athanasius the Great
CORRELATES TO DOCTRINE AND COVENANTS SECTION 13

May 15 on the Julian Calendar is the feast of Saint Athanasius the Great, one of the great theologians, or doctors, of the early Christian church. This was also the date on which John the Baptist appeared to Joseph Smith and Oliver Cowdery, conferring on these men the Aaronic Priesthood.

This correlation invites readers to consider how authority in the respective churches came about. Athanasius served both as Bishop and Patriarch of Alexandria (in Egypt) at different times. As such, he received authority that the Orthodox Church believes originated with the apostles. In contrast, Latter-day Saints believe that Joseph Smith received the Aaronic Priesthood with authority to baptize and administer the Sacrament (Lord's Supper) directly from John the Baptist, who appeared as an angel.

In Orthodoxy (May 15; Julian):

- Athanasius was born about AD 297 and died in 373.
- He is credited for identifying the twenty-seven books of the New Testament that are considered scriptural today.
- As a deacon, Athanasius assisted the bishop of Alexandria at the Council at Nicaea, which formulated the Nicene Creed (later supplemented in 381).
- Athanasius preached against Arianism, a branch of early Christianity that denied the divinity of Christ. He was exiled repeatedly by Roman emperors and endured threats against his life. He served as bishop and patriarch of Alexandria.
- Athanasius was a prolific writer of theological materials and was a staunch defender of Nicene Orthodoxy against Arianism and other heresies.
- He has been called the "Pillar of the Church."
- Athanasius wrote the biography of Saint Anthony the Great and was personally acquainted with Anthony.

- During the translation of the Book of Mormon, Joseph Smith and Oliver Cowdery came to verses that prompted them to pray concerning baptism.
- They took the matter to God in prayer on May 15, 1829, along the banks of the Susquehanna River in Pennsylvania.
- An angel appeared, declaring himself to be John the Baptist. He conferred upon them the Priesthood of Aaron and instructed them to baptize each other (see Joseph Smith—History 1:69).

May 6–Saint John before the Latin Gate
CORRELATION TO DOCTRINE AND COVENANTS SECTION 93

The date on which Doctrine and Covenants 93 was received (May 6, 1833) was the feast that commemorates Saint John before the Latin Gate. This feast marks an event involving John the Beloved (i.e., John the Apostle), who was thrown into a pot of boiling oil in Rome in AD 95, yet emerged unharmed. Interestingly, this Section also quotes several verses from a record of John that has not yet been fully revealed but will be in the future.

In Roman Catholicism (Roman Catholic; May 6):

- The website Catholicism.org provides this account for what is known of John's death and burial:

  Saint John died in the year 100, when he was eighty-eight years old. He was the youngest of all the Apostles, but the last to leave this world. His body as well as his soul have been assumed into Heaven, as Saint Robert Bellarmine assures us and as the tradition of the Faith clearly indicates. When his grave was opened, there was found nothing but bread, and in the eleventh century, Saint Peter Damian tells us that miraculous bread was still being renewed there whenever the tomb of Saint John was opened.[1]

In the Restored Church of Jesus Christ (May 6):

- Latter-day Saints believe that John the Apostle has been translated (see John 21:22 and D&C 7).
- Translated beings have power not to taste of death until Christ comes in glory (3 Nephi 28:7; D&C 7; Moses 7:21, 63).
- Doctrine and Covenants Section 93 specifically gives ten verses of holy scripture attributed to John, promising that "the fulness of John's record is hereafter to be revealed" (D&C 93:6).
- A further promise is given in verse 18:

  And it shall come to pass, that if you are faithful you shall receive the fulness of the record of John.

- Doctrine and Covenants 93 also contains themes related to divine light that are very similar to the teachings of Saint

352

Gregory Palamas and other Orthodox Saints, including Saint Seraphim of Sarov. Orthodoxy draws upon the Gospel of John in formulating these teachings (John 1 and 14).

- Doctrine and Covenants 93 seems to contain a reference the Orthodox teachings on the Uncreated or Tabor light in verse 29, which states:

  Man was also in the beginning with God. Intelligence, or the light of truth, was not created or made, neither indeed can be.

- By using the term "indeed," the wording of this Section seems to be replying to an assertion already made. But which church or theologian made the assertion that the light of Christ (or "Intelligence" or "light of truth") was "not created"? This seems to be an indirect reference to St. Gregory Palamas, who taught that the light or energies of God were "Uncreated."

---

[1] The Slaves of the Immaculate Heart of Mary, "Saint John Before the Latin Gate," Saint Benedict Center, May 6, 2000, accessed August 2, 2019 https://catholicism.org/saint-john-before-the-latin-gate-95.html. A Catholic martyrology gives this account for John's experience before the Latin Gate: "At Rome, the feast of St. John before the Latin Gate. Being bound and brought to Rome from Ephesus by the order of Domitian, he was condemned by the Senate to be cast, near the said gate, into a vessel of boiling oil, from which he came out more healthy and vigorous than before." See "Roman Martyrology (Martyrologium Romanum)," Boston Catholic Journal, Boston Catholic Journal, s.v. "May 6," accessed August 2, 2019 http://www.boston-catholic-journal.com/roman-martrylogy-in-english/roman-martyrology-may-in-english.htm#May_6th

May 7/20–The Sign of the Cross over Jerusalem
CORRELATION TO DOCTRINE AND COVENANTS SECTION 49

This date (Revised Julian) commemorates a great miracle that according to Christian tradition occurred on May 7, 351. In the days of Emperor Constantius (son of Constantine the Great), a vision of a cross was seen in the sky over Jerusalem, resulting in the conversion of many souls.

In Orthodoxy (May 7; Revised Julian):

- The website of the Orthodox Church in America gives this account of the event:

  The vision of the Cross over Jerusalem strengthened the Orthodox faithful and contributed to the return of many Arians to the Church. It is also a reminder of the awesome Second Coming of Christ, when "the sign of the Son of man shall appear in heaven" (Matthew 24:30).[1]

- Arianism was a branch of Christianity that denied the divinity of Christ. This teaching was condemned at the Council of Nicaea in AD 325 (for more on Arianism.

In the Restored Church of Jesus Christ (May 7):

- One of the themes in Doctrine and Covenants 49 may, indirectly, be a match to this miracle.
- Section 49, verse 8 states:

  Wherefore, I will that all men shall repent, for all are under sin, except those which I have reserved unto myself, holy men that ye know not of.

- At times, God shows marvelous miracles to encourage people to repent. Several such miracles are reported in the Book of Mormon (see for example, Helaman 16:13–14; 3 Nephi 1:15–19, 23).
- Who are the "holy men" of whom the Church "knows not"?
- This verse likely does not refer to the specific "translated beings" described in Latter-day Saint scripture, because their situations were known by the date of this revelation

(John the Apostle, the Three Nephites and the City of Enoch). See discussion in Chapter 3 of this book, under "Doctrine and Covenants 49:8."

- Translated beings have power not to taste of death until Christ comes in glory (3 Nephi 28:7; D&C 7; Moses 7:21, 63).
- Could it be that some of the Eastern Orthodox and Roman Catholic saints of whom I write are the *holy men* mentioned?
- If so, then their life stories, writings and tales of their miracles (and of other great miracles reported in Christian tradition)   are   worthy   of   study.

---

[1] "Commemoration of the Apparition of the Sign of the Precious Cross Over Jerusalem, in 351 AD," Orthodox Church in America, Orthodox Church in America, http://oca.org/saints/lives/1831/05/07/107787-commemoration-of-the-apparition-of-the-sign-of-the-precious-cross.

June 27 (1844)—The Prophet Amos
CORRELATION TO DOCTRINE AND COVENANTS SECTION 135

Joseph Smith shares a feast date with Saint Alexander of Svir of Russia (1448–1533). Joseph was killed in Carthage Jail on this day; Alexander was born on the day of this feast. Both men experienced remarkable visions of God. Joseph cited Amos 3:7 to support the idea that God speaks to the world through prophets.

Amos 3:7 states:

> "Surely the Lord God will do nothing, but he revealeth his secret unto his servants the prophets."

In Orthodoxy (June 27, 1844; exact match):

- Alexander was born on the feast day of Amos. His parents thus named him *Amos*.
- His name was changed to *Alexander* when he was tonsured a monk.
- He is revered for his vision of the Holy Trinity (1508).
- See Chapter 12 of this book for more on Alexander of Svir. See also this book's entry for August 30, correlation to Doctrine and Covenants Section 63.

In the Restored Church of Jesus Christ (June 27):

- Joseph was martyred at Carthage Jail on the feast day of Amos. June 27, 1844 was the very day when the Orthodox world was commemorating Amos.
- June 27 in the United States was June 15 in Russia and other Orthodox countries in the nineteenth century (twelve-day gap). Today, the feast of Amos falls on June 15/28 (thirteen-day gap).
- The day before Joseph's martyrdom, a book was advertised for sale in the *Nauvoo Neighbor* that contained a chapter on all the religious denominations in the United States. This book was entitled, *He Pasa Ekklesia: An Original History of the Religious Denominations of the United States.*[1] A chapter written by Joseph was included on "The Latter-day Saints." There was no Chapter on

Eastern Orthodoxy (there was no Orthodox presence in the United States at that time).

- Joseph opened this chapter by citing Amos 3:7, in support of the idea that God guides his Church through prophets.
- Thus, in Joseph's final published testimony, he cited this verse from Amos.

---

[1] See Joseph Smith, "The Latter Day Saints," in *He Pasa Ekklesia: An Original History of the Religious Denominations of the United States*, ed. I. Daniel Rupp (Philadelphia: J.Y. Humpreys, and Harrisburg: Clyde and Williams, 1844), 414, e-book, accessed August 2, 2019, https://archive.org/stream/hepasaekklesiaa00ruppgoog#page/n414/mode/2up. For background see "Latter Day Saints, 1844," The Joseph Smith Papers, Intellectual Reserve, Inc., under "Historical Introduction," http://www.josephsmithpapers.org/paper-summary/latter-day-saints-1844/1#historical-intro.

June 29/July 12–Saints Peter and Paul's Day
CORRELATION TO DOCTRINE AND COVENANTS 132

Joseph recorded this revelation on July 12, 1843, which since the early twentieth century is the date on the Julian calendar (Russian) for the commemoration of the feast of Saints Peter and Paul (it fell on July 11 in 1843). This feast is observed on June 29 on the Revised Julian calendar and on the Catholic calendar. It is one of the most ancient Christian feasts, dating back to at least AD 250.

Given that feasts begin at sundown, this feast would have covered parts of July 11 and 12 in Joseph's day.

The Lord conferred on Peter keys of authority, as recorded in Matthew 16:19:

> And I will give unto you [Peter] *the keys* of the kingdom of heaven; and whatsoever thou shalt bind on earth shall be bound in heaven; and whatsoever thou shalt loose on earth shall be loosed in heaven [emphasis added].

Peter's teaching on the divine nature is cited prominently by Orthodox writers in support of the idea of deification, or *theosis*. 2 Peter 1:4 states, "Whereby are given unto us exceeding great and precious promises: that by these ye might be partakers of the divine nature, having escaped the corruption that is in the world through lust." For an outline of Orthodox teachings on deification, see Chapter 2 of this book.

In Orthodoxy (July 12; Julian):

> *The Orthodox Study Bible* (s.v. Matthew 16:19) summarizes the Orthodox understanding of this verse:

> > *Keys of the kingdom* refers to a special authority that will be given to both Peter and the other apostles after the Resurrection. . . . Peter was not a leader over the others, but among them. This truth was confirmed at the Council of Jerusalem (Acts 15) where the apostles and presbyters met as equals, and where Peter advised, but James presided. Papal claims in later centuries must not be confused with the NT witness regarding Peter, nor should the role of Peter be diminished in opposition to these claims.

Binding and losing is a reference primarily to the authority to "absolve sins" . . . but also includes all the teaching, sacramental, and administrative authority of the apostles. *This authority was in turn transmitted to the bishops of the Church and continues in effect to this day* [emphasis added].

In the Restored Church of Jesus Christ (July 12):

- In Doctrine and Covenants 132, the Lord affirms that the faithful can become gods (132:19–20).
- In Doctrine and Covenants 132:45–46, the Lord also affirms that he has conferred the keys of the kingdom on Joseph Smith.

  45 *For I have conferred upon you the keys and power of the priesthood,* wherein I restore all things, and make known unto you all things in due time.

  46 And verily, verily, I say unto you, that whatsoever you seal on earth shall be sealed in heaven. . . . And whosesoever sins you remit on earth shall be remitted eternally in the heavens; and whosesoever sins you retain on earth shall be retained in heaven.

- The keys continue today in the restored Church of Jesus Christ, being held by all members of the Quorum of the Twelve and the First Presidency. The President, who is also the senior Apostle, presides over all; the President of the Church—the senior apostle—exercises all the keys.

20 July/2 August—The Prophet Elijah
CORRELATION TO MULTIPLE SECTIONS OF THE DOCTRINE AND COVENANTS

Elijah was one of the greatest Old Testament prophets. He appeared to Jesus along with Moses on the Mount of Transfiguration (Matthew 17). Malachi 4:5–6 records a prophecy that Elijah would come "before the great and dreadful day of the Lord" and will "turn the heart of the fathers to the children" (or "the father to his son" and before "great and glorious day," as translated in *The Orthodox Study Bible;* see Malachi 3:22–23).

Important correlations to the feast of Elijah are seen in four sections of the Doctrine and Covenants pertaining to temple ordinances for the living and the dead that seal couples and families for eternity.

In Orthodoxy (multiple correlations):

- In the Orthodox faith, Elijah is also greatly revered. Elijah along with Moses was present at the Transfiguration of Christ (Matthew 17), an event that has immense doctrinal importance in Orthodoxy.
- The light that shone from Christ on the mount is referred to as the "Uncreated light" or "Tabor light" in the Orthodox Church (see Chapter 2 above, *"Theosis* or Deification").
- Due to his fasting and secluded life in the wilderness (for example, 1 Kings 17:1–6), Elijah is also viewed as an Old Testament prototype for the early Christian Desert Fathers in Egypt (third century) and Christian monks.
- Under Orthodox teaching, Elijah and Enoch are the two prophets who will testify in the last days in the streets of Jerusalem, as prophesied in Revelation 11:2–12.

In the Restored Church of Jesus Christ (multiple correlations):

- Elijah appeared during the dedication of the Kirtland Temple, conferring sacred sealing keys on Joseph Smith and Oliver Cowdery (D&C 110:13–16).
- These keys continue today with the President of the Church, First Presidency, and Quorum of the Twelve;

however, only the President of the Church—the senior living Apostle—exercises all the keys.

- Temple presidents and sealers perform ordinances for the living and the dead by virtue of the authority that Elijah conferred.
- Sealing ordinances bind couples and families for eternity in fulfilment of Malachi's prophecy that he would "turn the hearts of the fathers to the children" (Malachi 4: 5-6).
- The first commandment to acquire a temple site was revealed on July 20, 1831, the feast of Elijah (Revised Julian and Roman Catholic Carmelite calendars). See Doctrine and Covenants 57:3.
- A further revelation pertaining to a temple site is seen in Doctrine and Covenants 58:57, dated to August 1, 1831. This corresponded to the exact day in the nineteenth century when the Orthodox world (on the Julian calendar of that century) observed the feast of Elijah.
- A revelation regarding the Kirtland Temple is dated August 2, 1831, which is the feast of Elijah on today's Julian calendar. Glorious promises are given in connection with the temple (D&C 97:15–19).
- Important promises were also given regarding a structure near the Kirtland Temple that was to be built for the work of the Presidency, where revelations were to be obtained (D&C 94:3). This revelation is also dated August 2, 1831, as was Section 97.

August 30/September 12—Saint Alexander of Svir
CORRELATION TO DOCTRINE AND COVENANTS 63

Saint Alexander of Svir is the only Russian Orthodox saint to have seen a vision of the entire Holy Trinity, or angels representing the Trinity. While praying one night in his hermitage (i.e., his cabin), a great light appeared, and Alexander saw three distinct heavenly persons. Each was wearing "most bright garments and clothed in white, beautiful in purity, shining more than the sun and illuminated with unutterable heavenly glory, and each holding a staff in his hand" (See Chapter 11, Saint Alexander of Svir).

Alexander spent part of his life in isolation, living as a hermit in a remote region near the eastern shore of Lake Ladoga in northwest Russia. Later, acting on divine command, he built up a monastery at this locale.

In Orthodoxy (August 30; Revised Julian):

- The ultimate transfiguration of the earth is a theme that has considerable importance in Orthodoxy. The monks who spread Orthodoxy though much of what today is Russia were seeking to prepare the earth for the Lord's Second Coming and the eventual transfiguration of the Earth.
- In his seminal work, *The Icon and the Axe,* author James Billington made these observations:

  Just as the apostles had seen a glimpse of the light from God at the Transfiguration of Christ, so could a true monk in Christ's universal church gain a glimmer of the coming *transfiguration of the cosmos.* . . . The hermit-monks who founded new monasteries on the northeastern frontier of Europe [i.e., in northwest Russia] thought of their new houses not so much as institutions designed to revivify the established church as transitory places in man's pilgrimage towards the second coming . . . the promised end was not just the resurrection of the dead but the *transfiguration of all creation* [emphasis added].[1]

- Orthodox scholar Kallistos Ware discusses the transfiguration of the

  earth in his classic work, *The Orthodox Church:*

Not only man's body but the whole of the material creation will eventually be transfigured: "Then I saw a new heaven and a new earth; for the first heaven and the first earth had passed away" (Revelation 21:1).[2]

In the Restored Church of Jesus Christ (August 30):

- Doctrine and Covenants 63:20–21 states:

  20 Nevertheless, he that endureth in faith and doeth my will, the same shall overcome, and shall receive an inheritance upon the earth *when the day of transfiguration shall come*;
  21 When *the earth shall be transfigured*, even according to the pattern which was shown unto mine apostles upon the mount; of which account the fullness ye have not yet received [emphasis added].

- Of all the Russian saints, Alexander was perhaps the greatest visionary of all. His vision of the Holy Trinity sets him apart from all others.
- Alexander started his monastic service in a monastery named for the Transfiguration of the Lord on Valaam Island in Lake Ladoga. His body now reposes in a church and cloister named for the Transfiguration.
- With these points in mind, it is fitting that the Lord chose to reveal Section 63 on his feast day.

---

[1] James H. Billington, *The Icon and the Axe: An Interpretive History of Russian Culture* (New York: Vintage Books, 1970), 52
[2] Timothy Ware (Bishop Kallistos of Kokleia), *The Orthodox Church* (London:

Table 1—Temple Correlations in the Doctrine and Covenants

The table below shows references to sections from the Doctrine and Covenants with key words such as the *temple* (also "house of prayer" and related phrases), *temple endowments*, and *baptism for dead*. Strong, doctrinally significant correlations to the Orthodox calendar are shown for each. The pattern of important temple-related correlations to the Orthodox (and Roman Catholic) calendars is pervasive and comprehensive. *Virtually every temple-related reference finds an appropriate theme on these calendars!*

Doctrine and Covenants Citation	Keyword	Description
57:3	Temple	**Elijah's feast. July 20. Revised Julian and Roman Catholic (Carmelite).** Commandment to acquire a specific parcel for temple site in Missouri.
58:57	Temple	**Elijah's feast. August 1. Exact Match.** Commandment to dedicate the temple site in Missouri.
94:3–9	House for work of the presidency	**Elijah's feast. August 2. Julian.** Instructions regarding the size and layout of a house for the work of the Church Presidency. The glory of the Lord to be present. These promises are similar to those for the Kirtland Temple which was built on an adjacent lot. This house for the work of the Presidency was never built.
97:15–19	Temple	**Elijah's feast. August 2. Julian.** Glorious promises regarding the temple in Missouri are made. In talks by Church authorities, these promises are treated as applicable to all Latter-day Saint temples.
38:8, 32	Endowed	**Saint Seraphim's feast (repose/death). January 2. Revised Julian.** This is the first promise of a spiritual endowment for Latter-day Saints. The fulfillment came in 1836 through the ordinances of the Kirtland

		Temple and in the Pentecostal outpouring that occurred during the dedication of this Temple.
38:1 and 109:79	Seraphs/ seraphims	**Saint Seraphim. January 2. Revised Julian**. The only two mentions in the Doctrine and Covenants of heavenly "seraphs" are 38:1 and 109:79, which mention "bright, shining seraphs" (the Russian translation says, "bright, shining seraphims"). Both of these verses have connections to Seraphim. He died on January 2 (the calendar date on which D&C 38 was revealed). He literally shined with heavenly light on more than one occasion, in well-documented events. See above regarding St. Seraphim and the endowment (D&C 38:8, 32). Section 109 is the dedicatory prayer for the Kirtland Temple. Seraphim died on January 2, 1833. This date fell within the calendar range of dates during which D&C 88 was revealed. D&C 88:119 contains the commandment to build the Kirtland Temple. During the dedication, miraculous outpourings of heavenly light were seen.

<u>124:22–</u> <u>31, 55</u>	House unto my name; baptism for dead	**Theophany (baptism of Christ). January 19. Julian.** This section gives the first commandment regarding baptism for the dead and the building of the Nauvoo Temple. At Theophany, the voice of the Father was heard and the Spirit descended. Similarly, temple ordinances help prepare people to meet God. Baptism of Christ shows all people need baptism; these can be performed in temples for deceased persons. The Theophany is one of twelve "great feasts" of Orthodoxy.
<u>127</u> (related to D&C 128 and 138)	Captives and setting at liberty; baptism for dead	**Entry of Christ into synagogue; and start of liturgical year. September 1. Revised Julian.** D&C 127 was revealed on September 1. Under Orthodox tradition of this date, the Savior entered the synagogue and quoted Isaiah 61:1–2, which mentions liberating the *captives* (see Luke 4:16–22). In Latter-day Saint teaching, the term "captives" is associated with the preaching of the gospel among the dead and with baptism for the dead. This is seen in D&C 138, in which Joseph Fielding Smith received a vision of Christ's ministry among the dead while his grave was in the tomb. See D&C 138: 18, 31 and 42. See also Doctrine and Covenants 128:22

		regarding the "prisoners."
128:21	Baptism for dead	**Feast of Archangel Michael. Revised Julian. September 6.** Joseph mentions the angels Michael, Raphael, and Gabriel. This ancient feast honors the Archangel Michael. Orthodox writers explain that it is intended also to honor the other archangels besides Michael, including Raphael and Gabriel.
132:19	Eternal marriage	**Feast of Saints Peter and Paul. July 12. Julian.** The Lord confers keys on Joseph using wording (132:45–46) similar to what Jesus told Peter (Matthew 16:19)
Excluded		**The following verses are excluded as they are figurative, or only in section headings. One has a historical reference to Herod's Temple in Jerusalem.** See Doctrine and Covenants 45:18, 20; 59; 60; 93:35; and 101:23. Doctrine and Covenants 43:16 also contains a reference to the temple endowment, but no precise date is given.

Glossary

Recommended Reading

Glossary of Orthodox Terms

Note: The terms given alphabetically below are, from left to right, English, Greek (where available, in Latin letters), and Russian. The Russian words are usually similar to Church Slavonic terms, which evolved from the religious language originally devised by Saints Cyril and Methodius in the ninth century. Church Slavonic is still used for Orthodox worship in several countries, in Russia, Serbia, Bulgaria and other countries. Where a term is described in detail in Part I or Part V of this book, the Glossary will refer back to the appropriate page.

Many definitions have been grouped below under the following special categories which are given in bold: (1) Orthodox Church Architecture; (2) Liturgical Vocabulary; (3) Liturgical Books; (4) Hymns; (5) Worship Services; (6) Priestly and Monastic Clothing; (7) Clergy and Priesthood; (8) Monk, Nun, Monastic titles and terms; (9) Monasteries and Convents. All other definitions are grouped alphabetically under *Other Terms.*

(1) Orthodox Church Architecture

Most Orthodox churches are built with a cross in a square shape. The altar is always on the east and worshippers always face that direction. Orthodox churches may have one or more domes on top. If the church has one dome, it represents Christ; if five, the four corners represent the four Gospels and the one in the center represents Christ.

Altar/Gr. hieron/Ru. престол

This term can refer to the entire sanctuary where the Eucharist (Holy Communion) is consecrated. The sanctuary is on the east end of the church. The holy table is also referred to as the altar. This table is in the middle of the sanctuary and represents the sepulcher of the Lord and is also thought of as a throne where Christ is present. On the altar are several objects, including a *corporal/antimens* cloth with an image of Christ's body being placed in the tomb, candles, a blessing cross, the Holy Gospel, and an ark or tabernacle in which the consecrated Holy Communion is stored (the "Holy Gifts") for the sick or for use during Great Lent. A separate table known as the *prosthesis* normally is positioned north of the holy table. This is where the actual bread and wine for the Holy Communion are placed, as well as the sacred utensils.

Bema

The raised platform on which the altar stands. This platform fills the sanctuary and extends partly into the nave. The part in the nave is referred to as the *solea* (Ru. солея).

Cathredral / Ru. кафедральный собор

A church that is the seat of the Bishop of the diocese. An Orthodox cathedral is not necessarily the largest or most noted church in the bishops's *eparchy* (diocese).

Choir area/Ru. клирос

Since Orthodox services often have two choirs singing antiphons, there are two areas designated for the choirs. These are on both ends of the *solea,* which is the part of the *bema* that extends into the nave. In some churches, they are positioned in the nave, on the north and south sides.

Iconostasis/Ru. иконостас

A screen of icons that separates the nave from the sanctuary or altar. This looks like a wall with icons in most Orthodox churches; however, the iconostasis is not intended as a wall. In earlier centuries, the icons were hung so that the sanctuary was visible to worshipers. Over time, more rows of icons were added, eventually obscuring the view of the sanctuary. The iconostasis has three sets of doors, the most important of which—the royal doors—are located in the middle of the iconostasis.

Narthex/Ru. притвор

The entry area in the church. An icon of the Theotokos, or Mother of God, is positioned at the left of a second door which leads into the Nave. To the right is an icon of Christ.

Nave/Ru. средняя часть

The main hall of the church. In the Russian tradition, worshipers stand during services. In the Greek tradition, worshipers are generally seated, though they do stand during designated portions of the Divine Liturgy. In Russian Orthodox churches, a few benches are often available at the back or on the sides for those who cannot stand.

Sobor/Ru. собор

In Russian Orthodoxy, a large church where the faithful of a given city can gather. The sobor is not necessarily the cathedral.

Temple/Ru. храм

> In Russian Orthodoxy, this term is often used when referring to a church. The term is also translated as *temple* when speaking of the Old Testament temples or temples of the Church of Jesus Christ of Latter-day Saints.

(2) Liturgical Vocabulary

Anaphora/Ru. анафора

> The portion of the Divine Liturgy during which the Holy Gifts (bread and wine) are consecrated.

Anathema or *anathematisma/Ru. анафема*

> A curse or suspension pronounced by the church against heretics or enemies on the first Sunday of Great Lent (the "Sunday of Orthodoxy"). This practice dates back many centuries, at least to the time when the heresy of iconoclasm was defeated (ca. 787).

Antidoron/Ru. антидор

> A portion of the *prosphora* (sacramental bread) that is left over after the Divine Liturgy service during which worshippers partake of the Eucharist or Holy Communion. The *antidoron* is distributed to worshippers to be eaten at home with reverence.

Antiphon/Ru. антифон

> Alternate singing by two choirs. In Orthodox services, this type of singing is included in vespers and matins in connection with a feast day. Antiphonal singing is also heard in the Divine Liturgy of Saint John Chrysostom. Antiphons are taken from the Psalms.

Corporal/Gr. antimension or antimens/Ru. антиминс

This is the altar cloth. It has an image of Christ's body being placed in the tomb. The *antimension* is signed by the bishop and constitutes the authority for the priest to celebrate the Divine Liturgy. Normally, the *antimension* contains relics, which could consist of small bone fragments of a saint or martyr pressed into a small bit of wax that is sewn into the hem of the *antimension*. With an *antimension*, a priest may celebrate the Divine Liturgy outside of a church. Without an *antimension*, the Divine Liturgy is not celebrated.

Diskarion/Ru. дискос

A plate where the Eucharistic bread is placed prior to its consecration as part of the Divine Liturgy. It may have an engraving of the Last Supper or of the infant Jesus.

Doxology/Ru. славословие

There are two Doxologies, a Greater and Lesser. These are prayers to the Father, Son, and Holy Ghost that are either read or sung. The Lesser Doxology is worded: "Glory to the Father, and to the Son, and to the Holy Spirit, for ever and ever. Amen." The Greater Doxology starts with Luke 2:14 and then continues with beautiful words of praise and invocations seeking God's blessings. It concludes with the words of the Trisagion, "Holy God, Holy Mighty, Holy Immortal, have mercy on us," which is thrice repeated. The term Doxology sometimes also refers to a special church service of praise and thanks following a great deliverance from evil or destruction.

Entrance/Gr. eisodos/Ru. вход

> The term *Entrance* refers to two movements in the Divine Liturgy, referred to as the Small Entrance and the Great Entrance. In the first, the clergy carry in the Gospel book, crying aloud: "Wisdom, let us attend!" In the second, the Holy Gifts (bread and wine) are carried out from the altar in a chalice as the cherubic hymn is chanted.

Eucharist/Ru. причастие

> The Holy Communion of bread and wine. The Eucharist or Holy Communion is consecrated not more than once a day, as part of the Divine Liturgy.

> During the season of Great Lent, the Eucharist is not celebrated during the weekdays. When the Divine Liturgy is celebrated during Great Lent, there is no *anaphora* (consecration of the Holy Communion); instead, the "presanctified gifts" are served. This is the bread and wine that were set aside following an earlier Sunday Divine Liturgy service.

Liturgy/Ru. литургия

> The term *liturgy* is based on two Greek words: *leitos*, meaning "people," and *ergeia*, meaning "working." The word thus suggests that participation in a liturgy is work, a service or duty that is given by the faithful. Liturgy is a work of prayer. The main liturgy in Eastern Orthodoxy is the Divine Liturgy of Saint John Chrysostom. It is during the Divine Liturgy that the Eucharist is consecrated.

Requiem for the Dead/Gr. pannychis/Ru. панихида

A brief church service held in remembrance of the deceased, often forty days or one year following death. The service usually follows the Divine Liturgy, or vespers or matins. *Pannychis* services are held at graveside, if for a specific person, or in the church. A bowl of boiled wheat with raisins and honey is blessed as part of the service and later eaten by those who attended the service.

Prosphoro, prosphora/Ru. просфора

Leavened bread made of wheat flour that is used in the Eucharist. In the Greek tradition, the *prosphora* consists of one loaf, often baked in two layers which represent the two natures of Christ, divine and human. In the Slavic tradition, five smaller loaves are used, representing the miracle that Jesus worked in feeding the multitude. The *prosphora* is stamped with a seal having a cross and the letters: IC XC NIKA ("Jesus Christ conquers"). The middle portion of the *prosphora* is called the Lamb; it is cut out for use in the Eucharist, while the remaining bread is the *antidoron*.

Sacred utensils

Utensils used in the Eucharist include a paten or *diskarion* (plate with a stem) on which the *prosphora* is placed; a spear, used to cut the portion of the *prosophora* known as the Lamb; a Chalice, into which the wine and bread particles are placed; and a spoon, for administering the Holy Gifts (bread mixed with the wine) to worshippers.

(3) Liturgical Books

In order for Orthodox services to be conducted, a small library of books is needed. This is a list of the key works that are used in Orthodox worship.

The Psalter or Psalms/ Ru. Псалтирь следованная

> Under the current pattern (of the Sabaite or Jerusalem *Typikon*), the Psalms are read in their entirety in Orthodox services each week. During Great Lent, they are read two times in a week.

The Horologion/ Ru. Часослов

> This book contains the psalms and prayers for the worship services held at set hours of the day (thus, *not* for the Divine Liturgy, which has no prescribed time).

The Octoechos/ Ru.Октоих

> This book contains hymns that are sung each week, organized according to the eight musical modes or tones that are used in singing Orthodox hymns.

The Menaia/ Ru. Минеи

> There are multiple volumes to this work, all containing hymns that are sung on the days of the annual cycle of fixed feasts.

The Triodion and Pentecostarion/ Ru.Триодь and Цветная Триодь

> These works contain, respectively, the hymns and Biblical readings that are used during the period of Great Lent (leading up to Easter) and the fifty-day period leading up to Pentecost.

The Typikon / Ru. Типикон

This work is considered the ultimate arbiter concerning all questions having to do with liturgical worship and the fasts.

The Euchologion and Hieratikon / Ru. Требник and Служебник

These works contain the litanies and priestly prayers for all the various offices of Orthodoxy.

The Epistle and Gospel Books / Ru. Апостол and Евангелие

The scriptural readings that are used for the various church services. The "Epistle" contains the Book of Acts and the Epistles; the Gospel Books include the four gospels.

(4) Hymns

Troparion / Ru. тропарь

An Orthodox hymn commemorating the feast day of a saint or specific event in Biblical or Christian history. The *troparia* are linked to the calendar. Embedded within their words are doctrines and teachings of the Orthodox faith, thus the *troparia* can be said to serve both a role in worship and in teaching.

Kontakion (Kondak)

The *kontakion* is a hymn about a biblical event having eighteen to twenty-four stanzas, with a short refrain at the end of each. In modern use, only the first stanza is sung during worship, normally on important religious feast days. This form of hymn is attributed to Saint Romanos the Melodist (sixth century AD). Romanos was a prolific composer. Tradition holds that his beautiful Nativity Kontakion was revealed to him by the Theotokos herself.

Sticheron/Ru. стихира

> A hymn based on a psalm, sung during matins or vespers.

Theotokion

> A hymn honoring the Theotokos, or Mother of God. These are included in all Orthodox services, often after the Trisagion, "Holy God, Holy Mighty, Holy Immortal, have mercy on us," which is thrice repeated.

(5) Worship Services – Daily Offices

Worship services normally follow this daily pattern:

> Vespers (sunset)/Gr. Espermos/ Ru. Вечерня
>
> Compline (after-dinner)/Ru. Повечерия
>
> Midnight Office (12:00 am)
>
> Matins/ Gr. Orthros (sunrise)/Ru. утреня
>
> First Hour (6:00 or 7 :00 am)
>
> Third Hour (9:00 am)
>
> Sixth Hour (12:00 pm)
>
> Ninth Hour (3:00 pm)

In addition, the Eucharist is consecrated and served as part of the Divine Liturgy of Saint John Chrysostom on Sundays. The Divine Liturgy often follows directly after matins, though it can be held later. Some churches may also have daily Divine Liturgy services. A few days per year, other liturgies are used, besides those of St. John Chrysostom.

(6) Priestly and Monastic Clothing

Monks and nuns wear a simple black habit or cassock. As they progress to higher levels of monastic devotion, items of clothing are added to the habit. Those who reach the highest level, the Great Schema, wear the *analav* (Ru. *аналав*), which is made of leather or wool and hangs from the shoulders, covering the back and front. The *analav* has a cross and figurative elements. It represents the monk or nun's lifelong commitment to the cross and to God.

Common items of clothing worn by monks and the clergy in Orthodox churches include:

> For the deacon: the *sticharion*, *stole*, and *cuffs*.

> For the priest: the *sticharion*, the *stole*, the *cuffs*, and the *chasuble*.

> For the bishop: the *sticharion*, the *sakkos*, the cuffs, the *omophorion*, and the *mantle*.

Chasuble/Gr. Phelonion, Phenolion/Ru. Фелонь

> A liturgical vestment worn by a priest over his other vestments. The *phelonion* does not have sleeves and the fabric on the front generally is shortened to facilitate the priest's service at the altar.

Crosier or Staff/Ru. Посох

> The pastoral staff of a bishop, also carried by senior monastic figures. The staff has two serpents toward the top, said to represent the brass serpent on the pole (Numbers 21:8–9; John 3:14; compare to Helaman 8:14–15).

380

Gr. sticharion / Ru. подризник

The long white (or yellow) undergarment of the clergy. The deacon wears it without other vestments except his stole and cuffs. The priest wears it under the chasuble. The bishop wears it under his *sakkos*. It is understood as the "robe of salvation and the garment of joy" (cf. Isaiah 61:3).

Mantle / Gr. mandia / Ru. мантия

A full cape worn by bishops and heads of monasteries, often blue or purple. It is an emblem of spiritual authority, reminiscent of the mantle passed from Elijah to Elisha as the former was taken to heaven.

Omophorion / Ru. омофор

A scarf worn by the bishop, symbolizing his authority. It is worn over the *sakkos*.

Sakkos / Ru. саккос

A tunic worn by a bishop during the Divine Liturgy. The sakkos is a brocade fabric with broad sleeves. This is worn by the bishop instead of the priest's *phelonion*.

Stole / Gr. epitrachelion / Ru. епитрахиль

Terms for a priest's stole

Stole / Gr. orarion / Ru. орарь) (a deacon's stole)

The stole typifies the priesthood. For a priest, it passes around his neck and is joined at front for its full length. A deacon's stole is worn on the left shoulder, sometimes crossed in front and in back as well.

381

Zone or girdle / Ru. пояс

A belt worn around clerical vestments.

(7) Clergy, Priesthood

Black Clergy, White Clergy

The term black clergy refers to the monastic clergy, meaning monks who have been ordained to the priesthood. Bishops and patriarchs are drawn from the black clergy. In contrast, the white clergy are parish priests. They are permitted to marry, as long as the marriage is contracted before their ordination.

Deacon, Hierodeacon

Some deacons serve on a volunteer basis; others are full-time clergy. A monk who has been ordained a deacon is a *hierodeacon.*

Priest; hieropriest or hieromonk / Ru. священник and иеромонах

The Divine Liturgy and other church offices are celebrated by a priest with the assistance of deacons and others. The priest is also able to perform the other sacraments of the Orthodox Church.

Bishop / Gr. episcopos / Ru. епископ

The bishop oversees the work of the Orthodox Church in a defined region called an eparchy. The bishops and priests serve full time.

Metropolitan/Ru. митрополит

> A metropolitan governs Orthodox Church affairs in an area comprised of several eparchies.

Patriarch/Ru. патриарх

> The head of most autocephalic Orthodox churches is called a patriarch. A few have the title of archbishop.

(8) Monk, Nun, Monastic titles and terms

The same levels of monasticism apply both to men and women. Novice and Rassophore nuns and monks are referred to, respectively, as "sister" or "brother"; Stavrophore and Great Schema nuns and monks are referred to as "mother" or "father."

Men: Abbot/Archimandrite, Hegumen/ Ru. Игумень

Women: Abbess or Prioress/Gr. Hegumene/Ru. Игуменья

> The titles Archimandrite and Hegumen both can be translated as Abbot, or the head of a monastery; however, the Archimandrite is the higher title of the two, indicating that the particular monk has authority over multiple monasteries or over a large and important monastery.

> An abbess has authority within her convent; nothing transpires in the convent without her blessing. In the Russian tradition, she wears a pectoral cross and can bless others by making the sign of the cross. She may also enter the altar area of the church to help maintain it and the vestments of the clergy.

Asceticism

A lifestyle involving abstinence, fasting, vigils, prayer, labor, and the disciplining of bodily appetites in pursuit of Christian virtue. An example is seen in Christ's admonition to take up the cross and follow him (Matthew 16:24). Orthodox writers see this as an invitation for believers to engage in self-denial and to follow Christ; both are aspects of Christian asceticism. In Orthodoxy, all believers are invited to engage in their own ascetic striving through fasting and other acts of religious devotion. The monastic lifestyle in particular is believed to embody Christian ascetic ideals.

Hermit

A monk who seeks spiritual development in wilderness seclusion.

Novice/ Ru. послушник

A man or woman living in a monastery who wishes to become a monk.

Rassophore/ Gr. rasophoro / Ru. рясофор

The first degree of monasticism.

Little or Lesser Schema/ Gr. stavrophoros/ Ru. крестоносец

The second degree of monasticism.

Great Schema/ Gr. megaloschemos/ Ru. Схима

The highest degree of monasticism. Schema monks wear the *analav*.

Stylite

A monk who spends an extended period of time on top of a pillar. Some famed monks in the early centuries of Christianity spent many years on top of pillars teaching and counseling people.

Tonsure

The formal act of clipping some or all the hair from the head of a man or woman entering monastic life.

(9) Monasteries and Female Monasteries (Convents)

Cell/Ru. Келья

A monk's personal quarters, normally shared with two or three others. Sometimes the cell is a separate hut, other times it is within a larger monastic structure.

Cenobitic

A communal form of monastic life.

Skete/Ru. скит

A small monastic residence that is part of a larger monastery. Sketes are located a good distance from the main monastery, giving the monks a measure of relative isolation, yet providing a convenient connection to the monastery.

Idiorrhythmic

A monastery where the monks retain their own personal property.

Lavra, Laura/Ru. лавра

A large and important monastery, originally composed of a collection of caves where monks resided. Only a relative few monasteries have this designation. Examples include the Monastery of the Great Lavra (Mount Athos, tenth century), the Lavra of Saint Sabbas (near Jerusalem, sixth century), the Trinity Lavra of Saint Sergius (near Moscow, fourteenth century), the Kyiv Pechersk Lavra or Kiev Lavra of the Caves (Kiev, eleventh century), the Pochayiv Lavra (Ukraine, sixteenth century), and the Neamt Lavra (Romania, 15th century).

Stavropegic monastery

A monastery that is directly under the authority of a patriarch. Most monasteries are under the authority of the local bishop.

Wilderness/Ru. пустынь

The land included within in or attached to a monastery in a remote location. The Russian term *pustyn'* can be translated as "desert" or "wilderness."

(10) Other terms

Apophatic

Seeking understanding by "not speaking"; or describing God in terms of what he is *not*. Some theologians assert that Orthodox theology of God is *apophatic* in nature; that is, God is beyond describing in human terms.

Apostle / Gr. Apostolos / Ru. Апостол

A book containing excerpts from the Acts of the Apostles and the Epistles for use during the Divine Liturgy. These readings are organized by readings based on the calendar. During the course of the liturgical year, Orthodox worshippers who consistently attend church services will hear much of the New Testament, Psalms, and portions of the Old Testament, in a language they can understand. This pattern has been followed since early Christian times.

Athos, Athonite

Mount Athos is known as the "Holy Mountain" in Orthodoxy. Athos is a peninsula in Greece that for over a thousand years has been home to monasteries with rich spiritual traditions. One of the largest Christian libraries in the world is found in Vatopaidi, one of the leading monasteries on Athos. Athos has a special status in the European Union. Only males may serve on Athos or visit. In Orthodox tradition, Athos is under the special care of the Theotokos, or Mother of God.

Autocephalous

Orthodox Churches that are self-governing are referred to as *autocephalous*. These include the Ecumenical Patriarchate of Constantinople, the Patriarchate of Alexandria, the Patriarchate of Antioch, the Patriarchate of Jerusalem, the Patriarchate of Russia, the Orthodox Church of Serbia, the Orthodox Church of Romania, the

Orthodox Church of Bulgaria, the Orthodox Church of Georgia, the Orthodox Church of Cyprus, the Orthodox Church of Greece, the Orthodox Church of Poland, the Orthodox Church of Albania, the Orthodox Church of the Czech lands and Slovakia, and the Ukrainian Orthodox Church. Some would consider the Orthodox Church in America to be autocephalous as well.

Byzantine, Byzantine Rite

The Christian form of worship that developed in the Byzantine Empire, which arose in the eastern provinces of the old Roman Empire. These forms of worship derived largely from those practiced in the early centuries of Christianity in and around Jerusalem and that were "synthesized" with practices in Constantinople (the capital of Byzantium).

Calendar

Gregorian Calendar

This is the modern calendar used in most of the world for civil purposes. It is named after Pope Gregory XIII, who introduced it in October 1582. In most Catholic countries of Europe, Thursday, October 4, 1582 was followed by Friday, October 15, 1582, resulting in ten days being skipped. The Gregorian Calendar was adopted in the British colonies of North America in 1752 and was in use in the United States during Joseph Smith's lifetime. Thus, dates he and his scribes recorded were based on the Gregorian calendar. The Gregorian calendar treats years that are multiples of four as leap years, except for years divisible by one hundred but not by four hundred.

Julian Calendar

This calendar was used since 46 BC, when it was introduced by Julius Caesar, until the pope introduced the Gregorian calendar in 1582. The Julian year is 365 days long, with a leap year every fourth year, without exception, making the Julian year on average 365.25 days long. The inaccuracy of the Julian Calendar arises due to there being too many leap years compared to the solar year. The Julian loses 11 minutes a year and thus falls back one day every 128 years compared to the solar year.

Greece followed the Julian Calendar until February 15, 1923, when thirteen days were dropped, making the next day March 1, 1923. In May of that same year, a church congress held in Greece authorized the adoption of a revised Julian calendar, which closely followed the logic of the Gregorian. Under the Revised Julian calendar, there will be no difference between its dates and those of the Gregorian Calendar for eight hundred years.

Since 1923, some Orthodox Churches follow the Revised Julian (such as the Greek Orthodox Church), while others follow the Julian by adding thirteen days to the Gregorian dates to preserve an equivalent Julian date.

Canonization or glorification/ *Ru. канонизация or прославление*

The process by which a particular deceased Christian is proclaimed a saint and thus is worthy of imitation by the faithful. The act of canonization is taken by a church synod and the leader of an autocephalous church. Individuals considered for canonization normally will either have died as Christian martyrs or may have shown gifts for working miracles such as healing, or miracles are associated with the tomb or relics of the deceased person. Others who accomplished notable missionary service, ascetic feats, or otherwise exemplified a Christian life may be canonized. Some saints are local (as opposed to church-wide), having been canonized under a bishop's authority. Normally, a deceased Christian is glorified only after his or her veneration has become widespread. There are no degrees of sainthood in Orthodoxy.

Church Slavonic, Old Church Slavonic

Saints Cyril and Methodius created the Old Church Slavonic language in the ninth century as part of a mission that they undertook to Moravia, a kingdom where a Slavic language was spoken. This language was intended originally to be understood by all speakers of Slavic languages and to be used in worship. Their achievement was the creation of a fully developed language, with grammar, vocabulary and spelling. Many scholars believe that the alphabet they created for this language was actually not what is known as the *Cyrillic,* but the *Glagolithic.* The language they created has evolved into Church Slavonic, which is still used (with local variations) particularly Orthodox churches in Russia, Bulgaria, and Serbia.

Church Councils

The Orthodox Church recognizes seven general councils known as "Ecumenical Councils" held between AD 325 and 787. These councils set forth basic dogmas of the church and principles of church law. The Holy and Great Council of the Orthodox Church (2016) seems to have been intended by its organizers to be the eighth such council, the first in over twelve hundred years; however, the Churches of Antioch, Russia, Bulgaria, and Georgia declined to attend. Other forms of councils also exist in the Orthodox faith. Some writers refer to the Orthodox Church as the "church of councils" due to their importance in church governance.

The Divine Ladder of Ascent

This is one of the most famous and influential works of Eastern Orthodox spirituality. It was written by Saint John Climacus, who is also known as "Saint John the Ladder" or John "Lestvichnik" (Иоанн Лествичник). This work describes thirty steps along the monk's path towards greater spirituality, culminating in "Love." Portions of John's book are still read in Orthodox churches during Great Lent. Copies of this book are widely available on the internet in many languages. It is said to have been the first book printed in the New World (1532 in Mexico).

Eastern Rite Catholics

Christians who recognize the authority of the Pope in Rome, but whose worship services are conducted according to the Byzantine Rite.

Ecumenical Patriarch

The Ecumenical Patriarch of Constantinople (modern Istanbul) is viewed as a "first among equals" and works to promote intra-Orthodox dialogue as well as dialogue with non-Orthodox faiths. While relatively few Greeks still remain in Istanbul (former Constantinople), the Patriarchate of Constantinople also has spiritual stewardship over roughly seven million Orthodox believers globally, chiefly in the Greek diaspora abroad.

Elder, starets/Gr. gerontas/Ru. старец

In Orthodoxy, an elder is not necessarily one who holds the priesthood. Rather, an elder is an older monk who has achieved a high degree of spiritual development. The elder serves as a mentor for younger monks.

Fasts

Fasting plays an important role in Eastern Orthodox worship. During the Holy and Great Council of the Orthodox Church (2016), a document entitled "The Importance of Fasting and its Observance Today" was adopted. Fasting normally involves abstinence from certain types of food. In the monastic tradition, the first three days of Great Lent are total fasts, meaning that those who are able to fast will skip all meals until Wednesday evening.

Feasts, Great Feasts

Every day on the liturgical calendar is a feast or commemoration for one or more saints or events in church history. These are called feasts. As used in Orthodoxy, this term does not imply that a banquet or special meal is prepared. Most are fixed on the calendar and do not change. Some move with reference to the date of Easter each year. There are twelve Great Feasts, eight of which commemorate events in Christ's life and four of which commemorate events related to Mary, the Theotokos.

Filioque

This term refers to words added to the Nicene Creed as recited in the Roman Catholic mass. The words were formally added in the eleventh century to clarify that the Holy Spirit proceeds not just from the Father, but from the Father and the Son. This change was a major cause of the schism between the churches in the East and West (i.e., Roman Catholicism and Eastern Orthodoxy). It still remains an obstacle to reunification of the two churches.

Gamos / Marriage (Brak)

See a description of Orthodox marriage under Chapter 8.

Great Lent/ Gr. Sarakosti/ Ru. великий пост

This is a forty-day period (not counting Sundays) of spiritual preparation leading up to Easter. Orthodox Christians are expected to deepen their religious devotion during this time through fasting (abstention from specified foods), prayer, and religious devotion. Great Lent begins on the Monday that comes before the seventh Sunday prior to Easter. This day is called Bright Monday or Clean Monday. Great Lent ends on the eve of Lazarus Saturday, the day that falls before Palm Sunday. Orthodox Christians also continue to observe prescribed fasts during Holy Week, leading up to Easter.

Hagia Sophia

The so-called Great Church in Constantinople, a massive domed Orthodox church that was the largest worship structure in the world in its day. Built in the sixth century, this church is an architectural wonder. It was converted into a mosque when Turkish forces took Constantinople in 1453. Today, it is a museum that attracts millions of visitors each year.

Hagiography

The writing of the life stories of the saints.

Heresy, heresies

Below are some heresies mentioned in this book. These particular heretical teachings have been condemned by Orthodox Church councils.

Arianism

A theology advanced by Arius of Alexandria (AD 256–336) under which Christ was created by the Father. Arius stated, "before he [the Son] was begotten, or created, or purposed, or established, he was not." Arianism called into question whether the Father and Son are divine in the same way. The Nicene Creed of AD 325 condemned this teaching.

Messalianism

A heretical movement within Christianity that rejected the need for sacraments and focused on prayer as the means of receiving the Holy Spirit. Some Messalians claimed they could see the Holy Trinity with their physical eyes. The Messalians were anathematized by the Third Ecumenical Council in AD 431.

Monophysitism

A heresy that arose in the fifth century AD which asserted that Christ only had one nature, the divine. This teaching was condemned at the Fourth Ecumenical Council in AD 451. Eastern Orthodox Christians believe that Christ had two natures and two wills, human and divine. A related heresy, Monothelitism, held that Christ had two natures but only one will. Monothelitism was rejected by the Sixth Ecumenical Council in AD 680.

Nestorianism

This is another heretical Christological belief which held that Christ was made of two persons—the physical man Jesus and that later, at the time of the Theophany, God began to dwell within the man Jesus. This belief was also condemned at the Third Ecumenical Council in AD 431 AD.

Hesychasm, Hesychast

A *hesychast* monk practices silent meditative prayer focused on Christ using the Jesus Prayer. The *Hesychast* tradition was revitalized in Slavic lands through the labors of Saint Paisius Velichkovsky (1722–1794), who translated the *Philokalia* into Slavonic.

Icon

Icons are an important part of Orthodox worship. They are more than works of art— they are seen as important channels for divine grace. Icons are normally painted in oil, on wood. They may depict Christ, Mary, various Biblical figures, martyrs, or events from biblical and Christian history. Their style and composition are not left to artistic creativity, but rather reflect many centuries of tradition governing how particular saints and events are depicted. Icons exhibit a style that emphasizes emotions and mysticism, rather than seeking to embody Renaissance or other Western artistic styles or ideals. By tradition, the Gospel writer Luke is said to have been the first iconographer.

Jesus Prayer

This prayer is practiced by *hesychast* monks and others seeking Christ-centered prayer. It its usual form, it is repeated on these words: "Lord

Jesus Christ, Son of God, have mercy on me, a sinner."

Mysteries

The Orthodox meaning of the term mystery is equivalent to sacrament, or a Gospel ordinance as that term is used by Latter-day Saints.

Old Believers/ Ru. Старообрядцы

A group that split from the Russian Orthodox Church in the seventeenth century due to changes introduced into the liturgy and worship. These changes were intended to better align Russian worship with the practices followed in the Greek Orthodox Church.

Orletz

A rug depicting an eagle with outstretched wings on which the bishop stands.

Pantocrator

An icon depicting Christ with his right hand raised bestowing a blessing and his left hand holding a Gospel book. Christ is represented as a mature, bearded man with a strong neck. His face is not symmetrical, with one half looking stronger and the other less so, seemingly embodying human frailty. This representation is thought to represent the two sides of Christ's nature and will: human and divine. The earliest surviving example of an Icon of *Christ Pantocrator* (sixth century) is found in the Saint Catherine's Monastery at the foot of Mount Sinai.

Philokalia

A collection of the writings of early and medieval Greek Church Fathers and saints. The Slavonic translation of this work was prepared under the supervision of Saint Paisius Velichkovsky (1722–1794). Among others, it includes excerpts from the writings of Saint Gregory Palamas (1296–1359) and Saint Symeon the New Theologian (949–1022) on topics relating to deification, vision of God, and the Tabor light.

Relics

The body or parts of the body of a saint. A small portion of the relics are stitched into the *antimension*. The grace of God is deemed to remain in the body or relics of saints even after their death. Miracles have sometimes been associated with the tombs and reliquaries of saints. The term *relic* is also used for sacred objects that are associated with Christ or saints. See 2 Kings 13:21; Mark 5:25–29; and Acts 19:12.

Sacraments

The Orthodox Church recognizes seven sacraments. See Chapter 8 for a discussion of the sacraments, or ordinances, of the Orthodox Church.

The Way of the Pilgrim

Entitled in English the "Way of a Pilgrim" or "Pilgrim's Tale," this work was first published anonymously in Kazan, Russia in 1884. This story tells the story of a Christian wanderer who reflects on the meaning of Paul's admonition to "pray without ceasing" (1 Thessalonians 5:17) and learns the Jesus Prayer. This book attests to the growing influence of the Bible and Eastern Orthodox spirituality within Russian society during the latter half of the nineteenth century.

Theotokos

The Mother of God, meaning Mary.

Recommended Reading

The sources cited in the chapter endnotes of this book are almost all from recognized Orthodox authors and publishers, or from other academic publishers. Many are found on websites maintained by Orthodox-affiliated organizations.

The lists below are provided for the benefit of general readers wishing to enhance their understanding of Eastern Orthodoxy. The "Short List" is presented in suggested order of priority.

Recommended "Short List"

Meyendorff, John. *St. Gregory Palamas and Orthodox Spirituality.* Crestwood, NY: St. Vladimir's Seminary Press, 1974.

Moore, Archimandrite Lazarus. *An Extraordinary Peace: St. Seraphim, Flame of Sarov.* Anaphora Press: Port Townsend, WA, 2009. **Note:** See especially Chapter 8.

Ware, Timothy (Bishop Kallistos of Diokleia). *The Orthodox Church.* Penguin Books: London and New York, 1997.

O'Grady, V. Rev. Patrick B. *Come, Let Us Worship: A Practical Guide to the divine Liturgy for Orthodox Laity.* Ancient Faith Publishing: Chesterton, IN, 2016.

Russell, Norman. *Fellow Workers With God: Orthodox Thinking on Theosis.* St. Vladimir's Seminary Press: Crestwood, NY, 2009.

Saint Symeon the New Theologian. *Life, Times, and Theology*, vol. 3 of *On the Mystical Life: The Ethical Discourses.* Popular Patristics Series no. 16. Edited and translated by Alexander Golitzin. St. Vladimir's Seminary Press: Crestwood, NY, 1996.

Other Recommended

Abdalah, Bishop John, and Nicholas G. Mamey, *Building an Orthodox Marriage: A Practical Commentary on the Eastern Orthodox Marriage Rite.* St. Vladimir's Seminary Press: Yonkers, NY, 2017.

Hapgood, Isabel Florence. *Service Book of the Holy Orthodox-Catholic Apostolic Church.* Forward by Patriarch Tikhon. Original publication 1906. Reprint by Antiochian Orthodox Christian Archdiocese of North America: Englewood, NJ, 1996. Available as an eBook, https://archive.org/details/ServiceBookOfHolyOrthodoxChurchBy Hapgood

Louth, Andrew. *Introducing Eastern Orthodox Theology*. InterVarsity Press: Downers Grove, IL, 2013.

Lossky, Vladimir. *The Mystical Theology of the Eastern Church*. St. Vladimir's Seminary Press: Crestwood, NY, 1976.

Saint John Climacus, *The Ladder of Divine Ascent*. Translated by Colm Luibheid and Norman Russell, introduction by Kallistos Ware. The Paulist Press: Mahwah, NJ, 1982.

Saint John Climacus. *The Divine Ladder of Ascent*. Translated by Lazarus Moore. Holy Transfiguration Monastery: Brookline, MA, 2012. Revised edition.

The Philokalia: The Complete Text. Compiled by St. Nikodimos of the Holy Mountian and St. Makarious of Corinth. Edited and translated by G. E. H. Palmer, Philip Sharrard, and Kallistos Ware. Faber & Faber: London, 1995, vol. 4.

Coniaris, Anthony M. *A Beginner's Guide to the Philokalia*. Light and Life Publishing Co.: Minnesota, MN, 2014.

Schmemann, Alexander. *For the Life of the World: Sacraments and Orthodoxy*. St. Vladimir's Seminary Press: Crestwood, NY, 1973.

About the Author

The author studied International Relations and Russian at Brigham Young University. He later earned a Juris Doctor from BYU and an MA in European Union Law from King's College of London. The author and his family have lived abroad extensively, including in Russia, China and Switzerland.

During the 1990s, the author worked for the the Historical Department of The Church of Jesus Christ of Latter-day Saints, where he helped edit and publish books on Church history.

Among the books the author has contributed to are:

Adrian W. Cannon and Richard E. Turley, Jr., gen. eds., Michael N. Landon, ed. *The Journals of George Q. Cannon, Volume I: To California in '49*. Salt Lake City: Deseret Book, 1999.

Adrian W. Cannon and Richard E. Turley, Jr., gen. eds., Chad M. Orton, ed. *The Journals of George Q. Cannon, Hawaiian Mission 1850-1854*. Salt Lake City: Deseret Book, 2014.

Gordon A. Madsen, Jeffrey N. Walker and John W. Welch, eds. *Sustaining the Law: Joseph Smith's Legal Encounters*. Provo, Utah: BYU Studies, 2014.

Made in the USA
Columbia, SC
06 September 2019